OBJECTIVE POLITICAL SCIENCE

SECTION-A

R. Gupta's[®]

Popular Master

Objective

POLITICAL SCIENCE

A COLLECTION OF HIGHLY USEFUL QUESTIONS FOR COMPETITIVE EXAMS

by

D.S. TIWARI

Ramesh Publishing House, New Delhi

Published by
O.P. Gupta *for* Ramesh Publishing House

Admin. Office
12-H, New Daryaganj Road, Opp. Officers' Mess,
New Delhi-110002 ① 23261567, 23275224, 23275124

E-mail: info@rameshpublishinghouse.com
Website: www.rameshpublishinghouse.com

Showroom
● Balaji Market, Nai Sarak, Delhi-6 ① 23253720, 23282525
● 4457, Nai Sarak, Delhi-6, ① 23918938

Book Code: R-786

ISBN: 978-93-5012-789-6

HSN Code: 49011010

16th Edition: 1907

CONTENTS

INTRODUCTION

1. Who among the following defines political science as the study of "the act of human and social control" or the "study of control relationship of wills"?
   (*a*) Robson   (*b*) Pollock
   (*c*) Maitland   (*d*) Catlin

2. ------- is the parent science of all the social sciences.
   (*a*) Sociology
   (*b*) History
   (*c*) Philosophy
   (*d*) None of the above

3. Which of the following deals with morality and formulates rules which should influence the behaviour of man while living in society?
   (*a*) Philosophy
   (*b*) Ethics
   (*c*) Sociology
   (*d*) None of the above

4. Ethics is concerned with man as a man and as such, it is prior to :
   (*a*) Society   (*b*) Science
   (*c*) Political Science (*d*) History

5. Who among the following prominent writers has given psychological explanations of almost all the political problems?
   (*a*) Le Bon   (*b*) Baldwin
   (*c*) Graham Wallas (*d*) All of the above

6. Political scientists have borrowed such, ideas as 'cultural relativism', 'social evolution', 'cultural diffusion' from :
   (*a*) Anthropology   (*b*) Sociology
   (*c*) Philosophy   (*d*) Economics

7. Who among the following said that politics has its roots, psychologically, in the study of mental habits and vocational activities of mankind?
   (*a*) Barker   (*b*) Plato
   (*c*) Bryce   (*d*) Wallas

8. Ivor Brown points out that economics deals mainly with ------- and politics is concerned with --------
   (*a*) Wealth, government
   (*b*) Business, state
   (*c*) Commodities, human beings
   (*d*) Production, administration

9. Which of the following theories of the origin of the state was accepted by liberalism?
   (*a*) Pluralist theory
   (*b*) Marxist theory
   (*c*) Historical theory
   (*d*) Institutional theory

10. Which of the following views believes that the state originated with class division and class struggle in society?
    (*a*) Liberal view   (*b*) Marxist view
    (*c*) Pluralist view (*d*) Traditional view

11. "It is not the consciousness of man which determines the material conditions of life but it is material conditions of life which determine their consciousness" – this statement is given by :
    (*a*) Gettell   (*b*) Karl Marx
    (*c*) Galbraith   (*d*) Catlin

12. "Politics is that part of social science which treats of the foundations of state and the principles of government". Who made this statement?
    (*a*) Willoughby   (*b*) Seeley
    (*c*) Paul Janet   (*d*) S.L. Wasby

13. Guild and Palmer strongly pleaded that the subject of politics should be :
(*a*) The political parties
(*b*) To secure obedience
(*c*) Negative
(*d*) Power instead of the state

14. The Father of modern sociology, A. Comte, portrayed society as a potentially harmonious and ordered structure in which all social classes
(*a*) worked for social change
(*b*) worked for the common good
(*c*) worked for the individual
(*d*) worked for capitalists

15. Socialist states are based on marxian ideology and are known as the :
(*a*) Blue world
(*b*) Green world
(*c*) Red world
(*d*) Yellow world

16. Which one of the following pairs is mismatched?
(*a*) Fascism — Mussolini
(*b*) Anarchism — Bakunin
(*c*) Socialism — Thomas Moore
(*d*) Pluralism — Kropotkin

17. Who has used the concept of "hegemony"?
(*a*) Laski
(*b*) MacIver
(*c*) Gramsci
(*d*) Marx

18. "Politics is struggle for power" was said by
(*a*) Morgenthau
(*b*) Quincy Wright
(*c*) Sprout
(*d*) Thomson

19. Kautilya wrote his Arthasastra on the subject of :
(*a*) History
(*b*) Practical politics
(*c*) Religion
(*d*) Science

20. Lord James Bryce is considered to be the best advocate of the :
(*a*) Experimental method
(*b*) Historical method
(*c*) Observational method
(*d*) Comparative method

21. The English word 'politics' originates from three Greek words like :
(*a*) Polis, Polity, Politico
(*b*) Polis, Polity, Politeia
(*c*) Polity, Political, Polis
(*d*) Politeia, Pol, Polis

22. Buckle said that "in the present state of knowledge, politics, far from being a science, is the most -------- of all arts".
(*a*) Forward
(*b*) Efficient
(*c*) Backward
(*d*) Obedient

23. Leacock says that without at least an unconscious political science, ------ will lose its main significance.
(*a*) Geography
(*b*) Economics
(*c*) Sociology
(*d*) History

24. Who conceived sociology as the all-inclusive Social Science?
(*a*) Lenin
(*b*) August Comte
(*c*) Lipson
(*d*) Garner

25. W.H.R. Rivers in his psychology and politics and Harold Lasswell in his psychopathology and politics present a study of politics based on :
(*a*) Political premises
(*b*) Economic premises
(*c*) Psychological premises
(*d*) Social premises

26. Who among the following appreciated the normative aspect of man's life in politics?
(*a*) Kant, Hegel, Green
(*b*) Garner, Joad, Bryce
(*c*) Barker, Catlin, Wilson
(*d*) Seeley, Garner, Lipset

27. In Sociology the unit of investigation is the :
(*a*) Conscious
(*b*) Socius
(*c*) Ardous
(*d*) Data

28. Charles Merriam, Lasswell and Morgenthau have preferred to make politics free from all ------ considerations
(*a*) Social
(*b*) Ethical
(*c*) Political
(*d*) Psychological

29. Plato and modern idealists have accepted the state as a/an ------ institution.
(*a*) Social
(*b*) Economic
(*c*) Ethical
(*d*) Political

30. According to traditional view, political science is a study of the ------ in its past, present and future aspects.
(*a*) Government   (*b*) Society
(*c*) State   (*d*) Power

31. Lord Bryce claims that "Political Science stands midway between -------- and -------- between the past and the present".
(*a*) Sociology, History
(*b*) History, Politics
(*c*) History, Geography
(*d*) Sociology, Psychology

32. According to Weber, -------- actions are motivated by the desire to acquire more and more ------
(*a*) Political, rights   (*b*) Human, power
(*c*) Social, freedom   (*d*) Economic, power

33. Plato considered politics a sub-division of
(*a*) Political Science   (*b*) Sociology
(*c*) Ethics   (*d*) History

34. Who among the following was the first writer in the western world who sharply separated politics from ethics?
(*a*) Plato   (*b*) Heymans
(*c*) Machiavelli   (*d*) Foy

35. A study of psychology, particularly of ------ psychology, is of inestimable value to the student of Political Science.
(*a*) Ethical   (*b*) Social
(*c*) Economic   (*d*) Historical

36. Who among the following said that "True politics cannot take a single step forward unless it has first done homage to morals"?
(*a*) Acton   (*b*) Lasswell
(*c*) Kant   (*d*) Gettell

37. According to Kautilya, the principles of morality :
(*a*) Should not be taken into consideration in politics
(*b*) Should be taken into consideration in politics
(*c*) Are the quintessence of politics
(*d*) None of the above

38. Lasswell defined political science as "an empirical discipline, as the study of the shaping and sharing of power" in his book
(*a*) Modern Democracies
(*b*) Power and Society
(*c*) Politics and the Social Sciences
(*d*) Elements of Politics

39. Who among the following applied the concept of culture to the study of social systems and presented the famous four fold functional analysis of the social systems?
(*a*) Giddings   (*b*) Talcott Parsons
(*c*) Lipset   (*d*) Max Weber

40. According to --------, "the application of the psychological clue to the reddles of human activity has indeed become the fashion of the day. If our forefathers thought biologically, we think psychologically".
(*a*) Wallas   (*b*) Woodworth
(*c*) Bryce   (*d*) Ernest Barker

41. Who among the following sociologists has made influential contributions in the field of political science?
(*a*) Durkheim   (*b*) Parsons
(*c*) Merton   (*d*) All of the above

42. Which of the following is the study and story of man's march towards political growth and development of social, economic and cultural institutions and organisations?
(*a*) Sociology   (*b*) Philosophy
(*c*) History   (*d*) Anthropology

43. President Lowell considered politics 'a/an --- and not an experimental science'.
(*a*) Moral   (*b*) Observational
(*c*) Social   (*d*) All of the above

44. According to August Comte, the principal methods by which political phenomena can be collected and classified include :
(*a*) Observation   (*b*) Experiment
(*c*) Comparison   (*d*) All of the above

45. In the words of Sidgwick, " ------- cannot determine the ultimate end and standard of good and bad, right and wrong, in political institutions".

(*a*) Sociology   (*b*) History

(*c*) Psychology   (*d*) Politics

46. Match List I with List II and select the correct answer using the codes given below the lists :

List I	List II
A. Hegel	1. Juridical
B. Austin	2. Sociological
C. MacIver	3. Descriptive
D. Garner	4. Metaphysical

Codes :

	A	B	C	D
(*a*)	1	2	3	4
(*b*)	4	1	2	3
(*c*)	4	3	2	1
(*d*)	4	1	3	2

47. Who among the following regarded political science a sub-division of ethics and the function of the state was to produce virtuous people?

(*a*) Aristotle   (*b*) Socrates

(*c*) Plato   (*d*) Garner

48. Who among the following emphasized the sociological evolution of the state and political institutions?

(*a*) Henry   (*b*) Morgan

(*c*) Laski   (*d*) Both (*a*) and (*b*)

49. The philosophy that stands diametrically opposite to liberalism is—

(*a*) Individualism   (*b*) Capitalism

(*c*) Marxism   (*d*) Fascism

50. In which of the following, the Departments of Political Science and Economics are combined together?

(*a*) London School of Economics and Political Science

(*b*) Canadian School of Economics and Political Science

(*c*) American School of Economics and Political Science

(*d*) Both (*a*) and (*b*)

51. "The art of looking for trouble, finding it whether it exists or not, diagnosing it wrongly and applying the wrong remedy". Who among the following gave the above definition of the politics?

(*a*) Ernest Barker   (*b*) Ernest Benn

(*c*) Frederick Pollock   (*d*) David Easton

52. Which of the following pairs are correct?

1. Jellinek : Political Science and Government
2. Gilchrist : Principles of Political Science
3. Pollock : An Introduction to the History of the Science of Politics
4. Francis Fucuyama : Games Nations Play

(*a*) 1 and 3   (*b*) 2 and 4

(*c*) Only 1   (*d*) 1, 2 and 3

53. Match List I (Definitions) with List II (Authors) and select the correct answer using the codes given below the lists :

List I	List II
A. Politics is both a science and an art	1. David Easton
B. Politics is the authoritative allocation of values that are binding on the society	2. Lasswell and Kaplan
C. Politics is the study of the shaping and sharing of power	3. Michael Curtis
D. Politics is organised dispute about power and its use	4. Treztschke

Codes :

	A	B	C	D
(*a*)	1	3	4	2
(*b*)	4	1	2	3
(*c*)	4	1	3	2
(*d*)	3	4	1	2

54. What philosophy is to the mental sciences, sociology is to the social sciences?

1. Both possess an all embracing character
2. Philosophy and Sociology are sister subjects

3. Sociology and Philosophy are inversely related to mental sciences and social sciences respectively

4. While philosophy is the 'mother' discipline with respect to mental sciences, sociology is the same with regard to social sciences.

    Which of the following are correct?

(*a*) 1 and 4   (*b*) 3 and 4

(*c*) 2 and 3   (*d*) 1 and 3

55. Who among the following pioneered the integration of the study of Political Science with psychology?

(*a*) S.M Lipset

(*b*) Walter Bagehot

(*c*) Eric Voeghin

(*d*) Harold Laski

56. Who among the following advocated that the central idea of the Political Science is power?

(*a*) David Apter   (*b*) Amos

(*c*) Max Weber   (*d*) Runciman

57. "I am not a part of a great symphony in which I realise myself only as an incident in the motif of the whole. I am unique. I am separate. I am myself."

    The above statement is made by :

(*a*) MacIver   (*b*) Austin

(*c*) Bryce   (*d*) Laski

58. Match List I (Works) with List II (Authors) and select the correct answer using the codes given below it :

List I (Works)	List II (Authors)
A. The social and Political thought of Karl Marx	1. Robert Dahl
B. An Introduction to comparative Government	2. Milton Friedman
C. Who Governs?	3. S.A. Vineri
D. Capitalism and Freedom	4. Jean Blondel

Codes :

	A	B	C	D
(*a*)	4	3	1	2
(*b*)	3	4	2	1
(*c*)	3	4	1	2
(*d*)	4	3	2	1

59. Who has termed the modern state an "Industrial State"?

(*a*) W.A. Robson   (*b*) S.M. Lipset

(*c*) H.D. Lasswell   (*d*) J.K. Galbraith

60. Which of the following pairs is not correctly matched?

(*a*) New Deal Programme   : Roosevelt

(*b*) Black Shirt Movement   : Mussolini

(*c*) Partyless democracy   : Jayaprakash Narayan

(*d*) Glasnost and Perestroika : Boris Yeltsin

61. Who among the following employed a biological method in the study of Politics?

(*a*) Lord Acton   (*b*) Milton

(*c*) T.H. Green   (*d*) Herbert Spencer

62. Which of the following pairs are NOT Correctly matched?

1. Introduction to Political Analysis   : David E. Apter

2. Systematic Politics   : G.E.G. Catlin

3. In Defence of Politics : Bernard Crick

4. The idea of Politics   : Carl J. Friedrich

Select the correct answer from below :

(*a*) Only 1   (*b*) 1 and 2

(*c*) Only 4   (*d*) 1, 2 and 4

63. Harold Lasswell's "Politics : Who Gets, What, When and How" discusses :

(*a*) Distributive justice

(*b*) Scientific method and Value-relativism

(*c*) Social implications of Capitalist Politics

(*d*) Fundamentals of Political-participation

64. "To teach the theory of the state to men who have not learned the first principles of sociology is like teaching astronomy or thermodynamics to men who have not learned the Newtonian Laws of motion".

    The above statement is made by :

(*a*) Giddings in "Principles of Sociology"

(*b*) Stuart Rice in 'Quantitative Methods in Politics'

(*c*) Kaplan in 'Power and Society'

(*d*) Arnold Brecht in 'Political theory'

65. The work 'Power and Society' is co-authored by :
   (*a*) Greenstein, Polsby and Nelson
   (*b*) Rieselbach and Balds
   (*c*) Girth and Mills
   (*d*) Harold Lasswell and Abraham Kaplan

66. The two remarks – "Political science is the science of state" and "Political science begins and ends with the state" have, respectively been made by :
   (*a*) Garner and Gilchrist
   (*b*) Laski and Gilchrist
   (*c*) Gettel and Laski
   (*d*) Gettel and Garner

67. The Keynote of liberalism is –
   (*a*) Individual
   (*b*) Liberty
   (*c*) Liberty of the individual
   (*d*) Personality

68. According to Marx, Politics is :
   (*a*) A devise to enhance class contradictions
   (*b*) An instrument of class domination
   (*c*) A mode of ensuring social harmony
   (*d*) A process aimed at welfare of the dominant class

69. The work 'Marxism and Politics' is authored by :
   (*a*) N. Poulantzas   (*b*) C. Wright Mills
   (*c*) Ralph Miliband   (*d*) Antonio Gramsci

70. Who held the view that society is federal in character?
   (*a*) MacIver   (*b*) Laski
   (*c*) Bentham   (*d*) Hannah Arendt

71. Who made the statement that, "in the present state of knowledge, politics far from being a science is one of the most backward of all arts"?
   (*a*) Henry Maine   (*b*) Roucek
   (*c*) Buckle   (*d*) Maitland

72. The present sociological impact on the study of Political Science can be traced back to :
   (*a*) Gaetamo Mosca
   (*b*) Max Weber
   (*c*) Vilfredo Pareto
   (*d*) Alasdair MacIntyre

73. The Famous 'Fourfold Functional analysis of the social system is made by :
   (*a*) Gabriel Almond   (*b*) Sidney Verba
   (*c*) James Coleman   (*d*) Talcott Parsons

74. A Scientific Sociological evolution of the state has been discussed by :
   (*a*) MacIver in the Modern State
   (*b*) Engels in Anti-Duhring
   (*c*) MacIver in the Web of Government
   (*d*) Engels in the Origin of the Family, Private Property and the State

75. Who among the following has underlined the importance of non-governmental factors for the explanation of political reality?
   (*a*) Ralph Miliband
   (*b*) Durkheim
   (*c*) Francis G. Castles
   (*d*) Antonio Gramsci

76. Which among the following are the scholars who have sought to give Psychological explanations of Political problems?
   (*a*) Mosca, Mills and Michaels
   (*b*) Barker and Laski
   (*c*) Graham Wallas, Trade and Le Bon
   (*d*) Aristotle and Plato

77. While analysing social conflicts who said that behind struggle there is a "castration complex"?
   (*a*) Abraham Kaplan
   (*b*) Lasswell
   (*c*) Walter Begehot
   (*d*) Lord Bryce

78. Who among the following held the view that without geography neither political nor strategical wisdom can go for?
   (*a*) Socrates
   (*b*) Plato
   (*c*) Aristotle
   (*d*) All of the above

79. Who among the following emphasised the influence of Physical environments on the forms of government and liberty of the people?

(*a*) Montesquieu
(*b*) Kant
(*c*) Hegel
(*d*) None of the above

80. In his book "History of Civilisation" who attributed the character of human inhabitants of a society completely to geographical and climatic conditions?
(*a*) Mosca
(*b*) Green
(*c*) Polymarchus
(*d*) Buckle

81. Its importance in the history of England has been emphasised by – Professor Shaler in his work "Nature and Man in America". It is :
(*a*) The Atlantic Ocean
(*b*) The Carpathians
(*c*) The English Channel
(*d*) All of the above

82. "Statistics contributes to the study of political and social institutions some what as microscopy contributes to Pathology". – is attributed to :-
(*a*) Garner
(*b*) Kant
(*c*) Sabine
(*d*) None of the above

83. The main contribution of statistics to Politics lies in :
(*a*) Bringing latter in the realm of sciences
(*b*) Imparting a mathematical orientation to the study of Politics
(*c*) Facilitating causal data analysis to increase Political understanding
(*d*) Both (*a*) and (*b*)

84. "Statistics, like real pies are good if you know the person who made them and are sure of the ingredients".
Who made the above comment?
(*a*) Laski
(*b*) Barker
(*c*) Lowell
(*d*) None of the above

85. Jurisprudence is :
(*a*) Law
(*b*) History of Law
(*c*) Anthology of Law
(*d*) Science of Law

86. It studies mankind in relation to Physical, Social and Cultural development. It is called –
(*a*) Physics
(*b*) Sociology
(*c*) Anthropology
(*d*) None of the above

87. Anthropology enriches political analysis by :
(*a*) Furnishing a full account of the past in which lie the roots of many contemporary customs and institutions
(*b*) Giving a scientific bend to political science
(*c*) Making the study of politics value free
(*d*) All of the above

88. The comment that – There are – institutions which like Plants, Flourish only on their hillside and under their own sunshine – is made by :
(*a*) Garner
(*b*) Bryce
(*c*) Gettel
(*d*) Sabine

89. Who among the following opines against stretching the analogy between the state and an Organism to extreme?
(*a*) Spencer
(*b*) Lord Acton
(*c*) T.H. Green
(*d*) Laski

90. Who opined that only government is stable which is in harmony with the mental constitution of the race?
(*a*) Mac Dougall
(*b*) Baldwin
(*c*) Le Bon
(*d*) None of the Above

ANSWERS

1	2	3	4	5	6	7	8	9	10
(d)	(a)	(b)	(c)	(d)	(a)	(c)	(c)	(c)	(b)

11	12	13	14	15	16	17	18	19	20
(b)	(c)	(d)	(b)	(c)	(d)	(c)	(a)	(b)	(c)

21	22	23	24	25	26	27	28	29	30
(b)	(c)	(d)	(b)	(c)	(a)	(b)	(b)	(c)	(c)

31	32	33	34	35	36	37	38	39	40
(b)	(b)	(c)	(c)	(b)	(c)	(a)	(b)	(b)	(d)

41	42	43	44	45	46	47	48	49	50
(d)	(c)	(b)	(d)	(b)	(b)	(c)	(d)	(c)	(d)

51	52	53	54	55	56	57	58	59	60
(b)	(d)	(b)	(a)	(b)	(c)	(d)	(c)	(d)	(d)

61	62	63	64	65	66	67	68	69	70
(d)	(c)	(b)	(a)	(d)	(d)	(b)	(b)	(c)	(b)

71	72	73	74	75	76	77	78	79	80
(c)	(b)	(d)	(d)	(c)	(c)	(b)	(c)	(a)	(b)

81	82	83	84	85	86	87	88	89	90
(c)	(a)	(c)	(c)	(d)	(c)	(a)	(b)	(b)	(c)

MEANING OF POLITICS

1. Robert Michels showed how 'democratic parties' are really :
   (a) Absurd Structures
   (b) Oligarchical Structures
   (c) Economic Structures
   (d) Authoritarian Structures

2. Who among the following is one of the advocates of the power theory in politics?
   (a) Catlin   (b) Kaplan
   (c) Lasswell   (d) All of the above

3. Who founded the structural-functional school in political science?
   (a) Apter   (b) Coleman
   (c) Plato   (d) Both (a) and (b)

4. Political Socialisation is the process of induction into the political culture and the psychological dimension of the :
   (a) Socio-economic System
   (b) Political System
   (c) Economic System
   (d) Social System

5. Who defines the political system as the "institutions, processes and interactions through which values are authoritatively allocated in a society"?
   (a) Almond   (b) Easton
   (c) Apter   (d) Pye

6. The liberal view of politics is based on the assumption that human beings are basically :
   (a) Independent   (b) Egoistic
   (c) Traditional   (d) Modern

7. The liberal view of politics is quite compatible with :
   (a) Conservatism   (b) Marxism
   (c) Fascism   (d) Nazism

8. Bernard Crick thinks that non-political conservatives, apolitical libera's and anti-political socialists do not know how to practise the art of :
   (a) Democracy   (b) Politics
   (c) Government   (d) Sociology

9. Marx approaches the question of politics from the point of view of :
   (a) Political Change
   (b) Cultural Change
   (c) Social Change
   (d) Administrative Change

10. In Marxist view of politics, conflict is inherent in the objective situation of the :
    (a) Social System
    (b) Class System
    (c) Political System
    (d) Economic System

11. In the last decades of which Century, politics was established as a separate and distinct subject?
    (a) Twentieth Century
    (b) Nineteenth Century
    (c) Eighteenth Century
    (d) Seventeenth Century

12. Greek philosophers never made a distinction between the :
    (a) Government and State
    (b) State and Society
    (c) Government and Society
    (d) Politics and Government

13. Who said that the State is a Union of Families and Villages having for its end Perfect and Self-sufficient life?
    (a) Aristotle   (b) Plato
    (c) Pollock   (d) Marx

14. Who among the following opined that life is a "perpetual and restless desire for power after power which ceases only in death"?
(*a*) Aristotle   (*b*) Nietzsche
(*c*) Hobbes   (*d*) Lasswell

15. Who was the first great political thinker who recognized the distinctive quality of politics as one of the basic human activities?
(*a*) Plato   (*b*) Aristotle
(*c*) Bernard Crick   (*d*) David E. Apter

16. Which notion characterizes the core of Marxist view of politics?
(*a*) The notion of class consciousness
(*b*) The notion of class conflict
(*c*) The notion of class determination
(*d*) The notion of ruling class

17. Who wrote the book 'In Defence of Politics'?
(*a*) Stephen Wasby
(*b*) Pareto
(*c*) Mosca
(*d*) Bernard Crick

18. Who founded the historical school of jurisprudence?
(*a*) Eichorn and Savigny
(*b*) John W. Burgess
(*c*) Francis Lieber
(*d*) John Hopkings

19. Which of the following systems of political analysis puts emphasis on legal and historical analysis, descriptive and comparative methods and interest group theory?
(*a*) Political philosophy
(*b*) Behaviourlism
(*c*) Pluralism
(*d*) Institutionalism

20. Who was the founder of the philosophical approach to politics?
(*a*) Plato   (*b*) Aristotle
(*c*) Hobbes   (*d*) Both (a) and (b)

21. Which view of politics suggests that political institutions realize philosophical ideals in governmental practices?
(*a*) Institutionalistic
(*b*) Pluralistic

(*c*) Marxist
(*d*) Behaviouralistic

22. The functionalist view of politics is professed by :
(*a*) David Easton   (*b*) Almond
(*c*) Talcott Parsons   (*d*) All of the above

23. Who propounded the elitist theory?
(*a*) Mosca   (*b*) Robert Dahl
(*c*) Lasswell   (*d*) Catlin

24. Liberalism coincides with the tradition of thought beginning with :
(*a*) John Locke   (*b*) Rousseau
(*c*) Hobbes   (*d*) Marx

25. The liberal view of politics upholds the pluralistic view of :
(*a*) Economy   (*b*) Polity
(*c*) State   (*d*) Society

26. According to the Marxist point of view ------ are the motive force behind all politics.
(*a*) Individual interests
(*b*) Social interests
(*c*) Conflicting economic interests
(*d*) Ruling class interests

27. The difficulty with the liberal approach is that it fails to distinguish between :
(*a*) Compromise and cooperation
(*b*) State and Society
(*c*) Society and government
(*d*) Compromise and Community

28. Behavioural approach to the study of politics insists on studying the actual behaviour of human beings in a :
(*a*) Social Situation
(*b*) Political Situation
(*c*) Particular Situation
(*d*) Crisis Situation

29. Which approach insists on making the achievements of political science subservient to human values and ends?
(*a*) Historical approach
(*b*) Modern approach
(*c*) Traditional approach
(*d*) Post-behavioural approach

30. Contemporary political science gives prominence to :
  (*a*) Modern approach
  (*b*) Empirical approach
  (*c*) Historical approach
  (*d*) Institutional approach

31. -------- was an Italian marxist and pioneer of neo-marxism.
  (*a*) MacIver   (*b*) Gramsci
  (*c*) Miliband   (*d*) Lenin

32. Who were probably the first to develop a new approach in social science which could be called a systematic interdisciplinary approach?
  (*a*) Dyke and Weldon
  (*b*) Marx and Engels
  (*c*) Marx and A. Ball
  (*d*) Popper and Dahl

33. Which one of the following is not the chief requisite of the empirical approach?
  (*a*) It deals with observable facts and data
  (*b*) It aims at explanation
  (*c*) It tends to make predictions
  (*d*) It deals with human values

34. Which of the following statement is correct?
  (*a*) The traditional view of politics deal with the study of state and government in their various aspects
  (*b*) Traditional thinking was characterised by a normative orientation
  (*c*) Traditional approach can be sub-divided into philosophical, institutional, historical, evolutionary and legal approaches
  (*d*) All of the above

35. Who among the following viewed that the institutional approach is concerned with the study of the central governmental institutions and their legal aspects and opinions?
  (*a*) Almond and Powell
  (*b*) Strauss and Merriam
  (*c*) Macridis and Dyke
  (*d*) Dahl and Easton

36. The works of -------- made a substantial contribution to the behavioural revolution.
  (*a*) Myron Weiner   (*b*) Sidney Verba
  (*c*) David Apter   (*d*) All of the above

37. Which of the following is not correct regarding behaviouralism?
  (*a*) It is a sort of a protest movement against the inadequacies of conventional political science
  (*b*) It has made the individual the centre of attention in the study of political phenomena
  (*c*) It lays emphasis on traditional outlook
  (*d*) It is pragmatic, catholic and eclectic

38. Which of the following is one of the criticisms made against behaviouralism?
  (*a*) The quantification of political phenomena is an unattainable goal
  (*b*) It is not possible to apply methodology of the natural sciences to the study of human behaviour
  (*c*) Value neutrality position is untenable
  (*d*) All of the above

39. The pioneer of the communication theory was :
  (*a*) Jean Blondel   (*b*) Deutsch
  (*c*) Robert Weiner   (*d*) O.R. Young

40. Prof. MacIver has analysed the nature of the state from the point of view of a sociologist in his book :
  (*a*) The Nature of Politics
  (*b*) Sociology and Political Theory
  (*c*) The Modern State
  (*d*) Principles of Sociology

41. Who was one of the first among the modern political scientists to challenge the traditional approaches?
  (*a*) Freud   (*b*) Lasswell
  (*c*) Bernard Crick   (*d*) Charles Merriam

42. Who is known for treating politics as a policy science?
  (*a*) Marx   (*b*) Mosca
  (*c*) Michels   (*d*) Lasswell

43. Match List I with List II and select the correct answer using the codes given below the lists :

	List I		**List II**
A.	Henry Sidgwick	1.	Systematic Politics
B.	S. Lipset	2.	The Principles of Politics
C.	G.E.G. Catlin	3.	The Elements of Politics
D.	J.R. Lucas	4.	Politics and the Social Sciences

Codes :

	A	**B**	**C**	**D**
(*a*)	3	4	1	2
(*b*)	3	2	1	4
(*c*)	2	4	1	3
(*d*)	4	3	2	1

44. Who said that politics is concerned with the 'authoritative allocation of values' for a society?
(*a*) B. Miller (*b*) David Easton
(*c*) Alan Ball (*d*) Ernest Benn

45. The liberal view of politics holds that politics is an instrument of reconciliation of the conflicting interests in :
(*a*) Castes (*b*) Classes
(*c*) Society (*d*) All of the above

46. According to marxists, what symbolizes not only the end of the conflict but the end of politics itself?
(*a*) A Pluralistic Society
(*b*) A Classless Society
(*c*) A liberal Society
(*d*) A Socialist Society

47. Traditional study of politics was dominated by :
(*a*) Behavioural approach
(*b*) Normative approach
(*c*) Marxist approach
(*d*) Power approach

48. The empirical approach seeks to discover and describe :
(*a*) Norms (*b*) Facts
(*c*) Values (*d*) Beliefs

49. The normative approach seeks to determine and prescribe :
(*a*) Values (*b*) Culture
(*c*) Facts (*d*) Rituals

50. Most of the classical political theories represent :
(*a*) Modern approach
(*b*) Philosophical approach
(*c*) Legal approach
(*d*) Empirical approach

51. Hobbes in his theory mainly focused on the grounds of :
(*a*) Social obligation
(*b*) Political obligation
(*c*) Economic obligation
(*d*) Psychological obligation

52. Who is regarded as the pioneer of individualism which later developed into liberalism?
(*a*) Locke (*b*) Hobbes
(*c*) Rousseau (*d*) Pareto

53. On what grounds T.H. Green developed his theory of rights?
(*a*) Liberal (*b*) Moral
(*c*) Social (*d*) Political

54. Who revived Kant's notion of 'rational negotiators to build his theory of justice?
(*a*) Aristotle (*b*) John Rawls
(*c*) Macpherson (*d*) Karl Popper

55. Who is the most outstanding contemporary champion of the philosophical approach to the study of politics?
(*a*) Socrates (*b*) Leo Strauss
(*c*) Dyke (*d*) Kant

56. ------ has described historical approach as historicism.
(*a*) Karl Popper (*b*) Karl Marx
(*c*) Dyke (*d*) Hobbes

57. Legal approach stands for an attempt to understand politics in terms of :
(*a*) Customs (*b*) Conventions
(*c*) Law (*d*) Procedures

58. Which of the following statements is not correct regarding drawbacks of the institutional approach?
(*a*) It neglects the role of informal groups and processes in shaping politics

(*b*) It is concerned with the established institutions

(*c*) It describes about international politics

(*d*) With its preoccupation with the institutions it neglects the individual

59. ------ is the most effective instrument of exercising power in the sphere of politics.
(*a*) Government   (*b*) Political Power
(*c*) Legitimacy   (*d*) Authority

60. Max Weber's definition of politics implies a focus on ------ in the context of national as well as international politics.
(*a*) Power   (*b*) State
(*c*) Society   (*d*) Democracy

61. Who is famous as the Founder of the Chicago School which made Substantial Contribution to the behavioural movement?
(*a*) Wallas   (*b*) Merriam
(*c*) Bentley   (*d*) Catlin

62. What were the twin slogans of post-behaviouralism?
(*a*) Relevance and Action
(*b*) Action and Values
(*c*) Facts and Values
(*d*) Relevance and Facts

63. "The state is considered to be the sole source of the 'right' to use violence. Hence, 'Politics' for us means striving to share power or striving to influence the distribution of power, either among states or among groups within a state" – who made this statement?
(*a*) Plato   (*b*) Weber
(*c*) Marx   (*d*) Hobbes

64. Political communication is the process whereby components of a ------ system. Such as, groups, institutions, transmit and receive information regarding the functioning of the political system.
(*a*) Social   (*b*) Political
(*c*) Economic   (*d*) Governmental

65. A ------ political system is characterized by differentiation of structures for the performance of specific functions.
(*a*) Developing   (*b*) Underdeveloped

(*c*) Developed   (*d*) Progressive

66. Who is the Chief exponent of communications theory approach?
(*a*) Almond   (*b*) Karl Deutsch
(*c*) Marx   (*d*) Coleman

67. Communication theory regards the function of communication as the centre of all :
(*a*) Social activity
(*b*) Political activity
(*c*) Economic activity
(*d*) Socio-economic activity

68. Decision-making analysis essentially follows ------ approach by drawing substantially on psychology, sociology, administrative theory and organization theory.
(*a*) Traditional   (*b*) Historical
(*c*) Empirical   (*d*) Interdisciplinary

69. According to the Marxist point of view, politics is only a part of :
(*a*) Structure   (*b*) Substructure
(*c*) Superstructure   (*d*) Class structure

70. Marx, Engels and Lenin argued that political systems should be compared and contrasted with reference to their respective
(*a*) Substructures   (*b*) Class structures
(*c*) Superstructures   (*d*) Caste structures

71. The traditional view of politics deals with :
(*a*) The study of state and government
(*b*) Groups and associations
(*c*) Ideologies
(*d*) Institutions

72. The work "Political Science : A Philosophical Analysis" is authored by :
(*a*) Oran Young
(*b*) Herbert Storing
(*c*) Vermon Van Dyke
(*d*) Leo Strauss

73. Traditional approaches dominated the study of Politics till :
(*a*) The outbreak of behavioural revolution after World War I
(*b*) The outbreak of behavioural revolution after World War II

(*c*) The advent of systems theory

(*d*) The revolutionary change in the thinking of the American Political Scientists

74. The oldest approach to politics is :
(*a*) Historical-Evolutionary approach
(*b*) Legal approach
(*c*) Institutional approach
(*d*) Philosophical approach

75. The Chief advocate of the Philosophical approach was :
(*a*) Vermon Van Dyke
(*b*) Socrates
(*c*) J.J. Rousseau
(*d*) Leo Strauss

76. "Philosophy, is the quest for wisdom and political philosophy is the attempt truly to know about the nature of Political things and the right or the good Political order".
The above statement is attributed to :
(*a*) R.H.S. Crossman (*b*) Karl Popper
(*c*) Leo Strauss (*d*) Macpherson

77. John Rawls revived the notion of negotiators to build his theory of justice. The nation of 'rational negotiators' originally belonged to :
(*a*) Hegel (*b*) Kant
(*c*) Nietzsche (*d*) Kafka

78. Who among the following developed his theory of rights on moral grounds and sought to limit the authority of the state?
(*a*) John Locke
(*b*) John Stuart Mill
(*c*) Thomas Hill Green
(*d*) Immanuel Kant

79. Leo Strauss, a champion of the Philosophical approach to political analysis is critical of :
(*a*) Idealism of Hegel and Green
(*b*) Utilitarianism of Bentham and Mill
(*c*) Hedonism of David Hume
(*d*) Historicism of Sabine and politivism of Catlin

80. Who among the following has built up a classic defence of libertarianism?
(*a*) Karl Popper (*b*) F.A. Hayek
(*c*) C.B. Macpherson (*d*) John Rawals

81. The concept of 'incremental change' is attributed to :
(*a*) Karl Popper (*b*) Hannah Arendt
(*c*) C.B. Macpherson (*d*) Alan R. Ball

82. Who among the following has built a neo-Marxist theory of freedom?
(*a*) Louis Althusser (*b*) Ralph Miliband
(*c*) Herbert Marcuse (*d*) George Lukas

83. Who among the following have – criticized the historical approach to political analysis?
(*a*) Hobbes and Locke
(*b*) Sidgwick and Barker
(*c*) Maxey and Sabine
(*d*) Lenin and Mao

84. The Historical-Evolutionary approach has been employed by Several Scholars. In this context, match List I (Books) with List II (Scholars) and select the correct answer from the codes given below the lists :

List I (Books)	List II (Scholars)
A. Ancient Law	1. John Seeley
B. The state and the Nation	2. E.M. Sait
C. Political Institutions	3. Henry Maine
D. Introduction to Political Science	4. Edward Jenkes

Codes :

	A	B	C	D
(*a*)	4	3	1	2
(*b*)	3	4	1	2
(*c*)	4	2	1	3
(*d*)	3	4	2	1

85. He has castigated the traditional approach to Political analysis for its emphasis on historicism and has warned against living "parasitically on ideas a century old".
(*a*) Gabriel Almond (*b*) Marian Levi
(*c*) David Easton (*d*) Sydney Webb

86. He has built theory of democracy by reverting to Aristotle and J.S. Mill while rejecting Bentham's utilitarianism and the contemporary elitism of Schumpeter and Dahl. He is :

(*a*) C.B. Macpherson (*b*) Giovanhi Sartori
(*c*) Raymond Aron (*d*) Karl Mannheim

87. Plato has been the source of inspiration for many later scholars. Which of the following group of scholars have been influenced by Plato?
(*a*) Mill, Marcuse and Locke
(*b*) Jenks, Seeley and Sait
(*c*) Kant, Hegel and Marx
(*d*) Crossman, Karl Popper and H.G. Wells

88. Which of the following pairs is correctly matched :
(*a*) Contemporary : C.J. Charlesworth
    Political Analysis
(*b*) Modern Politics : Garner
    and Government
(*c*) The Great Issues : John Austin
    of Politics
(*d*) Ideology and : Edward Shills
    Politics

89. Who among the following describe the institutional approach to Political analysis as "a routine description and pedestrian analysis of formal Political structures and processes ------"?
(*a*) Vermon Van Dyke
(*b*) Almond and Powell
(*c*) Somit and Tanenhaus
(*d*) A.F. Bentley

90. John Rawls has constructed his celebrated theory of Justice by drawing on the methodology of :
(*a*) Locke and Kant
(*b*) Mill and Kant
(*c*) Locke and Mill
(*d*) Rousseau and Kant

91. Which of the following works have NOT been authored by R.M. MacIver?
(*a*) The Web of Government
(*b*) Society : Its Structure and Changes
(*c*) The Modern state
(*d*) An Introduction to Politics

92. Which scholars among the following advocated an absolutist view of – Political

obligation
(*a*) Jeremy Bentham and James Mill
(*b*) Plato and Aristotle
(*c*) Thrasymachus and Machiavelli
(*d*) Hobbes, Rousseau and Hegel

93. He was the first to repudiate the absolutist view of Political obligation and to postulate rights of the individualism. He is :
(*a*) J.S. Mill (*b*) John Locke
(*c*) Adam Smith (*d*) Herbert Spencer

94. Scholars like Michael Oakeshott, Bertrand Jouvenel, Leo Strauss and Eric Voegelin, though diverse in their political orientations and areas of scholarship, stand together in :
(*a*) Criticising empiricism
(*b*) Supporting classical Political theory
(*c*) Castigating normativism of the traditional approaches
(*d*) Upholding modern approaches over the traditional ones.

95. Who among the following was the founder of the Chicago School which contributed significantly to the behavioural movement?
(*a*) G.E.G. Catlin (*b*) A.F. Bentley
(*c*) Heinz Eulau (*d*) C.E. Merriam

96. Match List I (Books) with List II (Authors) and select the correct answer using the codes given below the lists :

List I (Books)	List II (Authors)
A. Politics and Social Science	1. Stephen L. Wasby
B. Systems of Political Science	2. Allan R. Ball
C. Political Science – The Discipline and Its Dimensions	3. Seymour Martin Lipset
D. Modern Politics and Government	4. Oran R. Young

Codes :

	A	B	C	D
(*a*)	2	4	3	1
(*b*)	4	3	1	2
(*c*)	3	4	1	2
(*d*)	4	3	2	1

97. He was a pioneer of the behavioural approach to political analysis. He Sought to introduce a new findings of contemporary psychology. He was :
  (*a*) Arthur Bentley   (*b*) Charles Merriam
  (*c*) Graham Wallas   (*d*) Harold Lasswell

98. The author of 'Science and Method of Politics' is :
  (*a*) William Munro   (*b*) Kirk Patrick
  (*c*) G.E.G. Catlin   (*d*) Morgan

99. The Key-words of post-behaviouralism are :
  (*a*) Methodology and action
  (*b*) Relevance and action
  (*c*) Predictability and relevance
  (*d*) Analysis and action

100. Who defined behaviouralism as "a protest movement with in political science associated with a number of political scientists mainly American"?
  (*a*) Heinz Eulau   (*b*) David Truman
  (*c*) Robert A. Dahl   (*d*) Graham Wallas

101. Match List I (Behaviouralists) with List II (Books) and select the correct answer from the codes given below the lists :

List I (Behaviouralists)	List II (Books)
A. French Kent	1. A preface to Democratic theory
B. Herbert Tingston	2. Political Behaviour studies in Election Statistics
C. David Apter	3. Political Behaviour
D. Robert Dahl	4. Introduction to Political Analysis

Codes :

	A	B	C	D
(*a*)	2	3	4	1
(*b*)	3	2	4	1
(*c*)	3	2	1	4
(*d*)	1	3	2	4

102. The work 'Political Continuity and Change' is authored by :
  (*a*) Peter Markl   (*b*) Peter Odegard
  (*c*) Austin Ramney (*d*) John Austin

103. David Easton has enumerated seven major characteristics of post-behaviouralism and has described them as :
  (*a*) Theory of Organisation
  (*b*) Credo of pertinence
  (*c*) Doctrine of value-relativism
  (*d*) Credo of Relevance

104. Who among the following earliest behaviouralists sought not to describe political activity but to provide for new tools of investigation?
  (*a*) Harold Lasswell (*b*) G.E.G. Catlin
  (*c*) Arthur Bentley (*d*) Graham Wallas

105. Charles Merriam, the pioneer of the behavioural approach of the Chicago School authored :
  (*a*) Science and Method of Politics
  (*b*) Political Power and Social Change
  (*c*) New Aspects of Politics
  (*d*) Institutions and Processes

106. Who among the following argued that the rise of behaviouralism was symptomatic of a crisis in political theory – because of its failure to come to grip with normative issues?
  (*a*) Eric Voegelin   (*b*) Leo Strauss
  (*c*) David Easton   (*d*) Robert Dahl

107. Thomas Kuhn promoted the view that significance of scientific method lies in its capacity of problem solving and crists management and not in methodological sophistication in :
  (*a*) The Structure of Scientific Revolutions
  (*b*) The Making of Decisions
  (*c*) Value Systems and Social Process
  (*d*) Essays on the Scientific Study of Politics

108. Which one of the following pairs is correctly matched?
  (*a*) Nationality and Government : Sidgwick
  (*b*) Politics and Government : G.E.G. Catlin
  (*c*) A study of the Principles : G.E.G. Catlin of Politics
  (*d*) The Future of Political Science : Lasswell

109. Though Functionalism as an approach dates back to the days of Aristotle, in its modern form, the stress on functionalism is derived from the anthropological and sociological theories of :
(*a*) Karl Deutsch and O.R. Young
(*b*) Almond and Coleman
(*c*) Malinowski and Radcliff Brown
(*d*) Graham Wallas and Arthur Bentley

110. According to Structural-Functional approach, Structures are :
(*a*) Concrete institutions
(*b*) Relevant consequences
(*c*) Patterned behaviour
(*d*) Networks of the government

111. "Any collection of elements that – interact in some way with one another can be considered a system : a galaxy, a football team, a legislature, a political party".
The above statement is attributed to :
(*a*) Jean Blondel
(*b*) Karl Deutsch
(*c*) Leonard Binder
(*d*) Robert Dahl

112. Systems analysis was applied in the field of sociology by :
(*a*) Talcott Parsons
(*b*) Leonard Binder
(*c*) Myron Weiner
(*d*) Malinowski and Radcliff-Brown

113. 'Feedback' mechanism is associated with :
(*a*) Decision-making approach
(*b*) Structural-functionalism
(*c*) Systems analysis
(*d*) Kuhn's paradigm

114. The credit to develop structural functionalism as a tool of political analysis goes to :
(*a*) Robert Merton   (*b*) Marion Levy
(*c*) Gabriel Almond   (*d*) David Easton

115. The Nerves of Government : Models of Political Communication and Control is a pioneering work in the field of political analysis.
It is associated with :

(*a*) Decision-Making approach
(*b*) Structural-Functionalism
(*c*) Kuhn's Paradigm
(*d*) Communications theory

116. To postulate that the economic structure of society is responsible for creating and transforming its social structure including its legal and political structure a building like metaphor is used by :
(*a*) Communications theory
(*b*) Hannah Arendt's analysis of politics
(*c*) Marxist approach to political analysis
(*d*) Mao Zedong

117. The model of political system has served as a basis for :
(*a*) Structural-functional analysis
(*b*) Communications theory
(*c*) Both (*a*) and (*b*)
(*d*) Decision-making analysis

118. The idea of 'base' and 'superstructure' is expounded by :
(*a*) Marx in 'the Philosophy of Poverty'
(*b*) Marx and Engels in 'the Communist Manifesto'
(*c*) Marx in 'A Contribution to the-Critique of Political Economy'
(*d*) Engels in 'Anti-Duhring'

119. Decision-making approach was developed and popularised by :
(*a*) Leonard Binder
(*b*) Almond and Coleman
(*c*) Richard Synder and Charles Lindblom
(*d*) Robert Dahl

120. In political science, the Game theory is used to study :
(*a*) Issues of peace and conflict
(*b*) Cooperation among nations and organisations
(*c*) Problems of international relations and diplomacy
(*d*) International balance of power and division of labour

121. In David Easton's system analysis 'feedback' is :

(*a*) An organisational mechanism
(*b*) A communication process
(*c*) A motivational devise
(*d*) A tool of investigation

122. Who wrote in his work, 'Political Ideology' that political ideologies embrace a programme for the defence or reform of important social institutions and are normative in tone and content?
(*a*) Robert Walpole
(*b*) Robert Tucker
(*c*) Robert Lane
(*d*) Robert Dahl

123. The institutional approach is concerned with :
(*a*) Study of social institutions
(*b*) Study of the central governmental institutions and their legal aspects and opinions
(*c*) Study of political institutions
(*d*) Both (a) and (c)

124. Sabine's work 'A History of Political Theory' epitomises :
(*a*) Legal approach
(*b*) Historical Evolutionary approach
(*c*) Institutional approach
(*d*) Philosophical approach

125. The basic element/elements which comprise political theories is/are :
(*a*) Factual   (*b*) Causal
(*c*) Evaluative   (*d*) All of the above

126. The political behaviour approach became popular in :
(*a*) 1920s   (*b*) 1930s
(*c*) 1940s   (*d*) 1950s

127. Who opined that politics without the study of psychology of the individual is meaningless?
(*a*) Arthur Bentley
(*b*) Graham Walls
(*c*) David Held
(*d*) None of the above

128. Who among the following made a three fold classification of governmental output functions which are associated with policy making and implementation?

(*a*) Almond   (*b*) Coleman
(*c*) Binder   (*d*) Verba

129. The work Approaches to the study of Politics is edited by :
(*a*) Oran R.Young
(*b*) Roland Young
(*c*) Stephen Wasby
(*d*) None of the above

130. Thomas Kuhn devised paradigms in the field of :
(*a*) Sociology
(*b*) Physical Science
(*c*) Social Science
(*d*) Natural Science

131. According to Kuhn, there are number of phases through which a Science tends to pass. The first phase is :
(*a*) Normative Phase
(*b*) Pre-paradigmatic phase
(*c*) Upward phase
(*d*) None of the above

132. According to Thomas Kuhn, 'The history of science' has been characterised by :
(*a*) Growth of objectivity and decline of normativism
(*b*) Succession of distinct thought styles or paradigms
(*c*) Considerable influence of the paradigms on the kinds of problems scientists select for investigation
(*d*) Both (b) and (c)

133. The feature of pre-paradigmatic phase is that :
(*a*) No single theoretical approach or school predominates although a number of such schools of approaches compete for recognition
(*b*) Observers made use of crude methodologies
(*c*) A mix of theoretical approaches is practised
(*d*) None of the above

134. It is the characteristic feature of the paradigmatic phase, according to Thomas Kuhn that :

(*a*) Disciplines are separated

(*b*) Scientific community adheres to a dominant paradigm

(*c*) Theories are laid down after thorough revision

(*d*) Both (*a*) and (*c*)

135. Which of the following works is edited by Austin Ranney?

(*a*) Essays on the Behavioural study of Politics

(*b*) Approaches to the study of Political Science

(*c*) Political Research Methods : Foundations and Techniques

(*d*) None of the above

136. According to the thesis laid down by Thomas Kuhn, the third phase through which a science tends to pass is called :

(*a*) The amorphous phase

(*b*) The phase of final revision

(*c*) The crisis phase

(*d*) None of the above

137. It can be said that the most remarkable thing about Marxism is that :

(*a*) It laid down a step-by-step prescription to revolution

(*b*) It was accepted by million of people as their political creed

(*c*) Despite being scientific, it is suffused with humanism

(*d*) Both (*a*) and (*b*)

138. Who among the following is associated with the theoretical growth in cultural anthropology?

(*a*) David Easton

(*b*) Radcliffe Brown

(*c*) Malinowski

(*d*) Both (*b*) and (*c*)

139. The model of the open market has been borrowed from economics to analyse democratic politics by :

(*a*) Schumpeter

(*b*) Sartori

(*c*) Anthony Downs

(*d*) Both (*a*) and (*c*)

140. Which among the following scholars emphasised the sociological evolution of the state and its political institutions?

(*a*) Henry Maine

(*b*) L.H. Morgan

(*c*) J.J. Bachhofen

(*d*) All of the above

141. Whose view is that politics has got socialised and society has got politicised in modern times?

(*a*) Max Weber

(*b*) G. Sartori

(*c*) Antony Giddens

(*d*) All of the above

142. Who has analysed the nature of the state from the point of view of a sociologist in his work the Modern State?

(*a*) Laski

(*b*) MacIver

(*c*) Engels

(*d*) All of the above

143. Which of the following have been authored by Robert Dahl?

(*a*) A preface to Democratic theory

(*b*) Political Science – The discipline and its dimensions

(*c*) Modern Political Analysis

(*d*) Both (*a*) and (*c*)

144. Under the conflict theory, conflict is studied with reference to :

(*a*) Risks and strategies

(*b*) Pay offs and preferences

(*c*) Coalition forming rules and decision rules terminating conflicts

(*d*) All of the above

145. The communication theory starts with the presumption that :

(*a*) Government is a decision-making. system

(*b*) It is possible to communicate between the political and social systems

(*c*) Society is a form of administration of communication channels

(*d*) All of the above

ANSWERS

1	2	3	4	5	6	7	8	9	10
(b)	(d)	(d)	(b)	(b)	(b)	(a)	(b)	(c)	(b)
11	**12**	**13**	**14**	**15**	**16**	**17**	**18**	**19**	**20**
(b)	(b)	(a)	(b)	(b)	(b)	(d)	(a)	(d)	(d)
21	**22**	**23**	**24**	**25**	**26**	**27**	**28**	**29**	**30**
(a)	(d)	(a)	(a)	(d)	(c)	(a)	(b)	(d)	(b)
31	**32**	**33**	**34**	**35**	**36**	**37**	**38**	**39**	**40**
(b)	(b)	(d)	(b)	(a)	(d)	(c)	(d)	(c)	(c)
41	**42**	**43**	**44**	**45**	**46**	**47**	**48**	**49**	**50**
(b)	(d)	(a)	(b)	(c)	(b)	(b)	(b)	(a)	(b)
51	**52**	**53**	**54**	**55**	**56**	**57**	**58**	**59**	**60**
(b)	(a)	(b)	(b)	(b)	(a)	(c)	(c)	(d)	(a)
61	**62**	**63**	**64**	**65**	**66**	**67**	**68**	**69**	**70**
(b)	(a)	(b)	(b)	(c)	(b)	(b)	(d)	(c)	(b)
71	**72**	**73**	**74**	**75**	**76**	**77**	**78**	**79**	**80**
(a)	(c)	(b)	(d)	(d)	(c)	(b)	(c)	(d)	(b)
81	**82**	**83**	**84**	**85**	**86**	**87**	**88**	**89**	**90**
(a)	(c)	(b)	(d)	(c)	(a)	(d)	(d)	(c)	(a)
91	**92**	**93**	**94**	**95**	**96**	**97**	**98**	**99**	**100**
(d)	(d)	(b)	(b)	(d)	(c)	(c)	(c)	(b)	(c)
101	**102**	**103**	**104**	**105**	**106**	**107**	**108**	**109**	**110**
(b)	(a)	(d)	(c)	(c)	(b)	(a)	(c)	(c)	(c)
111	**112**	**113**	**114**	**115**	**116**	**117**	**118**	**119**	**120**
(d)	(a)	(c)	(c)	(d)	(c)	(c)	(c)	(c)	(c)
121	**122**	**123**	**124**	**125**	**126**	**127**	**128**	**129**	**130**
(b)	(c)	(b)	(b)	(d)	(a)	(b)	(a)	(b)	(b)
131	**132**	**133**	**134**	**135**	**136**	**137**	**138**	**139**	**140**
(b)	(d)	(a)	(b)	(a)	(c)	(c)	(d)	(d)	(d)
141	**142**	**143**	**144**	**145**					
(b)	(b)	(d)	(d)	(a)					

3

KEY CONCEPTS

1. ------ and ------ considerations are sometimes adduced in favour of imperialism.
   (*a*) Political, religious
   (*b*) Economic, humanitarian
   (*c*) Religious, humanitarian
   (*d*) Social, economic

2. Which of the following is not the indirect form of imperialism?
   (*a*) Sphere of influence
   (*b*) Tariff control
   (*c*) Leasehold
   (*d*) Nationalism

3. Who among the following idealist liberals emphasized on the creative form of citizenship?
   (*a*) J.S. Mill   (*b*) Bentham
   (*c*) T.H. Green   (*d*) Rousseau

4. During 20th century, liberalism equated citizenship with a/an :
   (*a*) Pluralist State
   (*b*) Egalitarian State
   (*c*) Liberal State
   (*d*) Individualistic State

5. The criticism of modern democratic citizenship has been the hallmark of :
   (*a*) Greek views on citizenship
   (*b*) Socialist views on citizenship
   (*c*) Marxist views on citizenship
   (*d*) Pluralist views on citizenship

6. In which book T.H. Marshal has explained the nature of citizenship in the context of Welfare State in Europe?
   (*a*) Politics
   (*b*) Six Books on the commonwealth
   (*c*) Citizenship and social class

7. (*d*) Citizenship

7. What has been the medium of extension of citizenship rights and the basis of the creation of an insulated economy, democracy and welfare state according to Gidden's?
   (*a*) Migration
   (*b*) Class conflict
   (*c*) Warfare
   (*d*) Egalitarian ideologies

8. In the 18th century Bentham maintained that the desire to have 'pleasures' is the basis of all :
   (*a*) Political activity
   (*b*) Social activity
   (*c*) Economic activity
   (*d*) Physical activity

9. Match List I with List II and select the correct answer by using the codes given below the lists :

List I	**List II**
A. Russell	1. Systematic politics
B. Catlin	2. The political system
C. Easton	3. Power : A New Social Analysis
D. Mosca	4. The Ruling Class

   Codes :

	A	**B**	**C**	**D**
(*a*)	3	1	2	4
(*b*)	1	2	3	4
(*c*)	4	3	2	1
(*d*)	3	1	4	2

10. Machiavelli's -------- is perhaps the most Fascinating study of power on record.
    (*a*) Republic
    (*b*) The Mind and Society

(c) Power

(d) The Prince

11. Who among the following writers wrote in praise of power of the state?

(a) Nietzsche   (b) Treitschke

(c) Bernhardi   (d) All of the above

12. Who maintains that power is not primarily a thing, a possession, but rather a relation?

(a) Easton   (b) Friedrich

(c) Wasby   (d) Parsons

13. Who among the following introduced the concept of dual citizenship?

(a) Romans   (b) Greeks

(c) Plato   (d) Republicans

14. Who devoted two chapters on citizenship in his book Six Books on the commonwealth?

(a) Kant   (b) Bodin

(c) Rousseau   (d) Hobbes

15. Parker T. Moon says that imperialism means domination of non-European native races by totally dissimilar :

(a) Commonwealth nations

(b) European nations

(c) Developing nations

(d) Developed nations

16. According to Hobson, imperialism is also known as :

(a) Exploitation

(b) Dollar imperialism

(c) Colonialism

(d) Yankee imperialism

17. When a rich country like the United States drags other states of the world into its area of influence by the power of money, it becomes :

(a) Protectorate

(b) Intervention

(c) Leasehold

(d) Dollar imperialism

18. For Aristotle, citizenship was concerned with securing stable government under the :

(a) State   (b) Constitution

(c) Law   (d) Leader

19. The idea of citizenship in the French Revolution was associated with the :

(a) Duties   (b) Rights

(c) Policies   (d) State

20. At the theoretical level, which of the following was a major factor for the rise of modern citizenship :

(a) German Revolution

(b) Russian Revolution

(c) French Revolution

(d) American Revolution

21. Which one of the following is not responsible for the growth of modern democratic citizenship?

(a) Migration ideologies

(b) Warfare

(c) Egalitarian ideologies

(d) Economic equality

22. According to Heatler, apart from the political needs participation and loyalty, which of the following major factors has been responsible for the rise of citizenship?

(a) Philosophical   (b) Military needs

(c) Economic   (d) All of the above

23. Greek concept of citizenship was :

(a) Limited   (b) Pragmatic

(c) Extensible   (d) None of the above

24. Match List I with List II and select the correct answer using the codes :

List I		List II
A. Coser and Rosenberg	1.	Power
B. Russell	2.	Comparative Government
C. Finer	3.	Sociological Theory
D. Beard	4.	Research in Social Science

Codes :

	A	B	C	D
(a)	3	1	2	4
(b)	1	2	4	3
(c)	3	2	1	4
(d)	4	2	1	3

25. Romans developed a form of citizenship which was more :

(*a*) Complex   (*b*) Flexible
(*c*) Legalistic   (*d*) All of the above

26. According to the Tables of Roman Civil law, which privilege was not entailed by citizenship?
(*a*) Service in the army
(*b*) Intermarriage
(*c*) Voting in the assembly
(*d*) Fundamental rights

27. When a rich country like the United States drags other states of the world into its area of influence by the force of militia, it becomes :
(*a*) Dollar imperialism
(*b*) Subjugation
(*c*) Yankee imperialism
(*d*) Leasehold

28. According to the Marxists, imperialism is the extension of the :
(*a*) Proletariat System (*b*) Capitalist System
(*c*) Socialist System   (*d*) Liberal System

29. Lenin says that imperialism is the final stage of :
(*a*) Liberalism   (*b*) Socialism
(*c*) Capitalism   (*d*) Marxism

30. Modern imperialism emerged :
(*a*) After Sixteenth Century
(*b*) Before Fifteenth Century
(*c*) After Seventeenth Century
(*d*) After Fifteenth Century

31. The motivating force behind the emergence of modern imperialism is :
(*a*) Political   (*b*) Economic
(*c*) Social   (*d*) Socio-Political

32. "What our great industries lack more is markets, because both Germany and the US have become protectionist to the extreme degree" – who made this statement in 1885?
(*a*) Monroe   (*b*) Jules Ferry
(*c*) Synder   (*d*) Moon

33. Who said that imperialism is a chief distortion of nationalism?
(*a*) Moon   (*b*) Amery
(*c*) Ebenstein   (*d*) Calvin

34. The concept of citizenship involves the concept of :
(*a*) Ethnicity   (*b*) Liberty
(*c*) Rights   (*d*) Duties

35. Who said that 'citizenship is man's basic right for it is nothing less than the right to have right?
(*a*) Earl Warren   (*b*) Gidden
(*c*) Marshal   (*d*) Lenin

36. The modern idea of citizenship includes not only civil and political dimensions but also a :
(*a*) Psychological component
(*b*) Social component
(*c*) Economic component
(*d*) Factual component

37. Who among the following advocates the group theory?
(*a*) Bentley   (*b*) Truman
(*c*) Kautsky   (*d*) All of the above

38. Politics is a study of the interaction of the economic, political and ideological dimensions of :
(*a*) Society   (*b*) Class
(*c*) State   (*d*) Power

39. ------ is the source of the economic dimension of power.
(*a*) Leadership   (*b*) Wealth
(*c*) Force   (*d*) Control

40. The ideological dimension of power emanates from the power exerted by :
(*a*) Religion   (*b*) Mass media
(*c*) Politicians   (*d*) Both (a) and (b)

41. Who said that politics is concerned among other things with conflicts over the proper use of force, power, authority?
(*a*) Apter   (*b*) Greaves
(*c*) Duverger   (*d*) Paul Janet

42. Who asserts that fundamental conception in social sciences is power in the same sense that energy is fundamental concept in physics?
(*a*) Russell   (*b*) Weber
(*c*) Macpherson   (*d*) Palmer

43. The 'power theory' finds its brilliant manifestation in the political philosophy of :
(*a*) Locke   (*b*) Hobbes
(*c*) Mill   (*d*) Rousseau

44. Which of the following was a 'protectorate' of the British Empire between 1922 and 1936?
(*a*) Israel   (*b*) Egypt
(*c*) Haiti   (*d*) Cuba

45. Advancements in science and technology as also the socio-economic processes, have made -------- more complex.
(*a*) Societies
(*b*) Human mind
(*c*) Politics
(*d*) None of the above

46. Which of the following is an example of societies that do not have organized state?
(*a*) Nuer in Southern Sudan
(*b*) Anuak in Anglo-Egyptian Sudan
(*c*) Tallensi in northern territory of Gold Coast
(*d*) All of the above

47. ------ is not restricted to any geographical area.
(*a*) State   (*b*) Nation
(*c*) Society   (*d*) Country

48. The relationship between state and society is --------, they determine and are, in turn, determined by each other.
(*a*) Reciprocal
(*b*) Controversial
(*c*) Contradictory
(*d*) None of the above

49. The word 'nation' is derived from the Latin word 'natio' which means :
(*a*) Common affiliation
(*b*) Common mother
(*c*) Common birth or race
(*d*) None of the above

50. During the French Revolution the term 'nation' came into great popularity and was used to mean :
(*a*) Patriotism
(*b*) Citizenship
(*c*) Liberation

(*d*) None of the above

51. Who said that revolution is that process by which a radical alteration of a particular society occurs over a time span?
(*a*) Moore   (*b*) Cohan
(*c*) Dunn   (*d*) Petee

52. Who said that power is "a relationship in which one group of persons is able to determine the actions of another in the direction of the Former's own ends"?
(*a*) Morgenthau   (*b*) Palmer
(*c*) Easton   (*d*) Duverger

53. The Elitist view maintains that in a democratic society political power resides in the :
(*a*) Bureaucratic elite   (*b*) Pluralist elite
(*c*) Liberal elite   (*d*) Socialist elite

54. "Politics is the possession and distribution of power" ------- who made this statement?
(*a*) Robson   (*b*) Becker
(*c*) Russell   (*d*) Disraeli

55. According to marxism, political power is a strong, organised and unified power of the economically :
(*a*) Weaker Section   (*b*) Dominant Class
(*c*) Backward Class   (*d*) Better off Section

56. What is meant by the "managerial revolution"?
(*a*) The revolution by which managers and not politicians became the controllers of political power
(*b*) Managers of industries have become so powerful that they can dictate the terms and conditions of their services
(*c*) The fact that in the modern western capitalist economics, ownership of capital and control of capital have been separated
(*d*) The industrial managers virtually control the economy of a country in the modern times

57. Ideological power helps the ruling class in maintaining the legitimacy of its :
(*a*) Ideological power   (*b*) Political power
(*c*) Economic power   (*d*) Social power

58. Who define power as 'the capacity in any relationship to command the service or compliance of others'?
(*a*) Weber
(*b*) MacIver
(*c*) Pareto
(*d*) Russell

59. Which of the following is not one of the types of authority prevalent in the modern state; according to Weber?
(*a*) Legal-rational authority
(*b*) Traditional authority
(*c*) Charismatic authority
(*d*) Nominal authority

60. Who among the following traditional thinkers brought out the significance of power in the political phenomenon?
(*a*) Hobbes
(*b*) Machiavelli
(*c*) Nietzsche
(*d*) All of these

61. Who defined political science as 'the study of the Shaping and Sharing of power'?
(*a*) Weber
(*b*) MacIver
(*c*) Lasswell and Kaplan
(*d*) Catlin

62. Match List I with List II and select the correct answer by using the codes given below :

List I	List II
A. Robert Dahl	1. Comparative Government and Politics
B. MacIver	2. Power and Society
C. Michael Curtis	3. Modern Political Analysis
D. Kaplan	4. The Web of Government

Codes :

	A	B	C	D
(*a*)	3	4	1	2
(*b*)	1	2	3	4
(*c*)	3	4	2	1
(*d*)	4	1	3	2

63. Which of the following is one of the traditionally recognized organs of power in the state?
(*a*) Legislature
(*b*) Executive
(*c*) Judiciary
(*d*) All of these

64. Leacock defines a nation or nationality as a body of people united by common descent and a common :
(*a*) Territory
(*b*) Customs
(*c*) Language
(*d*) None of the above

65. Who said that a nation is a community of persons living in definite territory and thereby bound together by the bonds of mutual love?
(*a*) Gilchrist
(*b*) Garner
(*c*) Bryce
(*d*) Barker

66. Who, in his work 'International Law,' emphasises that the idea of nation is associated with origin of birth, community of race, community of language, etc.?
(*a*) Leacock
(*b*) Hayes
(*c*) Calvo
(*d*) None of the above

67. Sidgwick has correctly said that some of the leading modern nations are "notoriously" of very mixed :
(*a*) Race
(*b*) Language
(*c*) System
(*d*) None of the above

68. Which of the following is not a form of closed door policy?
(*a*) Tariffs
(*b*) Shipping
(*c*) Concessions
(*d*) Mandate

69. What is the term used to explain control by two or more powers over a disputed territory in order to prevent colonial rivalry?
(*a*) Protectorate
(*b*) Alliance
(*c*) Condominium
(*d*) None of the above

70. The right of extra-territoriality was claimed and established in almost all ------ countries which give few rights to Christians.
(*a*) North-eastern
(*b*) Muslim
(*c*) Hindu
(*d*) Western

71. Modern imperialism places more reliance on :
(*a*) Downright conquest and annexation
(*b*) Diplomacy and international agreement
(*c*) Groupism and cold war
(*d*) Nuclear threat and hooliganism

72. Which of the following may be defined as "the complex of organised associations and institutions within a community"?
(*a*) Society
(*b*) Nation
(*c*) State
(*d*) None of the above

73. Who said that the global economy must be viewed as a collection of heterogeneous units with different agendas interacting with one-another in a variety of ways and thus changing its character over time?
(*a*) Adiseshiah
(*b*) Kurien
(*c*) Bruton
(*d*) Kruenger

74. Which of the following is defined as the value which labour produces beyond that which is socially necessary to sustain itself?
(*a*) Additional Value
(*b*) Labour Value
(*c*) Concealed Value
(*d*) Surplus Value

75. Which one of the following thinkers proposed the criterion of falsifiability as the measure of scientific truth?
(*a*) Levi-Strauss
(*b*) Max Weber
(*c*) Karl Popper
(*d*) Karl Marx

76. What does TRIPs stand for?
(*a*) Tariff-Related Intellectual Practices
(*b*) Trade-Related Intellectual Property Rights
(*c*) Trade-Related Interest Property Rights
(*d*) None of the above

77. Under ------ patents shall be available for any invention whether product or process in all fields of industrial technologies.
(*a*) GATT
(*b*) TRIMs
(*c*) TRIPs
(*d*) WTO

78. Who said that "state is particular portion of mankind viewed as an organised"?
(*a*) Bluntschelli
(*b*) Hegel
(*c*) Burgess
(*d*) Leacock

79. Who made no distinction between State and Society?
(*a*) Hegel
(*b*) Aristotle
(*c*) Plato
(*d*) Both (*b*) and (*c*)

80. Which theory considers the associations as important as the state itself?
(*a*) Institutionalistic theory
(*b*) Behaviouralistic theory
(*c*) Individualistic theory
(*d*) Pluralistic theory

81. ------ enjoys the power of coercion and ------ does not enjoy the powers of coercion
(*a*) State, Society
(*b*) Nation, State
(*c*) Association, Society
(*d*) Government, State

82. Society secures the cooperation of its members by :
(*a*) Coercion
(*b*) Persuasion
(*c*) Allurement
(*d*) None of the above

83. Who argues that trade liberalization brings about increasing returns, which in turn, would generate a higher rate of growth in the economy?
(*a*) Krueger
(*b*) Edwards
(*c*) Michaley
(*d*) Tayler

84. Which of the following means the extension of the neo-classical view of competition, 'the freedom of traders to use their resources where they will and exchange them at any price they wish' across the nations?
(*a*) Globalisation
(*b*) Privatisation
(*c*) Commercialisation
(*d*) None of the above

85. What does MIC stand for?
(*a*) Marginal Inquiry Commission
(*b*) Market Inquiry Commission
(*c*) Monopolies Inquiry Commission
(*d*) None of the above

86. The term 'nation' conveys the ideals of :
(*a*) Social independence
(*b*) Political independence
(*c*) Economic independence
(*d*) All of the above

87. Which of the following statements is true regarding nation?
   (*a*) A nation is a community which considers itself one
   (*b*) A nation means the population of a selfgoverning state
   (*c*) It is held together by many ties like territory language etc.
   (*d*) All of the above

88. Who said that a nation is a soul, a spiritual principle and "to have suffered, rejoiced and hoped together" makes a people a notion?
   (*a*) Hayes   (*b*) Ernest Renan
   (*c*) Burns   (*d*) Zimmern

89. The term nation emphasises the consciousness of unity due to :
   (*a*) Psychological Feelings
   (*b*) Political Feelings
   (*c*) Spiritual Feelings
   (*d*) Both (a) and (c)

90. Most of the political thinkers equate nation with :
   (*a*) Nationality
   (*b*) State
   (*c*) Society
   (*d*) None of the above

91. Which of the following are not the basis of the authority of society?
   (*a*) Social Customs   (*b*) Conventions
   (*c*) Laws   (*d*) Moral Pressure

92. The goals of the Indian Society have been spelt out in the :
   (*a*) Bhagavat Gita
   (*b*) Constitution
   (*c*) Religious Scriptures
   (*d*) All of the above

93. Who among the following modern writers brought out the significance of power in the political phenomenon?
   (*a*) Kaplan   (*b*) Merriam
   (*c*) Hobbes   (*d*) Both (a) and (b)

94. Ideological power provides a more subtle base of :
   (*a*) Economic power   (*b*) Political power
   (*c*) Traditional power (*d*) Physical power

95. Who define ideology as a 'systematic set of arguments and beliefs used to justify an existing or desired social order'?
   (*a*) Max Weber   (*b*) Joseph Dunner
   (*c*) Gramsci   (*d*) Dyke

96. Who among the following, uses the term 'Political System' instead of the state?
   (*a*) M.H. Fried   (*b*) G.H. Almond
   (*c*) Miss Follet   (*d*) Bakunin

97. Traditional political theory emphasises the study of :
   (*a*) Nation and civil society
   (*b*) State and government
   (*c*) Association and group
   (*d*) Government and nationality

98. Who among the following have given relatively the most satisfactory definitions of the state?
   1. Garner
   2. Oppenheim
   3. Gilchrist
   4. Sidgwick
   Select the correct answer from the following :
   (*a*) 1 and 2   (*b*) 2 and 3
   (*c*) 1 and 3   (*d*) 2 and 4

99. "Government is the agency or machinery through which common policies are determined, common affairs are regulated and common interests promoted".
   The above statement is attributed to :
   (*a*) Gettel   (*b*) Laski
   (*c*) Gilchrist   (*d*) Garner

100. Who among the following statements are 'communitarian'?
   (*a*) Ralph Miliband
   (*b*) Hannah Arendt
   (*c*) Hans J. Morgenthau
   (*d*) Louis Althusser

101. Consider the following statement : "---- the entire world has no right to silence a fool -----"
   The above statement was made by :
   (*a*) Niccollo Machiavelli
   (*b*) Jeremy Bentham

(*c*) James Mill

(*d*) John Stuart Mill

102. Which group of scholars among the following advocated that state has a personality of its own?

(*a*) Stahl, Gierke, Gerber, Treitschke and Bluntschli

(*b*) Green, Bradly, Aristotle and Bosanquet

(*c*) Max Stirner, Kropotkin and Tolstoy

(*d*) Nietzsche, Mussolini and Bernhardi

103. Which of the following views of state is the earliest in temporal order?

(*a*) Church-state view (*b*) Anarchist view

(*c*) Ethical view   (*d*) Organic view

104. In the tradition of the organic view of the state, who was the first among the following to clearly point out the interdependence of society and individual :

(*a*) Schaffle   (*b*) Fichte

(*c*) Rousseau   (*d*) Gumplowicz

105. The view which holds state as a 'necessary evil' seeks :

(*a*) Abolition of state

(*b*) Promotion of state

(*c*) Limited state

(*d*) Replacement of state by voluntary organisations

106. Who among the following first used the modern terms 'sovereign' and sovereignty'?

(*a*) English liberals like Locke

(*b*) German idealists like Hegel

(*c*) Chinese revolutionaries like Mao

(*d*) French jurists such as Beaumanoir and Loyseau

107. Jean Bodin claims to be the first modern writer to give the idea of sovereignty. He discussed it at length in :

(*a*) Lectures on Jurisprudence

(*b*) On Sovereignty

(*c*) Six Books on the Republic

(*d*) Recent Theories of Sovereignty

108. Who among the following suggested that the whole concept of sovereignty should be abandoned altogether?

(*a*) Barker   (*b*) MacIver

(*c*) Jenks   (*d*) Laski

109. He is sovereign only in name and not in fact. Although, outwardly the power is vested in him, the real power is enjoyed by another person or institution. He is a :

(*a*) De jure sovereign

(*b*) Legal sovereign

(*c*) Popular sovereign

(*d*) Titular sovereign

110. Who among the following is highly critical of the Austinian theory of sovereignty?

(*a*) Gilchrist   (*b*) Locke

(*c*) Henry Maine   (*d*) Hegel

111. The term 'nation' is derived from :

(*a*) Natio which means born

(*b*) Neten which means race

(*c*) Noton which means form

(*d*) Nail which means community

112. Who made the statement that ------ the, nation underlies the state ------ 'and' ------ the state is the nation organised in a certain way?

(*a*) Thomas Hill Green

(*b*) Lord Acton

(*c*) Henry Leocock

(*d*) Leslie Lipson

113. Which of the following is correctly matched?

(*a*) Woodrow Wilson : Politics Among Nations

(*b*) Ralph Miliband : Politics Among Nations

(*c*) Bluntschli   : Theory of the state

(*d*) Sidgwick   : Politics

114. The book 'The Hindrances to Good Citizenship' is authored by :

(*a*) R.M. MacIver   (*b*) James Bryce

(*c*) J.S. Mill   (*d*) De Tocqueville

115. Consider the following statement : "He who has the power to take part in deliberative or judicial administration is said by us to be a citizen of that state".

(*a*) Plato   (*b*) Aristotle

(*c*) Rousseau   (*d*) J.S. Mill

116. Naturalised citizens are citzens by :
(*a*) Training   (*b*) Birth
(*c*) Education   (*d*) Adoption

117. Who made the following statement? "Education is the best defence of citizenship".
(*a*) Laski   (*b*) Woodrow Wilson
(*c*) Lord Bryce   (*d*) Edmund Burke

118. Who says that the essence of good citizenship is "the contribution of one's instructed judgement to the public good"?
(*a*) Laski in 'A Grammar of Politics'
(*b*) MacIver in 'A Web of Government'
(*c*) Laski in 'Liberty in the Modern State'
(*d*) Thomas Paine in 'Rights of Man'

119. Who among the following is an authority on imperialism?
(*a*) Michael Sandel   (*b*) Parker T. Moon
(*c*) Rosa Luxemburg   (*d*) Both (a) and (b)

120. The comment – "The Empire is comerce" is attributed to :
(*a*) Andrew Carnegic
(*b*) Joseph Chamberlain
(*c*) Daniel Bell
(*d*) Parker T. Moon

121. Prominent critic of imperialism is :
(*a*) J.A. Hobson   (*b*) Lenin
(*c*) M.K. Gandhi   (*d*) All of the above

122. George Bernard Shaw has given his description of the British Imperialism in :
(*a*) The Third British Empire
(*b*) Imperialism and Civilization
(*c*) The Man of Destiny
(*d*) The Pattern of Imperialism

123. In Marxist theory, society is divided into dominant and dependent classes and the former controls the state which is an embodiment of :
(*a*) Political power
(*b*) Economic power
(*c*) Social power
(*d*) None of the above

124. The work 'History of freedom and other Essays' is authored by :

(*a*) Lord Hewart
(*b*) Lord Chesterfield
(*c*) Lord Acton
(*d*) None of the above

125. The pattern of social relations at any stage of social development is determind by :
(*a*) The forms of production at that stage
(*b*) The relations of production at that stage
(*c*) The mode of production at that stage
(*d*) All of the above

126. In the Marxist theory, the stage will wither away after :
(*a*) Revolution of workers takes place
(*b*) A classless society comes into existence
(*c*) Proletariat takes away the property of the capitalists
(*d*) None of the above

127. A great merit of the Marxist theory of state lies in the fact that :
(*a*) It emphasise the role of economic forces in shaping history
(*b*) It proclaims the advent of the rule of numerical majority
(*c*) It purges the liberal theory of its drawbacks
(*d*) Both (*b*) and (*c*)

128. Which of the following works is edited by R. Blackburn?
(*a*) Political Theory
(*b*) Political Thought in England from Spencer to Today
(*c*) Theory of the State
(*d*) Ideology in Social Science

129. The prominent criticism of the Marxian theory is that :
(*a*) There is no rigid division of society into two classes
(*b*) The size of the middle class has increased under the capitalist system instead of diminishing
(*c*) Both (*a*) and (*b*)
(*d*) Its prognosis has not been practicable anywhere, anytime

130. Among the early Greeks who held the view that the state is not a divine inspiration guiding the footsteps of men into Internal Truth but a device of his own making for the convenience of his social life?
(*a*) Socrates   (*b*) Pericles
(*c*) Plato   (*d*) Epicurus

131. According to early Romans 'Nomos' represents :
(*a*) State   (*b*) Society
(*c*) Internal Truth (*d*) Law

132. The view that the state was created by man was given a systematic and theoretical treatment during :
(*a*) Fourteenth Century
(*b*) Seventeenth Century
(*c*) Eighteenth Century
(*d*) Both (b) and (c)

133. According to early Romans 'Lex' signified :
(*a*) Body of Law created by man
(*b*) Social conventions followed by man
(*c*) Internal truth
(*d*) None of the above

134. The main exponents of the view that state is a man made institution, an artificial device were :
(*a*) Hobbes and Locke
(*b*) Locke and Bentham
(*c*) Hobbes, Locke and Bentham
(*d*) None of the above

135. The mechanistic view of the state gave rise to the doctrine of :
(*a*) Liberalism   (*b*) Anarchism
(*c*) Individualism (*d*) None of the above

136. Which of the following theories has facilitated the development of democratic institutions?
(*a*) Liberalism
(*b*) Guild-socialist view of the state
(*c*) Both (a) and (b)
(*d*) Machanistic view of the state

137. The work 'Self Government in Industry' is authored by :
(*a*) Herman Finer   (*b*) G.D.H. Cole
(*c*) R.G. Gettel   (*d*) A.J. Penty

138. Who among the following early Greeks compared the state to a man of great stature and pointed out the resemblance between the functions of the state and those of an individual?
(*a*) Plato   (*b*) Aristotle
(*c*) Socrates   (*d*) None of the above

139. Plato based his three fold classification of society, namely working classes, warriors and the rulers upon which of the following faculties of the human soul?
(*a*) Appetite   (*b*) Greed
(*c*) Wisdom   (*d*) All of these

140. Which of the following events challenged the view of the state as a natural institution?
(*a*) Renaissance
(*b*) Reformation
(*c*) Scientific revolution of the Seventeenth Century
(*d*) None of the above

141. Which of the following ignores the distinction between state and society?
(*a*) Machanistic view of the state
(*b*) Organic theory of the state
(*c*) Marxist view of the state
(*d*) None of the above

142. Who contended that society was an organism whose protoplasm or unit is man, the state or government in the one corresponding to the brain in the other?
(*a*) Fichte   (*b*) Schaffle
(*c*) Spencer   (*d*) Aristotle

143. Who among the following define the state as a community or society politically organised under one independent government within a definite territory?
(*a*) Dillon   (*b*) Leiden
(*c*) Steward   (*d*) All of these

144. Who held that a good citizen makes a good state and a bad citizen a bad state?
(*a*) Aristotle
(*b*) Plato
(*c*) Machiavelli
(*d*) None of the above

145. Who among the following was in favour of a small state?
    (*a*) Treitschke
    (*b*) Rousseau
    (*c*) Acton
    (*d*) None of the above

146. Who among the following did not make any differentiation between the state and government?
    (*a*) Stuart Kings of England
    (*b*) Louis XIV of France
    (*c*) Political thinkers like Hobbes
    (*d*) All of the above

147. The observation that, "The more the social bond is extended, the more it is weakened" is made by :
    (*a*) Lord Acton   (*b*) J.J. Rousseau
    (*c*) J.S. Mill   (*d*) James Stephen

148. Who opined that it was in small states that democracy first arose?
    (*a*) Lord Bryce
    (*b*) Lord Acton

    (*c*) Lord Hewart
    (*d*) None of these

149. Who among the following scholars held the view that the territory of a state should neither be very small nor very large?
    (*a*) Machiavelli   (*b*) Hobbes
    (*c*) Marx   (*d*) Aristotle

150. The book 'Nationality and Government' is authored by :
    (*a*) Zimmern   (*b*) Wiseman
    (*c*) Soltau   (*d*) D.L. Shills

151. Who among the following considers the state as the sole source of the right to use violence?
    (*a*) Marx   (*b*) Weber
    (*c*) Kant   (*d*) Hegel

152. The institution common to Saudi Arabia and Sweden is :
    (*a*) Ombudsman
    (*b*) Monarchy
    (*c*) Election commission
    (*d*) Local Judiciary

ANSWERS

1	2	3	4	5	6	7	8	9	10
(*c*)	(*d*)	(*c*)	(*b*)	(*c*)	(*c*)	(*b*)	(*b*)	(*a*)	(*d*)
11	**12**	**13**	**14**	**15**	**16**	**17**	**18**	**19**	**20**
(*d*)	(*b*)	(*a*)	(*b*)	(*b*)	(*c*)	(*d*)	(*c*)	(*b*)	(*c*)
21	**22**	**23**	**24**	**25**	**26**	**27**	**28**	**29**	**30**
(*d*)	(*d*)	(*a*)	(*a*)	(*d*)	(*d*)	(*c*)	(*b*)	(*c*)	(*d*)
31	**32**	**33**	**34**	**35**	**36**	**37**	**38**	**39**	**40**
(*b*)	(*b*)	(*c*)	(*c*)	(*a*)	(*b*)	(*d*)	(*d*)	(*b*)	(*d*)
41	**42**	**43**	**44**	**45**	**46**	**47**	**48**	**49**	**50**
(*b*)	(*a*)	(*b*)	(*b*)	(*a*)	(*d*)	(*c*)	(*a*)	(*c*)	(*a*)
51	**52**	**53**	**54**	**55**	**56**	**57**	**58**	**59**	**60**
(*b*)	(*c*)	(*b*)	(*d*)	(*b*)	(*c*)	(*b*)	(*b*)	(*d*)	(*d*)
61	**62**	**63**	**64**	**65**	**66**	**67**	**68**	**69**	**70**
(*c*)	(*a*)	(*d*)	(*c*)	(*d*)	(*c*)	(*a*)	(*d*)	(*c*)	(*b*)

71	72	73	74	75	76	77	78	79	80
(d)	(a)	(b)	(d)	(c)	(b)	(c)	(c)	(d)	(d)
81	**82**	**83**	**84**	**85**	**86**	**87**	**88**	**89**	**90**
(a)	(b)	(b)	(a)	(c)	(b)	(d)	(b)	(d)	(b)
91	**92**	**93**	**94**	**95**	**96**	**97**	**98**	**99**	**100**
(c)	(b)	(d)	(b)	(b)	(b)	(b)	(c)	(d)	(b)
101	**102**	**103**	**104**	**105**	**106**	**107**	**108**	**109**	**110**
(d)	(a)	(d)	(b)	(c)	(d)	(c)	(d)	(d)	(c)
111	**112**	**113**	**114**	**115**	**116**	**117**	**118**	**119**	**120**
(a)	(a)	(c)	(b)	(b)	(d)	(c)	(a)	(b)	(b)
121	**122**	**123**	**124**	**125**	**126**	**127**	**128**	**129**	**130**
(d)	(c)	(a)	(c)	(a)	(b)	(a)	(d)	(c)	(d)
131	**132**	**133**	**134**	**135**	**136**	**137**	**138**	**139**	**140**
(c)	(d)	(a)	(c)	(c)	(d)	(b)	(a)	(d)	(c)
141	**142**	**143**	**144**	**145**	**146**	**147**	**148**	**149**	**150**
(b)	(b)	(c)	(a)	(b)	(d)	(b)	(a)	(d)	(a)
151	**152**								
(b)	(b)								

———

4

POLITICAL IDEAS

1. Who said that "philosophers have so far interpreted the world, the problem is how to change it"?
(*a*) Lenin (*b*) Marx
(*c*) Rousseau (*d*) Miliband

2. In which book Lenin said that a socialist revolution would imply that the state under the fundamentally new conditions "is transformed into something which is no longer the state proper"?
(*a*) Marxism and Politics
(*b*) The Anatomy of Revolution
(*c*) State and Revolution
(*d*) Social Change

3. Who desired the 'fostering of revolution abroad as an essential part of the process'?
(*a*) Miliband (*b*) Lenin
(*c*) Cohan (*d*) Trotsky

4. The Communist Manifesto of Marx and Engels Frankly advocates the use of :
(*a*) Unfair methods
(*b*) Temporary methods
(*c*) Violent methods
(*d*) Non-violent methods

5. Which of the following is one of the kinds of revolution according to Johnson?
(*a*) Millenaria rebellion
(*b*) Jacquerie
(*c*) Anarchistic rebellion
(*d*) All of the above

6. Who makes a psychological study of the theme of revolution?
(*a*) Johnson (*b*) Sorokin
(*c*) Gurr (*d*) Tocqueville

7. Who among the following has propounded the theory of relative deprivation?
(*a*) Gurr (*b*) Nesvold
(*c*) Marx (*d*) Both (a) and (b)

8. Who discussed the causes of a revolution from the standpoint of psycho-analysis?
(*a*) Cohan (*b*) Friedrich
(*c*) Schwartz (*d*) Gurr

9. Who made the most significant contribution to the study of revolutions in modern times?
(*a*) Marx (*b*) Lenin
(*c*) Moore (*d*) Johnson

10. In his Eighteenth Brumaire of Louis Bonaparte, Marx produced a masterpiece of contemporary ------ revolutionary history.
(*a*) Russian (*b*) German
(*c*) French (*d*) Chinese

11. Match List I with List II and select the correct answer by using the codes :

List I	List II
A. Glorious Revolution	1. 1776
B. American Declaration of Independence	2. 1917
C. French Revolution	3. 1688
D. Russian Revolution	4. 1789

Codes :

	A	B	C	D
(*a*)	3	1	4	2
(*b*)	1	2	3	4
(*c*)	3	1	2	4
(*d*)	3	2	4	1

12. Who has sought to lay down some empirical observations on the basis of a case study of four great revolutions of the world?
(*a*) Cohan (*b*) Briton
(*c*) Aristotle (*d*) Lasswell

13. Who considers revolution to be 'a rapid, fundamental and violent domestic change in the dominant values and myths of a society'?
(*a*) Petee
(*b*) Kuhn
(*c*) Brinton
(*d*) Huntington

14. Who takes revolution as 'a shift in the class composition of the elites'?
(*a*) Lasswell
(*b*) Dunn
(*c*) Cohan
(*d*) Moore

15. According to Marxists, a revolution is taken as an inevitable development in which the essential factor is the change of :
(*a*) Class dominance
(*b*) Caste dominance
(*c*) Social dominance
(*d*) Political dominance

16. Who looks at revolutions as 'a sweeping fundamental change in the predominant myth of social order?
(*a*) Cohan
(*b*) Neuman
(*c*) Brinton
(*d*) Lenin

17. Who recognised the importance of historical accidents as a causative factor in revolutions?
(*a*) Lenin
(*b*) Sorokin
(*c*) Moore
(*d*) Marx

18. Which of the following is not one of the works of Marx?
(*a*) The German Ideology
(*b*) The Civil War in France
(*c*) The Communist Manifesto
(*d*) Revolutionary Change

19. Who said that social revolution is an ongoing process in which causes and effects are dialectically related?
(*a*) Huntington
(*b*) Karl Marx
(*c*) Johnson
(*d*) Miliband

20. For Marx, the ------ was the 'political form of social emancipation'.
(*a*) Communist League
(*b*) Paris Commune
(*c*) Revolution
(*d*) Communist Manifesto

21. Who among the following emphasized the human causes of revolution?
(*a*) Lenin
(*b*) Marx
(*c*) Almond
(*d*) Popper

22. Marx in his Address to the Communist League advocated the idea of :
(*a*) Mass revolution
(*b*) Temporary revolution
(*c*) Permanent revolution
(*d*) Class revolution

23. Which of the following statements is not correct regarding nature and meaning of revolution?
(*a*) Alteration of institution
(*b*) Alteration of social structures
(*c*) No changes in the leadership formation
(*d*) Alteration of values or myths of the society

24. Who said that political revolution occur because "the parties to a revolution differ about the institutional matrix within which political change is to be achieved and evaluated"?
(*a*) Kuhn
(*b*) Laski
(*c*) Moore
(*d*) Dunn

25. A revolution is certainly a result of :
(*a*) Political disequilibrium
(*b*) Economic disequilibrium
(*c*) Class disequilibrium
(*d*) Social disequilibrium

26. Who stressed the point that revolutions are destructive?
(*a*) Gurr
(*b*) Sorokin
(*c*) Johnson
(*d*) Cohan

27. The ------ law in England is regarded as a true embodiment of justice.
(*a*) Civil
(*b*) Constitutional
(*c*) Statute
(*d*) Common

28. Besides common law and the statute law, the English courts apply a certain type of rules which is known as
(*a*) Rationality
(*b*) Veracity
(*c*) Equity
(*d*) None of the above

29. What is regarded as the corner stone of the British system of government?
(*a*) Common law   (*b*) Civil law
(*c*) Rule of law   (*d*) Statute law

30. In which book Dicey developed the idea of Rule of law, published in 1885?
(*a*) The British Constitution
(*b*) Law and the Constitution
(*c*) An Introduction to the British Constitution
(*d*) None of the above

31. Who said that "rule, predominance or supremacy of the law" is an outstanding feature of the British Constitution?
(*a*) Dicey   (*b*) Harvey
(*c*) Tocqueville   (*d*) Barther

32. According to first proposition of Dicey, no person can be punished except for the :
(*a*) Crime of homicide
(*b*) Breach of law
(*c*) Breaking of taboos
(*d*) All of the above

33. Which of the following is not one of the sources of Administrative law?
(*a*) Constitution   (*b*) Custom
(*c*) Ordinance   (*d*) Superstition

34. Who divides the field of administrative law into the law of internal administration and the law of external administration?
(*a*) Goodnow   (*b*) Dicey
(*c*) James Hart   (*d*) Morgan

35. The distinction between constitutional law and Administrative law is very clear in countries like :
(*a*) USA   (*b*) Germany
(*c*) India   (*d*) Both (*a*) and (*c*)

36. Which article of the Indian constitution provided that the government or its agencies shall be subject to the jurisdiction of the Superior Courts?
(*a*) Article 300
(*b*) Article 136
(*c*) Article 226
(*d*) None of the above

37. According to which theory, participation represents the process by which goals are set and means are chosen in relation to all sorts of social issues?
(*a*) Socialist theory
(*b*) Marxist theory
(*c*) Democratic theory
(*d*) None of the above

38. Which of the following are the major types of participation, exercised by citizens in the decision-making process in government and administration?
1.   Democratic
2.   Administrative
3.   Social
4.   Community Development
Select the correct answer using the codes given below :
Codes :
(*a*) 1, 2 and 3   (*b*) 2, 3 and 4
(*c*) 1, 3 and 4   (*d*) 1, 2, 3 and 4

39. Who said that political participation is the activity by private citizens designed to influence governmental decision-making?
(*a*) Huntington Nelson
(*b*) Milton Esman
(*c*) Myron Weiner
(*d*) Lucian Pye

40. Which of the following statements is true regarding political participation?
(*a*) Electoral activities
(*b*) Protests, Strikes, Demonstrations
(*c*) The activities designed to influence the decisions of government through pressure or persuasion to attain ends
(*d*) All of the above

41. The system analysis would say that all types of participation-political, administrative and economic-would fall within the ambit of :
(*a*) Democratic participation
(*b*) Social participation
(*c*) Community development
(*d*) None of the above

42. Swaraj literally means :
(*a*) Ramrajya   (*b*) Self-rule
(*c*) Ahimsa   (*d*) Freedom

43. Swaraj implies the reign of complete :
(*a*) Social justice   (*b*) Equality
(*c*) Freedom   (*d*) All of these

44. What was the means adopted by Gandhiji for the attainment of freedom?
(*a*) Ahimsa   (*b*) Satyagraha
(*c*) Anashan   (*d*) Both (*a*) and (*b*)

45. The doctrine of the Rule of law was enunciated by :
(*a*) Rawls   (*b*) Dicey
(*c*) Bryce   (*d*) Barker

46. Which of the following is a source of law?
(*a*) Custom   (*b*) Religion
(*c*) Equity   (*d*) All of these

47. The most prolific source of law is :
(*a*) Equity   (*b*) Adjudication
(*c*) Legislation   (*d*) Custom

48. An informal method of making new law or altering an old one is :
(*a*) Legislation   (*b*) Equity
(*c*) Adjudication   (*d*) Arbitration

49. ------ law is concerned with the relationship between individuals.
(*a*) National   (*b*) Natural
(*c*) Private   (*d*) Public

50. Which theory considers law as eternal, constant, rational and immutable?
(*a*) Sociological theory
(*b*) Rational theory
(*c*) Natural theory
(*d*) Historical theory

51. The most widely accepted theory of law is :
(*a*) Historical theory
(*b*) Imperative theory
(*c*) Natural theory
(*d*) Sociological theory

52. The crux of citizenship is participation in the :
(*a*) Political Community
(*b*) Social Community
(*c*) Economic Community
(*d*) Social System

53. The foundations of modern citizenship were laid in the :
(*a*) 18th Century   (*b*) 19th Century
(*c*) 16th Century   (*d*) 17th Century

54. The law made by the King-in-Council or by the King-in-Parliament is known as the :
(*a*) Common law
(*b*) Statutory law
(*c*) Civil law
(*d*) None of the above

55. What is the "end of government" according to James Madison?
(*a*) Liberty   (*b*) Equality
(*c*) Justice   (*d*) Prosperity

56. Who said that the great merit of the common law is that it represents the survival of the fittest among the various legal rules which successive generations of men have tried?
(*a*) Neumann
(*b*) Munro
(*c*) Dicey
(*d*) None of the above

57. The two principal types of law in Great Britain are the :
(*a*) Common law, Civil law
(*b*) Statute law, Common law
(*c*) Constitutional law, Criminal law
(*d*) Civil law, Criminal law

58. In Britain, any dispute between a private person and an official is decided in the :
(*a*) Common Court of law
(*b*) Ordinary Court of law
(*c*) Lower Court of law
(*d*) None of the above

59. Who was among the chief critics of Dicey's exposition of rule of law?
(*a*) Harvey   (*b*) Ivor Jennings
(*c*) Neumann   (*d*) Both (*a*) and (*b*)

60. The most clear exposition of the 'rule of law' was provided by—
(*a*) George Washington
(*b*) Jean Bodin
(*c*) Ivar Jennings
(*d*) A.V. Dicey

61. Which of the following are the two great branches of public law?
(*a*) Constitutional law, Common law
(*b*) Common law, Administrative law
(*c*) Administrative law, Constitutional law
(*d*) Constitutional law, Administrative law

62. Who said that Administrative law is the sum total of the principles according to which the activity of the services (other than judicial) concerned with the execution of law is exercised?
(*a*) Dicey
(*b*) Barthelemy
(*c*) Robson
(*d*) None of the above

63. Constitutional law is concerned with the construction of the machinery of :
(*a*) Government
(*b*) Political parties
(*c*) State
(*d*) None of the above

64. According to Dicey, the basic principles of the English Constitution was the rule of law, which he contrasted with the :
(*a*) American Fundamental Rights
(*b*) French Droit Administratif
(*c*) German Democratic Principles
(*d*) None of the above

65. Who has every right to punish all those who Violate State laws, according to Hegel?
(*a*) Supreme Court   (*b*) State
(*c*) Judge   (*d*) Administrator

66. Who said that the Civil Society is an inferior state in which people perform functions not those which are private but which are selfregarding?
(*a*) Gettel   (*b*) Wayper
(*c*) Hegel   (*d*) Kant

67. According to Hegel, in ------ Society man worked for himself but in universal society he worked for all.
(*a*) Civil
(*b*) Singular
(*c*) Territorial

(*d*) None of these

68. What gives logical development to any individual in the civil society according to Hegel?
(*a*) Society   (*b*) Government
(*c*) State   (*d*) Nation

69. In his critique of Hegel's philosophy of Right, who argued about universal political participation as a means and end of the manifestation of human freedom?
(*a*) J.S. Mill   (*b*) Tocqueville
(*c*) Rousseau   (*d*) Karl Marx

70. Who believed that it was not possible for any civil society to exist without the agency and authority of state?
(*a*) Marx   (*b*) Rousseau
(*c*) Locke   (*d*) Hegel

71. The chief proponents of the theory of natural rights are :
(*a*) John Locke and Thomas Paine
(*b*) Lasswell and Kaplan
(*c*) Hegel and Kant
(*d*) Durkheim and Weber

72. He wrote a Whole Volume on Natural Rights and brought out the various sense in which the term 'Nature' has been used. His aim was to criticize the theory of Natural rights. He was :
(*a*) Norman Vincent Pearl
(*b*) D.G. Ritchie
(*c*) Auguste Comte
(*d*) Macpherson

73. Which one of the following pairs is correctly matched?
(*a*) Historical theory of rights : J.S. Mill
(*b*) Social Welfare theory of : Roscoe
   rights   Pound
(*c*) Idealistic theory of rights : Spencer
(*d*) Natural theory of rights   : Burke

74. Who among the following are the chief proponents of the legal theory of rights?
(*a*) Bentham and Hobbes
(*b*) Bentham and Mill

   (*c*) Mao and Che Guevera
   (*d*) Gramsci and Lukas

75. Which of the following is NOT correctly matched?
   (*a*) Hobhouse : The Elements of the social Justice
   (*b*) T. Rees : Equality
   (*c*) Dicey : An Introduction to the study of Law of the constitution
   (*d*) Laski : Principles of the Social and Political Theory

76. The historical theory of rights can be summed up in the sentence :
   (*a*) History makes right
   (*b*) What is rights is historical
   (*c*) History is the child of right
   (*d*) History and right are antithetical

77. Who among the following ridiculed the natural rights, as being 'nonsense upon stilts'?
   (*a*) Schapera   (*b*) Foucault
   (*c*) Jeremy Bentham (*d*) Karl Marx

78. Idealistic theory of rights upholds :
   (*a*) Individual's labour
   (*b*) Individual's family
   (*c*) Individual's wealth
   (*d*) Individual's personality

79. Who among the following laid down an elaborate defence of personal liberty?
   (*a*) Rawls   (*b*) Poulantzas
   (*c*) Robert Michels (*d*) John Stuart Mill

80. Civil liberty stands for :
   (*a*) Freedom to pursue one's desire
   (*b*) Freedom to exercise discretion in one's own domain
   (*c*) Liberty to a mass wealth
   (*d*) Liberty to free action and immunity from interference

81. Who among the following held the view that liberty and equality are opposed to each other?
   1. J.S. Mill
   2. Lord Hewart
   3. De Tocqueville
   4. Lord Acton

Select the correct answer from below :
   (*a*) Only 2   (*b*) Only 3
   (*c*) 3 and 4   (*d*) Only 4

82. "------ freedom exists only because there is restraint"
   (*a*) Dicey   (*b*) Seeley
   (*c*) Bryce   (*d*) Willoughby

83. Which of the following works are NOT authored by Harold J. Laski?
   1. The Dilemma of Our Time
   2. The Web of Our Time
   3. Democracy in Crisis
   4. The Elements of Social Justice
Select the correct answer from the following :
   (*a*) 1 and 2   (*b*) 1, 2 and 3
   (*c*) 2 and 4   (*d*) Only 3

84. Match List I (Authors) with List II (Books) and select the correct answer by using codes given below the lists :

List I (Authors)	List II (Books)
A. Plamenatz	1. Justice
B. Sidgwick	2. Man and Society
C. Spencer	3. Political Ideals
D. C.D. Burns	4. Elements of Politics

Codes :

	A	B	C	D
(*a*)	2	4	3	1
(*b*)	4	2	1	3
(*c*)	2	4	1	3
(*d*)	1	2	3	4

85. The author of Anarchy, State and Utopia is :
   (*a*) F.A. Hayek   (*b*) C.B. Macpherson
   (*c*) Robert Nozick (*d*) Neitzsche

86. The idea of 'Joining' or 'Fitting' is implied in the concept of :
   (*a*) Liberty   (*b*) Equality
   (*c*) Property   (*d*) Justice

87. Which of the following are the sources of law?
   (*a*) Custom, religion, scientific commentaries, adjudication, equity and legislation
   (*b*) Constitution, morality, religion, custom, public opinion and equity
   (*c*) Public opinion, custom, parliament, judicature and executive

(*d*) Judicature, equity, nature, religious commentaries and plebiscite

88. Which of the following pairs is correctly matched?
(*a*) Morris Ginsberg : Justice
(*b*) Rees : A theory of Justice
(*c*) Rawls : Equality
(*d*) D.D. Raphael : Problems of Political Philosophy

89. The idea of 'reverse discrimination' implies :
(*a*) Discrimination in a decreasing order
(*b*) Equating rich and poor as in the electoral arena
(*c*) Bestowing favoured treatment to the hitherto deprived sections
(*d*) Establishing institutional checks against arbitrary distinctions

90. Who among the following holds the view that rights are those conditions of social life without which man cannot be his best self?
(*a*) Green
(*b*) Laski
(*c*) Barker
(*d*) None of the above

91. Who among the following opines that a right is a power claimed and recognized as :
(*a*) Green
(*b*) Barker
(*c*) Laski
(*d*) None of the above

92. In their essence rights are :
(*a*) Legal injunction
(*b*) Moral imperatives
(*c*) Conditions of law
(*d*) Aspects of social life

93. Who among the following held the view that right is man's capacity of influencing the acts of another by means of the opinion and force of society?
(*a*) Bluntschli (*b*) Bodin
(*c*) Holland (*d*) Locke

94. "We have a right to the means that are necessary to the development of our lives in the direction of the highest good of the community of which we are a part" -------- Bosanquet
The above statement highlights :
(*a*) Importance of personality
(*b*) Linkage between development and community
(*c*) An aspect of rights
(*d*) All of the above

95. The work Law and Rights is authored by :
(*a*) W.E. Hocking
(*b*) L.T. Hobhouse
(*c*) Harold Laski
(*d*) None of the above

96. Rights are broadly divided into three categories: natural rights, moral rights and legal rights comprise :
(*a*) Civil rights (*b*) Political rights
(*c*) Economic rights (*d*) All of the above

97. Which of the following is the use to which the term 'liberty' can be put?
(*a*) Freedom from constraint, captivity or tyranny
(*b*) The unrestrained injoyment of natural rights
(*c*) Power of free choice
(*d*) All of the above

98. The concept of liberty has developed mainly in modern times and is closely associated with the philosophy of :
(*a*) Utilitarianism
(*b*) Liberalism
(*c*) Individualism
(*d*) None of the above

99. Who made the observation that : "We are unable to make a satisfactory distinction between the terms freedom and liberty; the only difference is that one is English, the other Latin"?
(*a*) T.H. Green
(*b*) R.H. Soltau
(*c*) MacIver
(*d*) None of the above

100. The concept of liberty in the present form was missing during :

(*a*) Ancient times
(*b*) Medieval times
(*c*) Both (*a*) and (*b*)
(*d*) None of the above

101. Who among the following refused to accept the nation of individual liberty against society or the state?
(*a*) Plato   (*b*) Socrates
(*c*) Aristotle   (*d*) Both (*a*) and (*b*)

102. According to Stoics, liberty was :
(*a*) Availability of conditions of the development of human personality
(*b*) Expression of self-restraint
(*c*) A tool of morality
(*d*) None of the above

103. As a result of Renaissance, a multi-dimensional demand for liberty was made against :
(*a*) Church and the Papacy
(*b*) Feudal economic order
(*c*) Monarchs
(*d*) All of the above

104. Inequality in society was supported by :
(*a*) Pericles   (*b*) Plato
(*c*) Aristotle   (*d*) Both (*b*) and (*c*)

105. The French Declaration of the Rights of Man and the Citizen was inspired by :
(*a*) Montesquieu   (*b*) Rousseau
(*c*) Marx   (*d*) All of the above

106. Who among the following considered equality as man's law of nature?
(*a*) Pericles   (*b*) Euripides
(*c*) Stoics   (*d*) All of the above

107. In the nineteenth century, a vigorous demand for socio-economic equality was raised by :
(*a*) Working class
(*b*) Peasantry
(*c*) Propertied class
(*d*) None of the above

108. Who among the following holds the view that no idea is more difficult in the whole realm of political science than equality?
(*a*) Sabine   (*b*) Dunning
(*c*) Laski   (*d*) All of the above

109. The work Liberty, Equality, Fraternity is authored by :
(*a*) J.F. Stephen
(*b*) J.F. Kennedy
(*c*) J.F. Ribero
(*d*) None of the above

110. Among other things, equality implies :
(*a*) Literal equalisation
(*b*) Balanced distribution of resources
(*c*) Progressive reduction of inequalities where they are thought to be unreasonable
(*d*) All of the above

111. Legal equality implies :
(*a*) Equal subjection of all citizens to the law
(*b*) Equal protection of the law for all citizens
(*c*) Equal distribution of material goods to all
(*d*) Both (*a*) and (*b*)

112. Which of the following works is authored by J.A. Corry?
(*a*) Democratic theory
(*b*) Democratic Government and Politics
(*c*) Equality
(*d*) Man Against Myth

113. Justice is a dynamic idea because :
(*a*) Its realization is a continuous process
(*b*) Progress towards its realization depends upon the development of social consciousness
(*c*) Both (*a*) and (*b*)
(*d*) The term justice suggests the quality of being just or right or resonable

114. The earliest concept of justice in Greek thought is found to be in the writings of :
(*a*) Pericles
(*b*) Socrates
(*c*) Sophists
(*d*) Early Pythagoreans

115. "There never was an absolute justice but only a convention made in mutual intercourse, in whatever region, from time to time providing against the infection or suffering of harm".

The above understanding of justice belongs to :

(*a*) Stoics   (*b*) Epicureans
(*c*) Liberals   (*d*) Anarchists

116. The concept of positive law is :
(*a*) Roman in Origin
(*b*) Greek in Origin
(*c*) Latin in Origin
(*d*) None of the above

117. Who among the following linked the idea of justice with religion and divinity?
(*a*) Bodin   (*b*) Cicero
(*c*) St. Augustine   (*d*) Machiavelli

118. Who opined that the term justice is derived from the Latin word Jus which embodies the idea of joining or fitting the idea of bond or tie?
(*a*) Laski   (*b*) Willoughby
(*c*) Barker   (*d*) Marx

119. He decried the talk of social justice in a capitalist society and socialists like Proudhon who preached social justice were criticised by him because they failed to realise the irrelevance of the idea of justice to the social problem. He was :
(*a*) Mao   (*b*) Hegel
(*c*) Max Stirner   (*d*) Karl Marx

120. Who among the following ridiculed the concept of natural justice and liberty and replaced those concepts by the principle of utility?
(*a*) Beccaria   (*b*) David Hume
(*c*) Thomas Acquinas   (*d*) J.S. Mill

121. Who has termed social consciousness as modern consciousness in the context of the determination of the meaning of justice?
(*a*) Barker   (*b*) D.D. Raphael
(*c*) Laski   (*d*) Sabine

122. Legal justice is broadly applied in the context of :
(*a*) Justice according to law
(*b*) Law according to justice
(*c*) Both (*a*) and (*b*)
(*d*) Law and justice according to morality

123. What is/are the other type of participation apart from the democratic type?
(*a*) Administrative
(*b*) Social
(*c*) Community Development
(*d*) All of the above

124. Democratic or political participation is the hall mark of democracy and
(*a*) Political modernization
(*b*) Political development
(*c*) Both (*a*) and (*b*)
(*d*) Political communication

125. In a traditional society, government and politics are the concern of :
(*a*) A narrow elite
(*b*) Middle classes
(*c*) Common people
(*d*) Trained politicians

126. Which among the following has gained wide acceptance in the politics of advanced nations?
(*a*) Aristocratic lineage of politicians
(*b*) Electoral decision making by a chosen few
(*c*) Principle of active citizenship
(*d*) All of the above

127. In the long run, broadened participation is a variable of :
(*a*) Political communication
(*b*) Social and economic modernization
(*c*) Cultural revolution
(*d*) Social justice

128. Who among the following have described political participation as "the activity by private citizens designed to influence governmental decision-making"?
(*a*) Sidney Verba
(*b*) S.P. Huntington
(*c*) John M. Nelson
(*d*) Both (*b*) and (*c*)

129. Which among the following cannot be reckoned as or associated with political participation?
(*a*) Citizen's attitudes, perceptions or knowledge or interest in politics

    (*b*) Electoral activities such as voting campaigning individually or collectively

    (*c*) The activities of professionals such as government officials, party officials, political candidates etc.

    (*d*) Both (*a*) and (*c*)

130. Which among the following scholars draw a distinction between 'participation' and 'mobilization'?
    (*a*) Myron Weiner
    (*b*) Norman Nie
    (*c*) Sydney Verba
    (*d*) All of the above

131. Participation takes place in :
    (*a*) Democratic political systems
    (*b*) Authoritarian political systems
    (*c*) Totalitarian political systems
    (*d*) All of the above

132. The work 'No easy choice' is authored by :
    (*a*) Soysal and Nelson
    (*b*) Huntington and Nelson
    (*c*) Recker and Nelson
    (*d*) Nelson

133. Depending upon the nature and tasks participation can take the shape of :
    (*a*) Consultation
    (*b*) Co-operation
    (*c*) Association
    (*d*) All of the above

134. Who among the following may say that all types of participation-political, administrative and economic would fall with in the ambit of social-participation?
    (*a*) Structural-Functionalists
    (*b*) Guild-Socialists
    (*c*) System analysts
    (*d*) None of the above

135. Sometimes social participation takes the form of social protests such as :
    (*a*) Demonstration
    (*b*) Strikes
    (*c*) Dharnas
    (*d*) All of the above

136. The work 'Maximum feasible Misunderstanding' is authored by :
    (*a*) Daniel P. Monyham
    (*b*) Daniel Lerner
    (*c*) Ramsay Mcdonald
    (*d*) None of the above

137. Which of the following states of society mainly developed social protests as a form of participation?
    (*a*) Middle classes
    (*b*) Neglected sections like Harijans, Tribals Women
    (*c*) Lower and upper middle classes
    (*d*) All of the above

138. Which of the following stand synonymous with administrative participation?
    (*a*) Programme participation
    (*b*) Community development
    (*c*) Political recruitment
    (*d*) Both (*a*) and (*b*)

139. Citizen participation in the decision making process mean :
    (*a*) Participation in policy-planning
    (*b*) Participation in programme-planning
    (*c*) Participation in implementation evaluation of policies and programmes
    (*d*) All of the above

140. Whatever form participation may take in the developmental process the Kingpin and the main actor in the whole drama of democratic development is :
    (*a*) Government
    (*b*) Common man
    (*c*) NGO
    (*d*) Local bodies

141. The book India's Development Experience is authored by :
    (*a*) Manmohan Singh
    (*b*) Atul Kohli
    (*c*) I.J. Ahluwalia
    (*d*) Tarlock Singh

ANSWERS

1	2	3	4	5	6	7	8	9	10
(b)	*(c)*	*(d)*	*(c)*	*(d)*	*(b)*	*(d)*	*(c)*	*(a)*	*(c)*
11	**12**	**13**	**14**	**15**	**16**	**17**	**18**	**19**	**20**
(a)	*(b)*	*(d)*	*(a)*	*(a)*	*(b)*	*(d)*	*(d)*	*(b)*	*(b)*
21	**22**	**23**	**24**	**25**	**26**	**27**	**28**	**29**	**30**
(b)	*(c)*	*(c)*	*(a)*	*(d)*	*(b)*	*(d)*	*(c)*	*(c)*	*(b)*
31	**32**	**33**	**34**	**35**	**36**	**37**	**38**	**39**	**40**
(c)	*(b)*	*(d)*	*(c)*	*(d)*	*(c)*	*(c)*	*(d)*	*(a)*	*(d)*
41	**42**	**43**	**44**	**45**	**46**	**47**	**48**	**49**	**50**
(b)	*(b)*	*(d)*	*(d)*	*(b)*	*(d)*	*(c)*	*(b)*	*(c)*	*(c)*
51	**52**	**53**	**54**	**55**	**56**	**57**	**58**	**59**	**60**
(b)	*(a)*	*(d)*	*(b)*	*(c)*	*(c)*	*(b)*	*(b)*	*(d)*	*(d)*
61	**62**	**63**	**64**	**65**	**66**	**67**	**68**	**69**	**70**
(d)	*(b)*	*(a)*	*(b)*	*(b)*	*(c)*	*(a)*	*(c)*	*(d)*	*(d)*
71	**72**	**73**	**74**	**75**	**76**	**77**	**78**	**79**	**80**
(a)	*(b)*	*(b)*	*(a)*	*(d)*	*(a)*	*(c)*	*(d)*	*(d)*	*(d)*
81	**82**	**83**	**84**	**85**	**86**	**87**	**88**	**89**	**90**
(c)	*(d)*	*(c)*	*(c)*	*(c)*	*(d)*	*(a)*	*(d)*	*(c)*	*(a)*
91	**92**	**93**	**94**	**95**	**96**	**97**	**98**	**99**	**100**
(a)	*(d)*	*(c)*	*(c)*	*(a)*	*(d)*	*(d)*	*(c)*	*(b)*	*(c)*
101	**102**	**103**	**104**	**105**	**106**	**107**	**108**	**109**	**110**
(d)	*(a)*	*(d)*	*(d)*	*(b)*	*(b)*	*(a)*	*(c)*	*(a)*	*(c)*
111	**112**	**113**	**114**	**115**	**116**	**117**	**118**	**119**	**120**
(d)	*(b)*	*(c)*	*(d)*	*(b)*	*(a)*	*(c)*	*(c)*	*(d)*	*(b)*
121	**122**	**123**	**124**	**125**	**126**	**127**	**128**	**129**	**130**
(b)	*(c)*	*(d)*	*(c)*	*(a)*	*(c)*	*(b)*	*(d)*	*(d)*	*(d)*
131	**132**	**133**	**134**	**135**	**136**	**137**	**138**	**139**	**140**
(d)	*(b)*	*(d)*	*(c)*	*(d)*	*(a)*	*(b)*	*(d)*	*(d)*	*(b)*
141									
(d)									

———————

5

DEMOCRACY

1. Which of the following theories of democracy indicates representative democracy?
(*a*) Classical-liberal theory
(*b*) Elitist theory
(*c*) Marxist theory
(*d*) Both (*a*) and (*b*)

2. Who elaborated the theory of separation of powers which had a great democratic appeal and influenced the making of American Constitution?
(*a*) Bentham　　　(*b*) Mill
(*c*) Locke　　　(*d*) Montesquieu

3. Locke's ideas about politics were complemented by Adam Smith in the realm of :
(*a*) Sociology　　　(*b*) Geography
(*c*) Psychology　　　(*d*) Economics

4. Macpherson has called ------ views on democracy as 'developmental democracy'.
(*a*) Mill's　　　(*b*) Locke's
(*c*) MacIver's　　　(*d*) Seelay's

5. A powerful critique of liberal democracy and a radically different image of good society was provided by :
(*a*) Liberalism　　　(*b*) Marxism
(*c*) Socialism　　　(*d*) Pluralism

6. Match List I with List II and select the correct answer using the codes given below :

List I	List II
A. Hobbes	1. Utopia
B. Thomas Moore	2. A preface to Democratic Theory
C. Sartori	3. Leviathan
D. Robert Dahl	4. Democratic Theory

Codes :

	A	B	C	D
(*a*)	1	2	4	3
(*b*)	3	1	4	2
(*c*)	3	1	2	4
(*d*)	4	3	1	2

7. Which of the following is one of the forms of accountability?
(*a*) Legislative accountability
(*b*) Judicial accountability
(*c*) Political accountability
(*d*) All of the above

8. Who is politically accountable to the political executive?
(*a*) Administration
(*b*) Judiciary
(*c*) Legislature
(*d*) None of the above

9. Who said that the best way of enforce accountability is to develop institutions that vigorously monitor the actions of public bureaucracy and punish those guilty of maladministration?
(*a*) Friedrich　　　(*b*) Finer
(*c*) Kingsley　　　(*d*) Levine

10. Which one of the following is vital to accountability?
(*a*) Decentralisation　　(*b*) Devolution
(*c*) Delegation　　(*d*) All of the above

11. ------ is interchangeably use with accountability.
(*a*) Control
(*b*) Delegation
(*c*) Responsibility
(*d*) None of the above

12. Which of the following is one of the examples of external formal controls?
   (*a*) Audit   (*b*) Span of Control
   (*c*) Judicial Review   (*d*) Both (*a*) and (*c*)

13. ------ is the principal means by which consent is granted or withdrawn in a democracy and rulers made accountable to the ruled.
   (*a*) Information   (*b*) Political Party
   (*c*) Participation   (*d*) Constitution

14. Who said that democracy is one of the most defused and pervasive concepts of history?
   (*a*) Macpherson   (*b*) Aristotle
   (*c*) Hagopian   (*d*) H.G. Wells

15. Which organisation sponsored an inquiry into the conflicts and ideals associated with the concept of democracy in 1949?
   (*a*) UNICEF   (*b*) UNESCO
   (*c*) WHO   (*d*) UNCTAD

16. Who defined democracy as 'the worst form of government less than tyranny'?
   (*a*) Cleon   (*b*) Plato
   (*c*) Laski   (*d*) Aristotle

17. The classical democratic element was provided by ------ who sought to free the individual from arbitrary government.
   (*a*) Locke   (*b*) Mill
   (*c*) Spencer   (*d*) Green

18. A classical theory of democracy was developed in :
   (*a*) Greece   (*b*) Athens
   (*c*) City-States   (*d*) China

19. Who provided the egalitarian element of democracy?
   (*a*) MacIver   (*b*) Rousseau
   (*c*) Marx   (*d*) Wilson

20. Who advocated right to vote and representative government in England?
   (*a*) Bentham   (*b*) J.S. Mill
   (*c*) Laski   (*d*) Both (*a*) and (*b*)

21. Who rejected the whole idea of liberal democracy, terming it as 'class democracy'?
   (*a*) Gandhism   (*b*) Communism
   (*c*) Marxism   (*d*) Socialism

22. Who said 'democracy is merely a mechanism for choosing and authorizing governments or in some other way getting laws and political decisions made?
   (*a*) Seelay   (*b*) Sartori
   (*c*) Lincoln   (*d*) Macpherson

23. Who said the democracy is only 'an experiment' in government?
   (*a*) Lindsay   (*b*) Rousseau
   (*c*) Macpherson (*d*) Lowell

24. Which of the following means to give an account of one's action and to report on the achievements and failures together with explanation of the declared objectives?
   (*a*) Accountability
   (*b*) Ordinance
   (*c*) Control
   (*d*) None of the above

25. ------ is the outcome of delegation of responsibility and authority.
   (*a*) Propriety
   (*b*) Accountability
   (*c*) Efficacy
   (*d*) None of the above

26. Which of the following is one of the limitations to accountability?
   (*a*) Professional ethics of a person may come into conflict with his administrative ethics
   (*b*) Administrative accountability is conditioned by the political structure of a country
   (*c*) Accountability, being culture oriented operates within the cultural atmosphere of a political system
   (*d*) All of the above

27. .... is the process by which of the administrative activities as a part of the management process.
   (*a*) Co-operation
   (*b*) Consultation
   (*c*) Association
   (*d*) None of the above

28. Which of the following is a new device of participation?

(*a*) Ombudsman
(*b*) Neighbourhood City Halls
(*c*) Model Cities Programme
(*d*) All of the above

29. Different forms of political participation have :
(*a*) Similar characteristics
(*b*) Different characteristics
(*c*) The same characteristics
(*d*) None of the above

30. Public participation can be of which of the following types?
(*a*) Direct or Indirect
(*b*) Formal or Informal
(*c*) Political or Social
(*d*) All of the above

31. Who among the following describes democracy as the government in which everyone has a share?
(*a*) Dicey　　　　(*b*) Lowell
(*c*) Seeley　　　　(*d*) Austin

32. Consider the following principles of liberal democracy as enumerated by Peter H. Merkl :
1. Government by Discussion
2. Majority Rule
3. Recognition of Minority Rights
4. Constitutional Government

Which of the above are correct? Choose the correct answer using the codes given below :
Codes :
(*a*) 1 and 2　　　　(*b*) 2 and 3
(*c*) 2, 3 and 4　　　(*d*) 1, 2, 3 and 4

33. Which of the following refers to those voluntary activities by which members of a society share in the selection of rulers and directly or indirectly, in the formation of public policy?
(*a*) Political Participation
(*b*) Economic Participation
(*c*) Social Participation
(*d*) None of the above

34. Which of the following are the active forms of political participaiton?
1. Canvassing and registering votes
2. Competing for public and party offices

3. Speech-writing and speech making
4. Formal enrolment in a party
Choose the correct answer using the codes given below :
Codes :
(*a*) 1 and 2　　　　(*b*) 1, 2, 3 and 4
(*c*) 2 and 3　　　　(*d*) 3 and 4

35. Milbraith suggested that political participation varies in relation to four major factors : the extent to which the individual receives political stimuli, individual's personal characteristics, individual's social characteristics, and
(*a*) The individual's ethnic affiliations
(*b*) The financial status of the individual
(*c*) The educational background of the individual
(*d*) The political environment in which the individual finds himself

36. Which of the following systems is regarded as the only system based on the will of the people desiring participating of as many people as possible in the struggle for power?
(*a*) Democratic System
(*b*) Socialist System
(*c*) Communist System
(*d*) None of the above

37. Consider the following major factors of political participation as suggested by Milbraith :
1. The extent to which the individual receives political stimuli
2. Individual personal characteristics
3. Individual social characteristics
4. Political setting or environment in which the individual finds himself
Which of the above are correct? Choose the correct answer from the codes given below :
Codes :
(*a*) 1 and 2　　　　(*b*) 1, 2, 3 and 4
(*c*) 2 and 3　　　　(*d*) 1, 2 and 4

38. Who among the following thinks that political participation is "the activity by private citizens designed to influence governmental decision-making"?

(*a*) Huntington   (*b*) Nelson
(*c*) Weiner   (*d*) Both (*a*) and (*b*)

39. Who among the following scholars drew a distinction between 'participation' and 'mobilization'?
(*a*) Weiner   (*b*) Norman Nie
(*c*) Verba   (*d*) All of the above

40. Which of the following is a method of participation?
(*a*) Consultation   (*b*) Co-operaton
(*c*) Association   (*d*) All of the above

41. "Democracy could be defined as a high flown name for something which does not exist". The above statement is made by :
(*a*) Giovanni Sartori   (*b*) J. Schumpeter
(*c*) Harold Laski   (*d*) Bernard Crick

42. Democracy has been variously interpreted by its exponents. Some scholars have treated democracy as a form of government. They are :
(*a*) Dicey, Lowell and Seeley
(*b*) Plato and Aristotle
(*c*) Rousseau and J.S. Mill
(*d*) Willoughby, Henry Maine and Laski

43. A.V. Dicey has given an account of democracy in :
(*a*) Democracy and Leadership
(*b*) Law and Opinion in England
(*c*) Consent and Consensus
(*d*) The Idea of Liberal Democracy

44. The system which enables the majority of a constituency in Switzerland to call back their representative from his office if they are not satisfied with his work is :
(*a*) Proportional representation
(*b*) Recall
(*c*) Spoil system
(*d*) Plebiscite

45. The work 'Ideology and Utopia' is authored by :
(*a*) Karl Mannheim   (*b*) S.M. Lipset
(*c*) Saint Simon   (*d*) A.F. Bentley

46. The statement that "Balance in the structure of society is a pre-requisite to the maintenance of democracy, " is made by :
(*a*) Gaetano Mosca   (*b*) Karl Mannheim
(*c*) C. Wright Mill   (*d*) Ernest Barker

47. Who among the following insists on the 'mono-national state' as a condition of successful democracy?
(*a*) Thomas Hobbes   (*b*) Hannah Arendt
(*c*) J.S. Mill   (*d*) Laski

48. He opines that two conditions are necessary for the successful working of democracy: 'material or external conditions' and 'mental or internal conditions'.
He is :
(*a*) Harold Laski
(*b*) Macpherson
(*c*) Ernest Barker
(*d*) W.W. Willoughby

49. The "iron law of oligarchy" was propounded by :
(*a*) James Burnham   (*b*) Robert Michels
(*c*) Gaetano Mosca   (*d*) Graham Wallas

50. The principle of concurrent majority is associated with the name of :
(*a*) John Locke   (*b*) John C. Calhon
(*c*) John Stuart Mill   (*d*) Bentham

51. De Tocqueville has enumerated the principal causes, which tended to maintain the democratic structure in the United States, in :
(*a*) Big Democracy
(*b*) The American Commonwealth
(*c*) Democracy in America
(*d*) None of the above

52. The names of Mably, Diderot, Helvetius and Holbach are associated with :
(*a*) Elitist theory of democracy
(*b*) Pluralist theory of democracy
(*c*) Classical liberal theory of democracy
(*d*) Redical theory of democracy

53. Joseph A. Schumpeter, and exponent of elitist theory of democracy has expounded his views on democracy in :
(*a*) The Idea of Liberal Democracy
(*b*) Political Elites

(*c*) Capitalism, Socialism and Democracy
(*d*) Consent and Consensus

54. The principal votaries of the liberal theory of representation are :
(*a*) Hobbes and Hamilton
(*b*) Locke and Thomas Jefferson
(*c*) Hayek and Oakesholt
(*d*) Burke and James Madison

55. He developed a model of the democratic process and described it as 'polyarchy' He is :
(*a*) Giovanni Sartori
(*b*) S.M. Lipset
(*c*) Robert Dahl
(*d*) None of the above

56. Who among the following condemned democracy as "an aristocracy of black guards"?
(*a*) Henry Maine (*b*) Lord Bryce
(*c*) Lecky (*d*) Talleyrand

57. Raymond Aron has given his views on democracy in :
(*a*) Social Structure and the Ruling Class
(*b*) Frontier of Democratic Theory
(*c*) The Group Basis of Politics
(*d*) None of the above

58. Who has described democracy as "government by the poorest, the most ignorant, the most-incapable who are necessarily the most-numerous"?
(*a*) Talleyrand (*b*) G.D.H. Cole
(*c*) Lecky (*d*) Bryce

59. In view of the Marxists, dictatorship of the proletariat is :
(*a*) True communist regime
(*b*) True democracy
(*c*) True dictatorship
(*d*) None of the above

60. The list system of proportional representation is employed in :
(*a*) Knesset of Israel
(*b*) Swiss National Council
(*c*) Italian Chamber of Deputies
(*d*) All of the above

61. Who among the following is a contemporary exponent of the radical theory of democracy?
(*a*) Karl Popper
(*b*) C.B. Macpherson
(*c*) Michael Oakesholt
(*d*) None of the above

62. Which of the following works have been authored by C.B. Macpherson?
(*a*) The Life and Times of Liberal Democracy
(*b*) Democratic Theory : Essays in Retrieval
(*c*) The real World of Democracy
(*d*) All of the above

63. Who among the following has dubbed Marxism as a totalitarian doctrine?
(*a*) Karl Popper
(*b*) Isaiah Berlin
(*c*) Hannah Arendt
(*d*) Both (*a*) and (*c*)

64. Democracy has been described, as 'an unbiological arrangement' by :
(*a*) A.L. Lowell
(*b*) Faguet
(*c*) C.D. Burns
(*d*) Maxey

65. Who among the following considers the dictatorship of the proletariat as "phantom alternative"?
(*a*) Lord Lothian (*b*) Hearnshaw
(*c*) Sartori (*d*) Popper

66. Who draws a distinction between 'developmental power' and 'extractive power' in the process of explicating his theory?
(*a*) Robert Dahl
(*b*) Karl Popper
(*c*) C.B. Macpherson
(*d*) None of the above

67. Who among the following hailed Hitler's Third Reich as "the most ennobled form of modern democratic state"?
(*a*) France
(*b*) Goebbles
(*c*) Nietzsche
(*d*) Both (*b*) and (*c*)

68. His view is that the Marxist theory of democracy gives birth to a closed society in which there is neither freedom nor democracy. He is :
(*a*) Karl Popper
(*b*) Giovanni Sartori
(*c*) Raymond Aron
(*d*) None of the above

69. Which of the following characteristics of a socialist country is instrumental in imparting it a totalitarian hue?
(*a*) Absence of plurality of parties and presence of only one party
(*b*) Absence of parliamentary system of government
(*c*) Strong bureaucracy
(*d*) All of the above

70. Democracy as an ideal can be achieved through :
(*a*) Political institutions
(*b*) Transformation of the mode of production
(*c*) Inculcation of new values of human equality
(*d*) All of the above

71. In Marxist view, periodical elections based on universal suffrage are an eyewash because-
(*a*) They are held only in name and not in spirit
(*b*) They cannot secure real liberty
(*c*) They cannot bring about an effective change in social relations
(*d*) None of the above

72. Bourgeois democracies emerged through :
(*a*) Socialist revolutions under the leadership of the working
(*b*) Revolutionary struggle of the bourgeoisie against the Papacy, Feudalism and Monarchy
(*c*) Coming into being of liberal democracy
(*d*) Both (*a*) and (*c*)

73. Which of the following is held as a transitional state in Marxian philosophy?
(*a*) Socialist state
(*b*) Liberal democratic state
(*c*) Fascist state
(*d*) Anarchist state

74. The work **'The New Image of the Common Man'** is authored by :
(*a*) Ernest Barker
(*b*) Carl Friedrich
(*c*) Macpherson
(*d*) None of the above

75. In the words of Woodrow Wilson, World War I was fought to make the world safe for :
(*a*) Representative government
(*b*) Liberty
(*c*) Democracy
(*d*) All of the above

76. It can be said that democracy is :
(*a*) A form of government
(*b*) A type of state
(*c*) An order of society
(*d*) All of the above

77. The work 'Considerations on Representative Government' is authored by
(*a*) Macpherson
(*b*) J.S. Mill
(*c*) Carole Pateman
(*d*) Marx

78. According to J.S. Mill, what are the conditions for the success of democracy?
(*a*) Voting by open of public ballot
(*b*) Indirect election
(*c*) State funding of election
(*d*) All the above

79. **Assertion (A) :** Preferential policies need not always violate the principle of fairness.
Reason (R) : Treating citizens as equals may require treating them differently.
(*a*) Both A and R are individually true and R is the correct explanation of A.
(*b*) Both A and R are individually true but R is **not** the correct explanation of A.
(*c*) A is true but R is false.
(*d*) A is false but R is true

80. Who defines democracy as a form of government in which the governing body is a comparatively large fraction of the entire nation?

(*a*) Lincoln
(*b*) Dicey
(*c*) Garner
(*d*) Laski

81. In addition to being a form of government and a type of state, democracy is an order of society. A democratic society is one in which :
(*a*) Government is popularly elected
(*b*) Liberty is given the highest value
(*c*) The spirit of equality and fraternity prevails
(*d*) All of the above

82. Democracy in its narrow sense means :
(*a*) Rule by the many
(*b*) A form of government
(*c*) A type of state
(*d*) An order of society

83. Early Greek city states experimented with different form of Government, prominent among them were :
(*a*) Monarchy and Tyranny
(*b*) Aristocracy and Oligarchy
(*c*) Democracy and Monarchy
(*d*) All of the above

84. As a form of government, Aristotle preferred :
(*a*) Aristocracy
(*b*) Tyranny
(*c*) Democracy
(*d*) Monarchy

85. The form of government in which all the freemen meet together in general assemblies, pass laws and execute them, receive ambassadors and act as jurymen is called :
(*a*) Plebiscitary democracy
(*b*) Direct democracy
(*c*) Representative government
(*d*) None of the above

86. A powerful eighteenth century advocate of direct democracy was :
(*a*) Rousseau
(*b*) Montesquieu
(*c*) Voltaire

(*d*) Diderot

87. Direct democracy was first practised in the Greek city states. In the medieval times this type of democracy was revived by :
(*a*) Chinese Kings
(*b*) Indian states
(*c*) Italian city states
(*d*) All of the above

88. Which of the following is the work authored by Lord Bryce?
(*a*) Political Science and Government
(*b*) State in Theory and Practice
(*c*) Modern Democracies
(*d*) Democratic Government

89. Which of the following practice direct democracy in modern times?
(*a*) Greece
(*b*) Forest Cantons of Switzerland
(*c*) German Lander
(*d*) Both (*b*) and (*c*)

90. Who remarked that all government are in fact aristocracies, in the sense that they are carried on by a relatively small number of persons?
(*a*) Mosca
(*b*) Pareto
(*c*) Durkheim
(*d*) Bryce

91. Who made the observation that, "Democracy in practice is the hypothesis, that all men are equal which is used in order to discover who are the best"?
(*a*) Kant
(*b*) C.D. Burns
(*c*) Fichte
(*d*) None of the above

92. Who among the following scholars authored the Work-Mind and Society?
(*a*) Edward Tufte
(*b*) Pareto
(*c*) Gaetano Mosca
(*d*) None of the above

ANSWERS

1	2	3	4	5	6	7	8	9	10
(*d*)	(*d*)	(*d*)	(*a*)	(*b*)	(*b*)	(*d*)	(*a*)	(*b*)	(*d*)
11	**12**	**13**	**14**	**15**	**16**	**17**	**18**	**19**	**20**
(*c*)	(*d*)	(*c*)	(*c*)	(*b*)	(*b*)	(*a*)	(*b*)	(*b*)	(*d*)
21	**22**	**23**	**24**	**25**	**26**	**27**	**28**	**29**	**30**
(*c*)	(*d*)	(*d*)	(*a*)	(*b*)	(*d*)	(*c*)	(*d*)	(*a*)	(*d*)
31	**32**	**33**	**34**	**35**	**36**	**37**	**38**	**39**	**40**
(*c*)	(*d*)	(*a*)	(*b*)	(*d*)	(*a*)	(*b*)	(*d*)	(*d*)	(*d*)
41	**42**	**43**	**44**	**45**	**46**	**47**	**48**	**49**	**50**
(*a*)	(*a*)	(*b*)	(*a*)	(*a*)	(*b*)	(*c*)	(*c*)	(*b*)	(*b*)
51	**52**	**53**	**54**	**55**	**56**	**57**	**58**	**59**	**60**
(*c*)	(*c*)	(*c*)	(*b*)	(*c*)	(*d*)	(*a*)	(*c*)	(*b*)	(*d*)
61	**62**	**63**	**64**	**65**	**66**	**67**	**68**	**69**	**70**
(*b*)	(*d*)	(*d*)	(*b*)	(*c*)	(*c*)	(*b*)	(*a*)	(*a*)	(*d*)
71	**72**	**73**	**74**	**75**	**76**	**77**	**78**	**79**	**80**
(*c*)	(*b*)	(*a*)	(*b*)	(*c*)	(*d*)	(*b*)	(*d*)	(*b*)	(*b*)
81	**82**	**83**	**84**	**85**	**86**	**87**	**88**	**89**	**90**
(*c*)	(*a*)	(*d*)	(*c*)	(*b*)	(*a*)	(*c*)	(*c*)	(*b*)	(*d*)
91	**92**								
(*b*)	(*b*)								

6

POLITICAL IDEOLOGIES

1. Whose teaching affected Gandhi's moral and political philosophy?
   (*a*) Doke
   (*b*) Plato
   (*c*) Vinoba Bhave
   (*d*) None of the above

2. Who said that non-violence means avoidance of violence in all forms?
   (*a*) Ruskin   (*b*) Tolstoy
   (*c*) Gandhiji   (*d*) Augustine

3. Who was the political Guru of Gandhiji?
   (*a*) Rabindranath Tagore
   (*b*) Dadabhai Naoroji
   (*c*) Gokhale
   (*d*) S.N. Banerjee

4. Who said that Gandhi's religion and morality were the same?
   (*a*) Gokhale   (*b*) Kripalani
   (*c*) Patel   (*d*) Jinnah

5. Who among the following gave priority to moral values in social and political life?
   (*a*) Gandhiji   (*b*) Kant
   (*c*) Cicero   (*d*) All of the above

6. Which of the following is not a requisite of Ahimsa?
   (*a*) Truth   (*b*) Fasting
   (*c*) Perseverance   (*d*) Satyagraha

7. Which of the following is not a form of satyagraha?
   (*a*) Non-cooperation
   (*b*) Civil disobedience
   (*c*) Picketing
   (*d*) Swarajya

8. ------ is an extreme form of satyagraha.
   (*a*) Non-cooperation
   (*b*) Fasting
   (*c*) Peace Brigade
   (*d*) Peaceful picketing

9. What is known as the voluntary exile from the permanent place of residence?
   (*a*) Fasting   (*b*) Hijrat
   (*c*) Hartal   (*d*) Picketing

10. Who describes Gandhi as a revolutionary leader on account of his "developing a technique for precipitating conflict and then resolving it non-violently"?
    (*a*) Hitler   (*b*) Donald E. Smith
    (*c*) Rousseau   (*d*) Hussain

11. Trusteeship provides a means of transforming the capitalistic order of society into a/an ---- one.
    (*a*) Socialist
    (*b*) Egalitarian
    (*c*) Bourgeois
    (*d*) None of the above

12. Who said that 'the concept of sarvodaya is the most original contemporary attempt at an Indian contribution to political thought'?
    (*a*) Gandhiji   (*b*) Vinoba Bhave
    (*c*) Dr. Ralph   (*d*) A. Appadorai

13. Who said that 'Gandhiji is one-third politician, one-third saint and one-third humbug'?
    (*a*) Andrews   (*b*) C.M. Joad
    (*c*) Marshall   (*d*) Marx

14. Who said about Gandhiji, "Generations to come, it may be, none will scarcely believe that such a one as this ever in flesh and blood walked upon this earth"?
    (*a*) Dr. Radhakrishnan

(*b*) Einstein
(*c*) Joad
(*d*) Pyarelal

15. The key of Gramsci's analysis of the failure of socialist revolution to take off in the west is the concept of—
(*a*) ideology   (*b*) intellectuals
(*c*) hagemony   (*d*) civil society

16. Which of the following is one of the organisational measures conceived to limit state control?
(*a*) A holding company structure
(*b*) Restructuring
(*c*) Leasing
(*d*) All of the above

17. Which of the following implies partial introduction of private ownership?
(*a*) Single ownership
(*b*) Public sector
(*c*) Joint venture
(*d*) None of the above

18. Which of the following is an obstacle to privatisation in a democratic society like India?
(*a*) In a democratic set-up it would not be possible to carry out privatisation in blatant disregard of the interest of workers
(*b*) It is a fraudulent practice on the part of the state to use book value of net assets
(*c*) The aim of privatisation is to encourage corporatisation to benefit the big industrialists
(*d*) All of the above

19. At which place a debate on 'the end of ideology' was held in the year 1955.
(*a*) Mumbai (India)   (*b*) Berlin (Germany)
(*c*) Milan (Italy)   (*d*) London (England)

20. The work 'Political Man' is authored by—
(*a*) S.M. Lipsel   (*b*) Karl Marx
(*c*) Daniel Bell   (*d*) V. Lenin

21. Who said that Gandhi's Ramrajya was a perfect anarchy, a stateless society which is governed by no other law except the moral law?
(*a*) Rousseau   (*b*) A. Hussain
(*c*) Nehru   (*d*) Tolstoy

22. The ideas that a man owed only a limited and relative loyalty to the state as he owed allegiance to other associations as well, takes Gandhiji very near to ------ thinkers.
(*a*) Socialist   (*b*) Pluralist
(*c*) Liberal   (*d*) Communist

23. Like ------, Gandhiji disliked concentration of power both in economic and political fields and opposed centralization of authority.
(*a*) Thoreau   (*b*) Ruskin
(*c*) Tolstoy   (*d*) Lao-Tse

24. ------ forms the basis of Gandhian economic philosophy.
(*a*) Universal equality
(*b*) Universal love
(*c*) Patriotism
(*d*) None of the above

25. Mahatama Gandhi learned the principle of reciprocity from :
(*a*) Ruskin   (*b*) Confucius
(*c*) Thoreau   (*d*) Vinoba Bhave

26. Who said that "Gandhi was an odd kind of pacifist, for he was an activist full of dynamic energy"?
(*a*) Pyarelal   (*b*) N.B. Sen
(*c*) Tolstoy   (*d*) Kabir

27. Acharya Kripalani regarded Mahatama Gandhi as essentially a ------ reformer.
(*a*) Spiritual   (*b*) Political
(*c*) Religious   (*d*) Social

28. Which word means that every person has to perform his allotted task in society in accordance with his capacities and training?
(*a*) Satyagraha
(*b*) Kartvyapalana
(*c*) Varnashramadharma
(*d*) None of the above

29. Mahatama Gandhi's new system of education known as the Nai Talim had at its bottom the two principle of :

(*a*) Truth and human dignity
(*b*) Ahimsa and varnashramadharma
(*c*) Satyagraha and swaraj
(*d*) Spiritualism and philanthropism

30. Which of the following aspects was not included in Gandhian economy?
(*a*) Individualism   (*b*) Anarchism
(*c*) Idealism   (*d*) Marxism

31. Gandhian economy emphasizes humanitarian and ------ values.
(*a*) spiritual   (*b*) cultural
(*c*) political   (*d*) socialist

32. Who among the following use to call himself a "born co-operator"?
(*a*) Rousseau   (*b*) Mahatma Gandhi
(*c*) Sardar Patel   (*d*) M.A. Jinnah

33. Who said that though Mahatama Gandhi's efforts were concentrated on India, he was a true internationalist?
(*a*) Rousseau   (*b*) Macpherson
(*c*) Barker   (*d*) Ralph Bunche

34. Among secular writers, who influenced Mahatama Gandhi the most?
(*a*) Ruskin   (*b*) Thoreau
(*c*) Rousseau   (*d*) Both (*a*) and (*b*)

35. Who remarked that 'Mahatama Gandhi is the spokesman for the conscience of all mankind?
(*a*) M.S. Buch   (*b*) George Marshall
(*c*) Joad   (*d*) Tandon

36. Non-violence, as taught and practised by Mahatama Gandhi is rooted in the Indian doctrine of :
(*a*) Satyagraha   (*b*) Ahimsa
(*c*) Swaraj   (*d*) Swadeshi

37. Who said that Ahimsa is a weapon of matchless potency?
(*a*) Catlin   (*b*) Rousseau
(*c*) Mahatama Gandhi (*d*) Tolstoy

38. Who thought that Gandhi's view on non-violence were absolute?
(*a*) Jinnah
(*b*) Abul Kalam Azad
(*c*) Jawahar Lal Nehru
(*d*) None of the above

39. Who said that morality is the basis of things and truth is the substance of morality?
(*a*) Tolstoy
(*b*) Jinnah
(*c*) Gandhi
(*d*) None of the above

40. According to Ray and Bhattacharya what are the structural components of Ideology?
(*a*) Its linkage with a grand philosophical system
(*b*) Its programme content derived from its philosophy
(*c*) Its strategy of achieving the programmatic goal
(*d*) All the above

41. Match List I with List II and select the correct answer by using the codes given below :

List I	List II
A. Bondurant	1. Hind Swarajya
B. Gandhi	2. Modern Political Theory
C. Joad	3. Conquest of Violence
D. Sampurnanand	4. Indian Socialism

Codes :

	A	B	C	D
(*a*)	3	1	2	4
(*b*)	3	1	4	2
(*c*)	4	3	1	2
(*d*)	1	3	4	2

42. Gandhiji rejects the system of :
(*a*) Indirect democracy
(*b*) Parliamentary democracy
(*c*) Direct democracy
(*d*) None of the above

43. Which of the following is not a step in Satyagraha campaign?
(*a*) Protest   (*b*) Negotiation
(*c*) Non-cooperation   (*d*) Violence

44. Who called Gandhi's concept of non-violence as the most foolish of all scheme's?
(*a*) Hobbes   (*b*) Nehru
(*c*) Lord Chelmsford (*d*) C.M. Case

45. The most appropriate name of Gandhian Socialism is :

(*a*) Satyagraha
(*b*) Sarvadharma Samanvaya
(*c*) Sanskritacharaya
(*d*) Sarvodaya

46. Sarvodaya aims at the ------ of politics
(*a*) Socialisation
(*b*) Spritualisation
(*c*) Democratization
(*d*) None of the above

47. Match List I with List II and select the correct answer by using the codes given below :

List I		**List II**
A. Labour	1.	Gramdan
B. Village property	2.	Bhoodan
C. Land	3.	Aparigraha
D. Non-possession	4.	Shramdan

Codes :

	A	B	C	D
(*a*)	4	1	3	2
(*b*)	4	1	2	3
(*c*)	3	4	1	2
(*d*)	2	3	4	1

48. Which of the following is not the main feature of the economic philosophy of sarvodaya as emphasised by Vinobaji?
(*a*) Elimination of poverty
(*b*) Helping world peace
(*c*) Cooperation of all political parties
(*d*) Revival of the old social order

49. Who describes Gandhi as "the type of the civilized and humanized man"?
(*a*) Moraes   (*b*) Fischer
(*c*) Stanely   (*d*) Carl Heath

50. ------ was the main source of inspiration for Gandhiji.
(*a*) Ramayana   (*b*) Mahabharata
(*c*) Upanishads   (*d*) Bhagawad Gita

51. Which of the following personalities are associated with Reformation, the great religious movement of the sixteenth century Europe which resulted in the establishment of Protestantism?
(*a*) Martin Luther   (*b*) Machiavelli
(*c*) Louis XIVth   (*d*) Garibaldi

52. Classical liberalism is also called negative liberalism because :
(*a*) It emphasised negative human values
(*b*) It insisted on the negative functions of the state
(*c*) It later proved to be antithesis of liberalism
(*d*) It found an echo in Marxism

53. The socio-cultural economic force/forces which made cardinal contribution of the birth and development of liberalism were :
(*a*) Renaissance and Reformation
(*b*) Enlightenment
(*c*) Scientific and Industrial Revolutions
(*d*) All of the above

54. The first exponent of political liberalism is :
(*a*) John Locke   (*b*) J.S. Mill
(*c*) Bentham   (*d*) T.H. Green

55. A prominent role in laying the economic foundations of the classical liberalism is played by :
(*a*) Adam Smith   (*b*) Thomas Malthus
(*c*) David Ricardo   (*d*) All of the above

56. In the religious sphere, liberalism upheld :
(*a*) Secularism and reason
(*b*) Revealed truth and reason
(*c*) Catholicism and Protestantism
(*d*) None of the above

57. The Sociological foundation of negative liberty was provided by :
(*a*) T.H. Green   (*b*) Jeremy Bentham
(*c*) John Locke   (*d*) Herbert Spencer

58. The idea of 'possessive individualism' is given by :
(*a*) Hannah Arendt   (*b*) C.B. Macpherson
(*c*) Karl Popper   (*d*) None of the above

59. A theory of 'social engineering' or 'piecemeal engineering' is advance by :
(*a*) Ernest Gellner   (*b*) L.T. Hobhouse
(*c*) Charles Taylor   (*d*) Karl Popper

60. Who among the following attached utmost importance to human dignity?

(*a*) Hegel   (*b*) Kant
(*c*) Marx   (*d*) Green

61. Which of the following is not a dimension of the 'felicific calculus' propounded by Bentham?
(*a*) Intensity   (*b*) Duration
(*c*) Probability   (*d*) Purity

62. Contributing significantly to the doctrine of utilitarianism, he said, "each to count as one, and no one for more than one". He is :
(*a*) J.S. Mill   (*b*) Jeremy Bentham
(*c*) James Mill   (*d*) David Hume

63. Felicific Calculus is :
(*a*) A device to analyse electoral behaviour
(*b*) A mode of computing feedback under systems analysis
(*c*) A multi-dimensional scale for the measurement of pleasure and pain
(*d*) None of the above

64. Who among the following observed that Bentham reduced the individual to a 'consumer of utilities'?
(*a*) Karl Popper   (*b*) Thomas H. Green
(*c*) J.S. Mill   (*d*) C.B. Macpherson

65. Bentham's formula that man's behaviour should be governed by advancement of pleasure and avoidance of pain, originally belonged to :
(*a*) Priestley   (*b*) Hume
(*c*) Epicurus   (*d*) Beccaria

66. Which of the following pairs is not correctly matched?
(*a*) Democratic theory : C.B. Macpherson
(*b*) Freedom : Maurice Cranston
(*c*) The Tyranny of Majority : L.T. Hobhouse
(*d*) Problems of Political Philosophy : D.D. Rapheal

67. A liberal who has postulated a 'clain connection' between the most advantaged and the least advantaged individuals in a Social Setting is :
(*a*) Rees
(*b*) Rawls

(*c*) Tawney
(*d*) None of the above

68. The concept of 'situated self' is advanced by :
(*a*) Liberals   (*b*) Communitarians
(*c*) Neo-Marxists   (*d*) Idealists

69. Antonio Gramsci establishes a strong link between which one of the following four sets of concepts?
(*a*) Ideology—Leadership—Domination—Religion
(*b*) Ideology—Leadership—War of Manoeuvre—Domination
(*c*) Ideology—Leadership—Domination—Passive Revolutions
(*d*) Ideology—Leadership—Domination—Intellectual

70. Who among the following announced that 'Marxism is a whole world-view'?
(*a*) Leon Trotsky
(*b*) G.V. Plekhanov
(*c*) Edward Said
(*d*) None of the above

71. Marx was influenced, among others, by French materialists like :
(*a*) Helvetius   (*b*) Voltaire
(*c*) Holbach   (*d*) Both (*a*) and (*c*)

72. The Statement , "The philosophers have only interpreted the world in various ways; the point however is to change it," is made by :
(*a*) Engels
(*b*) Bauer
(*c*) Marx
(*d*) None of the above

73. The country in which Marx spent more than half of his life and produced the major part of his scholarship was :
(*a*) Italy   (*b*) England
(*c*) Germany   (*d*) France

74. The author of 'Acquisitive Society' is :
(*a*) T. Rees
(*b*) R.H. Tawney
(*c*) J. Rawls
(*d*) None of the above

75. The concept of surplus value is centred on :
(*a*) Capital   (*b*) Technology
(*c*) Labour   (*d*) Organisation

76. The idea of 'moral individualism' is associated with the name of :
(*a*) T.H. Green   (*b*) Immanuel Kant
(*c*) Hegal   (*d*) Marx

77. In which of his works Marx discusses alienation?
(*a*) Philosophy of Poverty
(*b*) Economic and Philosophic Manuscripts
(*c*) Thesis on Feuerbach
(*d*) None of the above

78. The 'doctrine of permanent revolution' is laid down by :
(*a*) Antonio Gramsci   (*b*) George Lukas
(*c*) Joseph Stalin   (*d*) Mao Zedong

79. **Great Society** and **The Great Illusion** have been authored respectively by :
(*a*) Ritchie and Finer
(*b*) Graham Wallas and Norman Agell
(*c*) Finer and Ritchie
(*d*) Norman Agell and Graham Wallas

80. The noble concept of 'hegemony' is given by :
(*a*) Milton Friedman   (*b*) Isaiah Berlin
(*c*) F. Engels   (*d*) Antonio Gramsci

81. The author of **Two Concepts of Liberty** argues in favour of :
(*a*) Positive liberty
(*b*) Increase in the functions of state
(*c*) Equality
(*d*) Negative liberty

82. The Central idea of socialism is :
(*a*) Equality   (*b*) Society
(*c*) Justice   (*d*) All of these

83. The middle classes were designated as commercial despot by :
(*a*) Aristotle   (*b*) Marx
(*c*) Fourier   (*d*) Stalin

84. The idea of class war was originally spread by :
(*a*) Kautsky   (*b*) Marx
(*c*) Engels   (*d*) Saint Simon

85. Who among the following declared that property is theft?
(*a*) Ebenstein
(*b*) Joad
(*c*) Proudhon
(*d*) None of the above

86. Who said that: "Karl Marx is in a very real sense the father of socialism"?
(*a*) F.M. Watkins
(*b*) C.E.M. Joad
(*c*) Schumpeter
(*d*) None of the above

87. Which of the following is regarded as a landmark event in the development of socialism?
(*a*) The Glorious Revolution of 1688
(*b*) The Russian Revolution of 1917
(*c*) The French Revolution of 1789
(*d*) The American Declaration of Independence of 1776

88. The name of 'New Lanark' is associated with :
(*a*) Saint Simon
(*b*) William of Occam
(*c*) Robert Owen
(*d*) Laski

89. Which of the following names is associated with collectivism?
(*a*) Eduard Bernstein   (*b*) Jean Juares
(*c*) Karl Branting   (*d*) All of these

90. The Fabian Society was formed in :
(*a*) 1883   (*b*) 1884
(*c*) 1885   (*d*) 1886

91. Fabians were primarily influenced by :
(*a*) Engels and Lenin
(*b*) Lenin and Mao
(*c*) Aristotle and Saint Thomas Acquinas
(*d*) J.S. Mill, Henry George and Karl Marx

92. The name of "CGT" or "Confederation Generale du Travail" is relevant in connection with :
(*a*) Neo-liberalism
(*b*) Bolshevism
(*c*) Syndicalism
(*d*) None of the above

93. The Fabian Society was named after Fabius Cunctator who was the :
(*a*) Emperor of France
(*b*) Czar of Russia
(*c*) Dictator of ancient Rome
(*d*) None of the above

94. Who branded syndicalism as 'revisionism of the left'?
(*a*) Mosca   (*b*) Weber
(*c*) Marx   (*d*) Sorel

95. Which of the following works is authored by Herbert Spencer?
(*a*) A Plea for Liberty
(*b*) Social Statics
(*c*) Political Ideals
(*d*) All of the above

96. Who called guild socialism 'British variant of syndicalism'?
(*a*) Coker
(*b*) Poulantzas
(*c*) Florence Elliot
(*d*) None of the above

97. The view that rent is brigandage reduced to a system belongs to :
(*a*) Woolsey   (*b*) Davidson
(*c*) Engels   (*d*) Proudhon

98. Which of the following was totalitarian in character?
(*a*) Fascism   (*b*) Communism
(*c*) Nazism   (*d*) All of these

99. Nazism and Fascism arose respectively in :
(*a*) 1922 and 1933
(*b*) 1922 and 1932
(*c*) 1933 and 1922
(*d*) None of the above

100. The name of Sir Oswald Mosley is associated with :
(*a*) Mussolini's Cabinet
(*b*) Fascist Movement in England
(*c*) The Nazi Party
(*d*) None of the above

101. Mussolini borrowed the idea of constant struggle from :
(*a*) Nepolean Bonaparte
(*b*) Idealists
(*c*) Social Darwinists
(*d*) Adolf Hitler

102. The Fascist Philosophy of irrationalism was borrowed from :
(*a*) Treitschke and Bernhardi
(*b*) Hegel and Hume
(*c*) Schopenhauer and Nietzsche
(*d*) None of the above

103. Fascism believed in myths. In this regard Fascism was influenced by the social philosophy of :
(*a*) Nietzsche   (*b*) Sorel
(*c*) Kafka   (*d*) Kant

104. Who maintained that Fascism is a theory of liberal capitalist society in crisis?
(*a*) Gandhians   (*b*) Liberals
(*c*) Socialists   (*d*) Marxists

105. Who branded Fascist Party as "the Conscience of the state"?
(*a*) Mussolini
(*b*) Bergson
(*c*) Gentile
(*d*) None of the above

106. Goering's name is associated with :
(*a*) Italian Fascism
(*b*) German Nazism
(*c*) Japanese Militarism
(*d*) None of the above

107. In connection with Nazism 'Volk' refers to :
(*a*) State   (*b*) Race
(*c*) Nation   (*d*) Community

108. Hitler's notorious work **Mein-Kampf** literally mean :
(*a*) Nation-State   (*b*) Race and Nation
(*c*) My struggle   (*d*) My Nation

109. The 'Storm Troopers' and the 'Blackguards' are associated with :
(*a*) Fascism
(*b*) Militarism
(*c*) Nazism
(*d*) None of the above

110. Mahatma Gandhi owed his inspiration for civil disobedience and the non-payment of taxes to :
(*a*) Leo Tolstoy   (*b*) John Ruskin
(*c*) Thoreau   (*d*) Both (*b*) and (*c*)

111. The Keywords of Gandhian economy are :
(*a*) Self-sufficiency
(*b*) Decentralized production
(*c*) Equitable distribution
(*d*) All of the above

112. Who was the first writer to declare himself openly an Anarchist?
(*a*) Warren   (*b*) Thoreau
(*c*) Proudhon   (*d*) None of the above

113. Proudhon, a prominent anarchist discovered the origin of the state in :
(*a*) Dominant class   (*b*) Army and police
(*c*) Private property   (*d*) Both (*b*) and (*c*)

114. Who among the following popularised the theory of individualistic anarchism in the United states?
(*a*) Warren   (*b*) Tucker
(*c*) Schmidt   (*d*) Both (*a*) and (*b*)

115. An important anarchist, Kropotkin was inspired by :
(*a*) Ideas of Bakunin
(*b*) Darwin's biological principle of mutual aid
(*c*) Syndicalism
(*d*) Both (*a*) and (*b*)

116. Who among the following recommended both evolutionary and revolutionary techniques to achieve the anarchist goal?
(*a*) Bakunin
(*b*) Proudhon
(*c*) Hodgskin
(*d*) None of the above

117. The ideas of Proudhon, Bakunin and Kropotkin were popularised in France by :
(*a*) Elisee Reclus
(*b*) Guy de Moupassant
(*c*) Jean Grave
(*d*) both (*a*) and (*c*)

118. The work Reflections Violence is authored by :
(*a*) Pareto   (*b*) Sorel
(*c*) Proudhon   (*d*) Bakunin

119. Guild Socialism originated in :
(*a*) Post World-War I period
(*b*) The second decade of the twentieth century
(*c*) The inter-war period
(*d*) None of the above

120. In 1915, the Guild Socialists established the National Guilds League in:
(*a*) France   (*b*) U.S.A.
(*c*) Britain   (*d*) Germany

121. Who among the following tried to modify the ideas of Penty to suit modern conditions?
(*a*) G.D.H. Cole   (*b*) George Hobson
(*c*) A.R. Orage   (*d*) Both (*b*) and (*c*)

122. Who is said to be the "infant prodigy of guild socialism"?
(*a*) G.D.H. Cole   (*b*) Laski
(*c*) C.E.M. Joad   (*d*) Hobson

123. The term Syndicalism is derived from the word 'Syndicate' which is the French name for :
(*a*) Pressure Group
(*b*) Trade Union
(*c*) Political Party
(*d*) Secret Organisation

124. Syndicalism can be said to have drawn its inspiration from the words of :
(*a*) Karl Marx   (*b*) Proudhon
(*c*) Hegel   (*d*) Lenin

125. The Erfurt programme (1891) is associated with the name of :
(*a*) Bebel   (*b*) Liebknecht
(*c*) Singer   (*d*) All of these

126. Who said that, "Socialism is merely individualism retionalised organised, closed and in its right mind"?
(*a*) Sidney Olivier
(*b*) Edward Bernstein
(*c*) G.D.H. Cole
(*d*) Both (*b*) and (*c*)

127. It was an attempt to revise Marxism in the light of new experience which was not available to Marx. It was :
(*a*) Anarchism
(*b*) Fabianism
(*c*) Syndicalism
(*d*) Gandhism

128. The theory of anarchism was blended with Christian Socialism by :
(*a*) Graham Green
(*b*) Tolstoy
(*c*) Bakunin
(*d*) None of the above

129. The word anarchism is taken from the Greek Word Anarchia which means :
(*a*) Orderlessness   (*b*) Non-governance
(*c*) No-rule   (*d*) All of these

130. The Supreme goal of the Anarchist creed is :
(*a*) Liberty   (*b*) Equality
(*c*) Chaos   (*d*) All of these

ANSWERS

1	2	3	4	5	6	7	8	9	10
(*c*)	(*b*)	(*c*)	(*b*)	(*d*)	(*d*)	(*d*)	(*b*)	(*b*)	(*b*)
11	**12**	**13**	**14**	**15**	**16**	**17**	**18**	**19**	**20**
(*b*)	(*d*)	(*b*)	(*b*)	(*c*)	(*d*)	(*c*)	(*d*)	(*c*)	(*a*)
21	**22**	**23**	**24**	**25**	**26**	**27**	**28**	**29**	**30**
(*b*)	(*b*)	(*c*)	(*b*)	(*b*)	(*b*)	(*d*)	(*c*)	(*a*)	(*d*)
31	**32**	**33**	**34**	**35**	**36**	**37**	**38**	**39**	**40**
(*b*)	(*b*)	(*d*)	(*d*)	(*b*)	(*b*)	(*c*)	(*b*)	(*c*)	(*d*)
41	**42**	**43**	**44**	**45**	**46**	**47**	**48**	**49**	**50**
(*a*)	(*b*)	(*d*)	(*c*)	(*d*)	(*b*)	(*b*)	(*d*)	(*d*)	(*d*)
51	**52**	**53**	**54**	**55**	**56**	**57**	**58**	**59**	**60**
(*a*)	(*b*)	(*d*)	(*a*)	(*d*)	(*a*)	(*d*)	(*b*)	(*d*)	(*b*)
61	**62**	**63**	**64**	**65**	**66**	**67**	**68**	**69**	**70**
(*c*)	(*b*)	(*c*)	(*d*)	(*c*)	(*c*)	(*b*)	(*b*)	(*d*)	(*b*)
71	**72**	**73**	**74**	**75**	**76**	**77**	**78**	**79**	**80**
(*d*)	(*c*)	(*b*)	(*b*)	(*c*)	(*b*)	(*b*)	(*d*)	(*b*)	(*d*)
81	**82**	**83**	**84**	**85**	**86**	**87**	**88**	**89**	**90**
(*d*)	(*a*)	(*c*)	(*d*)	(*c*)	(*b*)	(*c*)	(*c*)	(*d*)	(*b*)
91	**92**	**93**	**94**	**95**	**96**	**97**	**98**	**99**	**100**
(*c*)	(*c*)	(*c*)	(*d*)	(*b*)	(*c*)	(*b*)	(*d*)	(*c*)	(*b*)
101	**102**	**103**	**104**	**105**	**106**	**107**	**108**	**109**	**110**
(*c*)	(*c*)	(*b*)	(*d*)	(*c*)	(*b*)	(*d*)	(*c*)	(*c*)	(*c*)
111	**112**	**113**	**114**	**115**	**116**	**117**	**118**	**119**	**120**
(*d*)	(*c*)	(*c*)	(*d*)	(*d*)	(*a*)	(*d*)	(*b*)	(*b*)	(*c*)
121	**122**	**123**	**124**	**125**	**126**	**127**	**128**	**129**	**130**
(*d*)	(*a*)	(*b*)	(*b*)	(*d*)	(*a*)	(*c*)	(*b*)	(*c*)	(*a*)

7

PARTY SYSTEM AND POLITICAL PROCESS

1. Which book published in 1908, is the first study of pressure groups?
   (*a*) The Process of Government
   (*b*) Comparative Politics
   (*c*) The Politics of the Developing Areas
   (*d*) Political Behaviour

2. The term 'coalition' is derived from the latin word 'coalitio'which means :
   (*a*) To merge   (*b*) To support
   (*c*) To grow together (*d*) To complement

3. Who among the following made the famous statement: "England does not love coalitions"?
   (*a*) K.C. Wheare   (*b*) Bertrand Russell
   (*c*) Disraeli   (*d*) Churchill

4. Which of the following is an important implication of the system of coalition?
   (*a*) Coalitions are formed for the sake of some reward, material or psychic
   (*b*) A coalition implies the existence of at least two partners
   (*c*) The underlying principle of a coalition system stands on the simple fact of temporary conjunction of specific interest
   (*d*) All of the above

5. Coalition governments continue to be :
   (*a*) Stable
   (*b*) undemocratic
   (*c*) Unstable
   (*d*) None of the above

6. Which of the following is one of the political and constitutional implications of the coalition politics?

   (*a*) Decline of the office of the Chief Minister
   (*b*) Mockery of Ministerial Responsibility
   (*c*) Heterogeneous character of the government
   (*d*) All of the above

7. In coalition governments the bureaucracy becomes :
   (*a*) Efficient
   (*b*) All powerful
   (*c*) Fair and just
   (*d*) None of the above

8. The most important factor in the formation of the coalitions is :
   (*a*) Power sharing
   (*b*) People's mandate
   (*c*) Political opportunism
   (*d*) Mutual understanding

9. Which of the following is one of the salient features of the coalition governments?
   (*a*) Lack of polarisation
   (*b*) Political opportunism
   (*c*) Political defections
   (*d*) All of the above

10. Who initiated the systematic study of pressure groups?
    (*a*) Powell   (*b*) Lenin
    (*c*) Grazia   (*d*) Bentley

11. Who said that institutional interest groups are "formal organisations, composed of professionally employed personnel, with designated political and social functions other than interest articulation"?

(*a*) Almond   (*b*) Greenstein
(*c*) Polsby   (*d*) Bingham

12. What according to Alfred de Grazia, are highly organized, claim large membership lists, have agents who are skilled in persuasion and public relations and insist that their interests are consonant with the public welfare?
(*a*) Anomic interest groups
(*b*) Lobbies
(*c*) Political parties
(*d*) Social institutions

13. Which is not a key feature of State?
(*a*) State is sovereign
(*b*) The State is an exercise in legislations
(*c*) The State is an instrument of domination
(*d*) The State is not a territorial associations.

14. Which of the following is not of the promotional groups in the world?
(*a*) Citizens for Democracy
(*b*) Anti-Saloon League (USA)
(*c*) Nair Society
(*d*) Public Union for Civil Liberties

15. Which of the following is a type of coalition categorised on the basis of mutual strength of coalition partners?
(*a*) One-party dominant Coalition
(*b*) Minority governmental Coalition
(*c*) Post-election Coalition
(*d*) Secular Coalition

16. Which of the following is not the type of coalition categorised on the basis of interaction of infrastructure and politics?
(*a*) Few party governmental coalition
(*b*) Secular coalition
(*c*) Post-election coalition
(*d*) Infrastructure dominated coalition

17. The group theory has been propounded by Arthur Bentley and :
(*a*) Almond   (*b*) David Truman
(*c*) W. Nelson   (*d*) Bingham

18. Who has defined interest as a conscious desire to have public policy or authoritatic allocation of values more in a particular, general or specific direction ?

(*a*) Alfred   (*b*) Peter
(*c*) Almond   (*d*) La Palombara

19. Who said Politics as the "authoritative allocation of values"?
(*a*) Easton
(*b*) Samuel Johnson
(*c*) Machiavelli
(*d*) Lord Acton

20. Which of the following states had formed coalition government on the basis of the strength of coalition partners vis-a-vis legislative strength-majority governmental coalition?
(*a*) West Bengal   (*b*) Uttar Pradesh
(*c*) Madhya Pradesh   (*d*) All of these

21. An interest group is a group which has a stake in the ------ process.
(*a*) Social   (*b*) Political
(*c*) Economic   (*d*) Governmental

22. The emergence of political parties has accompanied the :
(*a*) Growth of Parliament as an institution
(*b*) Diversification of political systems
(*c*) Growth of modern electorate
(*d*) All of the above

23. Who differentiated parties from authoritarian groups on the basis of the criterion that genuine parties rest upon "formally free recruiting"?
(*a*) Laski
(*b*) Max Weber
(*c*) Carl Friedrich
(*d*) None of the above

24. Who pointed out that, "the party system was in particular the mechanism by which the class state was transformed into the nation state"?
(*a*) Burke
(*b*) MacIver
(*c*) Laski
(*d*) None of the above

25. Who among the theorists of Marxian tradition gave prominent ideas on party?
(*a*) Stalin   (*b*) Lenin
(*c*) Trotsky   (*d*) Engels

26. Who among the following view interest groups as a phenomenon typical of capitalism and preclude their existence in the social order laid down by them?
(*a*) Anarchists (*b*) Marxists
(*c*) Neo-Liberals (*d*) Socialists

27. Lowell speaks of the tendency on men to run the cycle from radical to reactionary as they grow old, in his work :
(*a*) Public Opinion in War and Peace
(*b*) Modern democracies
(*c*) An Introduction to American Politics
(*d*) None of the above

28. Who holds the view that the term 'party' may be interchangeable with a 'faction' if it is not 'seditious'?
(*a*) Neumann (*b*) Willoughby
(*c*) Seeley (*d*) Sartori

29. Party is understood as a 'doctrine' by :
(*a*) Guild-socialism (*b*) Anarchism
(*c*) Marxism (*d*) Liberalism

30. In which of the following countries the two party system prevails?
(*a*) Canada (*b*) New Zealand
(*c*) South Africa (*d*) All of these

31. In his study of political parties Robert Michels focussed on :
(*a*) Organisation (*b*) Cadre
(*c*) Structure (*d*) Leadership

32. Who among the following does/do not favour existence of political parties?
(*a*) Rousseau (*b*) J.S. Mill
(*c*) Alexander Pope (*d*) Both (*a*) and (*c*)

33. The demarcation of parties as those of Left and those of Right can be traced in its origin to :
(*a*) Soviet Political Parties
(*b*) American Constituent Assembly
(*c*) Custom followed in the legislatures of European Continental Countries
(*d*) None of the above

34. Who has opined that the party system has broken down the great rigidity of the American Constitution?

(*a*) Garner (*b*) Gilchrist
(*c*) Gettel (*d*) Duverger

35. Who says that "a realistic survey of the British Constitution today must begin and end with parties and discuss them at length in the middle"?
(*a*) K.C. Wheare
(*b*) W.B. Munro
(*c*) Ivor Jennings
(*d*) None of the above

36. While discussing party system, Duverger uses the term 'indirect parties' to refer to :
(*a*) Pressure groups
(*b*) Organisations that play party-like role in a polity
(*c*) Non-government organisations
(*d*) All of the above

37. Who has compared parties with conduits that carry the process of social thought from the voluntary area of society into the area of government?
(*a*) MacIver (*b*) Barker
(*c*) Laski (*d*) None of the above

38. The term 'stasiology' refers to :
(*a*) Party Politics
(*b*) Scientific study of party politics
(*c*) Study of pressure group politics
(*d*) None of the above

39. Who has opined that a political party "is held together, primarily by its ideology and organisation"?
(*a*) Laski (*b*) Edmund Burke
(*c*) Roucek Huszar (*d*) Carl Friedrich

40. Who held the view about political parties that under a regime of universal suffrage, they are inevitable like the tides of the Ocean?
(*a*) Garner (*b*) Sartori
(*c*) Seeley (*d*) Sait

41. Who initiated the systematic study of pressure groups in the first decade of the twentieth century?
(*a*) Fertram Latham (*b*) David Truman
(*c*) Arthur Bentley (*d*) All of these

42. In the studies on political parties, the term used to imply dissidence and the illegitimate assertion of partisan aims is :
(*a*) Caucus   (*b*) League
(*c*) Cell   (*d*) Faction

43. Which among the following books contains the first systematic study of pressure groups?
(*a*) Interest Groups in American Society
(*b*) The Governmental Process
(*c*) The Process of Government
(*d*) The Nature of Politics

44. The names of Peter H. Odegard, Fertram Latham, V.O. Key Jr. and Charles B. Hagen are relevent in connection with the study of :
(*a*) Political parties
(*b*) Interest groups
(*c*) Political institutions
(*d*) Structural-Functional approach

45. The Human Nature Theory of the origin of political parties seeks to explain the phenomenon in terms of :
(*a*) Combative instinct
(*b*) Charisma of leaders
(*c*) Temperament
(*d*) All of the above

46. 'What is to be done'? is
(*a*) Lenin's critique of the Marxian theme of dialectical materialism
(*b*) Part of Rousseau's Confessions
(*c*) Lenin's first important theoretical work on party
(*d*) Trotsky's Critique of Lenin

47. Pressure groups were referred to as 'anonymous empire' by :
(*a*) MacIver
(*b*) Almond
(*c*) S.E. Finer
(*d*) None of the above

48. D.D. Mckean used the epithet invisible government to refer to :
(*a*) Political parties
(*b*) Bureaucracy
(*c*) Pressure groups
(*d*) None of the above

49. Who among the following did not look at political parties with favour and approval?
(*a*) Hamilton
(*b*) Laski
(*c*) George Washington
(*d*) Both (*a*) and(*c*)

50. Who says that victory is "the first commandment of a political party"?
(*a*) Alan Ball
(*b*) Barker
(*c*) Finer
(*d*) None of the above

51. One party system was established in :
(*a*) Germany by Hitler
(*b*) Russia by Lenin
(*c*) Italy by Mussolini
(*d*) All of the above

52. Who among the following visualised the party as a small compact care?
(*a*) Duverger   (*b*) Finer
(*c*) Lenin   (*d*) J.S. Mill

53. The significant work 'Interest Groups in Soviet Politics' is authored by :
(*a*) Alfred de Grazia
(*b*) Lenin
(*c*) Franklyn Griffiths and Gordon Skilling
(*d*) None of the above

54. Political parties are responsible for maintaining a continuous connection between :
(*a*) People and the Government
(*b*) President and the Prime Minister
(*c*) People and the Opposition
(*d*) Both (*a*) and (*c*)

55. Which among the following is distinguishing feature of a political party?
(*a*) Stable organisation
(*b*) Desirable objectives for the corporate body as a whole
(*c*) Recognised leadership
(*d*) All of the above

56. The work 'The British Constitution' is authored by :
(*a*) Carl Friedrich
(*b*) Ivor Jennings

(*c*) Richard Synder

(*d*) None of the above

57. Which of the following books is authored by C.A. Beard?

(*a*) American Government and Politics

(*b*) Modern Democracies

(*c*) Political Parties of Today

(*d*) All of the above

58. When a political party directs its activities in furthering sectional interests and selfish ends it degenerates into a :

(*a*) Pressure group

(*b*) Faction

(*c*) Interest group

(*d*) None of these

59. Who opined that a general will or a true public opinion cannot manifest itself in a country where parties or sects prevail?

(*a*) T.H. Green

(*b*) Rousseau

(*c*) Macpherson

(*d*) None of the above

60. Who made the observation that with or without universal suffrage, it is always an oligarchy which governs?

(*a*) C. Wright Mills

(*b*) Vilfredo Pareto

(*c*) Lowell

(*d*) None of the above

ANSWERS

1	2	3	4	5	6	7	8	9	10
(*a*)	(*c*)	(*c*)	(*d*)	(*c*)	(*d*)	(*b*)	(*c*)	(*d*)	(*d*)
11	**12**	**13**	**14**	**15**	**16**	**17**	**18**	**19**	**20**
(*a*)	(*b*)	(*d*)	(*c*)	(*a*)	(*c*)	(*b*)	(*d*)	(*a*)	(*d*)
21	**22**	**23**	**24**	**25**	**26**	**27**	**28**	**29**	**30**
(*b*)	(*c*)	(*b*)	(*b*)	(*b*)	(*b*)	(*a*)	(*d*)	(*d*)	(*d*)
31	**32**	**33**	**34**	**35**	**36**	**37**	**38**	**39**	**40**
(*d*)	(*d*)	(*c*)	(*b*)	(*c*)	(*b*)	(*b*)	(*b*)	(*c*)	(*d*)
41	**42**	**43**	**44**	**45**	**46**	**47**	**48**	**49**	**50**
(*c*)	(*d*)	(*c*)	(*b*)	(*d*)	(*c*)	(*c*)	(*c*)	(*d*)	(*c*)
51	**52**	**53**	**54**	**55**	**56**	**57**	**58**	**59**	**60**
(*d*)	(*c*)	(*c*)	(*d*)	(*d*)	(*b*)	(*a*)	(*b*)	(*b*)	(*b*)

8

FORMS OF GOVERNMENT

1. Who said the progress of transfer of administrative authority from a lower to a higher level of government is called "centralisation"?
 (*a*) White
 (*b*) Gulick
 (*c*) Simon
 (*d*) Fayol

2. Who is regarded as the father of local self-government in India?
 (*a*) Lord Mayo
 (*b*) Lord Lawrence
 (*c*) Lord Irwin
 (*d*) Lord Ripon

3. Which state government made drastic changes in the entire set-up of local self-government institutions in the state and introduced the Janapada set-up in 1948?
 (*a*) Gujarat
 (*b*) Manipur
 (*c*) Haryana
 (*d*) Madhya Pradesh

4. According to Structural Functional approach which of the following does not constitute 'input functions' of a political system?
 (*a*) Political socialisation
 (*b*) Political development
 (*c*) Interest aggregation
 (*d*) Political communication

5. Which of the following implies devolution of authority by a person to his agent or subordinate subject to his right of supervision and control?
 (*a*) Decentralisation
 (*b*) Centralisation
 (*c*) Delegation
 (*d*) None of the above

6. Decentralisation may be :
 (*a*) Political
 (*b*) Administrative
 (*c*) Moral
 (*d*) Both (*a*) and (*b*)

7. Which form of decentralisation means the setting up of new levels of government?
 (*a*) Political
 (*b*) Social
 (*c*) Legal
 (*d*) Economic

8. The term Panchayati Raj refers to a three-tier structure of rural local self-government in each :
 (*a*) Village
 (*b*) Block
 (*c*) District
 (*d*) None of the above

9. Who said that delegation means conferring authority from one executive or organisation unit to another?
 (*a*) Mooney
 (*b*) Terry
 (*c*) Follett
 (*d*) Dimock

10. Much of the delegation of work found in the departments and other organization is :
 (*a*) Formal
 (*b*) Conditional
 (*c*) Informal
 (*d*) None of the above

11. The work of the U.S.A. federal public services commission in matters of recruitment, classification etc. had been :
 (*a*) Delegated
 (*b*) Centralised
 (*c*) Decentralised
 (*d*) None of the above

12. An administrative thinker, M.P. Follett states that the concept of delegation is a mere myth of :
 (*a*) Bureaucratic theory
 (*b*) Organisational theory
 (*c*) Classical theory
 (*d*) Scientific theory

13. Without decentralisation ------ is impossible.
  (*a*) Comparative administration
  (*b*) Financial administration
  (*c*) Grass-roots administration
  (*d*) Personnel administration

14. Who said that vesting of much authority into the hands of elective local bodies makes the administrative system decentralized?
  (*a*) Taylor   (*b*) Riggs
  (*c*) White   (*d*) None of these

15. Decentralised agencies can be of various types depending upon their :
  (*a*) Status   (*b*) Authority
  (*c*) Accountability (*d*) All of these

16. Which form of decentralisation involves the problem of relationship between the headquarters and numerous field agencies?
  (*a*) Territorial
  (*b*) Functional
  (*c*) Administrative
  (*d*) None of the above

17. By the end of the ------ there was widespread disillusionment with centralised models of growth in developing countries.
  (*a*) 1970's   (*b*) 1960's
  (*c*) 1980's   (*d*) 1950's

18. Centralisation and decentralisation are not ------ principles of administration which can be universally applied to all types of administration.
  (*a*) Contextual
  (*b*) Axiomatic
  (*c*) Pragmatic
  (*d*) None of the above

19. Who recommended the vesting in the local agencies "not only the execution, but to a great degree the control of details"?
  (*a*) Laski   (*b*) Dimock
  (*c*) J.S. Mill   (*d*) Fayol

20. Too much of decentralisation may lead to
  (*a*) Anarchy
  (*b*) Grassroot democracy
  (*c*) Autocracy
  (*d*) None of the above

21. Which form of decentralisation signifies the central authority ceding specified decision-making functions to technical or professional bodies or experts?
  (*a*) Vertical   (*b*) Territorial
  (*c*) Horizontal   (*d*) Functional

22. Administrative decentralisation may be :
  (*a*) Vertical   (*b*) Horizontal
  (*c*) Territorial   (*d*) All of these

23. What facilitates the adjustment of national policies to the distinctive features of socio-cultural and economic conditions and characteristics?
  (*a*) Decentralisation
  (*b*) Delegation
  (*c*) Centralisation
  (*d*) None of the above

24. The centralisation versus decentralisation debate has been more insistent in the wake of new shifts in the development strategy of :
  (*a*) Developed countries
  (*b*) European countries
  (*c*) Third world countries
  (*d*) None of the above

25. Which of the following factors are relevant in opting for a centralised or decentralised system?
  1. Responsibility
  2. Function
  3. Administration
  4. External factors
  Choose the correct answer by using the codes given below :
  Codes :
  (*a*) 1, 2 and 3   (*b*) 2, 3 and 4
  (*c*) 1, 2, 3 and 4   (*d*) 1 and 3

26. Who among the following defines cabinet as a "hyphen that joins, the buckle that binds the executive and legislative departments together"?
  (*a*) Bryce   (*b*) Bagehot
  (*c*) Barker   (*d*) Garner

27. The works 'Modern Domocracies' and 'The English Constitution' are authored by :

    (*a*) James Bryce
    (*b*) Bryce and Bagehot respectively
    (*c*) Sir Walter Bagehot
    (*d*) Bagehot and Bryce respectively

28. Its members deliberate in secret to shape the policy of the government by mature, rational and independent discussion and to maintain harmony among its members. It is :
    (*a*) Party caucus   (*b*) Pressure group
    (*c*) Cabinet   (*d*) Militia

29. A parliamentary government is criticised as inefficient because :
    (*a*) It takes very long to take decisions
    (*b*) It breeds root tapism
    (*c*) It is not possible to fix responsibility for omissions and commissions clearly
    (*d*) It is a government by amateur

30. The most important and most characteristic feature each of the parliamentary and the presidential systems of governments respectively is :
    (*a*) Vitality and durability
    (*b*) Responsibility and independence
    (*c*) Harmony and longivity
    (*d*) Independence and responsibility

31. A great merit of the presidential system is :
    (*a*) Flexibility
    (*b*) Harmony
    (*c*) Stability
    (*d*) None of the above

32. Which form of government is based on the principle of "division of labour"?
    (*a*) Parliamentary system of government
    (*b*) Bureaucratic form of government
    (*c*) Presidential form of government
    (*d*) All of the above

33. Separation of powers, most of all ensures :
    (*a*) Stability   (*b*) Efficiency
    (*c*) Liberty   (*d*) All of these

34. Countries of which of the following regions have predominantly adopted the presidential form of government?
    (*a*) East Asia   (*b*) South-East Asia
    (*c*) Scandinavian   (*d*) Latin America

35. Consider the following political system—
    1. Czech Republic
    2. Malaysia
    3. South Africa
    4. Sri Lanka
What is the correct chronological sequence of the above opting to a sustained competitive electoral democracy?
    (*a*) 2, 4, 3 and 1   (*b*) 2, 3, 4 and 1
    (*c*) 4, 2, 1 and 3   (*d*) 4, 1, 2 and 3

36. The cabinet under a Presidential system is :
    (*a*) Part of the legislature
    (*b*) Controls the lower judiciary
    (*c*) A tool of the President
    (*d*) Both (*b*) and (*c*)

37. The Presidential system of government was adopted by Pakistan under :
    (*a*) General Zia-ul-Haq
    (*b*) General Yahya Khan
    (*c*) General Ayub Khan
    (*d*) None of the above

38. Political parties are extra-constitutional in :
    (*a*) U.S.A.
    (*b*) Great Britain
    (*c*) Republic of India
    (*d*) Both (*a*) and (*c*)

39. Over the laws passed by the Congress the American President has :
    (*a*) Absolute veto   (*b*) Rocket Veto
    (*c*) Both (*a*) and (*b*)   (*d*) Suspensive Veto

40. Which of the following countries have a unitary form of government?
    (*a*) Italy   (*b*) Nigeria
    (*c*) Japan   (*d*) Both (*a*) and (*c*)

41. Unitary government is, most of all, antithetical to :
    (*a*) International organisations
    (*b*) Non-government bodies
    (*c*) Local initiative
    (*d*) All of the above

42. The author of **Constitutional Government and Democracy** is :
    (*a*) Carl Friedrich   (*b*) Finer
    (*c*) Dicey   (*d*) None of the above

43. Who among the following opines that federalism, when successful, has generally been a stage towards a unitary government?
(*a*) Wheare
(*b*) Laski
(*c*) Dicey
(*d*) All of the above

44. The doctrine of 'dual federalism' was commonly used in the nineteenth century to describe :
(*a*) Australian federal system
(*b*) German federal system
(*c*) Both (*a*) and (*b*)
(*d*) American federal system

45. The notion of cooperative federalism emerged and got consolidated during the period of :
(*a*) Wilson and Roosevelt
(*b*) Taft
(*c*) Washington and Lincoln
(*d*) None of the above

46. In which of the following countries, the residuary power lie with the units?
(*a*) Australia
(*b*) India
(*c*) Canada
(*d*) Both (*a*) and (*c*)

47. Who among the following believe that the federal spirit is likely to expand worldwide and pervade the political structures of many a nation?
(*a*) Sidgwick
(*b*) Willoughby
(*c*) Wheare
(*d*) Both (*a*) and (*c*)

48. When did the real power slip away from the parliament into the hands of the cabinet which then assumed central importance?
(*a*) By the end of the seventeenth century
(*b*) By the end of the eighteenth century
(*c*) By the middle of the nineteenth century
(*d*) By the middle of the twentieth century

49. Which of the following developments expedited the decline of parliament and transfer of its power of the cabinet?
(*a*) Integration of pressure groups
(*b*) Strengthening of the judiciary
(*c*) Both (*a*) and (*b*)
(*d*) Rise of the party system

50. The most widely known model of parliamentary system of government is the :
(*a*) Indian model
(*b*) Westminster model
(*c*) French model
(*d*) Australian model

51. The term of office of the Mexican President is :
(*a*) Four years
(*b*) Five years
(*c*) Six years
(*d*) None of the above

52. The term 'presidential government' originated in :
(*a*) United States
(*b*) France
(*c*) Switzerland
(*d*) Great Britain

53. Which of the following events strengthened the American Presidency?
(*a*) The Great Depression
(*b*) The Korean War
(*c*) Both (*a*) and (*b*)
(*d*) The American Civil War

54. Which of the following set of countries does not have Presidential government?
(*a*) Italy and Canada
(*b*) Philippines and South Korea
(*c*) Indonesia and Egypt
(*d*) None of the above

55. In the United States of America, the election of President is :
(*a*) A direct popular election
(*b*) An indirect unpopular election
(*c*) An indirect popular election
(*d*) None of the above

56. The work **Government and Politics in Latin America** is authored by :
(*a*) R.A. Gomez
(*b*) Robert E. Scott
(*c*) Che Gwevera
(*d*) None of the above

57. The U.S. President heads :
(*a*) The armed forces
(*b*) Country's public administration
(*c*) National executive
(*d*) All of the above

58. Assertion (A) : T.H. Marshall divided citizenship rights as civil, political and social.
Reason (R) : The civic virtue of citizenship is regarded as an important supplement to theories of institutional justice today.
  (*a*) Both A and R are individually true and R is the correct explanation of A.
  (*b*) Both A and R are individually true but R is **not** the correct explanation of A.
  (*c*) A is true but R is false.
  (*d*) A is false but R is true.

59. Match the following

List-I	List-II
(Approach)	*(Scholar)*
(A) New Institutionalism	1. Michael Walzer
(B) Neo-Liberalism	2. David Apter
(C) Communitarianism	3. Milton Friedman
(D) Behaviouralism	4. Douglass North

codes

	A	B	C	D
(*a*)	4	3	1	2
(*b*)	2	3	1	4
(*c*)	2	1	3	4
(*d*)	4	1	3	2

60. Consider the following classics of Marxism—
  1. The German Ideology (Marx and Engels)
  2. The Paris Commune (Marx)
  3. The Critique of the Gotha Programme (Marx)
  4. State and Revolution (Lenin)
  Which of the above are a strong endorsement of direct democracy?
  (*a*) 1, 2 and 3
  (*b*) 2, 3 and 4
  (*c*) 1, 3 and 4
  (*d*) 1, 2 and 4

ANSWERS

1	2	3	4	5	6	7	8	9	10
(*a*)	(*d*)	(*d*)	(*b*)	(*c*)	(*d*)	(*a*)	(*c*)	(*b*)	(*c*)
11	12	13	14	15	16	17	18	19	20
(*c*)	(*b*)	(*c*)	(*c*)	(*d*)	(*a*)	(*b*)	(*b*)	(*c*)	(*a*)
21	22	23	24	25	26	27	28	29	30
(*d*)	(*d*)	(*a*)	(*c*)	(*c*)	(*b*)	(*b*)	(*c*)	(*d*)	(*b*)
31	32	33	34	35	36	37	38	39	40
(*c*)	(*c*)	(*c*)	(*d*)	(*c*)	(*c*)	(*c*)	(*d*)	(*d*)	(*d*)
41	42	43	44	45	46	47	48	49	50
(*c*)	(*a*)	(*c*)	(*d*)	(*a*)	(*a*)	(*d*)	(*c*)	(*d*)	(*b*)
51	52	53	54	55	56	57	58	59	60
(*c*)	(*d*)	(*c*)	(*a*)	(*c*)	(*a*)	(*d*)	(*b*)	(*a*)	(*a*)

9

BUREAUCRACY CONCEPT

1. The centralisation of bureaucracy was related to a trend of growing :
   (a) Nationalisation
   (b) Rationalisation
   (c) Commercialisation
   (d) None of the above

2. Marx's observations on the changing role of bureaucracy can be found eminently in his most brilliant political pamphlet :
   (a) Critique of political Economy
   (b) The Administrative State
   (c) The 18th Brumaire of Louis Bonaparte
   (d) Elements of Public Administration

3. Michels thought that all big organisations tended to develop a bureaucratic structure which ruled out the possibility of :
   (a) Internal democracy
   (b) External democracy
   (c) People's participation
   (d) Political interference

4. Who said that bureaucracy is just one of the three main types of personnel systems, viz, the Bureaucratic, the Aristocratic and the Democratic?
   (a) Max Weber   (b) Willoughby
   (c) Ogg   (d) Finer

5. Consider the following forms of bureaucracy according to Marx :
   1. The guardian bureaucracy
   2. The caste bureaucracy
   3. The patronage bureaucracy
   4. The merit bureaucracy

   Which of the above are correct? Choose the correct answer using the codes given below :
   (a) 1, 2 and 3   (b) 2 and 3

   (c) 3 and 4   (d) 1, 2, 3 and 4

6. Who identified bureaucracy with institutions and large scale organisations in society?
   (a) Laski   (b) Dimock
   (c) Davis   (d) Urwick

7. Which of the following developed in the eighteenth and nineteenth centuries, first in the countries of Western Europe and then in other countries of the world?
   (a) Public Administration
   (b) Development Administration
   (c) Bureaucracy
   (d) None of the above

8. Which of the following is a cause of bureaucracy, according to Weber?
   (a) Democracy
   (b) The emergence of money economy
   (c) The growth of the European population
   (d) All of the above

9. Which of the following features makes a public organisation bureaucratic, according to F. Heady?
   (a) Hierarchy
   (b) Defferentiation or specialisation
   (c) Qualification or competence
   (d) All of the above

10. The ------ bureaucracy has a class base and "arises from the class connection of those in the controlling positions".
    (a) Merit
    (b) Patronage
    (c) Caste
    (d) None of the above

11. What is another name for patronage bureaucracy?

Obj. Pol. Sc.-10

    (*a*) New bureaucracy
    (*b*) Spoils system
    (*c*) Traditional bureaucracy
    (*d*) Hierarchic system

12. Lenin agreed with Marx that bureaucracy is a parasite and is connected with :
    (*a*) Bourgeois society
    (*b*) Civil society
    (*c*) Proletariat society
    (*d*) None of the above

13. Which of the following forms of bureaucracy is neutral, anonymous and a political?
    (*a*) Committed bureaucracy
    (*b*) Depoliticised bureaucracy
    (*c*) Fully politicised bureaucracy
    (*d*) None of the above

14. Which of the following types of bureaucracy exists in single-party authoritarian structures?
    (*a*) Fully politicised bureaucracy
    (*b*) Committed bureaucracy
    (*c*) Depoliticised bureaucracy
    (*d*) Semi-politicised bureaucracy

15. According to Trotsky, bureaucratism is a :
    (*a*) Political Phenomenon
    (*b*) Social Phenomenon
    (*c*) Economic Phenomenon
    (*d*) None of the above

16. Who among the following has done a very detailed study of the negative aspects of bureaucracy?
    (*a*) Robert K. Merton   (*b*) Ralph P. Hummel
    (*c*) Riggs   (*d*) Both (*a*) and (*b*)

17. Weber's ideal type model advocates the separation of administrative staff from ownership of the means of
    (*a*) Distribution
    (*b*) Production
    (*c*) Communication
    (*d*) None of the above

18. To overcome the shortcomings of the bureaucratic model, Riggs introduced his ---- model of public administration.
    (*a*) Behavioural
    (*b*) Developmental
    (*c*) Ecological
    (*d*) None of the above

19. Bureaucratisation which tends to concentrate power in the hands of an administrative elite militates against the principles of :
    (*a*) Aristocracy
    (*b*) Democracy
    (*c*) Mobocracy
    (*d*) None of the above

20. Lloyd and Susanne Rudolph have argued that the weberian model is not necessarily the most rational and effective organisational structure in terms of :
    (*a*) Legitimacy   (*b*) Veracity
    (*c*) Efficiency   (*d*) None of the above

21. Who emphasised the point that administrative efficiency would be reduced by following Weber's structural approach?
    (*a*) Herbert Simon and Chester Barnard
    (*b*) Hewart
    (*c*) Laski
    (*d*) Merton

22. Who observed that bureaucracy is the most rationally known means of achieving imperative control over human beings?
    (*a*) Laski
    (*b*) Michels
    (*c*) Max Weber
    (*d*) None of the abvoe

23. The structural characteristics of bureaucracy according to Weber include :
    (*a*) Division of Labour
    (*b*) Rules
    (*c*) Hierarchy
    (*d*) All of the above

24. The behavioural characteristics of bureaucracy according to Weber include :
    (*a*) Rationality   (*b*) Neutrality
    (*c*) Impersonality   (*d*) All of the above

25. Who characterizes the power and authority of bureaucracy as new despotism?
    (*a*) Finer   (*b*) Marx
    (*c*) Lord Hewart   (*d*) Max Weber

26. Which of the following has been defined as "punctilious exactitude in the observance of regulations"?
(*a*) Nepotism　　　(*b*) Bureaucracy
(*c*) Red tape　　　(*d*) Administration

27. Who describes the growth of bureaucracies from structural-functional angle in colonial and non-colonial developing countries?
(*a*) Heady　　　(*b*) Riggs
(*c*) Fainsod　　　(*d*) Eisenstadt

28. A structural view of bureaucracy as an organisation was taken by :
(*a*) Max Weber　　　(*b*) Arthur K Davis
(*c*) Karl Marx　　　(*d*) Lenin

29. Who believes that bureaucracy contributes to the alienation of the people?
(*a*) Marx　　　(*b*) Weber
(*c*) Trotsky　　　(*d*) Rizzi

30. Much before Karl Marx, ------ had viewed bureaucracy as officials who governed in their own interests rather than in the interests of the governed.
(*a*) Spencer　　　(*b*) Mill
(*c*) Laski　　　(*d*) Saint Simon

31. Marx insisted that bureaucracy grew as a result of external and pathological :
(*a*) Political divisions
(*b*) Social divisions
(*c*) Economic divisions
(*d*) None of the above

32. The only thing for which Marx praised bureaucracy was its role in :
(*a*) Decentralising nations
(*b*) Ground level administration
(*c*) Centralising nations
(*d*) A political administration

33. Whose views are in sharp contrast to the Weberian conception of bureaucracy as rationalisation of organisation?
(*a*) Marx
(*b*) Lenin
(*c*) Merton
(*d*) None of these

34. Bureaucracy as an organisational model was first developed systematically by :
(*a*) Merton　　　(*b*) Hewart
(*c*) Laski　　　(*d*) Max Weber

35. Weber repeatedly stressed the fact that the ------ system has undeniably played a major role in the development of modern bureaucracy.
(*a*) Socialist
(*b*) Mixed
(*c*) Capitalist
(*d*) None of the above

36. Who has defined bureaucracy as "a system of government the control of which is so completely in the hands of officials that their power jeopardises the liberties of ordinary citizens"?
(*a*) Max Weber　　　(*b*) Laski
(*c*) Pfiffner　　　(*d*) Vieg

37. Merit bureaucracy aims at :
(*a*) Career open to affiliation
(*b*) Career open to experience
(*c*) Career open to talent
(*d*) Career open to politics

38. According to Bertrand Russel, bureaucracy everywhere tends to develop a negative psychology perpetually prone to :
(*a*) Prohibitions　　　(*b*) Injustice
(*c*) Corruption　　　(*d*) Impropriety

39. Who was the strongest critic of bureaucracy?
(*a*) Presthus　　　(*b*) Ramsay Muir
(*c*) Morrison　　　(*d*) Max Weber

40. Who developed a typology of authority and distinguished three pure types-traditional charismatic and legal?
(*a*) Mosca
(*b*) Michels
(*c*) Max Weber
(*d*) None of the above

41. Weber's conception of bureaucracy can be found in his ideas on :
(*a*) Power　　　(*b*) Authority
(*c*) Domination　　　(*d*) All of these

42. Who has defined power as "the probability that one actor within a social relationship will be in a position to carry out his own will despite resistance"?
(*a*) Marx   (*b*) Hegel
(*c*) Weber   (*d*) None of the above

43. Whose most extensive and systematic discussion of administration occurs within his sociology of Domination in Economy and Society?
(*a*) Weber   (*b*) Crozier
(*c*) Marx   (*d*) None of the above

44. Who regards bureau as an indispensable component of a society built on a complex distribution of labour, centralised administration and money economy?
(*a*) Lenin   (*b*) Max Weber
(*c*) Marx   (*d*) None of the above

45. ------ is considered as the most rational economic basis for bureaucratic administration by Weber.
(*a*) Liberalism   (*b*) Capitalism
(*c*) Socialism   (*d*) Gandhism

46. Who uses bureaucracy to mean "an organization that cannot correct its behaviour by learning from its errors"?
(*a*) T. Carlyle   (*b*) M. Crozier
(*c*) R. Shelton   (*d*) None of the above

47. Who said that bureaucracy is the price of parliamentary democracy?
(*a*) Morley   (*b*) Marx
(*c*) Finer   (*d*) Morrison

48. Match List I with List II and select the correct answer using the codes given below :

List I	List II
A. David Beetham	1. Bureaucracy and Development
B. Mohit Bhattacharya	2. Bureaucracy in Modern Society
C. Peter M. Blau	3. Critique of Political Economy
D. Marx	4. Max Weber and the Theory of Modern Politics

Codes :

	A	B	C	D
(*a*)	4	1	2	3
(*b*)	3	4	1	2
(*c*)	1	2	4	3
(*d*)	4	1	3	2

49. Marx examined bureaucracy as a set of relationships that arise in a specific ------ context.
(*a*) Political   (*b*) Socio-economic
(*c*) Administrative   (*d*) None of the above

50. Who defines the term bureaucracy as the systematic organization of tasks and individuals into a pattern which can most effectively achieve the ends of collective efforts?
(*a*) Gladden   (*b*) Pfiffner
(*c*) Max Weber   (*d*) Marx

51. The term bureaucracy is coined by :
(*a*) Hegel in 1821
(*b*) Vincent de Gourney in 1745
(*c*) Lenin in 1920
(*d*) None of the above

52. The structural view of bureaucracy as an organisation was taken by :
(*a*) Arther Bentley   (*b*) Bentham
(*c*) Arthur K. Davis   (*d*) None of the above

53. The work "The Revolution Betrayed" is authored by :
(*a*) Lenin   (*b*) Stalin
(*c*) Gorbachev   (*d*) Trotsky

54. Who preceded Karl Marx in viewing bureaucracy as officials who governed in their own interests rather than in the interests of the government?
(*a*) Charles Fourier   (*b*) Proudhon
(*c*) Saint Simon   (*d*) None of the above

55. The clause global new class theorists is associated with :
(*a*) Political parties
(*b*) Bureaucracy
(*c*) Capitalism and globalization
(*d*) Constitutionalism

56. Who among the following view bureaucrats as one of the several 'Veto groups' that function in a political system?
(*a*) Neo-liberals
(*b*) Feminists
(*c*) Anarchists
(*d*) Pluralist thinkers on bureaucracy

57. Who among the following is prominent global new class theorist?
(*a*) Andre Gunder Frank
(*b*) Weber
(*c*) Rizzi
(*d*) Martin Albrow

58. In the whole gamut of scholarship on bureaucracy the phrase 'governmental overload' is associated with :
(*a*) Pluralist theory of bureaucracy
(*b*) Soviet ideas on bureaucracy
(*c*) Neo-liberal views on bureaucracy
(*d*) None of the above

59. Who held that the two institutions— bureaucracy and standing army as most characteristic of the state machine and a parasite on the body of bourgeois society?
(*a*) Gandhi (*b*) Marx
(*c*) Lenin (*d*) Mao

60. Who among the following has made a very detailed study of the negative features of bureaucracy?
(*a*) Huntington (*b*) Weber
(*c*) Ralph P. Hummel (*d*) None of the above

61. The only thing for which Marx praised bureaucracy was :
(*a*) Its systematic hierarchical character
(*b*) Its performance in the Agrarian, Colonial societies
(*c*) Its role in centralizing nations
(*d*) All of the above

62. Who among the following regarded as Medieval Aristotle?
(*a*) St. Augustine
(*b*) St. Thomas Acq
(*c*) Marsiglio of Padue
(*d*) John Salisbury

63. Marx's observations on the changing role of bureaucracy can be prominently found in :
(*a*) Philosophy of Poverty
(*b*) Thesis on Feuerbach
(*c*) The 18th Brumaire of Louis Bonaparte
(*d*) All of the above

64. In modern times the rise and growth of bureaucracy is integrally associated with the emergence of :
(*a*) Political parties (*b*) Capitalist state
(*c*) Socialism (*d*) None of the above

65. The term 'soviets' was used and popularised by :
(*a*) Marx (*b*) Engels
(*c*) Lenin (*d*) Stalin

66. Who among the following have denounced bureaucracy and suggested its replacement by a new type of public services under people's bodies?
(*a*) Fabian Socialist (*b*) Marxists
(*c*) Liberals (*d*) Conservatives

67. The work **'How Britain is Governed'** is authored by :
(*a*) A.L. Lowell (*b*) A.V. Dicey
(*c*) Both (*a*) and (*b*) (*d*) Ramsay Muir

68. About which country it is said that the expansion of bureaucracy there under the imperial rule blocked the advent of industrial revolution?
(*a*) Japan (*b*) India
(*c*) China (*d*) Russia

69. Who among the following has shown that decision-making by bureaucrats is influenced by a host of factors like one's beliefsets, Socialization, feelings and emotions?
(*a*) Herbert Simon
(*b*) Hegel
(*c*) Weber
(*d*) Vincent de Gourney

70. The work **'The Politics of Under Development'** is authored by :
(*a*) Sigmund Neumann
(*b*) Gerald Heeger

   (*c*) Ramsay Muir
   (*d*) Samir Amin

71. Who among the following identified bureaucracy with institutions and large scale organisations in society?
   (*a*) Karl Marx
   (*b*) Engels
   (*c*) Harold Laski
   (*d*) Marshall E. Dimock

72. The 'traditional authority' according to Max Weber, rests on :
   (*a*) The long standing centres of power in society
   (*b*) The age old social institutions like caste
   (*c*) An established belief in the sanctity of memorial traditions and the legitimacy of the status of those exercising authority under them
   (*d*) All of the above

73. In which of his works Marx held that in a socialist society there would be no place for appointed officials, because the people would hold their power in their own hands and exercise it themselves?

   (*a*) Das Capital
   (*b*) Economic and Philosophic Manuscripts
   (*c*) Civil War in France
   (*d*) The Eighteenth Burmaire

74. Among the scholars who have contributed on the theme of bureaucracy, the name of Robert K. Merton is associated with :
   (*a*) Study of bureaucratic apparatus in the communist states including the Soviet Union
   (*b*) Make a class analysis of American bureaucracy
   (*c*) Study of dysfunctional aspects of bureaucracy
   (*d*) Both (*a*) and (*b*)

75. The inherent tendency of bureaucracy to accumulate power was a great cause of worry to Weber. He considered several mechanisms to limit the scope of bureaucracy. Important among them was :
   (*a*) Collegiality
   (*b*) Separation of powers
   (*c*) Direct democracy
   (*d*) All of the above

ANSWERS

1	2	3	4	5	6	7	8	9	10
(*b*)	(*c*)	(*a*)	(*b*)	(*d*)	(*b*)	(*c*)	(*d*)	(*d*)	(*c*)
11	**12**	**13**	**14**	**15**	**16**	**17**	**18**	**19**	**20**
(*b*)	(*a*)	(*b*)	(*a*)	(*b*)	(*d*)	(*b*)	(*c*)	(*b*)	(*c*)
21	**22**	**23**	**24**	**25**	**26**	**27**	**28**	**29**	**30**
(*a*)	(*c*)	(*d*)	(*d*)	(*b*)	(*c*)	(*d*)	(*b*)	(*a*)	(*d*)
31	**32**	**33**	**34**	**35**	**36**	**37**	**38**	**39**	**40**
(*b*)	(*c*)	(*a*)	(*d*)	(*c*)	(*b*)	(*c*)	(*a*)	(*b*)	(*c*)
41	**42**	**43**	**44**	**45**	**46**	**47**	**48**	**49**	**50**
(*d*)	(*b*)	(*a*)	(*b*)	(*b*)	(*c*)	(*d*)	(*a*)	(*b*)	(*b*)
51	**52**	**53**	**54**	**55**	**56**	**57**	**58**	**59**	**60**
(*b*)	(*c*)	(*d*)	(*c*)	(*b*)	(*d*)	(*c*)	(*a*)	(*c*)	(*c*)
61	**62**	**63**	**64**	**65**	**66**	**67**	**68**	**69**	**70**
(*c*)	(*b*)	(*c*)	(*b*)	(*c*)	(*b*)	(*d*)	(*c*)	(*a*)	(*b*)
71	**72**	**73**	**74**	**75**					
(*d*)	(*c*)	(*c*)	(*c*)	(*d*)					

THEORIES OF DEVELOPMENT

1. Which model of development was adopted by a number of European and Asian countries after the second world war?
   - (*a*) Liberal model
   - (*b*) Socialist model
   - (*c*) Welfare-state model
   - (*d*) None of the above

2. At the political level, the welfare state model believes that only a ------ state can perform the task of development.
   - (*a*) Socialist
   - (*b*) Communist
   - (*c*) Democratic
   - (*d*) Pluralist

3. Which of the following is one of the well-defined goals of the development strategy in India?
   - (*a*) Reduction in social disparities
   - (*b*) Providing minimum conditions of subsistence and survival
   - (*c*) Independence of economy from its reliance on strategic imports and foreign aid
   - (*d*) All of the above

4. Which of the following are the periods of development according to Marx?
   - (*a*) Feudalism and Communism
   - (*b*) Capitalism and Socialism
   - (*c*) Conservatism and modernism
   - (*d*) Both (*a*) and (*b*)

5. Which theory blames under-development on bad government, bad trade policies and political mismanagement?
   - (*a*) Pluralist theory
   - (*b*) Market theory
   - (*c*) Socialist theory
   - (*d*) None of the above

6. Which Political Scientist gave a new dimension to the concept of Justice, liberalism and Equality?
   - (*a*) John Rawls
   - (*b*) Arthur Bentley
   - (*c*) Karl Marx
   - (*d*) Hans Morgenthau

7. Which of the following models of development challenged the market model of development with freedom?
   - (*a*) Welfare model
   - (*b*) Liberal model
   - (*c*) Marxist model
   - (*d*) Both (*a*) and (*c*)

8. The market model of development has been an enemy of :
   - (*a*) Socio-economic equality
   - (*b*) Competition
   - (*c*) Political equality
   - (*d*) None of the above

9. Which model of development believes in development through the state?
   - (*a*) Marxist model
   - (*b*) Welfare model
   - (*c*) Liberal model
   - (*d*) None of the above

10. Who best explains the welfare theory of development?
    - (*a*) John Rawls
    - (*b*) Paul Baran
    - (*c*) J.M. Keynes
    - (*d*) Lucian Pye

11. Which of the following is not associated with political underdevelopment?
    - (*a*) Corruption
    - (*b*) Violent demonstrations
    - (*c*) Committed bureaucracy
    - (*d*) Territorial integration

12. The views of Marxism are more relevant in the context of underdevelopment of the :
(*a*) Developing countries
(*b*) Third-world countries
(*c*) Developed countries
(*d*) Asian countries

13. Which approach tried to study the nature of development in terms of evolution of the developed and under-developed societies?
(*a*) Historical approach
(*b*) Legal approach
(*c*) Comparative history approach
(*d*) Institutional approach

14. Who said that development is both political modernization and political institutionalization?
(*a*) Levy
(*b*) Jaguaribe
(*c*) Pierson
(*d*) Briggs

15. Which one of the following statements regarding the concept of development is not correct?
(*a*) Development is a very complex phenomenon
(*b*) Development is an asynchronous process
(*c*) The concept of development is also associated with ideology
(*d*) An undeveloped society is made up of certain social and political structures, processes and technologies and life-styles

16. The chief proponent of the theory of Natural Right are—
(*a*) John Locke and Thomas Paine
(*b*) Lasswell and Kaplan
(*c*) Hegel and Kant
(*d*) Durkheim and Weber

17. Which of the following is a significant model by which socio-economic development could be achieved?
(*a*) Market model
(*b*) Socialist model
(*c*) Welfare model
(*d*) All of the above

18. The ------ view of development considers market as central to development.
(*a*) Marxist
(*b*) Political
(*c*) Classical-liberal
(*d*) Socialist

19. In which book Adam Smith laid stress on the concept of an autonomous self-regulating economy described as civil society?

20. Adam Smith in his book 'The Wealth of Nations' equated development with :
(*a*) Consumer sovereignty
(*b*) Efficient production
(*c*) A positive movement
(*d*) A negative state

21. Who is the king in the market model of development?
(*a*) Consumer
(*b*) Retailer
(*c*) Producer
(*d*) None of the above

22. An important condition for the market model of development is :
(*a*) Manipulation
(*b*) Guild organisation
(*c*) Competition
(*d*) None of the above

23. Who said that development 'is a movement upward of a whole system of interdependent conditions as a complex process in which economic growth is only one of the several categories of causally relevant conditions'?
(*a*) Roger
(*b*) Gunnar Myrdal
(*c*) Walter
(*d*) None of the above

24. Which of the following does not mean development in the liberal capitalist world?
(*a*) Political participation
(*b*) Decentralisation of power
(*c*) Political defections
(*d*) National integration

25. Gandhi's view on development can be summed up as :
(*a*) Social Equilibrium
(*b*) Political Equilibrium
(*c*) Spiritual Equilibrium
(*d*) Moral Equilibrium

26. Gandhi made a distinction between ------ and ------ development.
(*a*) Real, moral
(*b*) Economic, real
(*c*) Political, social
(*d*) Moral, political

[The options for question 19:]
(*a*) Political Development and Political Decay
(*b*) Wealth of Nations
(*c*) Three World of Development
(*d*) None of the above

27. According to Gandhi, the root of happiness lies in :
(*a*) Materialism   (*b*) Hedonism
(*c*) Spiritualism   (*d*) Mysticism

28. Who said that underdevelopment theory erroneously overstresses the role of colonial and post-colonial economies in the development?
(*a*) John Rawls   (*b*) John Taylor
(*c*) Macpherson   (*d*) Walter

29. The Gandhian view of development was based upon his metaphysical ------ with emphasis on the supremacy of ethical values and a moral approach to the problem of development.
(*a*) Idealism
(*b*) Transcendentalism
(*c*) Theism
(*d*) None of the above

30. Which of the following statement is true regarding the socialist system of development?
(*a*) Public ownership of the means of production
(*b*) Centralisation of all sectors of economy
(*c*) All economic decisions are made by a central authority
(*d*) All of the above

31. According to whom, development consisted of four elements: adaptability, complexity, autonomy and coherence?
(*a*) Nye   (*b*) Huntington
(*c*) Briggs   (*d*) Pierson

32. Who gave the first system of social science framed primarily in terms of developmental models since it related development to social interests?
(*a*) Marx   (*b*) Myrdal
(*c*) Levy   (*d*) None of the above

33. Which of the following countries adopted the Marxist model of socialist development?
(*a*) China   (*b*) North Korea
(*c*) Cuba   (*d*) All of the above

34. Who said that while the socialist system was able to attain its initial goals, it could not adapt to the new challenges and requirements placed upon it?

(*a*) Roger   (*b*) Galbraith
(*c*) Pierson   (*d*) Levy

35. Who is the author of 'Two Concept of Liberty'?
(*a*) Mill   (*b*) Isciahs Berlin
(*c*) Laski   (*d*) Macpherson

36. Pain and pressure and the two Sovereign matter is said by–
(*a*) Hobbes   (*b*) Hegel
(*c*) Machiaveth   (*d*) Benthan

37. 'Pain and Pressure and the two Sovereign matter', is said by—
(*a*) Hobbes   (*b*) Hegel
(*c*) Machiavelli   (*d*) Bentham

38. Which theory was developed as a critique of welfare model of development in the context of post-colonial societies?
(*a*) Development theory
(*b*) Marxist theory
(*c*) Underdevelopment theory
(*d*) Socialist theory

39. Who among the following is not an advocate of underdevelopment theory?
(*a*) Paul Baran   (*b*) Andre Gunder
(*c*) Celso Furtando   (*d*) Simon

40. The major tenet of underdevelopment theory is also shared by :
(*a*) Dependency theory
(*b*) Socialist theory
(*c*) Development theory
(*d*) None of the above

41. Who best explains the welfare theory of development?
(*a*) John Rawls   (*b*) Paul Baran
(*c*) J.M. Keynes   (*d*) Lucian Pye

42. Which model of development believes in development through the state?
(*a*) Marxist model   (*b*) Welfare model
(*c*) Liberal model   (*d*) None of the above

43. The market model of development has been an enemy of :
(*a*) Socio-economic equality
(*b*) Competition
(*c*) Political equality
(*d*) None of the above

44. Which of the following models of development challenged the market model of development with freedom?
 (*a*) Welfare model   (*b*) Liberal model
 (*c*) Marxist model   (*d*) Both (*a*) and (*c*)

45. The ------ view of development considers market as central to development.
 (*a*) Marxist   (*b*) Political
 (*c*) Classical-liberal (*d*) Socialist

46. Which of the following is a significant model by which socio-economic development could be achieved?
 (*a*) Market model   (*b*) Socialist model
 (*c*) Welfare model   (*d*) All of the above

47. Who among the following propagated the idea of Cultural Revolution under Socialism?
 (*a*) Karl Marx   (*b*) Mao-Tse-Tung
 (*c*) V.I. Lenin   (*d*) J. Stalin

48. Who said that development is both political modernization and political institutionaliza-tion?
 (*a*) Levy   (*b*) Jaguaribe
 (*c*) Piercon   (*d*) Briggs

49. Which approach tried to study the nature of development in terms of evolution of the development and underdevelopment societies?
 (*a*) Historical approach
 (*b*) Legal approach
 (*c*) Comparative history approach
 (*d*) Institutional approach

50. An important condition for the market model of development is :
 (*a*) Manipulation
 (*b*) Guild organisation
 (*c*) Competition
 (*d*) None of the above

51. Who is the King in the market model of development?
 (*a*) Consumer   (*b*) Retailer
 (*c*) Producer   (*d*) None of the above

52. Consider the following statements : According to Max Weber, charisma refers to the ability to
 1. exercise authority on ground of holiness or bravery
 2. lead and inspire by sheer force of personality and conviction
 3. reason out and argue lucidly

 4. exercise power irrationally
 Which of the statements given above is/are correct?
 (*a*) 1 only   (*b*) 2 only
 (*c*) 1, 2 and 4   (*d*) 2, 3 and 4

53. Consider the following statements :
 1. Mosca divided all governments into two types : feudal and bureaucratic.
 2. Max Weber identified three types of authorities : charismatic, traditional, legal-rational.
 3. John Stuart Mill was the first scholar to have coined the term 'bureaucracy'.
 4. Frederick Engels wrote one of the early texts on the conditions of working classes in England.
 Which of the statements given above are correct?
 (*a*) 1, 2, 3 and 4   (*b*) 1, 2 and 4
 (*c*) 3 and 4   (*d*) 2 and 3

54. Which of the following is not associated with political underdevelopment?
 (*a*) Corruption
 (*b*) Violent demonstrations
 (*c*) Committed bureaucracy
 (*d*) Territorial integration

55. Which of the following does not mean development in the liberal capitalist world?
 (*a*) Political participation
 (*b*) Decentralisation of power
 (*c*) Political defections
 (*d*) National integration

56. Which of the following are correct about federalism?
 1. It implies protection and co-determination.
 2. It provides for additional controls of government, bureaucracy and parliament.
 3. It makes the process of government a continuing task of adjustment and coordination of competing interests.
 4. It ensures uniformity of law and administration.
 Select the correct answer using the codes given below :
 (*a*) 1, 2, 3 and 4   (*b*) 1, 2 and 3
 (*c*) 2 and 4   (*d*) 1, 3 and 4

57. Who among the following gave prominence to the size principle in his theory of political coalitions?
 (*a*) William Riker (*b*) Gabriel Almond
 (*c*) Lucian W Pye (*d*) V. O. Key

58. According to Gandhi, the root of happiness lies in :
 (*a*) Materialism (*b*) Hedonism
 (*c*) Spiritualism (*d*) Mysticism

59. Who said that underdevelopment theory erroneously overstresses the role of colonial and postcolonial economics in the development?
 (*a*) John Rawls (*b*) John Taylor
 (*c*) Macpherson (*d*) Walter

60. Which of the following statements is true regarding the socialist system of development?
 (*a*) Public ownership of the means of production
 (*b*) Centralisation of all sectors of economy
 (*c*) All economic decisions are made by a central authority
 (*d*) All of the above

61. In which one of the following countries was proportional representation system given up after a practice of nearly fifty years in favour of first-past the post system?
 (*a*) Germany (*b*) France
 (*c*) U.S.A. (*d*) Italy

62. Match List I (Idea) with List II (Thinker) and select the correct answer using the codes given below the lists :

List-I	List-II
A. Group theory	1. Robert Dahl
B. Polyarchy	2. G. Mosca
C. Elite theory	3. A.F. Bentley
D. Power elite	4. C. Wright Mills

Codes :

	A	B	C	D
(*a*)	3	4	2	1
(*b*)	2	1	3	4
(*c*)	3	1	2	4
(*d*)	2	4	3	1

63. Who points out that underdevelopment is systematically and everywhere associated with and produced by colonisation?
 (*a*) Paul Baran (*b*) Gunder Frank
 (*c*) C. Furtando (*d*) None of these

64. The theory of ------ can be traced to Lenin's theory of imperialism.
 (*a*) Underdevelopment
 (*b*) Colonialism
 (*c*) Development
 (*d*) None of the above

65. At the political level, the welfare state model believes that only a ------ state can perform the task of development.
 (*a*) Socialist (*b*) Communist
 (*c*) Democratic (*d*) Pluralist

66. Which of the following are the periods of development according to Marx?
 (*a*) Feudalism and Communism
 (*b*) Capitalism and Socialism
 (*c*) Conservatism and Modernism
 (*d*) Both (*a*) and (*b*)

67. Who said that while the socialist system was able to attain it initial goals, it could not adopt to the new challenges and requirements placed upon it?
 (*a*) Roger (*b*) Galbraith
 (*c*) Pierson (*d*) Levy

68. Which one of the following types of equality is not compatible with the liberal notion of equality?
 (*a*) Legal equality
 (*b*) Political equality
 (*c*) Social equality
 (*d*) Economic equality

69. Which one of the following principles is denoted by the Dicey's rule of law?
 (*a*) Equality before law and rule by law
 (*b*) Rule by law and law alone and due process of law
 (*c*) Equality before law and administrative law
 (*d*) Rule by law; equality before law and due process of law

70. A .... Political system is characterised by differentiation of structures for the performance of specific functions?
    (*a*) Developing   (*b*) Underdeveloped
    (*c*) Developed   (*d*) Progressive

71. Who pointed out that by denying redistribution of national wealth through the state, the market model fosters inequality and injustice?
    (*a*) Lucian Pye
    (*b*) Blake
    (*c*) Green and Tawney
    (*d*) Walter

72. Which one of the following pairs is not correctly matched?
    (*a*) Harmony between the parts of the society : Plato
    (*b*) Greatest good of the greatest number : J. Bentham
    (*c*) Greatest advantage of the least advantaged : John Rawls
    (*d*) Interest of the strongest : Aristotle

73. Which one of the following thoughts lays stress on right of recognition and belonging?
    (*a*) Neo-liberalism
    (*b*) Conservatism
    (*c*) Communitarianism
    (*d*) Democratic socialism

74. Which one *of* the following is the correct sequence in the political philosophy *of* John Locke?
    (*a*) State *of* Nature - Civil Society - Natural Rights Contract
    (*b*) Natural Rights - Contract - State *of* Nature - Civil Society
    (*c*) State *of* Nature - Contract - Civil Society - Natural Rights
    (*d*) Natural Rights - State *of* Nature - Contract - Civil Society

75. Who among the following thinkers are associated with early socialism sometimes termed as utopian socialism?
    1. Robert Owen   2. Saint Simon
    3. Charles Fourier   4. Proudhan
Select the correct answer using the codes given below :
    (*a*) 1, 2 and 3   (*b*) 1, 2 and 4
    (*c*) 3 and 4   (*d*) 1, 2, 3 and 4

ANSWERS

1	2	3	4	5	6	7	8	9	10
(*c*)	(*c*)	(*d*)	(*d*)	(*b*)	(*a*)	(*d*)	(*a*)	(*b*)	(*c*)
11	**12**	**13**	**14**	**15**	**16**	**17**	**18**	**19**	**20**
(*d*)	(*b*)	(*c*)	(*b*)	(*d*)	(*a*)	(*d*)	(*c*)	(*b*)	(*d*)
21	**22**	**23**	**24**	**25**	**26**	**27**	**28**	**29**	**30**
(*a*)	(*c*)	(*b*)	(*c*)	(*a*)	(*b*)	(*c*)	(*b*)	(*a*)	(*d*)
31	**32**	**33**	**34**	**35**	**36**	**37**	**38**	**39**	**40**
(*b*)	(*a*)	(*d*)	(*b*)	(*b*)	(*d*)	(*d*)	(*c*)	(*d*)	(*a*)
41	**42**	**43**	**44**	**45**	**46**	**47**	**48**	**49**	**50**
(*c*)	(*b*)	(*a*)	(*d*)	(*c*)	(*d*)	(*b*)	(*b*)	(*c*)	(*c*)
51	**52**	**53**	**54**	**55**	**56**	**57**	**58**	**59**	**60**
(*a*)	(*b*)	(*b*)	(*d*)	(*c*)	(*b*)	(*a*)	(*c*)	(*b*)	(*d*)
61	**62**	**63**	**64**	**65**	**66**	**67**	**68**	**69**	**70**
(*b*)	(*c*)	(*a*)	(*a*)	(*c*)	(*d*)	(*b*)	(*d*)	(*d*)	(*c*)
71	**72**	**73**	**74**	**75**					
(*c*)	(*d*)	(*b*)	(*d*)	(*a*)					

11

SOCIAL MOVEMENTS

1. ------ have for long been the language of protest, innovation and expression of individuality and separate identity.
   (a) Political ideas
   (b) Cultural ideas
   (c) Religious ideas
   (d) None of the above

2. The Virasaiva movement was organized by Basaveswara in the twelfth century A.D. in :
   (a) Karnatak
   (b) Bihar
   (c) Punjab
   (d) Madhya Pradesh

3. Whose account of a sect (Akhand Maha Yoga) in the making is based on direct observation in the real sense of the term as they actually became recruits?
   (a) Kolleen
   (b) Bali
   (c) Gar Kellom
   (d) Both (a) and (c)

4. The Akhand Maha Yoga Sangh was founded in :
   (a) Delhi
   (b) Varanasi
   (c) Patna
   (d) Bhopal

5. The Shah Wali Ullah movement emphasized :
   (a) Orthodoxy and purity of Islamic practices
   (b) Modernisation
   (c) Political values
   (d) None of the above

6. The Tabligh movement in late 1920s was started by :
   (a) Forbes
   (b) Joseph Troisi
   (c) Maulana Ilyas
   (d) Kolleen

7. The Kharwar movement, which emerged in the 1930s, was oriented towards reform in the direction of :
   (a) Westernization
   (b) Sanskritization
   (c) Political empowerment
   (d) Economic equality

8. ------ is considered to be a crucial aspect of any social movement.
   (a) Ideology
   (b) Population strength
   (c) Financial source
   (d) None of the above

9. Which of the following significant peasant movements emerged on the basis of communist ideology?
   (a) Tebhaga
   (b) Naxalite
   (c) Telangana
   (d) All of these

10. The Naxalbari peasant revolt owes its origin to the dying waves to Tebhaga movement in Bengal in the :
    (a) Thirties
    (b) Fifties
    (c) Forties
    (d) Sixties

11. Who was the founder of the Bharat Stree Mahamandal, 'Great Circle of Indian Women', in 1910?
    (a) Sarojini Naidu
    (b) Saraladevi Choudhurani
    (c) Saroj Dutt
    (d) Annie Besant

12. The character of social movement as an instrument of social change is quite different from an imitative or emulative process of :
    (a) Mobility and Change
    (b) Stasis and Kinesis
    (c) Strength and Weakness
    (d) None of the above

13. The social mobility and change that are brought about by social movements are based on :
    (*a*) Challenge   (*b*) Aggression
    (*c*) Protest   (*d*) All of the above

14. Which of the following is not a feature of social movements?
    (*a*) Collective mobilisation
    (*b*) Political affiliation
    (*c*) Ideology
    (*d*) Orientation to change

15. The ------ are a nomadic caste, engaged mainly in earthwork and stone work, who agitated in the 1930s in Karnataka claiming Kshatriya varna status for themselves.
    (*a*) Waddars   (*b*) Izhavas
    (*c*) Bhuyans   (*d*) Khonds

16. Which movement emerged among the peasants who started appropriating ownership of the land they were tilling in 1946?
    (*a*) Tabligh movement
    (*b*) Nijai Bol movement
    (*c*) Land-grab movement
    (*d*) None of the above

17. The Telugu literary movement introduced ideas of renaissance and set the tone of protest against :
    (*a*) Nizam administration
    (*b*) Tughlaq administration
    (*c*) Mughal administration
    (*d*) Lodhi administration

18. Many social movements among the scheduled castes and other backward classes emerged in the :
    (*a*) 19th and 20th Century
    (*b*) 17th and 18th Century
    (*c*) 18th and 19th Century
    (*d*) 16th and 17th Century

19. In which of the following countries, the phenomenon of non-governmental organisation is significant?
    (*a*) Asian   (*b*) African
    (*c*) Latin American   (*d*) All of the above

20. Which of the following is not included in the non-governmental organisations of the developing countries?
    (*a*) Church development agencies
    (*b*) Private hospitals and schools
    (*c*) Philanthropic foundations
    (*d*) Academic think-tanks

21. Which one of the following theories considers democracy not as a government of the people but as 'the iron law of oligarchy'?
    (*a*) The Pluralist   (*b*) The Marxist
    (*c*) The Elitist   (*d*) The Idealist

22. The public can private spheres came to be strongly demarcated in which one of the following ideological orientations?
    (*a*) Fascism   (*b*) Liberalism
    (*c*) Feminism   (*d*) Marxism

23. ------ are usually regarded as a subcategory of NGO.
    (*a*) People's organisations
    (*b*) Interest groups
    (*c*) Pressure groups
    (*d*) None of the above

24. Which of the following is included in people's organisations?
    (*a*) Peasant associations
    (*b*) Trade Unions
    (*c*) Cooperatives
    (*d*) All of the above

25. Who argues that in the place of large formal organisations, we find a myriad of small-scale dispersed movements engaged in an enormous variety of conflicts?
    (*a*) Carroll   (*b*) Fowler
    (*c*) Lehmann   (*d*) Fisher

26. Who considers NGOs as a third sector remedying the institutional weaknesses of both the state and private sector in promoting socio-economic development?
    (*a*) Marxist   (*b*) Socialist
    (*c*) Neo-Liberals   (*d*) Liberals

27. Which of the following is one of the ways to classify voluntary associations?
    (*a*) The orientation of the organisation

(*b*) Their history of creation and change
(*c*) The fields of intervention
(*d*) All of the above

28. Who among the following consider NGOs as part of the private sector, of socio-economic significance, mainly delivering services to the poor cheaply, equitably and efficiently?
(*a*) Neo-Liberals (*b*) Communists
(*c*) Marxists (*d*) Socialists

29. In which of the following states one of India's largest NGOs, "AWARE", is based :
(*a*) Maharashtra (*b*) Andhra Pradesh
(*c*) Madhya Pradesh (*d*) Uttar Pradesh

30. Who generally feel that NGOs are agents of capitalism and western political and cultural values throughout the developing world, articulating an agenda set by multilateral, bilateral and non-governmental donors?
(*a*) Traditional social movements
(*b*) Radical religious movements
(*c*) Radical social movements
(*d*) None of the above

31. Which of the following social organisations for women emerged in the cities and towns of British India between 1910 and 1920?
(*a*) Women's clubs (*b*) Mahila samitis
(*c*) Ladies societies (*d*) All of these

32. Who founded the Mahila Samiti movement in Bengal?
(*a*) Saroj Nalini Dutt
(*b*) Sarojini Naidu
(*c*) Annie Besant
(*d*) None of the above

33. Saroj Nalini's success in attracting women to these Mahila Samitis must be attributed to her sensitivity and tact in dealing with conservative :
(*a*) Muslim society
(*b*) Christian society
(*c*) Hindu society
(*d*) None of the above

34. Who became the first political mentor of Sarojini Naidu?
(*a*) Gokhale (*b*) Nehru
(*c*) Gandhi (*d*) Dadabhai Naoroji

35. The first All-India women's organisation (Women's Indian Association) was formed in :
(*a*) 1918 (*b*) 1917
(*c*) 1916 (*d*) 1919

36. Who had been critical of the women's organisations for not bringing the masses into their movement?
(*a*) Nehru (*b*) Gokhale
(*c*) Gandhi (*d*) S.N. Banerjee

37. Which of the following is not one of the three theories explaining the genesis of social movements?
(*a*) Strain theory
(*b*) Progressive theory
(*c*) Relative deprivation
(*d*) Revitalisation

38. ------ belong to a distinct category of social movements with the ideology of class conflict as their basis.
(*a*) Peasant Movements
(*b*) Women's Movements
(*c*) Tribal Movements
(*d*) None of the above

39. If social mobilisation has been demanding changes within the system, the changes that are likely to occur will be :
(*a*) Transformative (*b*) Alternative
(*c*) Accumulative (*d*) None of the above

40. If a social mobilisation is determined to replace one structure and substitute it by another, the changes should it materialise, would be :
(*a*) Alternative
(*b*) Transformative
(*c*) Accumulative
(*d*) None of the above

41. If the social mobilisation is directed towards creating new structures which by their existence would qualitatively affect the entire system, then the change, in the event that it is accomplished, will be :
(*a*) Alternative (*b*) Transformative
(*c*) Accumulative (*d*) None of the above

42. Which of the following is one of the features of the voluntary organisations?
  (*a*) A voluntary association is a non-profit organisation
  (*b*) A voluntary organisation is a grouping of several persons
  (*c*) A common use of resources aims at the realisation of specific or collective interests
  (*d*) All of the above

43. In which year Lador-Lederer's study suggested that NGOs were more accurately seen as non-state organisations, since they were intimately involved in governmental and intergovernmental processes?
  (*a*) 1963   (*b*) 1968
  (*c*) 1951   (*d*) 1979

44. In which country NGOs not only influence legislation and public policy but enjoy constitutional recognition of their roles?
  (*a*) Chile   (*b*) Philippines
  (*c*) Kenya   (*d*) Brazil

45. Who argues that NGOs are more likely to maintain the status quo than to change it?
  (*a*) Lewis   (*b*) Clarke
  (*c*) Fowler   (*d*) Gohlert

46. Council for the Advancement of People's Action and Rural Technology (CAPART) was established in the year :
  (*a*) 1984   (*b*) 1986
  (*c*) 1985   (*d*) 1983

47. Unlike interest or pressure groups NGOs are not usually :
  (*a*) Organised
  (*b*) Concerned with public sentiments
  (*c*) Membership-based
  (*d*) None of these

48. Most social movements theorists including Eckstein ------ the importance of institutional vehicles like NGOs in shaping political discourse and in mobilising collective interests.
  (*a*) Overlook   (*b*) Emphasise
  (*c*) Revive   (*d*) None of the above

49. Generally, social movements theory has ignored the :
  (*a*) Government Phenomenon
  (*b*) NGO Phenomenon
  (*c*) Political Phenomenon
  (*d*) None of the above

50. Which of the following means political action seen as stemming from calculated self-interest rather than obligation or duty?
  (*a*) Functionalism   (*b*) Contextualism
  (*c*) Reductionism   (*d*) Utilitarianism

51. Reductionism is a political phenomenon seen as the aggregate of consequences of :
  (*a*) Social behaviour
  (*b*) Political behaviour
  (*c*) Individual behaviour
  (*d*) Abnormal behaviour

52. Which of the following plays a vital role in facilitating political participation through their involvement in issue-based social movements and through their support to people's organisations?
  (*a*) NGOs
  (*b*) Political parties
  (*c*) Religious organisations
  (*d*) None of the above

53. Who argues that it is impossible to prove a connection between the withering of the authoritarian state in Latin America and the rise of NGOs and grassroots social movements?
  (*a*) Hojman   (*b*) Hirschman
  (*c*) Clarke   (*d*) Kay

54. The concept of civil disobedience is ***not*** central in the thought of the following—
  (*a*) John Rawls
  (*b*) M.K. Gandhi
  (*c*) Leo Tolstoy
  (*d*) Michel Foucault

55. Who of the following presidents of India was associated with the Trade Union Movement in India?
  (*a*) V.V. Giri   (*b*) N. Sanjiva Reddy
  (*c*) K.R. Narayanan   (*d*) Zakir Hussain

56. Which of the following is one of the generations of NGOs as distinguished by Korten?
 (*a*) NGOs committed to relief and welfare activities
 (*b*) NGOs committed to small-scale, local, development projects
 (*c*) NGOs committed to community organisation, mobilisation and coalition-building
 (*d*) All of the above

57. If a social mobilisation is determined to replace one structure and substitute it by another, the change should it materialise, would be :
 (*a*) Alternative
 (*b*) Transformative
 (*c*) Accumulative
 (*d*) None of the above

58. If social mobilisation has been demanding changes within the system, the changes that are likely to occur will be :
 (*a*) Transformative
 (*b*) Alternative
 (*c*) Accumulative
 (*d*) None of the above

59. ------ belong to distinct category of social movements with the ideology of class conflict as their basis.
 (*a*) Peasant Movement
 (*b*) Women's Movement
 (*c*) Tribal Movement
 (*d*) None of the above

60. Who had been critical of the women's organisations for not bringing the masses into their movement?
 (*a*) Nehru
 (*b*) Gokhale
 (*c*) Gandhi
 (*d*) S.N. Banerjee

61. Which of the following pairs is not correctly matched?
 (*a*) Mahatma Gandhi's Ideas—C.F. Andrews
 (*b*) The Gandhian Way—J.B. Kriplani
 (*c*) Marx, Gandhi and Socialism—Ram Manohar Lohia
 (*d*) Gandhi's political philosophy—B.R. Nanda

62. With which one of the following is the expression 'gift of grace' associated?
 (*a*) Legal-rational authority
 (*b*) Traditional authority
 (*c*) Charismatic authority
 (*d*) Autocratic authority

63. According to Paul Brass, Which one of the following was the crucial factor for the occurrence of communal riots in India?
 (*a*) Absence of social trust
 (*b*) Economic rivalry between communities
 (*c*) Organized riot system
 (*d*) Memories of Cultural Conflict

64. Which one of the following political theoriests finds the concept of 'imagined community' inadequate to describe nationalism in post-colonial societies?
 (*a*) Partha Chatterjee
 (*b*) V.R. Mehta
 (*c*) Hans Cohn
 (*d*) Ernest Gellner

65. Around the globe the proliferation of the non-governmental organisations is taking place most of all in :
 (*a*) Asia
 (*b*) Africa
 (*c*) Latin America
 (*d*) All of these

66. The largest NGO sector in the developing world belongs to :
 (*a*) India
 (*b*) Brazil
 (*c*) China
 (*d*) Argentina

67. Which of the following are distinguished from NGOs though usually regarded as their sub-category?
 (*a*) People's Organisation (POs)
 (*b*) Quasi-autonomous NGOs (QUANGOs)
 (*c*) Trade Unions
 (*d*) All of the above

68. Which one of the following was **not** identified by Almond as a stage of conversion process of a political system?
 (*a*) Interest articulation
 (*b*) Interest aggregation
 (*c*) Political recruitment
 (*d*) Rule adjudication

69. Which of the following phenomena is triggered by proliferation of NGOs?
 (*a*) Information revolution
 (*b*) Associational revolution
 (*c*) Industrial revolution
 (*d*) Participatory revolution

70. In Indonesia and Vietnam, NGOs have proliferated as a result of :
 (*a*) Hegemony of formal institutions
 (*b*) Weakness of formal institutions
 (*c*) Withering away of formal institutions
 (*d*) Both (*a*) and (*b*)

71. Which one of the following was the first country-wide pressure group of the organized Indian working class?
 (*a*) All India Trade Union Congress
 (*b*) Indian National Trade Union Congress
 (*c*) Indian Mining Federation
 (*d*) Hind Mazdoor Sabha

72. The largest group of NGOs in the developing world is of :
 (*a*) Environment NGOs
 (*b*) NGOs Working to eradicate child labour
 (*c*) Relief and Welfare NGOs
 (*d*) All of the above

73. The work 'The Latin America Left: from the Fall of Allende of Perostroika' is authored by :
 (*a*) S. Silliman
 (*b*) B. Loveman
 (*c*) Clark
 (*d*) None of the above

74. The 'Charity-development-empowerment typology of NGO orientation of the advanced nations is given by :
 (*a*) Korten
 (*b*) C. Elliot
 (*c*) Silliman
 (*d*) None of the above

ANSWERS

1	2	3	4	5	6	7	8	9	10
(*c*)	(*a*)	(*d*)	(*b*)	(*a*)	(*c*)	(*d*)	(*a*)	(*d*)	(*c*)
11	12	13	14	15	16	17	18	19	20
(*b*)	(*a*)	(*d*)	(*b*)	(*a*)	(*b*)	(*a*)	(*a*)	(*d*)	(*b*)
21	22	23	24	25	26	27	28	29	30
(*c*)	(*c*)	(*a*)	(*d*)	(*c*)	(*d*)	(*d*)	(*a*)	(*b*)	(*c*)
31	32	33	34	35	36	37	38	39	40
(*b*)	(*a*)	(*c*)	(*a*)	(*b*)	(*a*)	(*b*)	(*a*)	(*c*)	(*b*)
41	42	43	44	45	46	47	48	49	50
(*a*)	(*d*)	(*a*)	(*b*)	(*c*)	(*b*)	(*c*)	(*a*)	(*b*)	(*d*)
51	52	53	54	55	56	57	58	59	60
(*c*)	(*a*)	(*b*)	(*a*)	(*a*)	(*d*)	(*b*)	(*c*)	(*a*)	(*a*)
61	62	63	64	65	66	67	68	69	70
(*d*)	(*c*)	(*d*)	(*a*)	(*d*)	(*b*)	(*a*)	(*d*)	(*b*)	(*a*)
71	72	73	74						
(*a*)	(*c*)	(*b*)	(*b*)						

12

NATIONALISM AND INTERNATIONALISM

1. Identify the French author who coined the term 'Third World'?
   (*a*) J. P. Sartre
   (*b*) Alfred Sauvy
   (*c*) Franz Fanon
   (*d*) None of the above

2. Nationalism should be universalised so as to constitute real :
   (*a*) Nationalism
   (*b*) Nation
   (*c*) Internationalism
   (*d*) None of the above

3. ------ stands for a family of self-governing nations, united to each other by ties of equality and living at peace and concord with each other.
   (*a*) Internationalism
   (*b*) Hegemony
   (*c*) Imperialism
   (*d*) None of the above

4. The concept of internationalism desires a revision of the traditional doctrine of :
   (*a*) Liberty   (*b*) Sovereignty
   (*c*) Equality   (*d*) Fraternity

5. Which of the following organisations contains the essence of the concept of internationalism?
   (*a*) United Nations
   (*b*) League of Nations
   (*c*) NATO
   (*d*) Both (*a*) and (*b*)

6. Internationalism desires prevalence of sane and sensible :
   (*a*) Nationalism
   (*b*) Nationality

   (*c*) Nation
   (*d*) None of the above

7. Which of the following is largely a non-political concept and can exist even under foreign domination?
   (*a*) Nation
   (*b*) Nationalism
   (*c*) Nationality
   (*d*) None of the above

8. Ramsay Muir believes that language counts for more than race is the moulding of a :
   (*a*) Nation
   (*b*) Class
   (*c*) Society
   (*d*) None of the above

9. Who said that 'Nationality, like religion is subjective; psycological; a condition of mind; a spiritual possession; a way of feeling; thinking and living'?
   (*a*) Hayes
   (*b*) Burns
   (*c*) Zimmern
   (*d*) None of the above

10. ------ implies the exclusive right of a particular set of people of a country to lead an independent and separate life.
    (*a*) Nation
    (*b*) Nationalism
    (*c*) Nationality
    (*d*) None of the above

11. Who said that nationality is a nation in the making and as soon as a nationality secures political independence, it becomes a notion?

(*a*) Garner   (*b*) Laski
(*c*) Bryce   (*d*) Zimmern

12. Nationalism implies the exclusive right of the people of country to lead an independent and separate :
(*a*) Political life
(*b*) Economic life
(*c*) Social life
(*d*) None of the above

13. ------ is different from cosmopolitanism irrespective of the fact that both desire universal harmony and goodwill.
(*a*) Nationalism
(*b*) Internationalism
(*c*) Imperialism
(*d*) None of the above

14. Nationalism emerged in the ------ as a result of the decline of the papacy and the rise of sovereign secular states in the early modern period.
(*a*) West   (*b*) North
(*c*) East   (*d*) South

15. The term ------ signifies the consciousness of unity reinforced by psychological and spiritual feelings.
(*a*) Imperialism   (*b*) Nationality
(*c*) Nation   (*d*) None of the above

16. Nationalism came into its own in the early :
(*a*) 19th century   (*b*) 18th century
(*c*) 10th century   (*d*) 17th century

17. M.K. Gandhi subscribed to the ideal of a :
(*a*) World federation
(*b*) World religion
(*c*) World political party
(*d*) All of the above

18. Loyalty to the ------ is over whelmingly predominant over loyalty to the world community.
(*a*) Society   (*b*) Nation
(*c*) Government   (*d*) None of the above

19. Who was a relentless critic of the mononational state and the right of selfdetermination?

(*a*) Lord Acton   (*b*) R. Muir
(*c*) Hobson   (*d*) Laski

20. Which of the following is/are the major theme(s) of New International Economic Order (NIEO)?
1. Self-reliance
2. Globalization and liberalization
Select the correct answer using the codes given below :
codes :
(*a*) 1 only   (*b*) 2 only
(*c*) Both 1 and 2   (*d*) Neither 1 nor 2

21. The establishment of the league of Nations in 1920 represented the triumph of :
(*a*) Gandhian society
(*b*) Nehru socialism
(*c*) Wilsonian idealism
(*d*) None of the above

22. Fisher said that it is indisputable that of the greatest general contribution of the League of Nations was its influence in spreading the idea of international :
(*a*) Cooperation
(*b*) Justice
(*c*) Subordination
(*d*) None of the above

23. Who said that nationalism accepted the form, but changed it animating it with a new feeling of life and with a new religious fervour?
(*a*) Hayes   (*b*) Mill
(*c*) MacIver   (*d*) Hans Kohn

24. Who said that a nation is a culturally homogeneous social group which is at once conscious and tenacious of its unity of psychic life and possession?
(*a*) Hayes   (*b*) Acton
(*c*) Garner   (*d*) Kohn

25. A sovereign ------ remains the basic foundation of all international activity.
(*a*) Nation-state
(*b*) Democratic-state
(*c*) City-state
(*d*) None of the above

26. During the French Revolution, the term 'nation' came into great popularity. Then it was used to mean :
(*a*) Patriotism   (*b*) Racial unity
(*c*) Social solidarity   (*d*) Fraternity

27. A great advance in internationalism was made in the first quarter of the twentieth century. It was :
(*a*) End of the World War I
(*b*) Russian Revolution
(*c*) Formation of the League of Nations
(*d*) None of the above

28. Who among the following statesman played a cardinal role in the establishment of the League of Nations?
(*a*) Jawaharlal Nehru
(*b*) Winston Churchill
(*c*) Woodrow Wilson
(*d*) Robert Mcnamara

29. Who stated that, "To have suffered, rejoiced and hoped together" makes a people a nation?
(*a*) De Tocqueville
(*b*) Zimmern
(*c*) Ernest Renan
(*d*) None of the above

30. The original membership of the League of Nations was :
(*a*) 40   (*b*) 41
(*c*) 42   (*d*) 43

31. The work 'Essays on Nationalism' is authored by :
(*a*) Herry Hart
(*b*) H.A.L. Fisher
(*c*) C.J. Hayes
(*d*) None of the above

32. Most of all the word 'nation' signifies the existence of :
(*a*) Common racial stock
(*b*) Common historical traditions
(*c*) Common political consciousness
(*d*) None of the above

33. In several states of the US, the Jim Crow Legislation was responsible for—
(*a*) segregation of different communities
(*b*) reparation for previously segregated communities
(*c*) common schools for blacks and whites
(*d*) ban of civil rights movement

34. It can be said that the triumph of Wilsonian idealism manifested in :
(*a*) The establishment of the League of Nations
(*b*) The Treaty of Versailles
(*c*) The formation of the U.N.O.
(*d*) None of the above

35. Who branded the principle of national self-determination as a 'retrograde step in human history'?
(*a*) James Bryce   (*b*) Harold Laski
(*c*) Macpherson   (*d*) Lord Acton

36. Two prominent instances of people of different racial origins living together and forming a strong nationality are :
(*a*) Japan and China
(*b*) Switzerland and Canada
(*c*) Sri Lanka and Myanmar
(*d*) United States and Great Britain

37. Who called nationalism "man's other religion"?
(*a*) Hayes   (*b*) Hallowell
(*c*) Shillito   (*d*) None of the above

38. The league of Nations was brought into existence as a consequence of the :
(*a*) Russian Revolution
(*b*) World War I
(*c*) Treaty of Versailles
(*d*) All of the above

39. Who among the following regard language as the most important factor in the growth of nationalism?
(*a*) Mazzini   (*b*) Fichte
(*c*) Ramsay Muir   (*d*) All of these

40. It can be said that the earliest known idea on internationalism begin with :
(*a*) Machiavelli's The Prince
(*b*) Plato's Creto
(*c*) Dante's De Monarchia
(*d*) None of the above

41. The book 'Nationalism and Internationalism' is authored by :
(*a*) Ivor Jennings
(*b*) Ramsay Muir
(*c*) Ebenstein
(*d*) None of the above

42. Among the factors which hinder the growth of internationalism an important one is :
(*a*) Racism
(*b*) International division of labour
(*c*) Nationalism
(*d*) None of the above

43. Which among the following works is authored by J.A. Hobson?
(*a*) Imperialism and Civilization
(*b*) Nationalism, Myth and Reality
(*c*) Imperialism : A Study
(*d*) All of the above

44. Who said that over the period of time, nationality became, "one of the most powerful anaesthetics"?
(*a*) Gandhiji   (*b*) Lohia
(*c*) Tagore   (*d*) Vivekanand

45. Which among the following is said to be primarily responsible for revival of national sentiment?
(*a*) Glorious Revolution
(*b*) Industrial Revolution
(*c*) Russian Revolution
(*d*) French Revolution

46. Which of the following works is authored by Hans Kohn?
(*a*) A Democratic Process
(*b*) The Idea of Nationalism
(*c*) Representative Government
(*d*) International Politics

47. Who expounded the idea of the State as containing all the worth which the human being possessed?
(*a*) Kant   (*b*) Hegel
(*c*) Marx   (*d*) Schopenhaur

48. Who among the following has argued that the security of a multi-national state is always precarious as soldiers drawn from different nationalities lack the common incentive of oneness of interests and purposes?
(*a*) Barthelemy
(*b*) J.S. Mill
(*c*) Mosca
(*d*) None of the above

49. The doctrine of national self-rule was accepted and incorporated in :
(*a*) Preamble to the Constitution of India
(*b*) Charter of the United Nation
(*c*) NATO manual
(*d*) Both (*b*) and (*c*)

50. Around the world the contemporary opinion is in favour of :
(*a*) Nationalism   (*b*) Regionalism
(*c*) Internationalism   (*d*) Both (*a*) and (*c*)

51. Who held the view that the nation of a sovereign independent state, on the international side is fatal to the well-being of humanity?
(*a*) Laski
(*b*) Garner
(*c*) Woodrow Wilson
(*d*) None of the above

52. The book *Commonsense of World Peace* is written by :
(*a*) Christopher Hayes (*b*) H.G. Wells
(*c*) H.J. Laski   (*d*) H.J. Morgenthau

53. Who among the following was responsible for a scheme of an international league to enforce peace?
(*a*) Fichte   (*b*) Seeley
(*c*) Telleyrand   (*d*) None of the above

54. The principle of national self determination implies that every nation should be organised as an independent political entity. Which of the following are in some way associated with this principle?
(*a*) Congress of Vienna (1815)
(*b*) President Wilson's 14 Points (1917)
(*c*) French Revolution
(*d*) Both (*a*) and (*b*)

55. Which of the following have caused the growth of cooperative federalism in India?
   1. Union-State Collaboration in economic matters
   2. Union-State legislative relations
   3. Compulsion of development finance
   4. Dynamics of electoral politics

Select the correct answer using the codes given below :

Codes :
(*a*) 1 and 2   (*b*) 2 and 3
(*c*) 3 and 4   (*d*) 1 and 4

56. Which one of the following is suggested by the concept of universal citizenship?
(*a*) Identical rights for all persons
(*b*) Identical rights for all citizens
(*c*) Common rights for all with some special rights for minorities
(*d*) Single citizenship in the world

ANSWERS

1	2	3	4	5	6	7	8	9	10
(*b*)	(*c*)	(*a*)	(*b*)	(*d*)	(*a*)	(*c*)	(*a*)	(*c*)	(*b*)

11	12	13	14	15	16	17	18	19	20
(*c*)	(*a*)	(*b*)	(*a*)	(*c*)	(*a*)	(*a*)	(*b*)	(*a*)	(*d*)

21	22	23	24	25	26	27	28	29	30
(*c*)	(*a*)	(*d*)	(*c*)	(*a*)	(*a*)	(*c*)	(*c*)	(*c*)	(*c*)

31	32	33	34	35	36	37	38	39	40
(*c*)	(*c*)	(*c*)	(*a*)	(*d*)	(*b*)	(*c*)	(*c*)	(*d*)	(*c*)

41	42	43	44	45	46	47	48	49	50
(*b*)	(*c*)	(*c*)	(*c*)	(*d*)	(*b*)	(*b*)	(*b*)	(*b*)	(*c*)

51	52	53	54	55	56
(*a*)	(*b*)	(*a*)	(*d*)	(*c*)	(*d*)

13

THEORIES OF INTERNATIONAL RELATIONS

1. Political realism is contrary to the ------
   approach to international politics.
   (*a*) Pragmatic   (*b*) Legalistic
   (*c*) Moralistic   (*d*) Both (*b*) and (*c*)

2. According to Morgenthau, the laws by which
   man moves in the social world are :
   (*a*) Man-made   (*b*) Eternal
   (*c*) Temporary   (*d*) Obscure

3. Which theory is the result of the behavioural
   revolution in social sciences?
   (*a*) The Systems theory
   (*b*) The Realist theory
   (*c*) The Idealist theory
   (*d*) The Pluralist theory

4. Who treats equilibrium mainly in the context
   of balance of power system?
   (*a*) Fox   (*b*) Kaplan
   (*c*) Liska   (*d*) Merriam

5. Charles Mc Clelland's concept of system
   comes from :
   (*a*) Geography   (*b*) Biology
   (*c*) Economics   (*d*) History

6. Who treats six models of major international
   system?
   (*a*) Rosenau
   (*b*) Lasswell
   (*c*) Kaplan
   (*d*) None of the above

7. According to Kaplan, the most likely
   transformation of the balance power system
   is into a :
   (*a*) Bipolar System

(*b*) Unipolar System
(*c*) International System
(*d*) None of the above

8. Who produced formulations of the decision-
   making theory in 1738?
   (*a*) Anthony Downs   (*b*) Daniel Bernouli
   (*c*) David L. Sills   (*d*) Robinson

9. Who was the chief exponent of the realist
   theory?
   (*a*) Kennan   (*b*) Hans Morgenthau
   (*c*) Watkins   (*d*) Easton

10. Erich Kaufmann wrote in a book that the
    essence of the state was :
    (*a*) Development of power
    (*b*) Increase of power
    (*c*) Display of power
    (*d*) All of the above

11. Who said that the study of politics is the study
    of influence and the influential in his work
    on politics?
    (*a*) Kennan   (*b*) Lasswell
    (*c*) Morgenthau   (*d*) Watkins

12. Who gave theoretical orientation to realism?
    (*a*) Bross   (*b*) Burton
    (*c*) Morgenthau   (*d*) Lasswell

13. The two most vital concepts in which the
    inconsistency of Morgenthau's theory is most
    clearly revealed are :
    (*a*) Power and Society
    (*b*) Power and Statesmanship
    (*c*) Diplomacy and Society
    (*d*) Diplomacy and Statesmanship

14. According to Morgenthau, the best means of preserving peace in a society of sovereign nations is :
(*a*) National interest (*b*) Diplomacy
(*c*) Foreign trade (*d*) Autonomy

15. Who believes that a theory of International politics is "but a specific instance of a general theory of politics?
(*a*) Tucker (*b*) Morgenthau
(*c*) Kennan (*d*) Wasserman

16. Morgenthau's description of the drive for power as irrational is identical with that of :
(*a*) Hobbes (*b*) Locke
(*c*) Marx (*d*) J.S. Mill

17. According to Morgenthau, the social world is a projection of :
(*a*) Human nature (*b*) Society
(*c*) Classes (*d*) Caste

18. The model which the game theory employs is that of a game of :
(*a*) Amateurs (*b*) Strategy
(*c*) Chance (*d*) All of the above

19. Who was among the first to recognize the importance of the game theory in international politics?
(*a*) Martin Shubik (*b*) Karl Deutsch
(*c*) Kaplan (*d*) Both (*a*) and (*b*)

20. The most recent and notable contribution to an understanding of the decision-making theory has been made by :
(*a*) Joseph Frankel (*b*) John Burton
(*c*) Modelski (*d*) Lasswell

21. The first major attempt at introducing the decision-making analysis in the study of Foreign Policy was made by :
(*a*) Richard Synder (*b*) Oran R. Young
(*c*) Anthony Downs (*d*) A. Robinson

22. Which of the following writers brought about an enrichment of the decision-making approach to the study of political science?
(*a*) William Riker (*b*) James Robinson
(*c*) Herbert Simon (*d*) All of these

23. The systematic approach to international politics emphasises the significance of the interaction of behaviour of :
(*a*) Communities (*b*) States
(*c*) Cultures (*d*) All of these

24. Machiavelli suggested that the norms of behaviour for individuals in society and for statesmen in international relations are :
(*a*) Similar
(*b*) Different
(*c*) Contradictory
(*d*) None of the above

25. Who gave the first serious challenge to the scientific method giving rise to the controversy between science and traditionalism?
(*a*) P. Kurtz (*b*) Hedley Bull
(*c*) David Singer (*d*) Rosenau

26. A major difficulty with the scientific theorists lies in their overstress on :
(*a*) Values
(*b*) Precision
(*c*) Norms
(*d*) None of the above

27. Who defined power as comprising "anything that establishes and maintains the control of man over man"?
(*a*) Morgenthau (*b*) Strauss
(*c*) Wasserman (*d*) Tucker

28. What, according to Kaplan, could develop as a result of the extension of the functions of essential actors in a loose bipolar system?
(*a*) The system of hegemony
(*b*) Universal international system
(*c*) Colonial system
(*d*) None of the above

29. Which one of the following political philosophers is an advocate of positive liberty?
(*a*) Isaiah Berlin
(*b*) Iris Marion Young
(*c*) John Stuart Mill
(*d*) T.H. Green

30. Consider the following statements—
In his theory of Justice, John Rawls :

1. reconciles a liberal conception of political obligation with a redistributive conception of social justice.
2. affirms the utilitarian principle for determining what is good and desirable.
3. uses the instrument of the social contract to ensure fairness.
4. maintains that the concern for redistribution trumps individuals liberty.

Which of the statements given above are correct?

(*a*) 3 only   (*b*) 1 and 2
(*c*) 1 and 3   (*d*) 2 and 4

31. The theory of game has been developed mainly by :
(*a*) Mathematicians   (*b*) Economists
(*c*) Sociologists   (*d*) Both (*a*) and (*b*)

32. ------ was the cradle of Marxist-Leninist theory of international relations.
(*a*) China   (*b*) Soviet Union
(*c*) Japan   (*d*) America

33. Marxists seek to examine each issue of world politics, whether national or international, from the standpoint of :
(*a*) Historical materialism
(*b*) State
(*c*) Government
(*d*) None of the above

34. What is the essence of all politics, national or international, according to Morgenthau?
(*a*) Altruism
(*b*) List for power
(*c*) Patriotism
(*d*) None of the above

35. The whole case of idealism is based on the general ideal of evolutionary progress in :
(*a*) Culture
(*b*) Society
(*c*) Politics
(*d*) None of the above

36. Who points out that national interest is a matter of interpretation which differs from Statesman to Statesman?
(*a*) Sprout   (*b*) Spiro
(*c*) Kenneth   (*d*) Wassermann

37. Which approach is partial approach to the study of international politics?
(*a*) Decision-making Approach
(*b*) Realist Approach
(*c*) Idealist Approach
(*d*) Games Theory Approach

38. Who emphasised the importance of communications or flow of information for the proper understanding of international relations?
(*a*) Karl Marx   (*b*) Karl Deutsch
(*c*) Synder   (*d*) Palmer

39. Who emphasised the need of combining the classical and scientific approaches for the study of international relations?
(*a*) Morgenthau
(*b*) Palmer and Perkins
(*c*) Sprout
(*d*) Lasswell

40. In Marxian analysis, an important role is assigned to the production system and the :
(*a*) Economy
(*b*) Class relations
(*c*) International relations
(*d*) None of the above

41. Which of the following is not included in the Marxian theories about international politics?
(*a*) The theory of proletarian internationalism
(*b*) The theory of imperialism
(*c*) The theory of peaceful co-existence of states
(*d*) None of these

42. What, according to Marx, is the fundamental cause of the development of a thing?
(*a*) Its high origin
(*b*) Its inner harmony
(*c*) Its contradictoriness
(*d*) None of the above

43. Marxists have a ------ view of world politics.
(*a*) Static   (*b*) Prudent
(*c*) Dynamic   (*d*) None of the above

44. Which approach represents an attempt at applying mathematical models to International politics?

(*a*) Idealist approach
(*b*) Realist approach
(*c*) Game theory approach
(*d*) Decision-making approach

45. Which of the following account for the advent of the general system theory?
(*a*) Warld War II
(*b*) Communication revolution
(*c*) Behavioural revolution
(*d*) None of the above

46. To whose thinking can the origin of the general systems theory be traced?
(*a*) Oran Young
(*b*) Ludwig Von Bortalanffy
(*c*) David Easton
(*d*) None of the above

47. Who holds that a system is, "a whole which is compound of many parts ------ an ensemble of attributes"?
(*a*) J.W. Burton
(*b*) Colin Cherry
(*c*) Thomas Cook
(*d*) Ludwig Von Bortalanffy

48. Public institution may not cope with the expansion of democratic participation leading to political decay. Which one of the following scholars draws attention to such a consequence?
(*a*) Rajni Kothari
(*b*) Samuel Huntington
(*c*) Robert Dahl
(*d*) David Held

49. Who among the following was one of the earliest scholars to have produced formulations of the decision-making theory?
(*a*) Anthony Downs
(*b*) R. Handy
(*c*) Daniel Bernouli
(*d*) None of the above

50. According to Rawls, which of the following sets of social primary good is likely to be pursued by all human beings?
(*a*) Income and wealth, opportunities and powers, rights and liberties, and social bases of self respect

(*b*) Income and wealth, opportunities and powers, health and intelligence, and social bases of self-respect
(*c*) Right and liberties, income and wealth, health and intelligence, and social bases of self-respect
(*d*) Income and wealth, health and imagination, opportunities and powers, and social bases of self-respect

51. Which of the following theories represent an attempt at applying the art of model building to international politics?
(*a*) Decision making theory
(*b*) Communications theory
(*c*) Game theory
(*d*) All of these

52. Which one of the following books makes value and meaning crucial determinants of human action?
(*a*) Rousseau's 'Discourse on the origine of Inequality'
(*b*) Marx's 'on the Jewish Question'
(*c*) Weber's 'Protestant Ethic and the Spirit of Capitalism'
(*d*) Pain's 'Rights of Man'

53. The work 'Game Theory and Related Approaches to Social Behaviour' is authored by :
(*a*) James Robinson   (*b*) Harold Lasswell
(*c*) Martin Shubik   (*d*) None of the above

54. Among those who were the first to recognise the importance of the game theory in international politics is :
(*a*) Karl Deutsch
(*b*) Martin Shubik
(*c*) Oskar Morgenstern
(*d*) All of the above

55. Which of the following is/are among the leading realists of the post World War II period?
(*a*) George Kennan
(*b*) John Herz
(*c*) Hans Morgenthau
(*d*) Both (*a*) and (*c*)

56. On the question of the relationship between the national interest and morality Kennan projects the idea of :
(*a*) Moral relativism (*b*) Virtual relativism
(*c*) Reconciliation (*d*) None of the above

57. For realists, the supreme virtue of politics is :
(*a*) Idealism (*b*) Spiritualism
(*c*) Realism (*d*) Nationalism

58. Which of the following theorists regard power politics as only an abnormal or passing phase of history?
(*a*) Liberals (*b*) Marxists
(*c*) Idealists (*d*) Realists

59. The work 'Political Realism and Political Idealism' is authored by :
(*a*) John H. Herz (*b*) Condorcet
(*c*) Organski (*d*) None of the above

60. The crucial point on which political realism and political idealism are at cross purposes with each other is about the problem of :
(*a*) Nationalism (*b*) Justice
(*c*) Power (*d*) Law

61. Realist approach focusses attention on the units which it views as principal actors in international politics. These units are :
(*a*) MNCs (*b*) States
(*c*) Leaders (*d*) Organisations

62. The model which the game theory, employs is that of a :
(*a*) Game of chance
(*b*) Game of strategy
(*c*) Game of preparedness
(*d*) Game of durability

63. In the framework of the game theory, the principle kind of game which have been identified is :
(*a*) Games with identical interests
(*b*) Games with opposite interests
(*c*) Games with mixed interests
(*d*) All of the above

64. As in the games of chess, poker and bridge, there are parties to the game in politics also. Those parties are :

(*a*) Individuals (*b*) Institutions
(*c*) Power-brokers (*d*) Both (*a*) and (*b*)

65. Who among the following scholars tried to put the game theory into use?
(*a*) Mortan Kaplan
(*b*) Willam H. Riker
(*c*) Thomas C. Shelling
(*d*) All of the above

66. According to Mortan Kaplan physical force is necessary, at least as last resort to :
(*a*) Achieve the political goals
(*b*) To maintain a hold over the system
(*c*) To keep the political system intact
(*d*) None of the above

67. While laying down the norms of his systems theory, Kaplan divided the set of international actors into two categories :
(*a*) Corporations and nations
(*b*) Organisations and states
(*c*) National actors and supranational actors
(*d*) None of the above

68. Which of the following may be an instance of supranational actor?
(*a*) General Assembly of the UN
(*b*) President of the United States
(*c*) NATO
(*d*) All of the above

69. In the Western world, the balance of power system prevailed in :
(*a*) Eighteenth Century
(*b*) Nineteenth Century
(*c*) Twentieth Century
(*d*) Both (*a*) and (*b*)

70. An important rule of the balance of power system is that each essential actor should increase its capabilities which should be done through :
(*a*) Negotiation (*b*) War
(*c*) Colonization (*d*) None of the above

71. Ideally, how many essential actors should be there in Mortan Kaplan's balance of power system?
(*a*) Five (*b*) Six
(*c*) Either (*a*) or (*b*) (*d*) Ten

72. The work **Political Community at the International Level** is authored by :
 (*a*) Kenneth Boulding
 (*b*) Karl Deutsch
 (*c*) Joseph Frankel
 (*d*) None of the above

73. Who among the following expresses the opinion that the game theory does not give any basic information about international power politics and hence it is useless?
 (*a*) Mckinsley
 (*b*) Arthur Lee Burns
 (*c*) Warren Christofer
 (*d*) None of the above

74. The decision-making approach has its highest relevance in the :
 (*a*) Peace-time situation
 (*b*) Time of belligerencies
 (*c*) Bilateral negotiations
 (*d*) Crisis situation

75. Who has opined that the general systems theory is not so much a theory as a direction or a programme in the development of the scientific method?
 (*a*) Anatol Rapoport
 (*b*) Sydney Verba
 (*c*) Oran Young
 (*d*) None of the above

ANSWERS

1	2	3	4	5	6	7	8	9	10
(*d*)	(*b*)	(*a*)	(*b*)	(*b*)	(*c*)	(*a*)	(*b*)	(*b*)	(*d*)
11	**12**	**13**	**14**	**15**	**16**	**17**	**18**	**19**	**20**
(*b*)	(*c*)	(*d*)	(*b*)	(*b*)	(*a*)	(*a*)	(*b*)	(*d*)	(*b*)
21	**22**	**23**	**24**	**25**	**26**	**27**	**28**	**29**	**30**
(*a*)	(*d*)	(*b*)	(*b*)	(*b*)	(*b*)	(*a*)	(*b*)	(*d*)	(*c*)
31	**32**	**33**	**34**	**35**	**36**	**37**	**38**	**39**	**40**
(*d*)	(*b*)	(*a*)	(*b*)	(*b*)	(*d*)	(*a*)	(*b*)	(*b*)	(*b*)
41	**42**	**43**	**44**	**45**	**46**	**47**	**48**	**49**	**50**
(*b*)	(*c*)	(*c*)	(*c*)	(*c*)	(*b*)	(*b*)	(*b*)	(*c*)	(*a*)
51	**52**	**53**	**54**	**55**	**56**	**57**	**58**	**59**	**60**
(*c*)	(*c*)	(*c*)	(*d*)	(*d*)	(*a*)	(*c*)	(*c*)	(*a*)	(*c*)
61	**62**	**63**	**64**	**65**	**66**	**67**	**68**	**69**	**70**
(*b*)	(*b*)	(*d*)	(*d*)	(*d*)	(*c*)	(*c*)	(*c*)	(*d*)	(*a*)
71	**72**	**73**	**74**	**75**					
(*c*)	(*b*)	(*b*)	(*d*)	(*a*)					

14

STATE AND THE GLOBAL ORDER

1. The new Economic policy of India comprises the various policy measures and changes introduced since :
   - (*a*) June 1992
   - (*b*) July 1991
   - (*c*) May 1990
   - (*d*) July 1992

2. Who said that the best known economic system is the one that supplies the most of what people most want?
   - (*a*) Jacob
   - (*b*) Deane
   - (*c*) Galbraith
   - (*d*) Richard

3. ------ acts as a safety net for labour, which is regarded as a vital and concrete step, taken in the direction of Government's Exit policy.
   - (*a*) Consolidated fund
   - (*b*) National Renewal fund
   - (*c*) Contingency fund
   - (*d*) None of the above

4. What does NAFTA stand for?
   - (*a*) North Asian Free Trade Association
   - (*b*) North African Free Trade Association
   - (*c*) North Atlantic Free Trade Association
   - (*d*) North American Free Trade Association

5. ------ have become an increasingly important part of the foreign trade for both industrial and developing countries.
   - (*a*) Agricultural activities
   - (*b*) Services
   - (*c*) Cultural exchanges
   - (*d*) Educational institutes

6. The World Trade Organisation (WTO) is the successor to which one of the following institutional arrangements?
   - (*a*) World Trade Community
   - (*b*) International Trade and Development Association
   - (*c*) General Agreement on Trade and Tariffs
   - (*d*) Association for Economic and Social Reconstruction

7. What constitutes an important barometer of the health and performance of the economy?
   - (*a*) Prices
   - (*b*) Mergers
   - (*c*) Joint Ventures
   - (*d*) None of the above

8. Which of the following is a process by which prices rise and money value decreases?
   - (*a*) Deflation
   - (*b*) Stagnation
   - (*c*) Inflation
   - (*d*) None of the above

9. The outline of the perfectly competitive capitalist economy was first popularised by :
   - (*a*) Mill
   - (*b*) Adam Smith
   - (*c*) Laski
   - (*d*) Marx

10. What does TRIMs stand for?
    - (*a*) Trade-Related Investment Measures
    - (*b*) Tariff-Related Investment Measures
    - (*c*) Technology-Related Investment Measures
    - (*d*) Training-Related Investment Measures

11. Which of the following terms stands for opening the economy to the world by

removing protective barriers against free flow of trade technology and investment among countries?
(*a*) Liberalisation
(*b*) Globalisation
(*c*) Privatisation
(*d*) None of the above

12. Which of the following is the cause of the policy of globalisation?
(*a*) Crisis in balance of payments
(*b*) Crisis in exchange rate management
(*c*) Crisis in public sector management
(*d*) All of the above

13. What stands for the maximisation of economic efficiency and competitiveness of Indian industries without hampering the interests of the labour community on human face value with a view to capture the economic gains accrued from structural reforms initiated in the economy?
(*a*) New Economic Policy
(*b*) Micro-economics
(*c*) Macroeconomics
(*d*) None of the above

14. Leading neo-liberal institutionalists such as Axelrod, Keohane and Oye, developed their ideas in response to Kenneth Waltz's theory of neo-realism outlined in his 1979 work :
(*a*) Traditions of International Ethics
(*b*) Basic Texts and International Relations
(*c*) Theory of International Politics
(*d*) Our Global Neighbourhood

15. After the New Economic Policy, 1991 who opined that India would recover from her crisis and carry out adjustment programmes within a short duration itself, unlike other economies in a similar situation?
(*a*) America
(*b*) World Bank
(*c*) United Nations
(*d*) None of the above

16. Which of the following reports lists Seven Sins of privatisation?
(*a*) World Bank Report
(*b*) United Nations Report
(*c*) Appleby Report
(*d*) Human Development Report

17. Which of the following is a sin of privatisation?
(*a*) Making false promises to labour
(*b*) Using non-transparent and arbitrary procedures
(*c*) Replacing public monopolies with private ones
(*d*) All of the above

18. Who saw the seeds of prosperity in capitalism?
(*a*) Karl Marx   (*b*) Adam Smith
(*c*) Lenin   (*d*) Kautilya

19. Who said that the basic fact behind the price rise was the large volume of deficit finance undertaken to meet the development expenditure?
(*a*) Vakil   (*b*) David
(*c*) Goswami   (*d*) Kulkarni

20. ------ is the root cause of two evils, namely, inflation and the balance-of-payments deficit.
(*a*) Fiscal deficit
(*b*) Government Department
(*c*) Corruption
(*d*) None of the above

21. As a part of SAP (Structural Adjustment Policies), the economy was being ------ i.e. opened up to foreign goods and capital.
(*a*) Systematised
(*b*) Globalised
(*c*) Capitalised
(*d*) None of the above

22. Which of the following is the report that tried to examine all aspects relating to the structure, organisation, functions and procedure of the financial system?

    (*a*) Chakravorty Committee Report
    (*b*) Narsimhan Committee Report
    (*c*) Vaghul Group Report
    (*d*) All of the above

23. Which of the following is one of the broad features of the financial system?
    (*a*) The predominance of public sector institutions
    (*b*) The financial system has been subject to high degree of regulation motivated by socio-economic considerations
    (*c*) There has been a growing concern about the operational efficiency, productivity and profitability of the financial system
    (*d*) All of the above

24. The final outcome of the French Presidential election is on the completion of (run of election) second ballot among :
    (*a*) all the candidates
    (*b*) top two candidates
    (*c*) top three candidates
    (*d*) top four candidates

25. What is frequently referred to as the compelling reason for the sweeping economic reforms initiated in India?
    (*a*) The rapidly changing global economy
    (*b*) Civilization progress
    (*c*) Novelty of planning
    (*d*) Overcoming colonial influence

26. Which of the following criticisms has been levied against globalisation by Sukumar Basu?
    (*a*) Increasing debt burden
    (*b*) Increasing poverty
    (*c*) Erosion of economic sovereignty
    (*d*) All of the above

27. Who said that due to New Economic Policy India will find itself at the receiving end?
    (*a*) Sethi
    (*b*) Khushro
    (*c*) Jagmohan
    (*d*) Halleiner

28. Which model of economic development is advocated by L.M. Bhole, Ganguli and Prof. Dantwala as an alternative to globalisation?
    (*a*) The communist model
    (*b*) The mixed economy model
    (*c*) The laissez faire model
    (*d*) The Gandhian model

29. Whose New Industrial State and Economics and the Public Purpose divide the present day American Economy into two sectors – 'Market system' and 'Planning system'?
    (*a*) Richard's   (*b*) Galbraith's
    (*c*) Kurien's   (*d*) Gill's

30. India became a founder member of ------ by ratifying its agreement on 30 December 1994.
    (*a*) GATT   (*b*) WTO
    (*c*) OECD   (*d*) TRIPs

31. Very often ------ is recommended as an adjoint of globalisation.
    (*a*) Privatisation   (*b*) Openness
    (*c*) Liberalisation   (*d*) None of the above

32. Which of the following is the largest open market in the world?
    (*a*) ECM   (*b*) TRIPs
    (*c*) NAFTA   (*d*) TRIMs

33. Which of the following countries has open economy?
    (*a*) Hongkong   (*b*) Taiwan
    (*c*) Singapore   (*d*) All of these

34. Who among the following had established that globalisation and liberalization would result in better capacity utilization and economics of scale?
    (*a*) Kim   (*b*) Park
    (*c*) Bruton   (*d*) All of these

35. Which of the following is one of the main features of the TRIMs (Trade Related Investment Measures) text?
    (*a*) All restrictions on foreign capital/ investors/companies should be scrapped

(*b*) No restrictions will be imposed on any area of investment

(*c*) Imports of raw materials and components will be allowed freely

(*d*) All of the above

36. Which of the following is a bulwark of personal freedom?
   (*a*) Mandamus
   (*b*) Habeas Corpus
   (*c*) Quo-Warranto
   (*d*) Certiorari

37. The 8th round of Multi-lateral Trade Negotiations is popularly known as :
   (*a*) Berlin Round
   (*b*) Washington Round
   (*c*) Uruguay Round
   (*d*) None of the above

38. Which article of the Indian Constitution provides for the institution of Panchayati Raj?
   (*a*) Art. 36
   (*b*) Art. 39
   (*c*) Art. 40
   (*d*) Art. 48

39. Globalisation requires creation of ------ environment for free flow of direct foreign investment.
   (*a*) Conservative
   (*b*) Suitable
   (*c*) Special
   (*d*) Natural

40. Which of the following means globalisation of the Indian economy?
   (*a*) Adoption of market-friendly approach
   (*b*) Integration of it with the world economy
   (*c*) The industry has to face competition from outside, subject to some degree of protection which does not increase its efficiency
   (*d*) All of the above

41. Who said that the global economy must be viewed as a collection of heterogeneous units with different agendas interacting with one-another in a variety of ways and thus changing its character over time?
   (*a*) Awasthi
   (*b*) Kurien
   (*c*) Malcolm
   (*d*) Mody

42. Which of the following organisations defines globalisation as (a) gradual abolishment of import control over all items including consumption goods (b) reducing the rate of import duty and (c) privatising public sector enterprise?
   (*a*) World Bank
   (*b*) UNESCO
   (*c*) United Nations
   (*d*) UNICEF

43. What implies the equalisation of the domestic prices to international prices through the medium of competition?
   (*a*) Privatisation of the economy
   (*b*) Liberalisation of the economy
   (*c*) Globalisation of the economy
   (*d*) None of the above

44. Which act was passed in India to prevent restrictive trade practices?
   (*a*) GATT
   (*b*) MRTP
   (*c*) MFA
   (*d*) TRIMs

45. Globalisation gives primacy to unbridled :
   (*a*) Research
   (*b*) Trade
   (*c*) Development
   (*d*) Consumerism

46. ------ across the borders will be equalised by the opening of the economy to global competition.
   (*a*) Prices
   (*b*) Resources
   (*c*) Production
   (*d*) Capital

47. Who said that production is a social force in so far as it channelises human activity into useful ends?
   (*a*) Marx
   (*b*) Mill
   (*c*) Hegel
   (*d*) Smith

48. Which agreement encompasses a comprehensive overhaul of GATT'S dispute settlements, rules and procedures aimed at ensuring the prompt and efficient resolution of disputes?

(*a*) Seattle agreement
(*b*) Durban agreement
(*c*) Montreal agreement
(*d*) None of the above

49. The term 'international' was coined by :
(*a*) Jeremy Bentham   (*b*) Machiavelli
(*c*) Immanuel Kant   (*d*) John Stuart Mill

50. Precisely, the terms 'globalize' and 'globalism' were formally introduced in a printed text in the year :
(*a*) 1934   (*b*) 1984
(*c*) 1974   (*d*) 1944

51. Who said that, "Globalization refers to all those processes by which the peoples of the world are incorporated into single world society, global society"?
(*a*) Martin Albrow
(*b*) A.G. Frank
(*c*) Fucuyama
(*d*) None of the above

52. Who has made the observation that— "Globalization is what we in the Third World have for several centuries called colonization"?
(*a*) Hedley Bull
(*b*) Martin Khor
(*c*) Palmer and Perkins
(*d*) Both (*a*) and (*b*)

53. In terms of communications, globalization has been mainly occurring through :
(*a*) Computer networks
(*b*) Electronic Mass Media
(*c*) Telephony
(*d*) All of the above

54. In respect of organisations, globalization has been transpiring through :
(*a*) Proliferation and growth of companies
(*b*) Proliferation and growth of associations
(*c*) Proliferation and growth of regulatory agencies
(*d*) All of the above

55. Which of the following organisations have a global reach and treat the whole planet as their field of activity?
(*a*) Amnesty International
(*b*) Aid India Consortium
(*c*) World Intellectual Property Organization
(*d*) Both (*a*) and (*c*)

56. In respect of money and finance, globalization has unfolded mainly in terms of :
(*a*) Emergence of round-the-clock and round-the-world stock markets
(*b*) Spread of globally recognized credit cards
(*c*) Increasing use of currencies like the Yen and the Mark all over the world
(*d*) All of the above

57. Among other things, intercontinental ballistic missiles and spy satellites have served to globalize the world in :
(*a*) Technological terms
(*b*) Military terms
(*c*) Economic terms
(*d*) All of the above

58. It is difficult to determine a specific moment when globalization started because :
(*a*) Periodization is always imprecise and contentious as change and continuity are invariably intertwined
(*b*) History shows no exact water sheds on which everyone will agree
(*c*) Both (*a*) and (*b*)
(*d*) Globalization is an abstract phenomenon

59. Which of the following events were milestones on the road to globalization?
(*a*) First permanent transoceanic telegraph cable, 1866
(*b*) First global radio broadcast, 1930
(*c*) First photographs of planet Earth from outer space
(*d*) All of the above

60. Who among the following personalities coined the phrase 'global village'?

(*a*) James Rosenau

(*b*) Fucuyama

(*c*) Ledley Bull

(*d*) Marshall McLuhan

61. In which year appearance of a near complete 'ozon hole' over Antarctica was noticed and which raised global ecological awareness?

(*a*) 1970   (*b*) 1987

(*c*) 1977   (*d*) 1993

62. In which year the World Wide Web was introduced?

(*a*) 1971   (*b*) 1981

(*c*) 1991   (*d*) 1951

63. It can be said that globalization did not figure continually, comprehensively, intensely and with rapidly increasing frequency in the lives of a large proportion of humanity until around?

(*a*) 1940s   (*b*) 1950s

(*c*) 1960s   (*d*) 1970s

64. Who has defined globalization as, " the intensification of worldwide social relations which link distant localities in such a way that local happenings are shaped by events occuring many miles away and vice-versa"?

(*a*) Bendedict Anderson

(*b*) Anthony Giddens

(*c*) Philip O'Brion

(*d*) None of the above

65. Who among the following scholars asserted that – "Globalization does not simply refer to the objectiveness of increasing interconnectedness. It also refers to cultural and subjective matters [namely, the scope and depth of consciousness of the world as a single place"]?

(*a*) Raland Robertson

(*b*) Romain Rolland

(*c*) Ernest Gelner

(*d*) None of the above

66. Match List I (Scholars) with List II (Views on the beginning of globalization) and select the correct answer from the codes given below the lists :

List I	**List II**
A. Gamble	1. Start of the modern era
B. Modelski	2. Late 1950s
C. Harvey	3. Dawn of human civilisation
D. Rosenau	4. 1970s

Codes :

	A	**B**	**C**	**D**
(*a*)	4	3	2	1
(*b*)	3	1	4	2
(*c*)	1	3	2	4
(*d*)	4	1	2	3

67. Who wrote the article "The conditions of effective leadership in the industrial organisation"?

(*a*) Douglas Mc Gregor

(*b*) Sears

(*c*) Woodward

(*d*) Riggs

68. The United Nations is financed by :

(*a*) The contribution from the Member-States

(*b*) America

(*c*) Japan

(*d*) Russia

69. The number of judges in International Court of Justice are :

(*a*) 15   (*b*) 10

(*c*) 11   (*d*) 14

70. The centre-point of International Relation is:

(*a*) Struggle   (*b*) Power

(*c*) National Interest   (*d*) None of the above

71. Which is not a key feature of State?

(*a*) State is sovereign

(*b*) The State is an exercise in legislation

(*c*) The State is an instrument of domination

(*d*) The State is not a territorial association

72. Who said "A strong middle-class is the backbone of democracy"?
(*a*) Aristotle
(*b*) Garner
(*c*) Plato
(*d*) H.G. Wells

73. Which one of the following is the main feature of deliberative democracy?
(*a*) Parliamentary Sovereignty
(*b*) Executive Supremacy
(*c*) Judicial autonomy
(*d*) People' effective participation

74. Which one of the following is not the objective of WTO?
(*a*) Trade without discrimination
(*b*) Fair competition
(*c*) Price control
(*d*) Market access

75. The traditional view of the scope of International Politics does not include the study of :
(*a*) International Law
(*b*) International Organisations
(*c*) Geo-Politics
(*d*) Political Economy

76. A constitutional government stands for :
(*a*) A limited government
(*b*) A government run according to the provisions of the constitution
(*c*) A government run according to the wishes of the rulers
(*d*) A government run according to the wishes of the party bosses

77. Which one of the following are the devices of democracy which are commonly practised in modern times?
1. Widening of the Electorate
2. Frequent Election
3. Local Self Government
4. Responsibility of the Government to the majority party

Select correct answer from the following:
(*a*) 1 and 2
(*b*) 2 and 3
(*c*) 1, 2 and 3
(*d*) 1, 2, 3 and 4

78. "Nation is State plus nationality." Who said this?
(*a*) Garner
(*b*) Gilchrist
(*c*) Laski
(*d*) MacIver

79. The basic principle of Parliamentary Government is :
(*a*) Integration between Legislature and Executive
(*b*) Separation between Legislature and Executive
(*c*) Distribution of powers between the Centre and the State
(*d*) None of the above

80. In what respect is the American Federal System similar to that of the Indian Federal System?
1. Method of distribution of powers between the Centre and the States
2. Procedure of creation of new States
3. Position of judiciary
4. Representation of States in the Upper House of the Federal Legislative
Codes :
(*a*) 1, 3, 4
(*b*) 2, 3
(*c*) 3
(*d*) 4

81. Which one of the following is true about a Presidential form of Government?
(*a*) The President can be removed by the Legislature through impeachment
(*b*) The President cannot be removed by the Legislature
(*c*) The President can dissolve the Lower House of the Legislature
(*d*) None of the above

82. Single transferable vote system is known as :
(*a*) Plural voting system
(*b*) Direct voting system
(*c*) Hare system
(*d*) List system

83. Parliamentary Government operates on the Principle of secrecy which implies :
   (*a*) The time and date of meetings of the Cabinet are not made publicly known
   (*b*) The members of the Council of Ministers cannot divulge information regarding the proceedings of the Council of Ministers
   (*c*) The Prime Minister consults the various ministers in 'confidence' and takes decisions
   (*d*) None of the above

84. In the U.S. Federal System, a new State within State can be created by the :
   (*a*) Two Houses of the Congress
   (*b*) Senate
   (*c*) Congress with the consent of the concerned State
   (*d*) President

85. "Every State is known by the rights if maintains." Who said this?
   (*a*) Bryce   (*b*) Barker
   (*c*) Laski   (*d*) Garner

86. The nation state emerged :
   (*a*) After the fall of city states
   (*b*) After the fall of Roman empire
   (*c*) After the fall of Feudal state
   (*d*) After the fall of Oriental empire

87. According to pluralists, the main function of State is :
   (*a*) To promote welfare of its citizens
   (*b*) To harmonize the activities of various groups and associations
   (*c*) To provide social security
   (*d*) To remove inequality

88. Weak and unstable government is a feature of :
   (*a*) One party dominant system
   (*b*) One party authoritarian system
   (*c*) Two party system
   (*d*) Multi-party coalition system

89. Governments are classified as Parliamentary and Presidential on the basis of :
   (*a*) Relations between the Centre and the States
   (*b*) Relations between the Legislature and the Executive
   (*c*) Relations between the Executive and Judiciary
   (*d*) All the above

90. Which one of the following is not correctly matched?
   (*a*) Popular sovereignty — Rousseau
   (*b*) Political sovereignty — Locke
   (*c*) Legal sovereignty — Austin
   (*d*) External sovereignty — Bentham

91. A welfare State is based on :
   (*a*) A negative role of the State
   (*b*) A positive role of the State
   (*c*) A maximum role of the State
   (*d*) A minimum role of the State

92. A Socialist State stands for :
   (*a*) Free economic competition
   (*b*) Social control of the means of production and distribution
   (*c*) Class struggle
   (*d*) Abolition of State

93. Which of the following country has a Presidential form of Government?
   (*a*) Great Britain
   (*b*) United States of America
   (*c*) Japan
   (*d*) China

94. Consider the following statements :
   Assertion (A) : A federal system invariably provides for an independent judiciary
   Reason (R) : It settles the disputes between the centre and the constituent units
   Select your answer according to the following codes :

(*a*) Both (A) and (R) are correct and (R) is the right explanation of (A)

(*b*) Both (A) and (R) are correct, but (R) is not the right explanation of (A)

(*c*) (A) is correct, but (R) is false

(*d*) (R) is correct, but (A) is false

95. The power of Judicial Review is available to the Supreme Courts of which of these countries?

(*a*) India and U.S.A.

(*b*) Great Britain and France

(*c*) U.S.A. and Switzerland

(*d*) None of the above

96. Which of the following thinkers does not support democracy?

(*a*) Plato   (*b*) Locke

(*c*) Rousseau   (*d*) T.H. Green

97. Which of the following is not related to Economic Liberalism?

(*a*) Capitalism   (*b*) Socialism

(*c*) Privatization   (*d*) Globalisation

98. Which of the following is not a part of the welfare functions of the State?

(*a*) Raising standards of living

(*b*) Enactment of Labour laws

(*c*) Provide Social Justice

(*d*) Promoting Religious beliefs

99. Social Democracy is based on :

(*a*) Commitment to equality

(*b*) Support for Social Welfare State

(*c*) Ideal of Social Justice

(*d*) All of the above

100. In a unitary form of government the powers of the unit are derived from the :

(*a*) Constitution

(*b*) Centre

(*c*) Judiciary

(*d*) None of the above

ANSWERS

1	2	3	4	5	6	7	8	9	10
(*b*)	(*c*)	(*b*)	(*d*)	(*b*)	(*c*)	(*a*)	(*c*)	(*b*)	(*a*)
11	**12**	**13**	**14**	**15**	**16**	**17**	**18**	**19**	**20**
(*b*)	(*d*)	(*a*)	(*c*)	(*b*)	(*d*)	(*d*)	(*b*)	(*d*)	(*a*)
21	**22**	**23**	**24**	**25**	**26**	**27**	**28**	**29**	**30**
(*b*)	(*d*)	(*d*)	(*b*)	(*a*)	(*d*)	(*c*)	(*d*)	(*b*)	(*b*)
31	**32**	**33**	**34**	**35**	**36**	**37**	**38**	**39**	**40**
(*a*)	(*c*)	(*d*)	(*d*)	(*d*)	(*b*)	(*c*)	(*c*)	(*b*)	(*d*)
41	**42**	**43**	**44**	**45**	**46**	**47**	**48**	**49**	**50**
(*b*)	(*a*)	(*c*)	(*b*)	(*d*)	(*a*)	(*a*)	(*c*)	(*a*)	(*d*)
51	**52**	**53**	**54**	**55**	**56**	**57**	**58**	**59**	**60**
(*a*)	(*b*)	(*d*)	(*d*)	(*d*)	(*d*)	(*b*)	(*c*)	(*d*)	(*d*)
61	**62**	**63**	**64**	**65**	**66**	**67**	**68**	**69**	**70**
(*b*)	(*b*)	(*c*)	(*b*)	(*a*)	(*b*)	(*a*)	(*a*)	(*a*)	(*c*)

71	72	73	74	75	76	77	78	79	80
(d)	(d)	(d)	(c)	(d)	(b)	(c)	(b)	(d)	(c)
81	82	83	84	85	86	87	88	89	90
(a)	(c)	(b)	(c)	(c)	(c)	(b)	(d)	(b)	(d)
91	92	93	94	95	96	97	98	99	100
(b)	(b)	(b)	(a)	(a)	(a)	(b)	(d)	(d)	(b)

SECTION-B

Obj. Pol. Sc.-15

1

APPROACHES

1. Who among the following is associated with Liberal Political Economy approach?
   (*a*) Ricardo   (*b*) J.S. Mill
   (*c*) Adam Smith   (*d*) All of these

2. Which of the following approaches can be divided into two parts: Liberal political economy and Marxian political economy?
   (*a*) Political economy approach
   (*b*) Comparative approach
   (*c*) Legal approach
   (*d*) Philosophical approach

3. According to Marx, ------ depends upon comprehending economic categories as the theoretical expresssion of historical relations of production, corresponding to a particular stage of development of material production.
   (*a*) Metaphysics   (*b*) Dialectics
   (*c*) Politics   (*d*) None of these

4. Dialectic in Marxian theory was used as a synonym for :
   (*a*) Historical method
   (*b*) Scientific method
   (*c*) Comparative method
   (*d*) None of the above

5. Which approach seeks to understand the process of interaction between government and society, decision-making authorities and conflicting social forces and interests?
   (*a*) Legal approach
   (*b*) Behavioural approach
   (*c*) Institutional approach
   (*d*) Political Sociology approach

6. Who feels that politics depends on some settled order created by the state?
   (*a*) Dahl   (*b*) Greer

   (*c*) Crick   (*d*) Lasswell

7. Which of the following is not one of the approaches to the study of Governments?
   (*a*) Traditional approach
   (*b*) Sociological approach
   (*c*) Empirical approach
   (*d*) Economic approach

8. Which approach to the study of Governments is also known as Ethical approach?
   (*a*) Behavioural approach
   (*b*) Marxist approach
   (*c*) Philosophical approach
   (*d*) Sociological approach

9. The leaders of the Indian renaissance emphasised the importance of ------ values in politics.
   (*a*) Ethical   (*b*) Moral
   (*c*) Spiritual   (*d*) Social

10. Gandhi wanted ------ of politics.
    (*a*) Socialisation
    (*b*) Moralisation
    (*c*) Spiritualization
    (*d*) None of the above

11. Who among the following thinkers had a spiritual approach to politics?
    1. Vivekanand   2. Gokhale
    3. Aurobindo   4. Nehru

    Choose the correct answer using the codes given below :
    Codes :
    (*a*) 1 and 2   (*b*) 1 and 3
    (*c*) 1, 2, 3 and 4   (*d*) 3 and 4

12. Who believed that comparative approach is rather a supplement to the historical approach?

(*a*) Gandhi (*b*) Gilchrist
(*c*) Blunt (*d*) Powell

13. Which approach has been criticised for being too narrow?
(*a*) Historical approach
(*b*) Comparative approach
(*c*) Legal approach
(*d*) Institutional approach

14. Who explains that since the entire society is characterised by the interplay of influence, influential and influenced, politics pervades all society?
(*a*) J.S. Mill (*b*) Lasswell
(*c*) Marx (*d*) Dahl

15. Broadly speaking, political sociology is concerned with the social basis of power in all institutional sectors of :
(*a*) Government
(*b*) Country
(*c*) Society
(*d*) None of the above

16. Who among the following served as a central figure in empirical studies of elites and the sociology of political organisation?
(*a*) Parsons (*b*) Mosca
(*c*) Michels (*d*) Both (*b*) and (*c*)

17. ------ approach has laid emphasis on the collection and examination of 'facts' relating to the actual behaviour of man as a social and political being.
(*a*) Development (*b*) Behavioural
(*c*) Systems (*d*) Historical

18. Historical and Sociological approaches are ------ to each other.
(*a*) Complementary
(*b*) Irrelevant
(*c*) Contradictory
(*d*) None of the above

19. Which approach seeks to study the social relations that evolve between people in the process of production, distribution, exchange and consumption of the material goods and services?
(*a*) Behavioural approach

(*b*) System approach
(*c*) Political economy approach
(*d*) Historical approach

20. Graham Wallas of England and Arthur Bentley of the United States are prominent writers in the field of :
(*a*) Historical approach
(*b*) System approach
(*c*) Institutional approach
(*d*) Behavioural approach

21. Who said that political sociology starts with society and examines how it affects the state?
(*a*) Bendix and Lipset
(*b*) Max Weber
(*c*) Merriam and Lasswell
(*d*) Karl Marx

22. ------ is a branch of sociology that is mainly concerned with the analysis of the interaction between politics and society.
(*a*) Anthropology
(*b*) Political Sociology
(*c*) Structural Sociology
(*d*) None of the above

23. Who among the following accepted the view that state is more a social than a political institution?
(*a*) MacIver (*b*) Almond
(*c*) Easton (*d*) All of these

24. Consider the following characteristics of a system according to Almond?
1. Interdependence
2. Comprehensiveness
3. Existence of boundaries
4. Financial autonomy

Which of the above are correct? Choose the correct answer using the codes given below :
Codes :
(*a*) 3 and 4 (*b*) 2 and 1
(*c*) 1, 3, and 4 (*d*) 1, 2 and 3

25. Which of the following approaches is said to be 'value-laden'?
(*a*) Traditional approach
(*b*) Modern approach
(*c*) Systems approach
(*d*) None of the above

26. Which approach is criticised for being speculative and abstract?
(*a*) Systems approach
(*b*) Historical approach
(*c*) Comparative approach
(*d*) Philosophical approach

27. Which approach lays stress on the study of the formal structures of a political organisation like legislature, executive and judiciary?
(*a*) Legal approach
(*b*) Historical approach
(*c*) Institutional approach
(*d*) Sociological approach

28. Match the following Lists and choose the correct answer by using the codes given below:

List I	List II
A. Mosca	1. Complexity of elite Structure
B. C. Wright Mills	2. Empirical study of elites
C. Karl Mannheim	3. Mediating role of elites
D. Talcott Parsons	4. The concept of "power elite"

Codes :

	A	B	C	D
(*a*)	1	2	3	4
(*b*)	2	3	4	1
(*c*)	2	4	1	3
(*d*)	4	3	2	1

29. Who said that "an institution is any persistent system of activities and expectations or any stable pattern of group behaviour"?
(*a*) Dyke
(*b*) Finer
(*c*) Leo Strauss
(*d*) Macpherson

30. Legal approach stands for an attempt to understand politics in terms of :
(*a*) Law
(*b*) Conventions
(*c*) Customs
(*d*) Procedures

31. Which of the following views of politics suggests that political institutions realize philosophical ideals in governmental practices?
(*a*) Pluralist
(*b*) Marxist
(*c*) Behaviouralistic
(*d*) Institutionalistic

32. Who was one of the first among the modern political scientists to challenge the traditional approaches?
(*a*) Freud
(*b*) Lasswell
(*c*) Bernard Crick
(*d*) Charles Merriam

33. Contemporary political science gives prominence to :
(*a*) Modern approach
(*b*) Empirical approach
(*c*) Historical approach
(*d*) Institutional approach

34. The normative approach seeks to determine and prescribe :
(*a*) Values
(*b*) Customs
(*c*) Facts
(*d*) Rituals

35. Who among the following thinkers treat man as a selfish creature?
(*a*) Rousseau, Apter
(*b*) Machiavelli, Hobbes
(*c*) Mill, Locke
(*d*) Laski, Hobbes

36. Which of the following approaches is best represented by George H. Sabine?
(*a*) Sociological approach
(*b*) Philosophical approach
(*c*) Historical approach
(*d*) Integrated approach

37. Who said that politics included all activities which were carried out by the society?
(*a*) Sabine
(*b*) Catlin
(*c*) Dyke
(*d*) Andrews

38. Which of the following approaches has been expounded by Leo Strauss?
(*a*) Sociological approach
(*b*) Integrated approach
(*c*) Philosophical approach
(*d*) Normative approach

39. According to Apter, which of the following approaches helps in the study of laws, values and institutions?
(*a*) Normative approach

(*b*) Scientific approach

(*c*) Behavioural approach

(*d*) None of these

40. Which of the following is usually identified as a traditional approach?

(*a*) Legal approach

(*b*) Institutional approach

(*c*) Historical approach

(*d*) All of the above

41. Which approach aims at evolving standards of right and wrong for the purpose of a critical evaluation of the existing institutions laws and policies?

(*a*) Legal approach

(*b*) Philosophical approach

(*c*) Historical approach

(*d*) All of the above

42. The empirical approach remains largely

(*a*) Descriptive

(*b*) Prescriptive

(*c*) Non-committal

(*d*) None of the above

43. Who among the following UN Secretary General was the architect of preventive diplomacy?

(*a*) Trygave Lie

(*b*) Dag Hammarskjgoeld

(*c*) U. Thant

(*d*) Boutros-boutros Ghali

44. According to whom, normative approach can be (a) Historical (b) comparative and (c) structural?

(*a*) Dyke (*b*) Apter

(*c*) Andrews (*d*) Gillbert

45. Match List I with List II and select the correct answer by using the codes given below :

List I	List II
A. Dahl	1. Social Theory and Social Structure
B. Greer and Orleans	2. Modern Political Analysis
C. Merton	3. The Ruling Class
D. Mosca	4. Political Sociology

Codes :

	A	B	C	D
(*a*)	1	2	3	4
(*b*)	2	4	1	3
(*c*)	2	4	3	1
(*d*)	4	3	1	2

46. The names of Bentham, Savigny, Sir Henry Maine and A.V. Dicey are associated with :

(*a*) Historical approach to the study of government and politics

(*b*) Political economy approach to the study of government and politics

(*c*) Sociological approach to the study of government and politics

(*d*) Legal approach to the study of government and politics

47. The historical approach to the study of government stands on the assumption that :

(*a*) The process of history is the womb from which political processes and legal framework is born

(*b*) The stock of political theory comes out of socio-economic crises and the reaction they leave on the minds of the great thinkers

(*c*) The prime task of the study of politics is to find out the best social order for man

(*d*) Both (*a*) and (*c*)

48. It is said that under historical approach to the study of politics a scholar treats history as a genetic process. It means history is treated :

(*a*) As the study of how man got to be, what man once was and now is

(*b*) As the analysis of the anthropological growth of man from Homo Sapiens to human being

(*c*) As the study of the growth of institutions as dictable by human predilections

(*d*) None of the above

49. Institutional approach to the study of government and politics has been prominent through the history of political thought. Prominent ancient and modern thinkers giving allegiance to this approach are :

(*a*) Plato and Rousseau respectively

(*b*) Socrates and Kautilya respectively

(*c*) St. Thomas Acquinas and Machiavelli respectively

(*d*) Polybius and Finer respectively

50. Which of the following is correct about the scholars who take recourse to the legal approach to the study of government?

(*a*) They do not take into account the matters of state and confine their attention to laws

(*b*) They look at the early Greek thinkers for inspiration and intellectual guidance

(*c*) The view politics as a science of legal norms having nothing in common with the science of the state as a social organism

(*d*) All of the above

51. Which among the following liberal theorists talked of "uniform industrial society"?

(*a*) Aron (*b*) Smith

(*c*) Mill (*d*) Senior

52. Who among the following theorists of liberal political economy introduced the concept of "post-industrial society"?

(*a*) Daniel Bell (*b*) J.K. Galbraith

(*c*) Roman Rolland (*d*) None of these

53. Which of the following can be used synonymously to the term legal approach?

(*a*) Political approach

(*b*) Criminological approach

(*c*) Juridical approach

(*d*) Socio-cultural approach

54. Under the legal approach to the analysis of government and politics, the study of politics can be said to be mixed up with :

(*a*) Legal processes (*b*) Institutions

(*c*) Personalities (*d*) Both (*a*) and (*c*)

55. In the history of political thought, who among the following regarded state as primarily a corporation or a juridical person?

(*a*) Contractualists (*b*) Social Darwinists

(*c*) Analytical jurists (*d*) All of these

56. Legal approach has been employed by scholars both in ancient and modern times. Two such prominent ancient and modern

scholars are :

(*a*) Aristotle and Marx respectively

(*b*) Cicero and Dicey respectively

(*c*) Plato and Bodin respectively

(*d*) Thrasymachus and J.S. Mill respectively

57. Who among the following thinkers of the early modern period are associated with the doctrine of sovereignty?

(*a*) Jean Bodin (*b*) Hugo Grotius

(*c*) Thomas Hobbes (*d*) All of these

58. Who among the following was a distinguished student of the legal approach to the study of government and politics?

(*a*) Edward Jenks (*b*) Jellinek

(*c*) John Austin (*d*) John Stuart Mill

59. It can be maintained that the political scientists who employ legal approach to the study of politics look at the state as :

(*a*) The maintainer of a effective and equitable system of law and order

(*b*) Despenser of natural Justice and maintainer of the system of natural rights

(*c*) A machanism of maintaining equilibrium in the economic realm of society

(*d*) None of the above

60. Who among the following made the observation that the legal approach "treats the state primarily as an organisation for the creation and enforcement of law"?

(*a*) J.W. Garner (*b*) James Bryce

(*c*) Ernest Barker (*d*) V.V. Dyke

61. Who laid down the head of the state is the highest legal authority and his command is law that must be obeyed either to avoid punishment following its infraction, or to keep the dreadful state of nature away?

(*a*) Bentham (*b*) Locke

(*c*) Hobbes (*d*) Austin

62. The names of Ricardo, James Mill, J.S. Mill, Mc Culloch and Senior are associated with :

(*a*) Historical approach to the study of government and politics

(*b*) Political economy approach to the study of government and politics (*c*) Sociological approach to the study of government and politics

(*d*) Legal approach to the study of government and politics

63. The book **Introduction of the History of the Science of Politics** is written by :
(*a*) Leo strauss
(*b*) George H. Sabine
(*c*) Fredrick Pollock
(*d*) None of these

64. Who makes the observation that all great political theories are secreted in the interstices of political and social crises?
(*a*) Dumming
(*b*) Lowell
(*c*) Wayper
(*d*) Sabin

65. Which of the following books is written by Eugene Meehan?
(*a*) The Theory and Method of Political Analysis
(*b*) Theoretical Aspects of International Politics
(*c*) Philosophy of Politics
(*d*) All of the above

66. Who among the following made use of history for exalting the record of the Romans and thereby exhorting his people to restore the 'glory of Rome'?
(*a*) Cicero
(*b*) Sabin
(*c*) Bodin
(*d*) Machiavelli

67. Who associated history with the trend of conservatism?
(*a*) Hannah Arendt
(*b*) Michael Arendt
(*c*) Louis Gottschalk
(*d*) None of these

68. Who among the following criticises the historical approach to the study of government by saying that it is often loaded with superficial resemblances and historical parallels are misleading in most of the cases?
(*a*) A.V. Dicey
(*b*) James Bryce
(*c*) R.G. Gettell
(*d*) All of these

69. Institutional approach has also come to be known by the name of :
(*a*) Legal approach
(*b*) Socio-cultural approach
(*c*) Structural approach
(*d*) None of the above

70. Which of the following is included by modern writers among the structures of a political system which was not the case with ancient and medieval writers?
(*a*) Guild
(*b*) Party System
(*c*) Military
(*d*) All of these

71. About whom among the following it can be said that they have played with their emotions or prejudices while making the historical approach to the study of government and politics?
(*a*) Sabine
(*b*) Machiavelli
(*c*) Oakeshott
(*d*) Both (*b*) and (*c*)

72. Who opined that if political theory has a universal and respectable character, its reason should be traced in the affirmation that it is rooted in historical traditions?
(*a*) Machiavelli
(*b*) Sabine
(*c*) Oakeshott
(*d*) Bryce

73. The names of Walter Bagehot, F.A. Ogg, W.B. Munro, Richard Neustadt and C.F. Strong are associated with
(*a*) Legal approach
(*b*) Sociological approach
(*c*) Institutional approach
(*d*) Historical approach

74. The writing under the title – "From Sociology of Politics to Political Sociology" is authored by :
(*a*) Giovanni Sartori
(*b*) Richard Bendix
(*c*) Seymour Martin Lipset
(*d*) None of the above

75. Eminent writers like R.M. MacIver, David Easton and G.A. Almond subscribe to :
(*a*) Historical approach to the study of government and politics
(*b*) Psychological approach to the study of government and politics
(*c*) Sociological approach to the study of government and politics
(*d*) Both (*a*) and (*b*)

76. Which of the following concepts is popularised by the sociological approach to

the study of government and politics?
(*a*) Political Culture
(*b*) Political Communication
(*c*) Political Mobilization
(*d*) All of the above

77. Matters relating to the production and distribution of goods have an economic character. But they are very much involved in the political process because :
(*a*) Their regulation is done by the state
(*b*) Politics and economy are part of the same social process
(*c*) Both (*a*) and (*b*)
(*d*) State has ultimately an economic basis

78. Which of the following schools emerged because of the divergent interpretations of the role of the state in regulating economic matters?
(*a*) Liberalism   (*b*) Socialism
(*c*) Communism   (*d*) All of these

79. The work **'The State as a Concept of Political Science'** is authored by :
(*a*) Miller   (*b*) Watkins
(*c*) Robson   (*d*) O.R. Young

80. The chief exponent of the liberal political economy approach is :
(*a*) James Mill   (*b*) Nassau Senior
(*c*) Adam Smith   (*d*) None of the above

81. Apart from Adam Smith, who among the following identified hunting, pastoralism, agriculture and commerce as principal modes of transition?
(*a*) Hutchson   (*b*) Ferguson
(*c*) Hume   (*d*) All of these

82. Of the following who is regarded as intellectual god father of behavioural political science?
(*a*) Graham Wales
(*b*) Charles Merriam
(*c*) David Easton
(*d*) M.N. Roy

ANSWERS

1	2	3	4	5	6	7	8	9	10
(*d*)	(*a*)	(*b*)	(*b*)	(*d*)	(*c*)	(*d*)	(*c*)	(*a*)	(*c*)
11	**12**	**13**	**14**	**15**	**16**	**17**	**18**	**19**	**20**
(*c*)	(*b*)	(*d*)	(*b*)	(*c*)	(*d*)	(*b*)	(*a*)	(*c*)	(*d*)
21	**22**	**23**	**24**	**25**	**26**	**27**	**28**	**29**	**30**
(*a*)	(*b*)	(*d*)	(*d*)	(*a*)	(*d*)	(*c*)	(*c*)	(*a*)	(*a*)
31	**32**	**33**	**34**	**35**	**36**	**37**	**38**	**39**	**40**
(*d*)	(*b*)	(*b*)	(*a*)	(*b*)	(*c*)	(*b*)	(*c*)	(*a*)	(*d*)
41	**42**	**43**	**44**	**45**	**46**	**47**	**48**	**49**	**50**
(*b*)	(*a*)	(*b*)	(*b*)	(*b*)	(*d*)	(*b*)	(*a*)	(*d*)	(*c*)
51	**52**	**53**	**54**	**55**	**56**	**57**	**58**	**59**	**60**
(*a*)	(*a*)	(*c*)	(*d*)	(*c*)	(*b*)	(*d*)	(*b*)	(*a*)	(*a*)
61	**62**	**63**	**64**	**65**	**66**	**67**	**68**	**69**	**70**
(*c*)	(*b*)	(*c*)	(*d*)	(*a*)	(*d*)	(*b*)	(*b*)	(*c*)	(*a*)
71	**72**	**73**	**74**	**75**	**76**	**77**	**78**	**79**	**80**
(*d*)	(*b*)	(*c*)	(*a*)	(*c*)	(*a*)	(*a*)	(*d*)	(*b*)	(*c*)
81	**82**								
(*d*)	(*b*)								

CLASSIFICATION OF POLITICAL SYSTEM

1. Most of the third world countries have avoided involvement in superpower rivalries and adopted policy of :
   (*a*) Non-alignment
   (*b*) Appeasement
   (*c*) Isolation
   (*d*) None of the above

2. The third world countries have opposed all kinds of :
   (*a*) Nationalism
   (*b*) Imperialism
   (*c*) Internationalism
   (*d*) None of the above

3. What does the Greek word "Demos" mean?
   (*a*) Power
   (*b*) Democracy
   (*c*) People
   (*d*) None of the above

4. Who said the democracy is that government in which the supreme power of the state is vested in the entire people?
   (*a*) Weber   (*b*) Lincoln
   (*c*) Austin   (*d*) Herodotus

5. ------ play the dominant role in systematising and expressing the wishes of the people.
   (*a*) Pressure groups
   (*b*) Governments
   (*c*) Political parties
   (*d*) None of the above

6. The vital need of Third World Countries today is ------ development.
   (*a*) Economic

   (*b*) Political
   (*c*) Social
   (*d*) None of these

7. Who said that the states should not be distinguised so much on the basis of forms of government as on the basis of extent to which a country is governed?
   (*a*) Munro   (*b*) Bryce
   (*c*) Easton   (*d*) Aristotle

8. Authoritarian conservative system support ------ values.
   (*a*) Modern   (*b*) Traditional
   (*c*) Moral   (*d*) None of the above

9. ------ do not develop or are not allowed to grow in conservative authoritarian systems.
   (*a*) Interest groups   (*b*) Political parties
   (*c*) Pressure groups   (*d*) All of these

10. The general characteristics of the developing countries are not ------ found in all the states.
    (*a*) Uniformly
    (*b*) Often
    (*c*) Heterogeneously
    (*d*) None of the above

11. ------ is considered as a perverted form of government by Aristotle.
    (*a*) Dictatorship   (*b*) Monarchy
    (*c*) Democracy   (*d*) Aristocracy

12. Who defines democracy as "a government in which every one has a share"?
    (*a*) Bryce   (*b*) MacIver
    (*c*) Laski   (*d*) Seeley

13. ------ democracy can exist and function only in small states with a limited, homogeneous population where people can conveniently meet and deliberate together.
 (*a*) Direct
 (*b*) Representative
 (*c*) Indirect
 (*d*) None of the above

14. Which of the following is one of the characteristics of dictatorship?
 (*a*) Autocratic (*b*) Despotism
 (*c*) Tyranny (*d*) All of these

15. ------ is a form of government in which a person or group of persons possesses absolute power without effective constitutional limitations.
 (*a*) Autocracy (*b*) Dictatorship
 (*c*) Tyranny (*d*) Totalitarianism

16. Which of the following implies an absolute sovereign monarch ruling without restriction?
 (*a*) Absolutism (*b*) Despotism
 (*c*) Autocracy (*d*) Dictatorship

17. Who described democracy as the paradise of the shrieker, babbler, word-spinner, flatterer and tuft-hunter?
 (*a*) Garner (*b*) Hartmann
 (*c*) Godkin (*d*) Laski

18. Who defined democracy as 'aristocracy of black guards'?
 (*a*) Maine (*b*) Barker
 (*c*) Talleyrand (*d*) Aristotle

19. Which of the following is one of the principles on which the democratic form of government is organised?
 (*a*) Freedom (*b*) Majority rule
 (*c*) Equality (*d*) All of these

20. Which of the following is associated with dictatorship?
 (*a*) Autocracy (*b*) Authoritarianism
 (*c*) Despotism (*d*) All of the above

21. Which of the following is a demerit of dictatorship?

 (*a*) It stands for imperialism
 (*b*) It is an unstable form of government
 (*c*) It destroys liberties of the individual
 (*d*) All of the above

22. The twin phenomena of non-participation and over-participation are the main concerns of the :
 (*a*) Pluralists (*b*) Liberals
 (*c*) Marxists (*d*) Socialists

23. Authoritarianism is more of a tendency where power comes to be :
 (*a*) Delegated
 (*b*) Centralised
 (*c*) Decentralised
 (*d*) None of the above

24. Who said that dictatorship is the government of one man who has not obtained his position by inheritance but by force or consent, or a combination of both?
 (*a*) Godkin (*b*) Maine
 (*c*) Cobban (*d*) Carlyle

25. Who, in his comparing political systems analysed the governments and constitutional systems of the developing countries?
 (*a*) Aristotle (*b*) Jean Blondel
 (*c*) Laski (*d*) Bryce

26. Which of the following is the type of government found in the developing countries?
 (*a*) Liberal democracies
 (*b*) Military regimes
 (*c*) Communist regimes
 (*d*) All of the above

27. ------ is an outstanding example of populist political system.
 (*a*) Egypt (*b*) Japan
 (*c*) Bangladesh (*d*) Somalia

28. ------ is a merit that is often mentioned as a quality of an authoritarian government.
 (*a*) Efficiency
 (*b*) Popularity
 (*c*) Representativeness
 (*d*) None of the above

29. Who said that one of the great merits of democracy is that it minimises the dangers of discontent and revolution?
(*a*) Garner   (*b*) Mill
(*c*) Gettell   (*d*) Laski

30. Match List I with List II and select the correct answer by using the codes given below :

List I	**List II**
A. Cobban	1. Politics
B. Ford	2. Dictatorship
C. Aristotle	3. Democracy and Liberty
D. Lecky	4. Dictatorship in the Modern world

Codes :

	A	**B**	**C**	**D**
(*a*)	2	4	3	1
(*b*)	1	2	3	4
(*c*)	2	4	1	3
(*d*)	1	2	4	3

31. In the twentieth century a number of democracies crumbled and yielded to dictatorships during :
(*a*) The cold war period
(*b*) The post cold war period
(*c*) The inter world war period
(*d*) Pre-world war I period

32. Who among the following gave a three fold classification of governments viz, perfect state, imperfect state and state of ignorance?
(*a*) Thomas Acquinas
(*b*) Aristotle
(*c*) Plato
(*d*) None of the above

33. Polybius classified governments into :
(*a*) Monarchy, aristocracy and democracy
(*b*) Plutocracy, bureaucracy and aristocracy
(*c*) Dictatorship, democracy and oligarchy
(*d*) None of the above

34. In their classifications of governments the common feature is that both believe that various forms of governments along with their corrupt form follow one another in a cycle. They are :
(*a*) Gilchrist and Burgess
(*b*) Aristotle and Polybius

(*c*) Plato and Aristotle
(*d*) None of the above

35. Bodin based his classification of governments solely on :
(*a*) The prevailing institutional order
(*b*) The number of men in whose hands the sovereign power resided
(*c*) The oriental scheme of governments
(*d*) None of the above

36. Rousseau divided governments into monarchies, aristocracies and democracies. He sub-divided aristocracies into :
(*a*) Natural, elective and hereditary
(*b*) Unitary, non-unitary and democratic
(*c*) Oligarchic, democratic and bureaucratic
(*d*) None of the above

37. Who among the following find Aristotle's classification of governments sound and logical?
(*a*) John Seeley   (*b*) Gilchrist
(*c*) Burgess   (*d*) Both (*b*) and (*c*)

38. The statement—"Everything for the state, nothing against the state, nothing outside the state" ------ is attributed to :
(*a*) Hitler
(*b*) Mussolini
(*c*) General Franco
(*d*) None of the above

39. In the opinion of Marriott, the bases of classification of governments are :
(*a*) Unitary and federal
(*b*) Rigid and flexible
(*c*) Monarchical, presidential and parliamentary
(*d*) All of the above

40. Who regards "balance in the structure of society" as a pre-requisite to the maintenance of democracy?
(*a*) Barker
(*b*) Mannheim
(*c*) C.D. Burns
(*d*) None of the above

41. Which of the following works are critical of democracy?

(*a*) Laski's A Grammer of Politics
(*b*) Maine's Popular Government
(*c*) Lecky's Democracy and liberty
(*d*) Both (*b*) and (*c*)

42. Which of the following generally characterise an authoritarian regime?
(*a*) Ideological uniformity
(*b*) Monism
(*c*) Elitism
(*d*) All of the above

43. The work 'The Sociology of Developing Societies' is authored by :
(*a*) M.M. Hoogvelt
(*b*) Eugene J. Kolb
(*c*) A.G. Frank
(*d*) None of the above

44. In the international politics, the third world countries have been following the policy of :
(*a*) Isolationism
(*b*) Neutrality
(*c*) Alliance-Formation
(*d*) Non-alignment

45. The work 'The Politics of the Developing Areas' is authored by :
(*a*) Gabriel Almond   (*b*) James Coleman
(*c*) Carl Friedrich   (*d*) Both (*a*) and (*b*)

46. Which of the following countries have been used by the United States as backyards for American industry?
(*a*) East-European countries
(*b*) Island states of the pacific ocean
(*c*) Latin American nations
(*d*) All of the above

47. The outstanding features of the political system of the developed countries are :
(*a*) Conflict and controversy
(*b*) Coalition and defection
(*c*) Modernisation and stability
(*d*) None of the above

48. V.I. Lenin enunciated his theory of imperialism in :
(*a*) The State and Revolution
(*b*) Todayisms

(*c*) Imperialism: The Highest Stage of Capitalism
(*d*) None of the above

49. Which of the following intellectuals are associated with the dependency theory?
(*a*) Andre Gunder Frank
(*b*) Ralph Miliband
(*c*) Samir Amin
(*d*) Both (*a*) and (*c*)

50. The developing countries will develop themselves into developed countries, when they will acquire
(*a*) Two-party system
(*b*) Social stability
(*c*) Modern political culture
(*d*) Economic prosperity and political stability

51. Aspects of Political development is authored by :
(*a*) A.G. Frank   (*b*) Hannah Arendt
(*c*) Samir Amin   (*d*) Lucian Pye

52. Which among the following regimes cannot be termed as dictatorial?
(*a*) Turkey under Kemal Ataturk
(*b*) Indonesia under Sukarno
(*c*) Russia under Stalin
(*d*) Spain under Franco

53. In essence, dictatorship is :
(*a*) The assumption of extra-legal authority by the head of the state
(*b*) The rule of a man in a partyless polity
(*c*) Absence of civilian control over military
(*d*) All of the above

54. In the post World War II period an authoritarian government was established in Portugal under :
(*a*) Idi Amin
(*b*) Salazar
(*c*) General Albuqurque
(*d*) None of the above

55. The work 'Dictatorship' is authored by :
(*a*) Alfred Cobban
(*b*) Michael R. Curtis
(*c*) Gettel
(*d*) Rodee, Christol and Anderson

56. An absolute sovereign, a monarch ruling without restriction can best be termed as :
(*a*) Despot
(*b*) Autocrat
(*c*) Aristocrat
(*d*) None of the above

57. In the history of England, dictatorship was established under :
(*a*) Louis XIV   (*b*) Charles XV
(*c*) Oliver Cromwell   (*d*) Queen Elizabeth I

58. Absolute rule of a single person who occupies his position by means of force and, as such, is not accountable to any popular institution, it can best be described as :
(*a*) Totalitarianism   (*b*) Authoritarianism
(*c*) Autarchy   (*d*) Dictatorship

59. Among the well known dictatorial governments of the world that emerged after World War II with which country the name of 'Newin' is associated?
(*a*) Thailand
(*b*) Yugoslavia
(*c*) Burma (presently Myanmar)
(*d*) Uganda

60. Who among the following accepted the classification of Aristotle but added to it a fourth form called Theocracy, with its perverted form known as Idolocracy?
(*a*) Plato   (*b*) Marsilio of Padua
(*c*) Saint Augustine   (*d*) Bluntschli

ANSWERS

1	2	3	4	5	6	7	8	9	10
(*a*)	(*b*)	(*c*)	(*d*)	(*c*)	(*a*)	(*c*)	(*b*)	(*d*)	(*a*)
11	**12**	**13**	**14**	**15**	**16**	**17**	**18**	**19**	**20**
(*c*)	(*d*)	(*a*)	(*d*)	(*b*)	(*c*)	(*b*)	(*c*)	(*d*)	(*d*)
21	**22**	**23**	**24**	**25**	**26**	**27**	**28**	**29**	**30**
(*d*)	(*b*)	(*b*)	(*c*)	(*b*)	(*d*)	(*a*)	(*a*)	(*a*)	(*c*)
31	**32**	**33**	**34**	**35**	**36**	**37**	**38**	**39**	**40**
(*c*)	(*c*)	(*a*)	(*b*)	(*b*)	(*a*)	(*d*)	(*b*)	(*d*)	(*b*)
41	**42**	**43**	**44**	**45**	**46**	**47**	**48**	**49**	**50**
(*d*)	(*d*)	(*a*)	(*d*)	(*d*)	(*c*)	(*c*)	(*c*)	(*c*)	(*d*)
51	**52**	**53**	**54**	**55**	**56**	**57**	**58**	**59**	**60**
(*d*)	(*b*)	(*a*)	(*b*)	(*a*)	(*b*)	(*c*)	(*d*)	(*c*)	(*d*)

TYPOLOGIES OF CONSTITUTIONS

1. Who among the following is of the opinion that England has no constitution?
   (a) Freeman (b) Thomas Paine
   (c) Tocqueville (d) Both (b) and (c)

2. Which of the following is not one of the important statutes of the British Parliament?
   (a) Reform Act of 1832
   (b) Representation of People's Act, 1918
   (c) Magna Carta,1215
   (d) Indian Independence Act, 1947

3. ------ are the judgements and interpretations of the British courts which define the scope and limitations of the different charters, statutes and common Law of England.
   (a) Conventions
   (b) Judicial decisions
   (c) Common Law
   (d) None of the above

4. Who said that cabinet in England is a hyphen that joins, the buckle that binds, the executive and legislative departments together?
   (a) Bagehot (b) J.S. Mill
   (c) Ogg (d) Dicey

5. Which of the following are the rules for determining the mode in which the descretionary powers of the crown ought to be exercised?
   (a) Laws
   (b) Customs
   (c) Conventions
   (d) None of the above

6. Who said that the prerogatives are the residue of the descretionary or autocratic powers which have been left legally with the crown?
   (a) Finer (b) Dicey

   (c) Ogg (d) Mill

7. Who refers to cabinet as the pivot round which the whole political machinery revolves?
   (a) Marriott (b) Ramsay Muir
   (c) Lowell (d) Gladstone

8. What was issued by King John at Runnymede on the Thames in 1215?
   (a) Bill of Rights
   (b) Magna Carta
   (c) Petition of Rights
   (d) None of the above

9. The parliament of Great Britain is a/an ------ legislature which has no parallel in the democratic world.
   (a) Sovereign (b) Non-political
   (c) Authoritarian (d) All of these

10. Which of the following is used to describe the orders, rules and regulations issued by the executive departments to supplement and elaborate the laws passed by the parliament?
    (a) Delegation
    (b) Delegated Legislation
    (c) Decentralisation
    (d) None of the above

11. The evolution of delegated legislation began in the :
    (a) Eighteenth Century
    (b) Sixteenth Century
    (c) Nineteenth Century
    (d) Seventeenth Century

12. Which law was described by Blackstone as the best birthright, the noblest inheritance of mankind?
    (a) Public Law

(*b*) Constitutional Law
(*c*) Private Law
(*d*) Common Law

13. The two principal types of Law in Great Britain are the :
(*a*) Public and Private Law
(*b*) Common and Statute Law
(*c*) Constitutional and Common Law
(*d*) None of the above

14. The ------ law is regarded as a true embodiment of justice.
(*a*) Common   (*b*) Public
(*c*) Private   (*d*) None of the above

15. Which French Scholar had said that rule, predominance or supremacy of the law is an outstanding feature of the British constitution?
(*a*) Munro   (*b*) Morrison
(*c*) Tocqueville   (*d*) Laski

16. The Reforms Act of ------ was the first in the series of many enactments that tried to regulate the right to vote in Great Britain.
(*a*) 1867   (*b*) 1832
(*c*) 1911   (*d*) 1932

17. The most important feature of the British constitution is its ------ character.
(*a*) Unwritten
(*b*) Rigid
(*c*) Written
(*d*) None of the above

18. England has a ------ form of government.
(*a*) Presidential   (*b*) Dictatorial
(*c*) Parliamentary   (*d*) Federal

19. The British constitution is a classic example of ------ constitution.
(*a*) Written   (*b*) Flexible
(*c*) Rigid   (*d*) None of the above

20. ------ play (s) a vital role in the British political system.
(*a*) Conventions
(*b*) Judicial Review
(*c*) The Crown
(*d*) None of the above

21. Which of the following is one of the sources of the British constitution?
(*a*) Statutes   (*b*) Conventions
(*c*) Common Law   (*d*) All of these

22. The British constitution does not exist in real sense as there is no set :
(*a*) Social System
(*b*) Economic System
(*c*) Political System
(*d*) None of the above

23. The British constitution is a queer mixture of the :
1. Monarchical principles
2. Democratic principles
3. Aristocratic principles
4. Socialist principles

Which of the above are correct? Choose the correct answer using the codes given below :
(*a*) 2 and 4   (*b*) 1 and 3
(*c*) 1, 2 and 3   (*d*) 1, 2, 3 and 4

24. Which term, according to Munro is an attempt to lay out the districts in such a way that the interests of the dominant party will be served?
(*a*) Filibustering
(*b*) Gemeinschaft
(*c*) Gerrymandering
(*d*) None of the above

25. In U.S.A., the House of Representatives holds ------ session (s) in a year.
(*a*) Two   (*b*) Three
(*c*) Four   (*d*) One

26. Who is the presiding officer of the senate in U.S.A.?
(*a*) Speaker   (*b*) Vice-President
(*c*) President   (*d*) Chairman

27. Which of the following means a parliamentary device of long-winded speeches, not necessarily relevant, to obstruct, delay or bargain over a measure under consideration for voting?
(*a*) Mudslinging
(*b*) Gerrymandering
(*c*) Filibustering
(*d*) None of these

28. Who has the power to appoint the inferior officers of the union in the American constitution?
(*a*) Council of Ministers
(*b*) President
(*c*) Prime Minister
(*d*) Parliament

29. Which constitution seeks to avoid the undesirable 'Spoils System'?
(*a*) Indian Constitution
(*b*) American Constitution
(*c*) British Constitution
(*d*) None of the above

30. Who is the ex-officio chairman of the senate in U.S.A.?
(*a*) President   (*b*) Speaker
(*c*) Vice-President (*d*) Deputy Speaker

31. Who said that pressure seek to influence the men who weild power, not to place their own men in power, at least not officially?
(*a*) Carr   (*b*) Laski
(*c*) Johnson   (*d*) Duverger

32. Which term is used to indicate the technique of establishing contacts with the members of congress and state legislatures to influence them to vote for or against a measure to suit the interest of a pressure group?
(*a*) Interest group
(*b*) Lobbying
(*c*) Propaganda
(*d*) None of the above

33. Who said that the American Electoral System is unfair, inaccurate, uncertain and undemocratic?
(*a*) Laski   (*b*) Munro
(*c*) Sidney   (*d*) Mac Gregor

34. The constitution of the United States is the oldest ------ constitution in existence in the world.
(*a*) Written   (*b*) Rigid
(*c*) Unwritten   (*d*) Flexible

35. The American constitution gives recognition to the principles of :

(*a*) Military sovereignty
(*b*) Presidential sovereignty
(*c*) Religious sovereignty
(*d*) Popular sovereignty

36. The president is chief executive, but he can make no appointments without approval of the :
(*a*) House of Representatives
(*b*) Federal Court
(*c*) Senate
(*d*) None of the above

37. The constitution of the United States has guaranteed certain fundamental rights to the people which are :
(*a*) Impeachable   (*b*) Justiciable
(*c*) Unimpeachable   (*d*) Non-justiciable

38. The constitution of the United States is described as :
(*a*) Flexible
(*b*) Rigid
(*c*) Conventional
(*d*) None of the above

39. The ------ have assumed very influential role in the political system of America.
(*a*) Political parties   (*b*) Government
(*c*) State   (*d*) Conventions

40. The U.S. constitution is based on the doctrine of :
(*a*) Balance of power
(*b*) Unification of power
(*c*) Isolation of power
(*d*) Separation of power

41. Which of the following is the power of the federal judiciary in U.S.A. to declare any legislation or executive action null and void if the same is found to be inconsistent with the provisions of the constitution?
(*a*) Judicial Activism
(*b*) Judicial Immunity
(*c*) Judicial Review
(*d*) None of the above

42. The U.S. constitution provides for :
(*a*) Dual citizenship

(*b*) Multiple citizenship
(*c*) Single citizenship
(*d*) None of the above

43. Who said that "the constitution of the USA is the most completely federal constitution in the world"?
(*a*) Jennings   (*b*) Strong
(*c*) Munro   (*d*) Gilbert

44. In U.S.A., which of the following is one of the causes of the senate being the most powerful second chamber?
(*a*) It enjoys direct executive powers
(*b*) The senators are directly elected
(*c*) Senior politicians belong to this House
(*d*) All of the above

45. The Supreme Court in which country is probably the strongest of all judicial tribunals in the world?
(*a*) U.K.   (*b*) France
(*c*) U.S.A.   (*d*) Switzerland

46. Who defines a political party as groups of citizens more or less organised, who act as a political unit and who by the use of their political power aim at controlling the government and carrying out their policies?
(*a*) Bryce   (*b*) Gettel
(*c*) Gladstone   (*d*) Morrison

47. Whose consent is obligatory before a constitutional revision can be brought about?
(*a*) President   (*b*) Senate
(*c*) Prime Minister   (*d*) Judge

48. Consider the following forms of government ascribed to the French constitution :
1. Parliamentary form of government
2. Dictatorial form of government
3. Presidential form of government
4. Federal form of government

Which of the above are correct? Choose the correct answer using the codes given below :
Codes :
(*a*) 1, 2 and 3   (*b*) 1 and 3
(*c*) 1 and 2   (*d*) 2 and 4

49. In France, the 1958 constitution ------ the traditional relationship between the legislative and the rule-making authorities.
(*a*) Reverses
(*b*) Involves
(*c*) Endorses
(*d*) None of the above

50. Under the 1958 constitution, the premier of France is ------ by the President.
(*a*) Elected
(*b*) Terminated
(*c*) Nominated
(*d*) None of the above

51. In France, the concept of 'community' is an important innovation of the constitution of the :
(*a*) Fourth Republic   (*b*) Fifth Republic
(*c*) Second Republic   (*d*) Third Republic

52. Which council has been given the function of deciding on the constitutionality of Governmental or parliamentary acts?
(*a*) Bar Council
(*b*) Executive Council
(*c*) Security Council
(*d*) Constitutional Council

53. In France, an important feature of the 1958 constitution is constitutional recognition of :
(*a*) Pressure groups
(*b*) Political parties
(*c*) Fundamental rights
(*d*) None of the above

54. Which Article of the French constitution speaks that political parties and groups shall be instrumental in the exercise of the suffrage?
(*a*) Article 2   (*b*) Article 3
(*c*) Article 4   (*d*) Article 5

55. The ------ of the Fifth Republic is the Keystone of the new parliamentary regime in France.
(*a*) President
(*b*) Council of Ministers
(*c*) Prime Minister
(*d*) Vice-President

56. Who was the first President of the fifth Republic in France?

(*a*) Philip
(*b*) Michel
(*c*) Louisix
(*d*) General de Gaulle

57. The constitution of the French fifth Republic provides for a ------ form of government with a strong president.
(*a*) Parliamentary   (*b*) Authoritarian
(*c*) Presidential   (*d*) Dictatorial

58. Which of the following is true regarding constitution of the fifth French Republic?
(*a*) Quasi-monarchical
(*b*) Quasi-presidential
(*c*) A parliamentary Empire
(*d*) All of the above

59. The 'Declaration of 1789' was based on the doctrine of :
(*a*) Natural liberty   (*b*) Natural law
(*c*) General will   (*d*) Both (*b*) and (*c*)

60. Which Article of the French constitution declares France as an indivisible, secular, democratic and social Republic?
(*a*) Article 5   (*b*) Article 6
(*c*) Article 2   (*d*) Article 7

61. Who said that the constitution of the fifth Republic of France was 'tailor-made for General de Gaulle'?
(*a*) Dorothy Pickles   (*b*) Finer
(*c*) Harrison   (*d*) Strong

62. The French legal and judicial system bears the imprint of :
(*a*) British law
(*b*) Constitutional law
(*c*) Greek law
(*d*) Roman law

63. In France, which Courts have been constituted to administer law that is called 'Administrative Law'?
(*a*) Civil Courts
(*b*) Administrative Courts
(*c*) Ordinary Courts
(*d*) None of the above

64. Which of the following is one of the features of the system of administrative Law in France?

(*a*) It relieves the public officials of the jurisdiction of ordinary courts
(*b*) It distinguishes official acts from personal acts
(*c*) It deals with rules relating to the validity of administrative decrees
(*d*) All of the above

65. Which of the following are the two kinds of administrative courts in France?
(*a*) Civil and Criminal Courts
(*b*) Ordinary and Constitutional Courts
(*c*) Lower Court and High Court
(*d*) Regional Councils and Council of States

66. Which courts is the highest appellate court for Administrative Law in France?
(*a*) Regional Councils (*b*) Council of State
(*c*) Civil Court   (*d*) High Court

67. Which of the following are the two houses of the French parliament under the fifth Republic?
(*a*) Congress, Senate
(*b*) Senate, House of Representatives
(*c*) House of Lords, House of Commons
(*d*) National Assembly, Senate

68. Which of the following is the lower and popular chamber of the French parliament?
(*a*) Senate
(*b*) House of Representatives
(*c*) National Assembly
(*d*) None of the above

69. In France, the term of the Senate is :
(*a*) Three years   (*b*) Six years
(*c*) Two years   (*d*) Nine years

70. Who controls the finances of the nation in France?
(*a*) Parliament
(*b*) Prime Minister
(*c*) President
(*d*) Council of Ministers

71. In France, the parliament meets ipso jure ------ in a year.
(*a*) Thrice   (*b*) Twice
(*c*) Once   (*d*) None of the above

72. The most important feature of local government in France is extreme type of :
   (*a*) Centralisation
   (*b*) Decentralisation
   (*c*) Bureaucratisation
   (*d*) None of the above

73. Who said that "A natural consequence of the tight integration of nation and local government is a rigid uniformity of local government arrangements throughout the length and breadth of the country"?
   (*a*) Bryce   (*b*) Zink and Ogg
   (*c*) Munro   (*d*) Finer

74. Which of the following statements is correct regarding the concept of community as innovated in the constitution of the fifth Republic in French?
   (*a*) It is a sort of association between French Republic and its overseas territories and departments
   (*b*) It is something between a federation and a commonwealth
   (*c*) The members of the community have equal status
   (*d*) All of the above

75. Who is the highest ceremonial functionary of the State in China?
   (*a*) Prime Minister
   (*b*) Chairman
   (*c*) President
   (*d*) None of the above

76. In China, the President is elected by the :
   (*a*) People   (*b*) NPC
   (*c*) Vice-President   (*d*) Congress

77. The communist party is the vanguard of the :
   (*a*) People
   (*b*) Followers of communism
   (*c*) Rich men's property
   (*d*) None of the above

78. The Chinese state is built on the principles of :
   (*a*) Bureaucratic centralism
   (*b*) Democratic centralism
   (*c*) Authoritarian centralism
   (*d*) None of the above

79. Who said that Chinese political system has a high degree of centralism but is based on a high degree of democracy?
   (*a*) Mao Tse-tung   (*b*) Zhao Ziyang
   (*c*) Chou Keng-sheng (*d*) Liu Shao Chi

80. Which chapter of the Chinese constitution incorporates fundamental rights and duties?
   (*a*) Chapter 3   (*b*) Chapter 1
   (*c*) Chapter 2   (*d*) Chapter 4

81. China has opted for a ------ legislature.
   (*a*) Unicameral   (*b*) Tricameral
   (*c*) Bicameral   (*d*) None of the above

82. Which is the highest organ of Chinese Judiciary?
   (*a*) Supreme Court
   (*b*) Supreme People's Court
   (*c*) High Court
   (*d*) Constitutional Court

83. All power in China, according to the Chinese constitution, belongs to the :
   (*a*) State
   (*b*) Government
   (*c*) People
   (*d*) None of the above

84. China is a multi-national :
   (*a*) Unitary state
   (*b*) Federal state
   (*c*) Capitalist state
   (*d*) Authoritarian state

85. Which of the following means that local units can do exactly as they like so long as the agents of the governments which are above them do not object?
   (*a*) Democratic Centralism
   (*b*) Authoritarian Centralism
   (*c*) Bureaucratic Centralism
   (*d*) None of the above

86. Who said that the communist party is the ultimate political authority and the source of all decision making on the mainland China today?
   (*a*) Waller   (*b*) Schumann
   (*c*) Bernett   (*d*) Whitling

87. The highest organ of the communist party of China is the :
(*a*) NPC
(*b*) Cell
(*c*) State Council
(*d*) Supreme People's Court

88. All the legislative powers in China are vested in the :
(*a*) State Council
(*b*) Supreme People's Court
(*c*) NPC
(*d*) None of the above

89. Which of the following is one of the important institutions in the Chinese constitutional structure?
(*a*) The State Council
(*b*) The Supreme People's Court
(*c*) The NPC
(*d*) All of the above

90. Which of the following is true regarding the National People's Congress in China?
(*a*) It has the power to amend the constitution
(*b*) It is the sole law-making body for the country
(*c*) A number of officials of the state are elected by the NPC
(*d*) All of the above

91. Who proposes the name of the premier of the state council in China, according to the constitution?
(*a*) President
(*b*) Vice-Premier
(*c*) Standing Committee
(*d*) None of the above

92. Which of the following is not one of the committees established by the NPC of China?
(*a*) Nationalities Committee
(*b*) Ethic Committee
(*c*) Law Committee
(*d*) Education Committee

93. In China, the Functions of the President are :
(*a*) Nominal
(*b*) Non-official

(*c*) Real
(*d*) None of the above

94. The state council of the people's Republic of China is the :
(*a*) Lower organ of state power
(*b*) Provincial people's Government
(*c*) Central people's Government
(*d*) None of the above

95. Which of the following are included in the different categories of rights of the Chinese people?
(*a*) Economic Rights
(*b*) Social and Cultural Rights
(*c*) Political and Civil Rights
(*d*) All of the above

96. The most dominant role is played by the pressure groups in the administrative system of :
(*a*) U.K.   (*b*) France
(*c*) U.S.A.   (*d*) Russia

97. Who suggested mass campaigns as a means of maintaining the revolutionary fevour and of creating a new society?
(*a*) Mao Zedong   (*b*) Deng
(*c*) Strong   (*d*) Hua Guo-Feng

98. Which politics is a unique feature of the Chinese system?
(*a*) Popular   (*b*) Mass-Line
(*c*) Socialist   (*d*) Secular

99. The most widely discussed of all the mass campaigns in China was :
(*a*) Great Leap Forward
(*b*) The Communist Revolution
(*c*) The Freedom Movement
(*d*) None of the above

100. Which Article of the Chinese constitution speaks of equality of all the nationalities?
(*a*) Article 3   (*b*) Article 9
(*c*) Article 6   (*d*) Article 4

101. The constitution of the people's Republic of China is based on the definite ideology of :
(*a*) Marx   (*b*) Lenin
(*c*) Engels   (*d*) All of the above

102. ------ does not promote any specific electoral system in Germany.
 (*a*) Civil Law
 (*b*) Basic Law
 (*c*) Constitutional Law
 (*d*) Public Law

103. The German electoral system is one of personalised.
 (*a*) List system
 (*b*) Non-transferable voting system
 (*c*) Proportional representation
 (*d*) None of the above

104. In Germany, the number of constituencies corresponds to ------ the number of seats in the Bundestag (Federal parliament).
 (*a*) Two-third
 (*b*) One-Fourth
 (*c*) Half
 (*d*) None of the above

105. Which of the following is one of the functions of the Bundestag in Germany?
 (*a*) To enact legislation
 (*b*) To determine the budget
 (*c*) To initiate committees investigating specific acts of the executive
 (*d*) All of the above

106. In Germany, the Bundesrat (Federal Council) is not a ------ elected organ.
 (*a*) Representatively
 (*b*) Legally
 (*c*) Democratically
 (*d*) None of the above

107. Which of the following is one of the functions of the federal council in Germany?
 (*a*) To introduce bills
 (*b*) To comment on bills introduced by the Federal Government
 (*c*) To consent of object to legislation adopted by Federal Parliament
 (*d*) All of the above

108. Which of the following was the first important German constitution that was drafted as a result of revolution of 1848?
 (*a*) Weimar constitution

 (*b*) The Nazi constitution
 (*c*) German Reich constitution
 (*d*) None of the above

109. In Germany, the Weimar constitution introduced the political system of a :
 (*a*) Presidential Democratic Republic
 (*b*) Parliamentary Federal Republic
 (*c*) Parliamentary Unitary Republic
 (*d*) None of the above

110. At the end of the First World War, the 1871 constitution was replaced by the :
 (*a*) Weimar constitution
 (*b*) The Nazi constitution
 (*c*) German Reich constitution
 (*d*) None of the above

111. In Germany, one of the problems of the Weimar constitution was the extent of power vested in the :
 (*a*) Cabinet
 (*b*) Prime Minister
 (*c*) Parliament
 (*d*) President of the Reich

112. Which of the following is included among the powers of the President of the German Reich :
 (*a*) Representative of the state
 (*b*) Head of the state
 (*c*) The right to dissolve the legislature and to enact emergency legislation
 (*d*) All of the above

113. When did a statutory instrument abolish the most important basic rights in the German constitution?
 (*a*) 28 Feb, 1933 (*b*) 10 Feb, 1933
 (*c*) 20 Feb, 1934 (*d*) 11 Feb, 1932

114. The Eastern part of Germany was under the occupation of :
 (*a*) Italy (*b*) England
 (*c*) Soviet Union (*d*) America

115. In which year the socialist order of East Germany collapsed and the question of reunification of the two German states arose?
 (*a*) 1987 (*b*) 1986
 (*c*) 1989 (*d*) 1990

116. Into how many zones Germany was divided after the capitulation of the German army at the end of the second World War?
(*a*) Three   (*b*) Four
(*c*) Five   (*d*) Six

117. In Germany, the parliamentary council enacted the ------ on 8th May, 1949.
(*a*) Basic Law
(*b*) Public Law
(*c*) Constitutional Law
(*d*) Civil Law

118. Which of the following are the important constitutional organs of Germany?
(*a*) Federal Parliament, Federal Constitutional Court
(*b*) Federal Council, Federal President
(*c*) Federal Government, Federal Chancellor
(*d*) All of the above

119. Which of the following are the two main legislative bodies at the federal level in Germany?
(*a*) Bundestag and Bundesrat
(*b*) Bundestag and Bunderegierung
(*c*) Bundesrat and Bundeskanzler
(*d*) None of the above

120. In Germany, the Bundestag is made up of elected representatives called :
(*a*) Councillors   (*b*) Deputies
(*c*) Chancellors   (*d*) None of the above

121. The Bundestag is formed by regular, periodic :
(*a*) Elections   (*b*) Competitions
(*c*) Nominations   (*d*) None of the above

122. ------ can now be regarded as the permanent constitution of the German state.
(*a*) Public Law
(*b*) Constitutional Law
(*c*) Common Law
(*d*) Basic Law

123. Who is the Head of the German state?
(*a*) Deputies
(*b*) Federal Chancellor
(*c*) Federal Prime Minister
(*d*) Federal President

124. The Federal President of Germany is elected for a term of :
(*a*) 5 years   (*b*) 6 years
(*c*) 4 years   (*d*) 3 years

125. What is an important characteristic of the German legal and political system?
(*a*) Rule of Law
(*b*) Judicial Review
(*c*) Separation of Powers
(*d*) None of the above

126. The Bundeskanzler/in can be ousted from office :
(*a*) By a simple majority vote of no confidence
(*b*) By giving a majority vote in favour of a successor
(*c*) By a two-third majority vote, ratified by the Bundespresident/in
(*d*) By impeachment in the presence of the Federal Court Chief Justice

127. Who is the Chairperson and head of the government?
(*a*) Federal President
(*b*) Prime Minister
(*c*) Federal Chancellor
(*d*) Councillor

128. In Germany, who chooses the ministers and determines their numbers and responsibilities?
(*a*) Federal Chancellor
(*b*) Prime Minister
(*c*) Federal President
(*d*) Councillor

129. According to which Article of the German constitution, the Federal Government or an individual Federal Minister may be authorised by a statute to issue statutory instruments?
(*a*) Article 56 BL   (*b*) Article 76 BL
(*c*) Article 29 BL   (*d*) Article 80 (1) BL

130. Which of the following is the most important principle of the German state set out in Article 20 BL?
(*a*) Democracy   (*b*) Republicanism
(*c*) Federalism   (*d*) All of the above

131. Which Article defines Germany as a democratic state?
(*a*) Article 20 (I) BL (*b*) Article 25
(*c*) Article 21 BL (*d*) Article 30

132. Which principle declares that Germany is a republic, as opposed to a monarchy?
(*a*) Federalism (*b*) Republicanism
(*c*) Democracy (*d*) Social State

133. Germany consists of ------ lander (German States)
(*a*) Fourteen (*b*) Fifteen
(*c*) Sixteen (*d*) Seventeen

134. In South Africa, the council of provinces which replaced the ------ under the new constitution, was inaugurated on 6 February 1997.
(*a*) Senate
(*b*) Federal Council
(*c*) House of Representatives
(*d*) None of the above

135. In South Africa, the National Council of provinces comprises of :
(*a*) 80 members (*b*) 70 members
(*c*) 90 members (*d*) 60 members

136. The Republic of South Africa is one sovereign democratic state founded on which of the following values?
(*a*) Non-racialism and non-sexim
(*b*) Supremacy of the constitution and the rule of law
(*c*) Human dignity
(*d*) All of the above

137. In South Africa, the National Assembly has between ------ members.
(*a*) 300 and 350 (*b*) 250 and 300
(*c*) 350 and 400 (*d*) 400 and 450

138. In South Africa, the rights that are enshrined in the constitution of the Republic include :
(*a*) Protection against detention without trial, torture of any inhuman form of treatment or punishment
(*b*) The right to privacy
(*c*) Freedom of conscience
(*d*) All of the above

139. In South Africa, the judicial authority of the Republic is vested in the courts, which comprise the :
(*a*) Constitutional court
(*b*) High court
(*c*) Supreme court of Appeal
(*d*) All of the above

140. In South Africa, no person may hold office as president for more than :
(*a*) Four terms (*b*) Three terms
(*c*) Two terms (*d*) None of the above

141. In which year the Republic of South Africa adopted an interim constitution, which contains the basic elements of the final constitution of the Republic?
(*a*) 1992 (*b*) 1993
(*c*) 1994 (*d*) 1995

142. Which of the following is one of the indispensable elements of the state order?
(*a*) Pluralistic democracy
(*b*) Separation of powers, including a bicameral parliament
(*c*) A civil rights section emphasising the basic right of the individual to get access to an independent judiciary
(*d*) All of the above

143. Which of the following is a federative state?
(*a*) Switzerland (*b*) Austria
(*c*) Australia (*d*) All of these

144. The provincial constitution of 1993 establishes in chapter 9, ------ provinces as federal elements of the Republic in South Africa.
(*a*) Eight (*b*) Six
(*c*) Nine (*d*) Three

145. In a federal state, the residual legislative power is normally vested in the :
(*a*) Units
(*b*) Centre
(*c*) Parliament
(*d*) Leader of the majority party

146. Which of the following are the major sources of financial income of the whole republic in South Africa?
(*a*) House tax and Income tax
(*b*) Entertainment tax and Income tax

(*c*) Income tax and Value-Added tax
(*d*) None of the above

147. The new constitution of Republic of South Africa was adopted by the constituent Assembly on :
(*a*) 10 June 1997 (*b*) 8 May 1996
(*c*) 3 December 1996 (*d*) 17 June 1997

148. In South Africa Legislative power is vested in a bicameral parliament comprising :
(*a*) Upper Chamber and Lower Chamber
(*b*) A National Assembly and a National Council of provinces
(*c*) House of Lords and House of commons
(*d*) None of the above

149. In South Africa National and provincial legislatures are elected separately, under a :
(*a*) 'Multiple-ballot' electoral system
(*b*) 'Single-ballot' electoral system
(*c*) 'Double-ballot' electoral system
(*d*) None of the above

150. In South Africa National Assembly is elected by :
(*a*) Proportional representation
(*b*) Single non-transferable voting
(*c*) Direct representation
(*d*) None of the above

151. In South Africa, each provincial legislature appoints ------ permanent delegates and nominates ------ special delegates to the National Council of provinces.
(*a*) Six, Four (*b*) Two, Four
(*c*) Three, Six (*d*) Three, Five

152. In South Africa, the Head of the state is the president who is elected by the ------ from among its members.
(*a*) National Council
(*b*) Provincial Council
(*c*) National Assembly
(*d*) None of the above

153. Which of the following courts ensures that the executive, legislative and judicial organs of government adhere to the provisions of the interim constitution in South Africa?
(*a*) Civil Court
(*b*) Constitutional Court

(*c*) Criminal Court
(*d*) None of the above

154. The new constitution of the Republic of South Africa came into Force on :
(*a*) 29 June, 1998 (*b*) 25 May, 1996
(*c*) 4 February, 1997 (*d*) 15 April, 1997

155. How many provinces are there in the Republic of South Africa?
(*a*) Nine (*b*) Six
(*c*) Four (*d*) Three

156. In South Africa, the local sphere of government consists of municipalities, with executive and legislative authority vested in the :
(*a*) Provincial Council
(*b*) Municipal Council
(*c*) Chairman of the municipality
(*d*) None of the above

157. In South Africa, the objectives of local government include :
(*a*) To provide democratic and accountable government for local communities
(*b*) To ensure the provision of services to communities
(*c*) To promote social and economic development
(*d*) All of the above

158. The 'Petition of Right', the 'Bill of Rights', the 'Act of Settlement', the 'Parliament Act of 1911' are associated with :
(*a*) English Constitution
(*b*) American Constitution
(*c*) French Constitution
(*d*) Canadian Constitution

159. In the constitutional-political history of the United States, the political parties made their maiden appearance in the year :
(*a*) 1800 (*b*) 1866
(*c*) 1796 (*d*) 1789

160. Who made the observation that "If the constitution consists of institutions and not of the paper that describes them, the British constitution has not been made but has grown and there is no paper"?

(*a*) James Bryce
(*b*) Ivor Jennings
(*c*) Lord Hewart
(*d*) None of the above

161. The work studies in History and Jurisprudence is authored by :
(*a*) James Bryce
(*b*) H.J. Laski
(*c*) R.N. Gilchrist
(*d*) None of the above

162. Who among the following has compared the amending process of a constitution with the safety valve of an engine?
(*a*) Garner   (*b*) Gilchrist
(*c*) Gettell   (*d*) None of the above

163. The term 'New Deal' is associated with :
(*a*) Franklin Madison
(*b*) James Jackson
(*c*) Andrew Jackson
(*d*) Theodore Roosevelt

164. They are of the opinion that England has no constitution. One declares that, "where a constitution cannot be produced in a visible form, there is none". The other says that in "England the constitution may go on changing continually or rather it does not exist". The two scholars respectively are :
(*a*) Burke and Mill
(*b*) Thomas Paine and Henry Maine
(*c*) Thomas Paine and De Tocqueville
(*d*) None of the above

165. Of the following, which is the features of the British Constitution?
(*a*) Parliamentary Supremacy
(*b*) Two Party System
(*c*) Hereditary Character
(*d*) All the above

166. It has been opined that without them, the British constitution is like a skeleton without blood and flesh. They are :
(*a*) Works of eminent jurists
(*b*) Conventions
(*c*) Statutes
(*d*) All of the above

167. Which of the following amendments to the American constitution granted suffrage to women?
(*a*) 14th amendment (1868)
(*b*) 15th amendment (1870)
(*c*) 19th amendment (1920)
(*d*) 21st amendment (1933)

168. Who was the first to suggest a new scheme of the classification of constitutions into flexible and rigid?
(*a*) E.M. Sait
(*b*) James Bryce
(*c*) K.C. Wheare
(*d*) None of the above

169. The British North America Act of 1867 determined the constitution of :
(*a*) Mexico   (*b*) U.S.A.
(*c*) Canada   (*d*) Alaska

170. The era of constitutionalism is said to have been heralded by :
(*a*) The British Constitution
(*b*) The Russian Constitution
(*c*) The American Constitution
(*d*) The French Constitution

171. A constitution is eminently desirable to :
(*a*) Curb the powers of governments by a fundamental law
(*b*) Restrain the government on behalf of the individual
(*c*) Limit the vagaries of present and future generation
(*d*) All of the above

172. In England the membership of the House of Commons and the House of Lords respectively is :
(*a*) 450 and 775   (*b*) 500 and 650
(*c*) 355 and 900   (*d*) 650 and 805

173. Who among the following hold the opinion that an unwritten constitution "is suitable to a people who have a strong sense of tradition and a profoundly conservative spirit"?
(*a*) Esmein   (*b*) Judge Jameson
(*c*) Judge Story   (*d*) Both (*a*) and (*b*)

174. Match List I (Scholars) with List II (Works) and select the correct answer from the codes given below the lists :

List I		List II
A. A.L. Lowell	1.	The statute of westminster
B. H. Finer	2.	The Government of England
C. K.C. Wheare	3.	Studies in Jurisprudence
D. J. Bryce	4.	The Theory and practice of modern Government

Codes :

	A	B	C	D
(*a*)	4	2	3	1
(*b*)	2	1	4	3
(*c*)	2	4	3	1
(*d*)	2	4	1	3

175. That the constitution grow instead of being made is the dictum of :
(*a*) Ivor Jennings
(*b*) Sir James MacIntosh
(*c*) Herman Finer
(*d*) None of the above

176. The working of the Cabinet Government in U.K. is based upon :
(*a*) Parliamentary laws
(*b*) Constitution
(*c*) Well-established customs and usages
(*d*) All of the above

177. Who observed that the classification of constitutions into written and unwritten should be discarded and the better distinction can be made between countries which have a written constitution and those which have no written constitution?
(*a*) Finer
(*b*) Bryce
(*c*) Laski
(*d*) Wheare

178. The often-quoted observation about the American constitutional system that, "we are under the constitution but the constitution is what judges say it is", is mady by :
(*a*) Chief Justice Marshall
(*b*) Herman Finer
(*c*) Chief Justice Hughes
(*d*) Theodore Roosevelt

179. The constitution of the United States is represented as the best type of a written constitution. Still, much of it, in practice has come to be unwritten and in legal terms extra – constitutional, the most notable example of which is :
(*a*) Growth of Political parties
(*b*) Working of the Senate
(*c*) Judicial review
(*d*) All of the above

180. The work 'American Government in Action' is authored by—
(*a*) H.J. Laski   (*b*) M.E. Dimock
(*c*) W.B. Munro   (*d*) A.L. Lowell

181. How many states ratified the present constitution of the United States of America which was adopted at the philadelphia convention in 1787 and which came into force in 1789?
(*a*) 8   (*b*) 9
(*c*) 10   (*d*) 11

182. The constitution of the United States of America is regarded as one of the briefest constitutions in the world. Originally it consisted of how many articles?
(*a*) 7   (*b*) 8
(*c*) 9   (*d*) 10

183. The constitution of the United States of America presents a classic example of rigid variety of constitutions. While the constitution of India has undergone more than hundreds amendments during its history of 70 years, how many amendments have been effected on the U.S. constitution?
(*a*) 26   (*b*) 32
(*c*) 17   (*d*) 49

184. Who has commented on the U.S. constitution that – "yet, after all deductions, it ranks above every other written constitution for the intrinsic excellence of its scheme, its adaptation to the circumstances of the people, its simplicity and precision of language, its judicious mixture of definiteness in principle with elasticity in details"?

(*a*) Dicey
(*b*) Laski
(*c*) Bryce
(*d*) None of the above

185. The Work 'Essentials of American Government' is authored by :
(*a*) F.A. Ogg
(*b*) A.V. Dicey
(*c*) F.O. Ray
(*d*) Both (*a*) and (*c*)

186. Match List I (English Charters) with List II (Years) and select the correct answer from the codes given below the lists :

List I	List II
A. Magna Carta	1. 1701
B. Petition of Rights	2. 1215
C. Act of Settlement	3. 1707
D. Act of Union with Scotland	4. 1628

Codes :

	A	B	C	D
(*a*)	3	4	2	1
(*b*)	2	4	1	3
(*c*)	4	3	1	2
(*d*)	4	3	2	1

187. Who among the following has termed the British constitution as a judge-made constitution?
(*a*) Lowell
(*b*) Seeley
(*c*) Dicey
(*d*) None of the above

188. The work 'English Government and politics' is authored by :
(*a*) Anson
(*b*) Dicey
(*c*) Ogg
(*d*) None of the above

189. Who among the following strongly defended the existence of the British constitution?
(*a*) Edmund Burke
(*b*) Thomas Paine
(*c*) Harold Laski
(*d*) All of these

190. It made the parliament the supreme law-making body and declared that it should be called regularly. It also provided a list of individual rights. It was passed in 1689. It is called :

(*a*) Bill of Rights
(*b*) Petition of Rights
(*c*) Act of Settlements
(*d*) None of the above

191. The work 'Politics and Government in U.S.' is authored by :
(*a*) David Truman
(*b*) Bill Clinton
(*c*) Redford Truman
(*d*) Both (*a*) and (*c*)

192. The book 'The Government of United States' is authored by :
(*a*) Harold Laski
(*b*) James Bryce
(*c*) W.B. Munro
(*d*) None of the above

193. The remark that ------ "The President of the United States is both more or less than a King, he is both more or less than a Prime Minister, The more carefully his office is studied the more does its unique character appear" ------ is made by :
(*a*) Abraham Lincoln
(*b*) Laski
(*c*) George Washington
(*d*) Bryce

194. Who among the following propounded the doctrine of separation of powers?
(*a*) Dicey
(*b*) Ogg and Zink
(*c*) Ivor Jennings
(*d*) Montesquieu

195. The works 'The American Presidency and the American President' have been authored by :
(*a*) Harold Laski
(*b*) Harold Laski and Haymen Sindney respectively
(*c*) O. Johnson Aludius
(*d*) O. Johnson Aludius and Harold Laski respectively

196. Which among the following put a stop to the spoils system in the United States of America?
(*a*) Pendleton Act
(*b*) Gerrymandering
(*c*) 26th Constitutional Amendment
(*d*) None of the above

197. Which of the following institutions in the United States has been termed as 'a continuous constitutional convention'?
(*a*) Senate   (*b*) Congress
(*c*) Presidency   (*d*) Supreme Court

198. Cabinet is an extra-constitutional institution in the United States of America. It was brought into existence by :
(*a*) Abraham Lincoln
(*b*) George Washington
(*c*) Ronald Reagan
(*d*) None of the above

199. General de Gaulle was the first President of the fifth Republic. Who was the first premier?
(*a*) Delere
(*b*) Mabley
(*c*) Diderot
(*d*) None of the above

200. How many constitutions have made appearance in France since the French Revolution of 1789?
(*a*) 10   (*b*) 13
(*c*) 17   (*d*) 21

201. The work 'The Fifth French Republic' is authored by :
(*a*) Dorothy Pickles
(*b*) S.E. Finer
(*c*) Neumann
(*d*) None of the above

202. Which of the following articles of the constitution of the Fifth Republic declare France as an indivisible, secular, democratic and social Republic?
(*a*) Article 1   (*b*) Article 2
(*c*) Article 3   (*d*) Article 4

203. In China, the constitution of 1954 remained in force till :
(*a*) 1974   (*b*) 1977
(*c*) 1978   (*d*) 1981

204. China has been under the governance of the Communist Party since :
(*a*) 1948   (*b*) 1949
(*c*) 1950   (*d*) 1951

205. Which dynasty's rule in China is said to be a period of glory and also degradation for China?
(*a*) Ching dynasty   (*b*) Manchu dynasty
(*c*) Ming dynasty   (*d*) Sung dynasty

206. Presently China is governed according to the constitution of :
(*a*) 1975
(*b*) 1978
(*c*) 1982
(*d*) None of the above

207. Which of the following articles of the constitution of Fifth Republic of French provide for revision?
(*a*) Article 1   (*b*) Article 25
(*c*) Article 89   (*d*) Article 91

208. The government system of people's Republic of China can be said to be :
(*a*) Authoritarian
(*b*) Totalitarian
(*c*) Dictatorial
(*d*) None of the above

209. "The constitution of the fifth Republic is tailor-made for "General de Gaulle".
The above statement is made by :
(*a*) Michel Delere
(*b*) Herman Finer
(*c*) Dorothy Pickles
(*d*) None of the above

210. Which of the constitutional documents is regarded as 'the worst drafted in French constitutional history'?
(*a*) Constitution of the Fifth Republic
(*b*) Constitution of the Fourth Republic
(*c*) Constitution of the Third Republic
(*d*) Constitution of the Second Republic

211. "There lies a sleeping giant. Let it sleep for when he wakes he will shake the world". Who made the above statement about China?
(*a*) Hitler   (*b*) Mussolini
(*c*) Napoleon   (*d*) Mark Twain

212. During the cold war period China had ideological differences mainly with :

(*a*) United States of America
(*b*) North Korea
(*c*) Union of Soviet Socialist Republic
(*d*) All of these

213. The period of which dynasty is called the golden period in China's history of art, philosophy and prosperity?
(*a*) Tang dynasty
(*b*) Sui dynasty
(*c*) Sung dynasty
(*d*) None of the above

214. When did the National People's Congress adopt the draft constitution of China?
(*a*) November 30, 1953
(*b*) January 1, 1952
(*c*) September 20, 1954
(*d*) None of the above

215. In which year did the constitutional framework, engineered and adopted in early 1950s, undergo a radical change?
(*a*) 1977   (*b*) 1978
(*c*) 1987   (*d*) 1988

216. 'Bundesprasident' is :
(*a*) Head of the Land
(*b*) Head of the German State
(*c*) Head of the German Judiciary
(*d*) None of the above

217. Which of the following are among the most important principles of the German State as set out in the Basic law?
(*a*) Democracy   (*b*) Republicanism
(*c*) Both (*a*) and (*b*)   (*d*) Judicial Review

218. After the capitulation of the German army at the end of the World War II, Germany was divided into several zones, each of which was governed by one of the allied forces. In all how many zones were created?
(*a*) Four   (*b*) Five
(*c*) Six   (*d*) Seven

219. In Germany, the terms 'Bundestag' and 'Bundesregierung' refer to :
(*a*) Federal Council and Parliament
(*b*) Federal Parliament and Federal Government

(*c*) Federal Chancellor and Federal Council
(*d*) None of the above

220. Which among the following introduced in Germany the political system of a parliamentary federal republic?
(*a*) Constitution of 1848
(*b*) Constitution of 1871
(*c*) Weimar Constitution
(*d*) None of the above

221. In 1871 the German Reich was established under :
(*a*) Bismarck   (*b*) Garibaldi
(*c*) Kafka   (*d*) Hegel

222. First important German constitution was the German Reich constitution drafted as a result of :
(*a*) First World War, 1914-1918
(*b*) Revolution of 1848
(*c*) Rise of Hitler during the inter-war period
(*d*) None of the above

223. Under the constitution of 1982, the Prime Minister of China can hold office for a maximum two terms. This amounts to a total duration of :
(*a*) 8 years   (*b*) 9 years
(*c*) 10 years   (*d*) 11 years

224. Which of the following articles of the German constitution defines Germany as a democratic state and states that all state authority emanates from the people and is to be exercised by means of elections and voting?
(*a*) Article 20   (*b*) Article 30
(*c*) Article 31   (*d*) Article 40

225. Which article of the Chinese constitution of 1954 refers to the determination of the people's Republic to ensure the gradual abolition of systems of exploitation and the building up of a socialist society?
(*a*) Article 1   (*b*) Article 2
(*c*) Article 3   (*d*) Article 4

226. How many articles does the Chinese constitution of 1982 consist of?
(*a*) 103   (*b*) 203
(*c*) 303   (*d*) 30

227. Administratively, China is divided into how many provinces and autonomous regions?
(*a*) 21 and 5 respectively
(*b*) 10 and 20 respectively
(*c*) 30 and 2 respectively
(*d*) None of the above

228. Chinese constitution of 1982 says that all power in China belong to the people. It is exercised through :
(*a*) National People's Congress
(*b*) Provincial People's Congress
(*c*) Local People's Congress
(*d*) Both (*a*) and (*c*)

229. The real executive authority in China vests in :
(*a*) President
(*b*) Prime Minister
(*c*) State Council headed by the Prime Minister
(*d*) National People Congress

230. Which of the following constitutions reiterate Chinese faith, inter alia, in the five principles of 'panchsheel'?
(*a*) Constitution of 1954
(*b*) Constitution of 1975
(*c*) Constitution of 1978
(*d*) Constitution of 1982

231. In the constitution of 1954, the fundamental rights of the Chinese people were enumerated in :
(*a*) Chapter I   (*b*) Chapter II
(*c*) Chapter III   (*d*) Chapter IV

232. In which year did the Allied powers who were in occupation of the western part of Germany made provisions to convene a constitutional assembly to draft a constitution?
(*a*) 1947   (*b*) 1948
(*c*) 1949   (*d*) 1950

233. The German term 'Abgeordnete' refers to :
(*a*) Deputy Federal Chancellor
(*b*) Elected representatives of the Bundestag
(*c*) Governor of the Lander
(*d*) None of the above

234. The interim constitution of the Republic of South Africa was ratified on 22 December, 1993 and officially came into effect on :
(*a*) 1 January, 1994   (*b*) 22 January, 1995
(*c*) 27 April, 1994   (*d*) 27 April, 1995

235. The membership of the National Assembly of the Republic of South Africa is :
(*a*) 350
(*b*) 400
(*c*) Between 350 and 400
(*d*) None of the above

236. How many ministers can be there at the most in the cabinet of the Republic of South Africa?
(*a*) 25   (*b*) 27
(*c*) 35   (*d*) 37

237. How many terms a person, can hold office of the president of the Republic?
(*a*) Two
(*b*) Three
(*c*) Four
(*d*) None of the above

238. How many members are there in the National Council of Provinces in South Africa?
(*a*) 80   (*b*) 90
(*c*) 100   (*d*) 150

239. The judicial authority of the Republic of South Africa is vested in :
(*a*) The Constitutional Court
(*b*) The Supreme Court of Appeal
(*c*) The High Courts and the Magistrates Courts
(*d*) All of the above

240. In the Republic of South Africa, cabinet decisions at the apex are :
(*a*) Essentially prerogative of the President
(*b*) Voted upon by members of the National Assembly
(*c*) Reached by consensus
(*d*) All of the above

241. The President of the Republic of South Africa may be removed by :
(*a*) An executive order by the deputy president made in consultation with the National Assembly

   (*b*) A motion of no-confidence
   (*c*) Impeachment
   (*d*) Both (*b*) and (*c*)

242. The constitutional Assembly which adopted the new constitution of the Republic of South Africa comprised of :
   (*a*) The National Assembly
   (*b*) The National Assembly and the Senate
   (*c*) The Senate
   (*d*) Council of state and the central legislature

243. To be entitled to proportional number of ministerial portfolios, what is the minimum Number of seats that a party must hold in the National Assembly?
   (*a*) 20
   (*b*) 30
   (*c*) 40
   (*d*) None of the above

244. Who among the following appointed Hitler as Chancellor or Head of the Government in Germany?
   (*a*) Kroger
   (*b*) Hindenburg
   (*c*) Katz
   (*d*) None of the above

245. Adolf Hitler became the Chancellor of the German state on :
   (*a*) 22 January, 1931
   (*b*) 15 January, 1932
   (*c*) 30 January, 1933
   (*d*) 31 December, 1934

246. In the Weimar constitution, the emphasis was on :
   (*a*) Federalism   (*b*) Centralisation
   (*c*) Fundamental law   (*d*) All of these

247. Which of the following rights have been granted by the constitution of 1954 in China?
   (*a*) Right to work
   (*b*) Right to rest and leisure
   (*c*) Right to education
   (*d*) All of the above

248. The preamble of the Chinese constitution declares China to be :
   (*a*) A multi – ethnic Federal State
   (*b*) A multi – national Unitary State
   (*c*) A multi – ethnic Unitary State
   (*d*) A Federation of Federations

249. Which Article of the Chinese constitution of 1982 provides for equality of nationalities?
   (*a*) Article 4   (*b*) Article 6
   (*c*) Article 8   (*d*) Article 30

250. The work 'The Governments of Europe' is authored by :
   (*a*) Ogg   (*b*) E.M. Sait
   (*c*) W.B. Munro   (*d*) W.R. Anson

ANSWERS

1	2	3	4	5	6	7	8	9	10
(*d*)	(*c*)	(*b*)	(*a*)	(*c*)	(*b*)	(*a*)	(*b*)	(*a*)	(*b*)
11	**12**	**13**	**14**	**15**	**16**	**17**	**18**	**19**	**20**
(*c*)	(*d*)	(*b*)	(*a*)	(*c*)	(*b*)	(*a*)	(*c*)	(*b*)	(*a*)
21	**22**	**23**	**24**	**25**	**26**	**27**	**28**	**29**	**30**
(*d*)	(*c*)	(*c*)	(*c*)	(*d*)	(*b*)	(*c*)	(*b*)	(*a*)	(*c*)
31	**32**	**33**	**34**	**35**	**36**	**37**	**38**	**39**	**40**
(*d*)	(*b*)	(*b*)	(*a*)	(*d*)	(*c*)	(*c*)	(*b*)	(*a*)	(*d*)
41	**42**	**43**	**44**	**45**	**46**	**47**	**48**	**49**	**50**
(*c*)	(*a*)	(*b*)	(*d*)	(*c*)	(*b*)	(*b*)	(*b*)	(*a*)	(*c*)

51	**52**	**53**	**54**	**55**	**56**	**57**	**58**	**59**	**60**
(*b*)	(*d*)	(*b*)	(*c*)	(*a*)	(*d*)	(*a*)	(*d*)	(*d*)	(*c*)
61	**62**	**63**	**64**	**65**	**66**	**67**	**68**	**69**	**70**
(*a*)	(*d*)	(*b*)	(*d*)	(*d*)	(*b*)	(*d*)	(*c*)	(*d*)	(*a*)
71	**72**	**73**	**74**	**75**	**76**	**77**	**78**	**79**	**80**
(*b*)	(*a*)	(*b*)	(*d*)	(*c*)	(*b*)	(*a*)	(*b*)	(*d*)	(*c*)
81	**82**	**83**	**84**	**85**	**86**	**87**	**88**	**89**	**90**
(*a*)	(*b*)	(*c*)	(*a*)	(*a*)	(*c*)	(*a*)	(*c*)	(*d*)	(*d*)
91	**92**	**93**	**94**	**95**	**96**	**97**	**98**	**99**	**100**
(*a*)	(*b*)	(*a*)	(*c*)	(*d*)	(*c*)	(*a*)	(*b*)	(*a*)	(*d*)
101	**102**	**103**	**104**	**105**	**106**	**107**	**108**	**109**	**110**
(*d*)	(*b*)	(*c*)	(*c*)	(*d*)	(*c*)	(*d*)	(*c*)	(*b*)	(*a*)
111	**112**	**113**	**114**	**115**	**116**	**117**	**118**	**119**	**120**
(*d*)	(*d*)	(*a*)	(*c*)	(*c*)	(*b*)	(*a*)	(*c*)	(*a*)	(*b*)
121	**122**	**123**	**124**	**125**	**126**	**127**	**128**	**129**	**130**
(*a*)	(*d*)	(*d*)	(*a*)	(*c*)	(*b*)	(*c*)	(*a*)	(*d*)	(*d*)
131	**132**	**133**	**134**	**135**	**136**	**137**	**138**	**139**	**140**
(*a*)	(*b*)	(*c*)	(*a*)	(*c*)	(*d*)	(*c*)	(*d*)	(*d*)	(*c*)
141	**142**	**143**	**144**	**145**	**146**	**147**	**148**	**149**	**150**
(*b*)	(*d*)	(*d*)	(*c*)	(*a*)	(*c*)	(*c*)	(*b*)	(*c*)	(*a*)
151	**152**	**153**	**154**	**155**	**156**	**157**	**158**	**159**	**160**
(*a*)	(*c*)	(*b*)	(*c*)	(*a*)	(*b*)	(*d*)	(*a*)	(*c*)	(*b*)
161	**162**	**163**	**164**	**165**	**166**	**167**	**168**	**169**	**170**
(*a*)	(*c*)	(*a*)	(*c*)	(*d*)	(*b*)	(*c*)	(*b*)	(*c*)	(*c*)
171	**172**	**173**	**174**	**175**	**176**	**177**	**178**	**179**	**180**
(*d*)	(*d*)	(*d*)	(*d*)	(*b*)	(*c*)	(*d*)	(*c*)	(*a*)	(*b*)
181	**182**	**183**	**184**	**185**	**186**	**187**	**188**	**189**	**190**
(*b*)	(*a*)	(*a*)	(*c*)	(*d*)	(*b*)	(*c*)	(*c*)	(*a*)	(*a*)
191	**192**	**193**	**194**	**195**	**196**	**197**	**198**	**199**	**200**
(*c*)	(*c*)	(*b*)	(*d*)	(*b*)	(*a*)	(*d*)	(*b*)	(*a*)	(*b*)
201	**202**	**203**	**204**	**205**	**206**	**207**	**208**	**209**	**210**
(*a*)	(*b*)	(*a*)	(*b*)	(*b*)	(*c*)	(*c*)	(*b*)	(*c*)	(*a*)
211	**212**	**213**	**214**	**215**	**216**	**217**	**218**	**219**	**220**
(*c*)	(*c*)	(*c*)	(*c*)	(*b*)	(*b*)	(*c*)	(*a*)	(*b*)	(*c*)
221	**222**	**223**	**224**	**225**	**226**	**227**	**228**	**229**	**230**
(*a*)	(*b*)	(*c*)	(*a*)	(*d*)	(*a*)	(*a*)	(*d*)	(*c*)	(*d*)
231	**232**	**233**	**234**	**235**	**236**	**237**	**238**	**239**	**240**
(*c*)	(*b*)	(*b*)	(*c*)	(*c*)	(*b*)	(*a*)	(*b*)	(*d*)	(*c*)
241	**242**	**243**	**244**	**245**	**246**	**247**	**248**	**249**	**250**
(*d*)	(*b*)	(*a*)	(*b*)	(*c*)	(*b*)	(*d*)	(*b*)	(*a*)	(*c*)

4

CONSTITUENT ASSEMBLY

1. A special session of the Constituent Assembly was held at midnight on 14-15 August 1947 in connection with the :
   - (a) Independence resolution
   - (b) Partition of India
   - (c) Transfer of Power
   - (d) None of the above

2. Which committee was appointed to prepare guidelines for the Constituent Assembly?
   - (a) Drafting committee
   - (b) Congress Expert Committee
   - (c) Advisory Committee
   - (d) Union powers Committee

3. The elections to the Constituent Assembly were :
   - (a) Indirect
   - (b) Held twice
   - (c) Direct
   - (d) None of the above

4. Members of the Constituent Assembly were elected by the elected members of the :
   - (a) Legislative Councils
   - (b) Parliament
   - (c) Legislative Assemblies of the provinces
   - (d) All of the above

5. Who described Constituent Assembly as "a body of Hindus" in the House of Lords?
   - (a) Churchill
   - (b) V. Simon
   - (c) Mountbatten
   - (d) Attlee

6. Who Labelled the Drafting Committee as a drifting Committee?
   - (a) Jinnah
   - (b) Kunzru
   - (c) Naziruddin Ahmed
   - (d) Jayakar

7. The demand for the establishment of a Constituent Assembly was first embodied in a resolution of the Indian National Congress passed at its Faizpur session on :
   - (a) December 8, 1936
   - (b) July 5,1938
   - (c) January 2, 1936
   - (d) August 4, 1936

8. Which committee was set up to prepare a draft constitution on August 29, 1947?
   - (a) Staff Committee
   - (b) Union Constitution Committee
   - (c) Drafting Committee
   - (d) Union powers committee

9. The constitution-making body was not in Fact a...body.
   - (a) Democratic
   - (b) Legal
   - (c) Temporary
   - (d) Sovereign

10. One of the earliest demands for Constituent Assembly was by the :
    - (a) Cripps Mission
    - (b) Nehru Report
    - (c) Cabinet Mission
    - (d) Simon Commission

11. The elections to the Constituent Assembly were held in :
    - (a) June 1946
    - (b) July 1946
    - (c) August 1946
    - (d) July 1947

12. Who acted as president of the Constituent Assembly on 9 December, 1946?
    - (a) Rajendra Prasad
    - (b) Sardar Patel
    - (c) Sachidanand Sinha
    - (d) K.M. Munshi

13. Which of the following is included in the Committees on procedural Affairs?

(*a*) Training and staff committee
(*b*) Credentials committee
(*c*) Hindi Translation Committee
(*d*) All of the above

14. Which of the following resolutions forms the basis of the new constitution passed in second plenary session?
(*a*) Objective Resolution
(*b*) Independence Resolution
(*c*) August Resolution
(*d*) None of the above

15. Which of the following is one of the main principles of the objectives Resolution?
(*a*) To frame a constitution which should secure for India, a due place in the comity of nations.
(*b*) That India is to be an independent, sovereign, republic
(*c*) That India is to be a democratic union with an equal level of self- government in all the constituent parts.
(*d*) All of the above

16. Which of the following is included in the Committees on Substantive Affairs?
(*a*) Union powers committee
(*b*) Drafting committee
(*c*) Advisory committee on minorities
(*d*) All of the above

17. The Constituent Assembly had a total of more than...Committees with a membership of greater than eighty individuals.
(*a*) Sixteen   (*b*) Twenty
(*c*) Fifteen   (*d*) Thirteen

18. Sir Krishnaswami Ayyangar, K.M. Munshi, B.L. Mittar, Saiyad Mohammed Sadulla were the members of the :
(*a*) Advisory committee
(*b*) Drafting committee
(*c*) Union powers committee
(*d*) Committee on minorities

19. Which of the following is a criticism of the Constituent Assembly?
(*a*) Congress Domination
(*b*) An unrepresentative Body

(*c*) Dominated by the legal Luminaries
(*d*) All of the abaove

20. The total number of seats fixed in the proposed Constituent Assembly for British India, Chief Commissioner's provinces, and the Indian states respectively are :
(*a*) 290, 6 and 93 seats
(*b*) 280, 16 and 93 seats
(*c*) 292, 4 and 93 seats
(*d*) 292, 7 and 90 seats

21. Who said that the father of the Indian Constitution conceived of a Constituent Assembly as something dynamic, not merely a body of representatives but "a nation on the move"?
(*a*) Ivor Jennings   (*b*) J.L. Nehru
(*c*) Sardar Patel   (*d*) B.R. Ambedkar

22. Who referred to the philadelphia convention, the French experiment and the Russian revolution as sources of inspiration?
(*a*) Rajendra Prasad
(*b*) Jawahar Lal Nehru
(*c*) Sardar Patel
(*d*) B.R. Ambedkar

23. Which of the following is a representative body chosen for the purpose of considering and either adopting or proposing a new constitution or changes in the existing constitution?
(*a*) Legislative
(*b*) Cabinet
(*c*) Election Commission
(*d*) Constitutent Assembly

24. The modern concept of Constituent Assembly is a/an...political contribution to the science of government.
(*a*) Eastern   (*b*) Southern
(*c*) Western   (*d*) Northern

25. Whose idea of the general will influenced the rise of the concept of Constitutional Government?
(*a*) Laski's   (*b*) Mill's
(*c*) Rousseau's   (*d*) MacIver's

26. The earliest Constituent Assemblies the philadelphia convention of 1787, which framed the constitution of the USA, and the National Assembly of France were the products of...and registered a break with the past.
 (*a*) Evolution　　(*b*) Revolutions
 (*c*) Revivalism　　(*d*) None of the above

27. The demand for a Constituent Assembly was for the first time authoritatively conceded by the British Government, though in an indirect way and with important reservations,in what is known as the :
 (*a*) August offer, 1940
 (*b*) Cripps mission, 1942
 (*c*) Cabinet mission, 1946
 (*d*) Quit India movement, 1942

28. "The Constituent Assembly declares its firm and solemn resolve the proclaim India as an Independent sovereign Republic and to draw up for her future governance a constitution". This statement is related to :
 (*a*) Independence Resolution
 (*b*) August Resolution
 (*c*) Cabinet Resolution
 (*d*) Objectives Resolution

29. Which of the following is one of the features of the working process of the Constituent Assembly, according to G. Austin?
 (*a*) Decision-making by consensus
 (*b*) The principle of Accommodation
 (*c*) The act of selection and modification
 (*d*) All of the above

30. Which of the following proposal were recommended by the Cabinet mission during its stay in India?
 (*a*) To form a Constituent Assembly
 (*b*) To form an interim government
 (*c*) To introduce adult Franchise
 (*d*) To form an Estimates Committee
 Choose the correct answer using the codes given below :
 (*a*) 1 and 2　　(*b*) 2 and 4
 (*c*) 1, 2 and 3　　(*d*) 3 and 4

31. The demand for a Constituent Assembly was for the first time authoritatively conceded by the British Government, though in an indirect way, through :
 (*a*) Shimla Conference
 (*b*) August Offer
 (*c*) Wavell Plan
 (*d*) None of the above

32. Broadly, the duration during which the Constituent Assembly drafted the constitution for India was :
 (*a*) December 1945 to December 1949
 (*b*) December 1946 to December 1949
 (*c*) November 1946 to January 1949
 (*d*) November 1947 to January 1950

33. Over how many sessions the Constituent Assembly drafted the Constitution for India?
 (*a*) 11　　(*b*) 12
 (*c*) 13　　(*d*) 14

34. While drafting the Constitution for India how many days of actual work was undertaken by the Constituent Assembly?
 (*a*) 900 days　　(*b*) 200 days
 (*c*) 188 days　　(*d*) 165 days

35. How many Articles and schedules were there in the draft Constitution?
 (*a*) 355 Articles and 8 schedules
 (*b*) 315 Articles and 13 schedules
 (*c*) 295 Articles and 13 schedules
 (*d*) None of the above

36. First attempt by Indians to frame a constitution of their country was in the form of :
 (*a*) Round Table conference
 (*b*) Nehru Report
 (*c*) Macdonald Award
 (*d*) Government of India Act, 1919

37. The elections to the Constituent Assembly were :
 (*a*) Indirect
 (*b*) Held Twice
 (*c*) Direct
 (*d*) None of the above

38. The Nehru committee was appointed and the Nehru Report was submitted respectively on :

(*a*) May 19, 1928 and 10 August, 1928
(*b*) May 19, 1928 and 10 August, 1929
(*c*) May 19, 1927 and 10 August, 1928
(*d*) June 1, 1929 and August 31, 1929

39. Jawaharlal Nehru's proposal of a Constituent Assembly was for the first time formally accepted by the Congress in the year :
(*a*) 1934 (*b*) 1935
(*c*) 1936 (*d*) 1937

40. Which of the following most influenced the Constitution of India?
(*a*) Government of India Act, 1919
(*b*) Indian Independence Act, 1947
(*c*) Government of India Act, 1935
(*d*) All of the above

41. Fundamental duties have been introduced in the Constitution by :
(*a*) 42nd Amendment Act, 1976
(*b*) 44th Amendment Act, 1978
(*c*) 73rd Amendment Act, 1993
(*d*) None of the above

42. The Dominion status of India was established under :
(*a*) Government of India Act, 1919
(*b*) Government of India Act, 1935
(*c*) Both (*a*) and (*b*)
(*d*) Indian Independence Act, 1947

43. Parts XVII, XVI and XVIII of the constitution of India are related respectively to :
(*a*) Official language, SCs, STs and OBCs and Emergency provisions
(*b*) SCs, STs and OBCs, official language and Emergency provisions
(*c*) SCs, STs and OBCs, emergency provisions and official language
(*d*) None of the above

44. The work 'Constituent Assemblies of the World' is authored by :
(*a*) Subhash Kashyap
(*b*) T.S. Venkataraman
(*c*) Pattabhi Sitaramaiyya
(*d*) None of the above

45. Which of the following is one of the features of the working process of the Constituent Assembly, according to Granville Austin?
(*a*) Decison-making by consensus
(*b*) The principle of Accomodation
(*c*) The act of selection and modification
(*d*) All of the above

46. 'Politbureau is a term associated with—
(*a*) Communist Party
(*b*) Samajwadi Party
(*c*) Congress Party
(*d*) Bhartiya Janta Party

47. The Constitution of India superimposes an elected president upon the parliamentary system of responsible government. Another constitution which prescribes a similar governmental pattern is :
(*a*) The Constitution of France
(*b*) The Constitution of Germany
(*c*) The Constitution of Eire
(*d*) All of the above

48. Article 51 A which constitutes the part IVA of the constitution of India and which contain the fundamental duties was introduced in the constitution in the year :
(*a*) 1976 (*b*) 1977
(*c*) 1978 (*d*) 1979

49. Which of the following need to be considered to have a full view of the law of citizenship in India?
(*a*) The citizenship Act, 1955
(*b*) Articles 5, 6, 7 and 8
(*c*) Article 11
(*d*) All of the above

50. Protection of Civil Rights Act, 1955 pertains to :
(*a*) Human rights
(*b*) Citizenship
(*c*) Untouchability
(*d*) Freedom of expression

51. Which of the following articles made a mention of the sueability of the state :
(*a*) Article 100 (*b*) Article 200
(*c*) Article 300 (*d*) All of these

52. Prior to Independence the territory of India was divided into :
   (*a*) 9 Governor's provinces, 600 states and some Centrally Administered areas
   (*b*) 12 Governor's provinces, 552 states and 15 centrally Administered areas
   (*c*) 6 Governor's provinces, 562 states and 2 centrally Administrated areas
   (*d*) 552 provinces, 12 states and 10 centrally Administered Areas.

53. For preparing the draft, who was the advisor of the constituent Assembly?
   (*a*) B.N. Rao
   (*b*) B.R. Ambedkar
   (*c*) K.M. Munshi
   (*d*) J.L. Nehru

54. For the consitituent Assembly, who was the chairman of the steering Committee?
   (*a*) B.N. Rao
   (*b*) B.R. Ambedkar
   (*c*) K.M. Munshi
   (*d*) J.L. Nehru

ANSWERS

1	2	3	4	5	6	7	8	9	10
(*c*)	(*b*)	(*a*)	(*c*)	(*b*)	(*c*)	(*a*)	(*c*)	(*d*)	(*b*)
11	12	13	14	15	16	17	18	19	20
(*b*)	(*c*)	(*d*)	(*a*)	(*d*)	(*d*)	(*c*)	(*b*)	(*d*)	(*c*)
21	22	23	24	25	26	27	28	29	30
(*b*)	(*b*)	(*d*)	(*c*)	(*c*)	(*b*)	(*a*)	(*d*)	(*d*)	(*a*)
31	32	33	34	35	36	37	38	39	40
(*b*)	(*b*)	(*a*)	(*d*)	(*b*)	(*b*)	(*a*)	(*a*)	(*a*)	(*c*)
41	42	43	44	45	46	47	48	49	50
(*a*)	(*d*)	(*c*)	(*b*)	(*d*)	(*a*)	(*c*)	(*a*)	(*d*)	(*c*)
51	52	53	54						
(*c*)	(*a*)	(*a*)	(*c*)						

5

NATURE OF INDIAN FEDERALISM

1. One of the most important forms of regionalism is :
   (a) Political consciousness
   (b) Demand for decentralisation
   (c) Linguism
   (d) None of the above

2. The existence of inter-state boundary and water disputes is also a manifestation of :
   (a) Regionalism   (b) Linguism
   (c) Racism   (d) Individualism

3. Which of the following is one of the forms of regionalism?
   (a) Demand for state autonomy
   (b) Demand for a full statehood
   (c) Demand for Intra-regional autonomy within states
   (d) All of the above

4. Which of the following theories is another form of regionalism?
   (a) Liberal theory
   (b) Marxist theory
   (c) 'Sons of soil' theory
   (d) Regional theory

5. Special provisions regarding Jammu and Kashmir, Nagaland, Sikkim clearly accept the principle of :
   (a) Separatist theory
   (b) 'Sons of soil' theory
   (c) Regional theory
   (d) None of the above

6. ------ movements in some states is an extreme form of regionalism.
   (a) Cultural
   (b) Secessionist
   (c) National

   (d) None of these

7. Each zonal council has as its chairman the ------ of India.
   (a) Finance Minister
   (b) Prime Minister
   (c) Home Minister
   (d) None of the above

8. Which of the following implies an agreement between two or more communities which as between themselves are independent and autonomous?
   (a) Federation   (b) Protectorate
   (c) Coalition   (d) Detente

9. In which of the following countries the residuary powers are assigned to the Federating units?
   (a) United States   (b) Australia
   (c) Switzerland   (d) All of these

10. The control theme of the criticism levelled before the sarkaria commission against the working of union-state legislative relations is :
    (a) Centralisation
    (b) Decentralisation
    (c) Over-centralisation
    (d) Unequal treatment of states

11. Who stated that "the administrative autonomy of the states is almost equal to the administrative autonomy of centre"?
    (a) Pylee   (b) Santhanam
    (c) White   (d) Brecher

12. The states Reorganisation Act of 1956 grouped the states into------ zonal councils.
    (a) Five   (b) Three
    (c) Four   (d) Six

13. Which of the following commissions stated that Federalism is more a functional arrangement for co-operative action, than a static institutional concept?
(*a*) Rajamannar Commission
(*b*) Finance Commission
(*c*) Sarkaria Commission
(*d*) None of the above

14. Who among the following is responsible for the maintenance of audit of union and state accounts?
(*a*) The Attorney-General
(*b*) The Comptroller and Auditor-General
(*c*) The Secretary General
(*d*) None of the above

15. In which of the following countries, the residuary powers are vested in the union?
(*a*) India
(*b*) Canada
(*c*) Switzerland
(*d*) Both (*a*) and (*b*)

16. Federalism as a political theory is based on the principles of------ and ------.
(*a*) Equality, egalitarianism
(*b*) Relativity, empiricism
(*c*) Legality, elitism
(*d*) Nationality, collectivism

17. Who among the following said that decentralisation and lack of cohesion in the party system is the natural outcome of the structural fact of Federalism?
(*a*) D.B. Truman
(*b*) K.C. Wheare
(*c*) M.J. Vile
(*d*) Myron Weiner

18. The erosion of state autonomy can be observed in which of the following spheres?
(*a*) President's rule
(*b*) Appointment of Governors
(*c*) President's assent to state Bills
(*d*) All of the above

19. The term 'Federal' is derived from the Latin word 'Foedus' which means :
(*a*) Separation
(*b*) Distribution
(*c*) Covenant
(*d*) None of the above

20. Who defines Federalism as a union of groups that may be union of states or communities such as political parties, trade unions, etc?
(*a*) Wheare
(*b*) Friedrich
(*c*) Laski
(*d*) Bombwall

21. Which of the following constitutions is Federal in its formulations but operated in a unitary style?
(*a*) Brazil
(*b*) Argentina
(*c*) Venezuela
(*d*) All of these

22. The United States confers residuary powers on the :
(*a*) Centre
(*b*) States
(*c*) Both (*a*) and (*b*)
(*d*) Supreme Court

23. Which of the following Federations influenced the founding father of the Indian constitution?
(*a*) American Federation
(*b*) Canadian Federation
(*c*) Australian Federation
(*d*) All of the above

24. Which of the following is one of the approaches to the study of Indian Federal System?
(*a*) Historical approach
(*b*) Institutional approach
(*c*) Legal approach
(*d*) All of the above

25. Which model of Federalism is prevalent in the newly independent countries of Asia and Africa?
(*a*) Operative Federalism
(*b*) Unitarian Federalism
(*c*) Bargaining Federalism
(*d*) Co-operative Federalism

26. Which of the following is not a Federal feature of the Indian Constitution?
(*a*) Written Constitution
(*b*) Independent Judiciary
(*c*) Rigid Constitution
(*d*) Single Citizenship

27. Which commission has examined the process of economic planning in the context of union-state relations?
(*a*) Sarkaria Commission
(*b*) Administrative Reforms Commission

(*c*) Planning Commission
(*d*) None of the above

28. Which of the following committees was appointed in 1971 to review the Federal structure under the retired Chief Justice of the High Court?
(*a*) Santhanam Committee
(*b*) Financial Committee
(*c*) Rajamannar Committee
(*d*) None of the above

29. Which among the following refers to ties which bind the people of a particular country into one unified relationship?
(*a*) Nation
(*b*) National integration
(*c*) Citizenship
(*d*) Unionism

30. Which of the following was the first linguistic state in India, formed in 1953?
(*a*) Andhra Pradesh (*b*) Goa
(*c*) Punjab (*d*) Haryana

31. Which of the following is a defined territorial unit including particular language or languages, jatis, ethnic groups or tribes, particular social setting and cultural pattern, Folk dance, music, folk arts, etc?
(*a*) Area
(*b*) Region
(*c*) Village
(*d*) All of the above

32. Which of the following commission was appointed in 1953 in order to reorganise the states on linguistic grounds?
(*a*) State Reorganisation commission
(*b*) Linguistic Commission
(*c*) Fazal Ali Commission
(*d*) None of the above

33. ------ led to the centralisation of political decisions or the unbalanced progress of different parts with the same state.
(*a*) Capitalism
(*b*) Regionalism
(*c*) Separatism
(*d*) None of the above

34. Which of the following Articles of the constitution says "India, that is Bharat, shall be a 'Union of States'"?
(*a*) Article 6 (*b*) Article 9
(*c*) Article 1 (*d*) Article 21

35. Who among the following described the Indian constitution as quasi-federal?
(*a*) Wheare (*b*) Jennings
(*c*) Bombwall (*d*) Merkl

36. In which of the following countries the boundaries of the states cannot be changed without the consent of the state legislature concerned?
(*a*) U.S.A (*b*) Switzerland
(*c*) Australia (*d*) All of these

37. Which of the following constitutions authorities the National Governments to see that the democratic government's function in the states and that the constitution and federal laws are executed by the State officers?
(*a*) Chinese (*b*) Mexican
(*c*) American (*d*) German

38. Frustrated with slow economic progress and the dominant congress party rule, the leaders of the regional parties in the states have consistently clamoured for :
(*a*) More and more financial grants
(*b*) More and more autonomy for the states
(*c*) More and more share in the parliament
(*d*) More and more interference in national policies

39. Which one of the following does not find mention in the preamble to the constitution?
(*a*) Dignity of the individual
(*b*) Dignity of the constitution
(*c*) Fraternity
(*d*) Unity and integrity of the Nation

40. Which of the following indicates non-interference of the centre in the prescribed domain of the states?
(*a*) Regional autonomy
(*b*) State autonomy
(*c*) Commercial autonomy
(*d*) None of the above

41. Which one of the following political parties is older than the other three?
   (*a*) DMK   (*b*) BJP
   (*c*) AIDMK   (*d*) Telugu Desam

42. Who among the following observes that Federalism is a system of government in which neither level of government is wholly dependent on the other nor wholly independent of the other?
   (*a*) Wheare   (*b*) Vile
   (*c*) White   (*d*) Pylee

43. The question of ------ was examined at great length by the supreme court in the case of state of West Bengal Vs. Union of India (1962).
   (*a*) Territoriality
   (*b*) Legality
   (*c*) Sovereignty of the states
   (*d*) None of the above

44. Who decides whether a bill is a Money Bill or not?
   (*a*) The President
   (*b*) The Speaker
   (*c*) The Finance Secretary
   (*d*) None of these

45. The Indian Constitution is regarded as :
   (*a*) Federal
   (*b*) Unitary
   (*c*) Parliamentary
   (*d*) Federal in form, Unitary in spirit

46. India is a Federal State because its constitution provides for :
   (*a*) Single citizenship
   (*b*) Single judiciary
   (*c*) Sharing of powers between states and centre
   (*d*) A written constitution

47. The source of all political power in India lies with—
   (*a*) Parliament
   (*b*) The Lok Sabha
   (*c*) The People
   (*d*) The Constitution

48. A renowned British authority on Federalism has classified India as "a Unitary state with subsidiary Federal principles rather than a Federal state with subsidiary unitary principles".
He is :
   (*a*) Ivor Jennings
   (*b*) Harold Laski
   (*c*) K.C. Wheare
   (*d*) None of the above

49. Which part of the constitution of India elaborates the basic provisions regarding the distribution of powers between the central and provincial governments?
   (*a*) Part X   (*b*) Part XI
   (*c*) Part XII   (*d*) Part XIV

50. The committee set up by the Constituent Assembly for the purpose of preparing the basic principles for distribution of powers was :
   (*a*) Union powers committee
   (*b*) Union constitution committee
   (*c*) Rules committee
   (*d*) All of the above

51. Who talks of Federalism in India as an example of the concept of competitive bargaining?
   (*a*) W.H.M. Jones
   (*b*) Rajni Kothari
   (*c*) Francine frankel
   (*d*) None of the above

52. In contemporary times, the bargaining model of Federalism is prevalent mainly in :
   (*a*) East European Countries
   (*b*) East Asian Countries
   (*c*) Post-Colonial Societies of Asia and Africa
   (*d*) None of the above

53. Which of the following subjects are part of the Union list?
   1. Banking, insurance, elections
   2. Public health, forests, estate duty
   3. Drugs, trade unions and stamp duties
   4. Airways, telephones, customes and excise duties

Select the correct answer from the following :
(*a*) 1 and 2   (*b*) 1, 2 and 3
(*c*) 1 and 4   (*d*) 2, 3 and 4

54. The residuary powers under the Indian constitution are vested in the union. This feature has been incorporated from :
(*a*) American Federation
(*b*) Canadian Federation
(*c*) Australian Federation
(*d*) Swiss Federation

55. Which of the following articles empowers parliament to make laws on any item included in the state list for the whole or any part of India while a proclamation of Emergency is in operation?
(*a*) Article 384   (*b*) Article 272
(*c*) Article 250   (*d*) Article 352

56. Which of the following constitutions despite laying down a federal framework for the respective countries use the term union?
(*a*) U.S. Constitution of 1787
(*b*) The British North America Act which contained constitutional provisions for Canada.
(*c*) Soviet Constitution of 1977
(*d*) All of the above

57. In vesting the residuary power in the union, the constitution of India has followed the Canadian system. The provision related to the residuary powers are mentioned under :
(*a*) Article 245   (*b*) Article 246
(*c*) Article 252   (*d*) Article 248

58. Under which article of the constitution, legislation by a state shall be subject to disallowance by the president when reserved by the Governor for his consideration?
(*a*) Article 101
(*b*) Article 201
(*c*) Article 301
(*d*) None of the above

59. Which Article of the constitution lays down that, "Full faith and credit shall be given throughout the territory of India to public acts, records and judicial proceedings of the union and every state"?
(*a*) Article 162
(*b*) Article 245
(*c*) Article 261
(*d*) None of the above

60. Zonal Councils have been established :
(*a*) On the recommendations of the Sarkaria commission
(*b*) By the states Reorganisation Act 1956
(*c*) Finance commission (Miscellaneous provisions) Act, 1951
(*d*) None of the above

61. The work 'Some characteristics of the Indian Constitution' is authored by :
(*a*) K.C. Wheare   (*b*) Granville Austin
(*c*) Ivor Jennings   (*d*) None of the above

62. Which of the following articles state that parliament may by law provide for the adjudication of any dispute with respect to the use, distribution or control of the waters of any inter-state river?
(*a*) Article 263   (*b*) Article 261
(*c*) Article 264   (*d*) Article 262

63. Which among the several legislative Acts passed during the pre-independence period first time introduced the Federal concept and used the expression 'Federation of India'?
(*a*) Indian Councils Act, 1909
(*b*) Government of India Act, 1919
(*c*) Government of India Act, 1935
(*d*) Indian Independence Act, 1947

64. Who was the harbinger of the view that the Constituent Assembly of India was the first assembly which adopted from the very start what is called as the concept of co-operative Federalism?
(*a*) A.H. Birch
(*b*) K.C. Wheare
(*c*) Granville Austin
(*d*) None of the above

65. Which among the Acts reduced the Control of Secretary of State?
  (*a*) Indian Councils Act, 1909
  (*b*) Indian Councils Act, 1892
  (*c*) Govt. of India Act, 1919
  (*d*) Govt. of India Act, 1935

66. The Constituent Assembly was to consist of—
  (*a*) 275 members
  (*b*) 389 members
  (*c*) 325 members
  (*d*) 425 members

ANSWERS

1	2	3	4	5	6	7	8	9	10
(*c*)	(*a*)	(*d*)	(*c*)	(*b*)	(*b*)	(*c*)	(*a*)	(*d*)	(*c*)

11	12	13	14	15	16	17	18	19	20
(*b*)	(*a*)	(*c*)	(*b*)	(*d*)	(*b*)	(*a*)	(*d*)	(*c*)	(*b*)

21	22	23	24	25	26	27	28	29	30
(*d*)	(*b*)	(*d*)	(*d*)	(*c*)	(*d*)	(*a*)	(*c*)	(*b*)	(*a*)

31	32	33	34	35	36	37	38	39	40
(*b*)	(*c*)	(*b*)	(*c*)	(*a*)	(*d*)	(*b*)	(*b*)	(*b*)	(*b*)

41	42	43	44	45	46	47	48	49	50
(*a*)	(*b*)	(*c*)	(*b*)	(*d*)	(*c*)	(*d*)	(*c*)	(*b*)	(*c*)

51	52	53	54	55	56	57	58	59	60
(*a*)	(*c*)	(*c*)	(*b*)	(*c*)	(*d*)	(*d*)	(*b*)	(*c*)	(*b*)

61	62	63	64	65	66
(*c*)	(*d*)	(*c*)	(*c*)	(*c*)	(*b*)

6

FUNDAMENTAL RIGHTS

1. According to the Constituent Assembly Debates Directive principles is merely another name for the :
   (*a*) Bill of Rights
   (*b*) Human Rights Character
   (*c*) Instruments of Instructions
   (*d*) Governmental Accountability

2. Which Article of the Constitution states that the state shall organise village panchayats as units of self-government?
   (*a*) Article 43   (*b*) Article 40
   (*c*) Article 45   (*d*) Article 42

3. In which of the following cases, the Directive principles were accorded a more subsidiary and subordinate position than was contemplated by the founding father of the constitution?
   (*a*) Cow Slaughter case
   (*b*) Kerala Education Bill case
   (*c*) Champakam Dorairajan's case
   (*d*) All of the above

4. The Golak Nath case was heard by a special Bench of 11 judges as the validity of three constitutional amendments------- , -------- and ----- was challenged.
   (*a*) 3rd, 4th, 5th   (*b*) 1st, 4th, 17th
   (*c*) 1st, 2nd, 8th   (*d*) 2nd, 3rd, 4th

5. The case of Gopalan Vs. State of Madras was relevant to :
   (*a*) Article 21   (*b*) Article 12
   (*c*) Article 16   (*d*) Article 14

6. In Bijoy cotton mills Vs. State of Ajmer case, the supreme court upheld the constitutional validity of minimum wages Act, 1948 by taking into consideration Article 43 which provides for :
   (*a*) "Minimising inequalities in income"
   (*b*) "Eliminating inequalities in status"
   (*c*) "Living wages for workers"
   (*d*) None of the above

7. In state of Bombay Vs. F.N. Balasara case, the supreme court gave full weight to ------, which directs the state to bring about prohibition of intoxicating drinks.
   (*a*) Article 43   (*b*) Article 47
   (*c*) Article 29   (*d*) Article 13

8. Which of the following Articles deals with the right to property has already been deleted by the 44th Amendment Act of 1978?
   (*a*) Article 30   (*b*) Article 29
   (*c*) Article 31   (*d*) Article 32

9. The expression "procedure established by law" has been taken from Article XXXI of the :
   (*a*) British Constitution, 1946
   (*b*) American Constitution, 1963
   (*c*) German Constitution, 1987
   (*d*) Japanese Constitution, 1946

10. How can a citizen protect his Fundamental Rights?
    (*a*) By a writ in the Supreme court of India
    (*b*) By approaching the president of India
    (*c*) Through police action
    (*d*) They are already protected

11. Which of the following is not a Fundamental Rights?
    (*a*) Right against exploitation
    (*b*) Equal pay for equal work
    (*c*) Equality before law
    (*d*) Right to freedom of religion

12. The Supreme Court of India gave the verdict that the original structure of the constitution as embodied in the preamble, could not be changed under any circumstances, in the case of :
 (*a*) Sajjan Singh   (*b*) Minerva Mills
 (*c*) Keshvananda   (*d*) Golaknath

13. The Gandhian principles have been enumerated in the :
 (*a*) Fundamental Rights
 (*b*) Preamble
 (*c*) Directive Principles
 (*d*) Fundamental Duties

14. An interpretation of the Indian constitution is based on the spirit of the :
 (*a*) Preamble
 (*b*) Fundamental Duties
 (*c*) Fundamental Rights
 (*d*) None of the above

15. Fundamental Duties were incorporated in the Constitution of India by the :
 (*a*) 43rd Amendment Act
 (*b*) 42nd Amendment Act
 (*c*) 41st Amendment Act
 (*d*) None of the above

16. Which of the following rights provided the necessary guidance to the framers of our constitution in selecting a set of rights which could best suit the social and political conditions in India?
 (*a*) The French Declaration of Rights
 (*b*) The Bill of Rights of the U.S.
 (*c*) The Universal Human Rights charter
 (*d*) All of the above

17. Which of the following are those conditions of social life without which no man can seek to be himself at his best?
 (*a*) Duties
 (*b*) Rights
 (*c*) Sociability
 (*d*) Civilised behaviour

18. In which of the following cases the question of amendability of Fundamental Rights came before the supreme court of India?

 (*a*) Shankari prasad Vs. Union of India
 (*b*) Sajjan Singh Vs. State of Rajasthan
 (*c*) Golak Nath Vs. State of Punjab
 (*d*) All of the above

19. In which of the following cases the validity of the first constitutional Amendment Act was challenged?
 (*a*) Golak Nath's case
 (*b*) Shankari Prasad's case
 (*c*) Sajjan Singh's case
 (*d*) Maneka Gandhi's case

20. Which of the following articles not only lays down the procedure but also confers power on the parliament to abridge or modify Fundamental Rights?
 (*a*) Article 360   (*b*) Article 358
 (*c*) Article 368   (*d*) Article 362

21. In which of the following cases the competence of parliament to enact 17th amendment was challenged before the constitution Bench comprising of five judges?
 (*a*) Minerva mill's case
 (*b*) Sajjan Singh's case
 (*c*) Golak Nath's case
 (*d*) None of the above

22. In which of the following decisions supreme court held that parliament's amending power is limited?
 (*a*) Sajjan Singh's case
 (*b*) Shankari Prasad's case
 (*c*) Minerva Mills, case
 (*d*) Keshvananda Bharti's case

23. Which part of the constitution provides the Directive principles of state policy?
 (*a*) Part IV   (*b*) Part II
 (*c*) Part III   (*d*) Part V

24. The Directive principles represent some what the pattern of instrument of instructions provided in the :
 (*a*) Government of India Act, 1935
 (*b*) Government of India Act, 1919
 (*c*) Independence Act, 1947
 (*d*) None of the above

25. Who among the following declared that the Indian Constitution is "First and Foremost a social document"?
(*a*) Jawaharlal Nehru
(*b*) Granville Austin
(*c*) M.K. Gandhi
(*d*) None of the above

26. Which of the following components of the Constitution has also been referred to as "the conscience of the constitution"?
(*a*) Preamble
(*b*) Fundamental Rights
(*c*) Directive principle of state policy
(*d*) Both (*b*) and (*c*)

27. In which of its sessions the congress party passed a resolution which declared that "the basis of the future constitution of India must be a declaration of Fundamental Rights"?
(*a*) Surat session of 1907
(*b*) Lucknow session of 1916
(*c*) Madras session of 1927
(*d*) Both (*a*) and (*b*)

28. Right to property has been eliminated from the fundamental rights by :
(*a*) 42nd Constitutional Amendment Act of 1976
(*b*) 44th Constitutional Amendment Act of 1978
(*c*) 43rd Constitutional Amendment Act of 1977
(*d*) 24th Constitutional Amendment Act of 1971

29. Which year does the "Golak Nath Vs the state of Punjab" case belong to?
(*a*) 1962   (*b*) 1965
(*c*) 1969   (*d*) 1967

30. Which of the following document rejected the idea of Fundamental Rights?
(*a*) Nehru Report
(*b*) Simon Commission and joint parliamentary committee which were responsible for the Government of India Act, 1935
(*c*) Objectives Resolution of Pt. Jawaharlal Nehru

(*d*) Both (*a*) and (*b*)

31. Article 300 A has :
(*a*) The vestiges of the erstwhile right to property
(*b*) Provision for the machinery of audit and account
(*c*) The power to review the acts of the state legislature
(*d*) All of the above

32. The terminology "equality before law and equal protection of laws" is found under :
(*a*) Article 13   (*b*) Article 14
(*c*) Article 15   (*d*) Article 16

33. The fundamental duties have been incorporated in Article 51A of the constitution. At present, the total number of Fundamental duties are :
(*a*) 9   (*b*) 10
(*c*) 11   (*d*) 12

34. Fundamental duties enjoin upon a person to respect :
(*a*) Mother Tongue   (*b*) National Flag
(*c*) National Anthem   (*d*) Both (*b*) and (*c*)

35. The people residing in India are asked by Constitution via its part IVA to preserve :
(*a*) National monuments
(*b*) Communal Harmony
(*c*) Political structure
(*d*) Rich heritage of the composite culture of the country

36. Which of the following comments are correct about enforcement of the Fundamental Duties?
(*a*) They can be only indirectly enforced
(*b*) They can be enforced if a proper suit is brought before the highest court of the country
(*c*) There is no provision in the constitution for direct enforcement of any of the Fundamental Duties
(*d*) All of the above

37. The constitution enjoins upon a person via Article 51A to protect and improve :
(*a*) Natural environment

(*b*) Unity and integrity of the nation

(*c*) Public property

(*d*) Ethnic composition of society

38. As part of the fundamental duties that a resident of India is expected to fulfill she or he should cherish and follow :

(*a*) Gandhian values and Nehruvian principles

(*b*) Noble ideals which inspired our national struggle for freedom

(*c*) Congress ideology

(*d*) None of the above

39. Article 51A makes it incumbent upon a person residing in India to promote :

(*a*) Communal harmony

(*b*) The spirit of common brotherhood amongst all the people of India

(*c*) Economic well-being of the nation

(*d*) All of the above

40. Which of the following is the country that has adopted the western model of liberal democracy and has also included a number of basic duties in its constitution.

(*a*) France   (*b*) U.S.A.

(*c*) Germany   (*d*) Japan

41. A committte that was appointed by the Government of India to make recommendations about Fundamental Duties was headed by :

(*a*) Sardar Swaran Singh

(*b*) Manmohan Singh

(*c*) Khushwant Singh

(*d*) Sanjay Gandhi

42. It is a fundamental Duty of a citizen of India to develop :

(*a*) Her or his economic status and social standing

(*b*) The understanding between different communities

(*c*) Scientific temper and spirit of enquiry

(*d*) All of the above

43. Which of the following works are authored by K.R. Bombwall?

(*a*) Constitutional law of India

(*b*) Indian political system

(*c*) Foundations of political science

(*d*) All of the above

44. The constitution of India through its part IVA enjoins upon the citizens of India of strive towards excellence in :

(*a*) One's occupational area

(*b*) One's economic and social endeavours

(*c*) All spheres of individual and collective activity

(*d*) None of the above

45. The power to issue writs for the enforcement of the fundamental rights is given by the constitution to the High Courts under :

(*a*) Article 32   (*b*) Article 123

(*c*) Article 226   (*d*) Article 339

46. Article 23, among other things, prohibits traffic in human beings. This expression includes :

(*a*) Slavery

(*b*) Use of women and children for immoral purposes

(*c*) Conscription

(*d*) Both (*a*) and (*b*)

47. Special provision for the protection of children is made in :

(*a*) Article 23   (*b*) Article 24

(*c*) Article 39(b)   (*d*) All of these

48. Which among the following constitutional offices are to a certain extent immune from the impact of Article 14?

(*a*) President

(*b*) Governor

(*c*) Speaker of Lok Sabha,

(*d*) Both (*a*) and (*b*)

49. Which of the following cases is popularly known as Mandal Commission case?

(*a*) Indra Sawhney V. Union of India, 1992

(*b*) Bommai V. Union of India, 1994

(*c*) Ramsharan V. Union of India, 1989

(*d*) None of the above

50. Which of the following Articles provides for abolition of untouchability?

(*a*) Article 17   (*b*) Article 18
(*c*) Article 26   (*d*) Article 27

51. Who raised protest in 1970s against conferment of decorations like Bharat Ratna by the Government?
(*a*) Jai Prakash Narayan
(*b*) Ram Manohar Lohia
(*c*) Acharya Kripalani
(*d*) Vinobha Bhave

52. Freedom to reside and settle in any part of the territory of India is conferred by :
(*a*) Article 19(1)(e)   (*b*) Article 18(4)
(*c*) Article 19(1)(d)   (*d*) Article 19(1)(F)

53. Which of the following does not compose a ground for restriction on the freedom of speech and expression as given under the constitution?
(*a*) Defamation   (*b*) Insolvency
(*c*) Contempt of court (*d*) Public order

54. 'Equality before the law', is an expression of
(*a*) English common law
(*b*) French Administrative law
(*c*) American Constitutional law
(*d*) None of the above

55. The expression 'equal protection of laws' owes its origin to :
(*a*) French Constitution
(*b*) English Constitution
(*c*) American Constitution
(*d*) None of the above

56. Equality before the law is a corollary of the concept of the rule of law given by :
(*a*) Dicey   (*b*) Lord Bryce
(*c*) Lincoln   (*d*) Churchill

57. Under Article 14 if there is any reasonable basis for classification, the legislature would be entitled to make a different treatment. In order to be 'reasonable' a classification must be :
(*a*) Unarbitrary
(*b*) Rational
(*c*) Both (*a*) and (*b*)
(*d*) Fair and just

58. Which of the following articles provides for prohibition of discrimination on grounds of religion, race, caste, sex and place of birth?
(*a*) Article 16
(*b*) Article 19(1)(C)
(*c*) Article 15
(*d*) None of the above

59. Under the constitution of India freedom of the press is deemed as included under :
(*a*) Article 19   (*b*) Article 19(1)
(*c*) Article 19(1)(a)   (*d*) Article 19(2)

60. The term 'double jeopardy' pertains to :
(*a*) Article 19   (*b*) Article 20
(*c*) Article 21   (*d*) Article 22

61. Freedom of a person or personal liberty is sought to be ensured by the constitution of India by means of :
(*a*) Article 19   (*b*) Article 20
(*c*) Article 21   (*d*) Article 21 and 22

62. Which of the following chapters of the Indian constitution is the most comprehensive and detailed one?
(*a*) Chapter III   (*b*) Chapter IV
(*c*) Chapter V   (*d*) Chapter VII

63. Who among the following is the guardian of the fundamental rights guaranteed by the constitution of India?
(*a*) Parliament   (*b*) Judiciary
(*c*) Lok Sabha   (*d*) President

64. Which of the following rights is guaranteed to every person whether citizen or foreigner?
(*a*) Rights relating to protection of life
(*b*) Freedom of religion
(*c*) Right against exploitation
(*d*) All of the above

65. Equal protection of laws implies equal treatment in :
(*a*) Privileges conferred
(*b*) Liabilities imposed
(*c*) Both privileges conferred and liabilities by the law imposed
(*d*) Neither privileges conferred nor liabilities imposed

66. Which article provides for residential qualification in certain catagory of public employment?

    (*a*) Article 16 (3)   (*b*) Article 16 (2)

    (*c*) Article 15 (4)   (*d*) None of the above

67. Which article deals with the Right to Freedom?

    (*a*) Article 15 to 18   (*b*) Article 19 to 22

    (*c*) Article 17 to 21   (*d*) None of the above

ANSWERS

1	2	3	4	5	6	7	8	9	10
(*c*)	(*b*)	(*d*)	(*b*)	(*a*)	(*c*)	(*b*)	(*c*)	(*d*)	(*a*)
11	**12**	**13**	**14**	**15**	**16**	**17**	**18**	**19**	**20**
(*b*)	(*d*)	(*c*)	(*a*)	(*b*)	(*d*)	(*b*)	(*d*)	(*b*)	(*c*)
21	**22**	**23**	**24**	**25**	**26**	**27**	**28**	**29**	**30**
(*b*)	(*d*)	(*a*)	(*a*)	(*b*)	(*d*)	(*c*)	(*b*)	(*d*)	(*b*)
31	**32**	**33**	**34**	**35**	**36**	**37**	**38**	**39**	**40**
(*a*)	(*b*)	(*c*)	(*c*)	(*d*)	(*c*)	(*a*)	(*b*)	(*b*)	(*d*)
41	**42**	**43**	**44**	**45**	**46**	**47**	**48**	**49**	**50**
(*a*)	(*c*)	(*c*)	(*c*)	(*c*)	(*d*)	(*b*)	(*d*)	(*a*)	(*a*)
51	**52**	**53**	**54**	**55**	**56**	**57**	**58**	**59**	**60**
(*c*)	(*a*)	(*b*)	(*a*)	(*c*)	(*a*)	(*c*)	(*c*)	(*c*)	(*b*)
61	**62**	**63**	**64**	**65**	**66**	**67**			
(*c*)	(*a*)	(*b*)	(*d*)	(*c*)	(*a*)	(*b*)			

7

THE UNION EXECUTIVE

1. Which of the following is included in the Union Executive?
   (a) President
   (b) Council of ministers
   (c) Prime Minister
   (d) All of the above

2. Which Article states that the Prime Minister shall be 'at the head' of the council of ministers?
   (a) Article 57
   (b) Article 74
   (c) Article 72
   (d) Article 73

3. The real executive in India is the :
   (a) Prime Minister
   (b) Speaker of Lok Sabha
   (c) President
   (d) Governor

4. Which of the following Articles of the constitution defines the duties of the prime minister in the discharge of which he acts as a link between the president and the cabinet?
   (a) Article 75
   (b) Article 78
   (c) Article 77
   (d) Article 73

5. Which of the following commission is an extra-constitutional advisory body under the chairmanship of the PM?
   (a) Finance Commission
   (b) Sarkaria Commission
   (c) Planning Commission
   (d) Pay Commission

6. The Council of Ministers comprises of :
   (a) Cabinet Ministers
   (b) Ministers of State
   (c) Deputy Ministers
   (d) All of the above

7. A/An------ is a quasi-judicial procedure in parliament.
   (a) Prorogation
   (b) No-confidence motion
   (c) Impeachment
   (d) Censure motion

8. The vice-president shall be elected by an electoral college consisting of member of :
   (a) State legislatures
   (b) Both houses of parliament
   (c) Lok Sabha and Vidhan Sabha
   (d) None of the above

9. A veto is suspensive when the executive veto can be overridden by the legislature by an :
   (a) Ordinary majority
   (b) Two-third majority
   (c) Absolute majority
   (d) None of the above

10. The veto power of the Indian president is categorised as :
    (a) Absolute
    (b) Suspensive
    (c) Pocket
    (d) All of these

11. The president shall have the pardoning power in respect of :
    (a) All cases of punishment by a court martial
    (b) Offences against laws made under the Union and concurrent lists
    (c) A sentence of death
    (d) All of the above

12. Who said that "it is most useful to look upon the executive as the residuary legatee, for that explains the mixed nature of its functions and parts"?
    (a) Finer
    (b) Laski
    (c) Gilchrist
    (d) White

13. Who cannot be a member of parliament or a state legislature?
(*a*) Prime Minister　(*b*) President
(*c*) Minister　(*d*) Speaker

14. According to which article of the constitution the executive power of the Union is vested in the President who is empowered to exercise it either directly or through officers subordinate to him?
(*a*) Article 52　(*b*) Article 51
(*c*) Article 54　(*d*) Article 53

15. Who is empowered to declare three different types of emergency?
(*a*) President　(*b*) Prime Minister
(*c*) Parliament　(*d*) Governor

16. The President of India is elected by :
(*a*) Direct election
(*b*) Nomination
(*c*) Indirect election
(*d*) None of the above

17. Which of the following is included in the electoral college for electing the President?
(*a*) The elected members of the both Houses of Parliament
(*b*) The elected members of the Legislative Assemblies of the States
(*c*) The elected members of the Legislative Assemblies of Union Territories of Delhi and Pondicherry
(*d*) All of the above

18. Which of the following Articles of the constitution talks about the President's term of office?
(*a*) Article 52-53　(*b*) Article 56-57
(*c*) Article 51-52　(*d*) Article 57-58

19. Which Article of the constitution lays down a detailed procedure for the impeachment of the President?
(*a*) Article 57　(*b*) Article 58
(*c*) Article 62　(*d*) Article 61

20. The President is elected by the system of proportional representation by means of :
(*a*) Single transferable vote
(*b*) Single non-transferable vote

(*c*) Double transferable vote
(*d*) None of the above

21. Who nominates the Chairman of the Public Account Committee of Indian Parliament?
(*a*) The Prime Minister
(*b*) The President
(*c*) The Speaker of the Lok Sabha
(*d*) The Chairman of the Rajya Sabha

22. In case of 'private' member's Bills the President of India enjoys the powers of :
(*a*) Suspensive veto　(*b*) Pocket veto
(*c*) Absolute veto　(*d*) Qualified veto

23. The President of India is a :
(*a*) Real executive
(*b*) Titular executive
(*c*) De-facto executive
(*d*) None of the above

24. The President can dissolve the Lok Sabha on :
(*a*) Advice of the Chief Justice of India
(*b*) Recommendation of the Lok Sabha
(*c*) Advice of the Prime Minister
(*d*) Recommendation of the Rajya Sabha

25. The following have held office of the President of India :
(1) V.V. Giri
(2) N. Sanjiva Reddy
(3) Dr. Zakir Hussain
(4) Fakhruddin Ali Ahmed
The Chronological order in which they held office is :
(*a*) 3, 1, 4 and 2　(*b*) 2, 1, 3 and 4
(*c*) 1, 2, 3 and 4　(*d*) 1, 3, 4 and 2

26. Who was the first Vice-President of India?
(*a*) Dr. S. Radhakrishnan
(*b*) V.V. Giri
(*c*) Dr. Zakir Hussain
(*d*) N. Sanjiva Reddy

27. Who among the following prime ministers of India did not face the Lok Sabha even once?
(*a*) Indira Gandhi　(*b*) Rajiv Gandhi
(*c*) Charan Singh　(*d*) V.P. Singh

28. The Constitution of India provides for the nomination of two members to the Lok Sabha, by the President to represent :

(*a*) Men of eminence in arts, science etc.
(*b*) Parsis
(*c*) The Anglo-Indian community
(*d*) None of the above

29. Who among the following describes the position of the prime minister as 'primus inter pares', i.e. 'first among equals.

(*a*) Morely (*b*) Appleby
(*c*) Leacock (*d*) White

30. Which of the following Acts defines "Minister" as a "Member of the Council of Ministers, by whatever name called, and includes a Deputy Minister"?
(*a*) Customs Act, 1962
(*b*) Salaries and Allowances of Minister Act, 1952
(*c*) Income-tax Act, 1961
(*d*) Monopolies and Restrictive Trade Practices Act, 1969

31. The ordinance-making power will be available to the President only when :
(*a*) The two Houses of Parliament have been prorogued
(*b*) The two Houses of Parliament are not in session
(*c*) Either (*a*) or (*b*)
(*d*) None of the above

32. The Rajya Sabha can take initiative in—
(*a*) Censuring a Minister
(*b*) Creating a New All India Service
(*c*) Considering Money Bill
(*d*) Appointing Judges

33. A veto is ------ when the executive veto can be overridden by the legislature by an ordinary majority.
(*a*) qualified (*b*) absolute
(*c*) pocket (*d*) suspensive

34. The executive vetoes from the stand-point of effect on the legislation can be classified as :
1. Absolute veto   2. Qualified veto
3. Suspensive veto 4. Pocket veto
5. Multiple veto

Which of the above correct? Choose the correct answer from the codes given below :
(*a*) 1, 2, 3 and 4 (*b*) 2, 3 and 4
(*c*) 1, 2 and 4 (*d*) 2, 4 and 5

35. Which of the following steps is taken by the President when a Bill is presented to him, after its passage in both Houses of Parliament?
(*a*) He may declare his assent to the Bill
(*b*) He may declare that he withholds his assent to the Bill
(*c*) He may, in the case of Bills other than Money Bills, return the Bill for reconsideration of the Houses, with or without a message suggesting amendments
(*d*) All of the above

36. Which of the following vetoes is a useful device in the United States where the executive has no power of control over the legislature, by prorogation, dissolution or otherwise?
(*a*) Absolute veto (*b*) Pocket veto
(*c*) Suspensive veto (*d*) Qualified veto

37. The Vice-President acts as the President of India when :
(*a*) President is sick
(*b*) President is unable to discharge his duties
(*c*) President is absent from the country
(*d*) All of the above

38. Every Proclamation issued under Article 352 is to be laid before :
(*a*) Lok Sabha
(*b*) Each House of Parliament
(*c*) Rajya Sabha
(*d*) Vice-President

39. Who among the following represents Indian in international affairs?
(*a*) Union Minister for external affairs
(*b*) Prime Minister
(*c*) President
(*d*) All of the above

40. Which of the following amendments substituted the words 'armed rebellion' for 'internal disturbance' in the Article 352?
(*a*) 42nd Amendment, 1976

(*b*) 44th Amendment, 1978
(*c*) 24th Amendment, 1971
(*d*) None of the above

41. To whom the President can refer any matter of constitutional law for advice?
(*a*) Attorney-General
(*b*) Union Law Minister
(*c*) Supreme Court
(*d*) Any of the above

42. No Money Bill can be introduced in Parliament with the previous recommendation of :
(*a*) Prime Minister
(*b*) President
(*c*) Lok Sabha Speaker
(*d*) Public Accounts Committee

43. What is the period within which an ordinance promulgated by the President should be laid before both Houses of Parliament after they assemble?
(*a*) Six months   (*b*) Six weeks
(*c*) Six days   (*d*) Two months

44. The President has the power to summon or prorogue :
(*a*) Only Lok Sabha
(*b*) Only Rajya Sabha
(*c*) Any House of the Parliament
(*d*) None of the above

45. When a Bill is presented to the president after its passage in both Houses of Parliament, he shall be entitled to :
(*a*) Declare his assent
(*b*) Declare that he withholds his assent
(*c*) Return the non-money bills for reconsideration of the Houses.
(*d*) Take any of the steps enumerated in (*a*) (*b*) and (*c*).

46. Who summons a joint sitting of both Houses of Parliament in case of a deadlock between them?
(*a*) Lok Sabha Speaker
(*b*) President of the Republic
(*c*) Prime Minister
(*d*) Either (*a*) or (*b*)

47. Which of the following Articles lays down that "the executive power of the Union shall be vested in the President"?
(*a*) Article 53   (*b*) Article 63
(*c*) Article 73   (*d*) Article 83

48. Which of the following Articles lay down the Ministers can be appointed by the President only on the advice of the Prime Minister?
(*a*) Article 62   (*b*) Article 71
(*c*) Article 74   (*d*) Article 75

49. The executive power which is vested by the Constitution on the President, means :
(*a*) Execution of the laws enacted by the lagislature
(*b*) The power of carrying on the business of government
(*c*) The administration of the affairs of the state
(*d*) All of the above

50. Which article lays down that all officers of the Union shall be President's subordinates?
(*a*) Article 75   (*b*) Article 53
(*c*) Article 78   (*d*) None of the above

51. Disputes cannot be raised in connection with the election of a President or Vice-President on the ground of :
(*a*) Age of the incumbent
(*b*) Domicile status of the incumbent
(*c*) Any vacancy in the electoral college
(*d*) All of the above

52. Who among the following is neither appointed, nor removed by the President?
(*a*) Attorney-General of India
(*b*) Comptroller and Auditor-General
(*c*) Speaker of State Assembly
(*d*) Chairman of a State Public Service Commission

53. In order to be Vice-President, a person must be qualified for election as :
(*a*) A member of the Council of States
(*b*) Speaker of Lok Sabha
(*c*) Chief Election Commissioner
(*d*) None of the above

54. Which of the following Articles prescribed the qualifications for election as Vice-President of India?
(*a*) Article 65   (*b*) Article 66
(*c*) Article 72   (*d*) Article 78

55. The election of the Vice-President shall be indirect and in accordance with :
(*a*) The first-past the post system
(*b*) The list system
(*c*) The system of proportional representation
(*d*) None of the above

56. Which of the following bodies will have no part to play in the election of the Vice-President?
(*a*) Rajya Sabha   (*b*) State Legislatures
(*c*) Lok Sabha   (*d*) None of the above

57. In which of the following ways a vacancy may arise in the office of the President?
(*a*) Loss of an essential qualification by the incumbent
(*b*) Long and unaccounted absence from the office
(*c*) Setting a side of his election as President
(*d*) All of the above

58. What will happen if the sitting President's term expires while his successor is yet to enter upon his office?
(*a*) Vice-President shall begin to act as President
(*b*) The incumbent shall continue to hold office
(*c*) The incumbent's term shall be increased for one year
(*d*) None of the above

59. Who was the first Vice-President to have been elected for a second term?
(*a*) Dr. S. Radhakrishnan
(*b*) B.D. Jatti
(*c*) Neelam Sanjeeva Reddy
(*d*) Shanker Dayal Sharma

60. Which of the following Articles lay down the norms for the Vice-President?
(*a*) Article-66   (*b*) Article-67

(*c*) Article- 68   (*d*) Article-78

61. When the Vice-President discharges the functions of the President he gets the emoluments :
(*a*) Of the President only
(*b*) Of the Vice-President only
(*c*) Both (*a*) and (*b*)
(*d*) None of the above

62. Determination of doubts and disputes relating to the election of a President or Vice-President is dealt within :
(*a*) Article 71   (*b*) Article 72
(*c*) Article 73   (*d*) Article 74

63. When the Vice-President acts as President his duties as Chairman of the Council of State are performed by :
(*a*) Speaker of Lok Sabha
(*b*) Deputy Speaker of Lok Sabha
(*c*) Deputy Chairman of the Council of States
(*d*) None of the above

64. Under which article of the Constitution, the qualifications for election to the office of the President find mention?
(*a*) Article 55   (*b*) Article 56
(*c*) Article 57   (*d*) Article 58

65. Which article of the Constitution lay down that the President's term of office is five years though he is eligible for re-election?
(*a*) Article-56   (*b*) Article 57
(*c*) Article 56-57   (*d*) Article 58

66. Which of the following Articles prescribe that the President shall not hold any other office of profit?
(*a*) Article 50   (*b*) Article 57
(*c*) Article 59   (*d*) Article 60

67. Which of the following is not a manner in which a vacancy may arise in the office of the President?
(*a*) President's demise
(*b*) President's resignation
(*c*) President's long absence
(*d*) President's removal by impeachment

68. The normal function of the Vice-President is to act as :
- (*a*) President, when the President is not able to discharge the duties of his office
- (*b*) Deputy Chief of Indian Armed forces
- (*c*) Ex-officio Chairman of the Council of States
- (*d*) None of the above

69. Article 91 lays down :
- (*a*) Conditions necessary for the office of the speaker of the Lok Sabha
- (*b*) The situation when the Vice-President may discharge the functions of the President
- (*c*) The role of the Deputy Chairman of the Council of States when Vice-President acts as President
- (*d*) None of the above

70. President's office may terminate within the term of five years due to his resignation. President has to address the resignation to :
- (*a*) Vice-President
- (*b*) Prime Minister
- (*c*) Speaker of Lok Sabha
- (*d*) Any of the above

ANSWERS

1	2	3	4	5	6	7	8	9	10
(*d*)	(*b*)	(*a*)	(*b*)	(*c*)	(*d*)	(*c*)	(*b*)	(*a*)	(*d*)
11	**12**	**13**	**14**	**15**	**16**	**17**	**18**	**19**	**20**
(*d*)	(*a*)	(*b*)	(*d*)	(*a*)	(*c*)	(*d*)	(*b*)	(*d*)	(*a*)
21	**22**	**23**	**24**	**25**	**26**	**27**	**28**	**29**	**30**
(*c*)	(*c*)	(*b*)	(*c*)	(*a*)	(*a*)	(*c*)	(*c*)	(*a*)	(*b*)
31	**32**	**33**	**34**	**35**	**36**	**37**	**38**	**39**	**40**
(*c*)	(*b*)	(*d*)	(*a*)	(*d*)	(*d*)	(*d*)	(*b*)	(*c*)	(*b*)
41	**42**	**43**	**44**	**45**	**46**	**47**	**48**	**49**	**50**
(*c*)	(*b*)	(*b*)	(*c*)	(*d*)	(*b*)	(*a*)	(*d*)	(*d*)	(*b*)
51	**52**	**53**	**54**	**55**	**56**	**57**	**58**	**59**	**60**
(*c*)	(*c*)	(*a*)	(*b*)	(*c*)	(*b*)	(*c*)	(*b*)	(*a*)	(*b*)
61	**62**	**63**	**64**	**65**	**66**	**67**	**68**	**69**	**70**
(*a*)	(*a*)	(*c*)	(*d*)	(*c*)	(*c*)	(*c*)	(*c*)	(*c*)	(*a*)

8

PARLIAMENT

1. Which of the following Articles of the constitution states that the parliament of India consists of the President and two Houses?
   (*a*) Article 64   (*b*) Article 79
   (*c*) Article 74   (*d*) Article 80

2. How many members of the Council of States are the representatives of the States and the Union Territories?
   (*a*) 245   (*b*) 240
   (*c*) 235   (*d*) 237

3. Which of the following postpones the further transaction of business for a specified time hours, days or weeks?
   (*a*) Dissolution
   (*b*) Adjournment
   (*c*) Prorogation
   (*d*) None of the above

4. What merely terminates a session?
   (*a*) Dissolution
   (*b*) Adjournment
   (*c*) Prorogation
   (*d*) None of the above

5. The Constitution provides an elaborate definition of a Money Bill in :
   (*a*) Article 110   (*b*) Article 112
   (*c*) Article 111   (*d*) Article 109

6. Who among the following has the power to Summon a 'joint sitting' of both the Houses for the purpose of deliberation and voting on the Bill?
   (*a*) Prime Minister   (*b*) President
   (*c*) Speaker   (*d*) Chairman

7. All Bills which are not constitution Amendment Bills and Money Bills, are :
   (*a*) Special Bills   (*b*) General Bills
   (*c*) Original Bills   (*d*) Ordinary Bills

8. A Parliamentary committee may be defined as one that :
   (*a*) Is appointed or elected by the House or nominated by the Speaker/Chairman
   (*b*) Works under the direction of the Speaker/Chairman
   (*c*) Presents its report to the House or to the Speaker/Chairman
   (*d*) All of the above

9. Which of the following are standing committees?
   (*a*) Financial committees
   (*b*) Scrutiny committees
   (*c*) Enquiry committees
   (*d*) All of the above

10. Which of the following are the two types of Parliamentary Committees in India?
    (*a*) Subject and Service Committees
    (*b*) Enquiry and Scrutiny Committees
    (*c*) Standing and Ad hoc Committees
    (*d*) Select and Financial Committees

11. Which of the following types of committees are elected by the House or nominated by the Speaker/Chairman every year or from time-to-time, as the case may be, and are permanent in nature?
    (*a*) Standing Committees
    (*b*) Service Committees
    (*c*) Ad hoc Committees
    (*d*) Select Committees

12. Which of the following is included in scrutiny committees?
    (*a*) Committee on Government Assurances
    (*b*) Committee on Subordinate Legislation

Obj. Pol. Sc.-22

(*c*) Committee on the Welfare of SCs and STs

(*d*) All of the above

13. Which of the following committees are constituted by the House or by the Speaker/Chairman, to consider and report on specific matters and become functus officio as soon as they have completed their work on these matters?

(*a*) Service committees

(*b*) Adhoc committees

(*c*) Subject committees

(*d*) Financial committees

14. Which of the following is the oldest Financial Committee?

(*a*) Committee on public undertakings

(*b*) Assurance committee

(*c*) Public Accounts committee

(*d*) None of the above

15. Which of the following is a question which relates to a matter of urgent public importance and can be asked with notice shorter than the ten days prescribed for an ordinary question?

(*a*) Unstarred Questions

(*b*) Short Notice Questions

(*c*) Starred Questions

(*d*) None of the above

16. The institutions, Sabha and Samiti, mentioned in ------- , may be said to have contained rudiments of a modern parliament.

(*a*) Yajurveda   (*b*) Rigveda

(*c*) Atharvaveda   (*d*) Samveda

17. Which of the following refers specially to a kind of democratic polity where in the supreme power vests in the body of people's representatives called Parliament?

(*a*) Republican   (*b*) Communist

(*c*) Parliamentary   (*d*) Socialist

18. Who among the following summons the two Houses of Parliament to meet from time to time?

(*a*) Speaker

(*b*) President

(*c*) Prime Minister

(*d*) Council of Ministers

19. The number of representatives from each state in India depends largely on its :

(*a*) Population

(*b*) Location

(*c*) Area

(*d*) None of the above

20. Who among the following is the ex-officio Chairman of Rajya Sabha?

(*a*) President   (*b*) Speaker

(*c*) Prime Minister   (*d*) Vice-President

21. Which of the following is a limitation on the powers of Rajya Sabha?

(*a*) A Money Bill cannot be introduced in Rajya Sabha

(*b*) Whether a particular Bill is a Money Bill or not is to be decided by the speaker of Lok Sabha

(*c*) Rajya Sabha has no power to pass a vote of no-confidence in the Council of Ministers

(*d*) All of the above

22. ------- is the pivot on which the political system of the country revolves.

(*a*) President

(*b*) Parliament

(*c*) Judiciary

(*d*) None of the above

23. Who among the following nominates 12 members to the Rajya Sabha from amongst persons having special knowledge or practical experience in respect of such matters as literature, science, art and social service?

(*a*) Prime Minister   (*b*) Speaker

(*c*) Vice-President   (*d*) President

24. Which of the following are the functions of Parliament?

(*a*) Law-making, development, social engineering and legitimatizational functions

(*b*) Representational, grievance ventilation, educational and advisory functions

(*c*) Informational functions

(*d*) All of the above

25. Want of Parliamentary confidence in the Government may be expressed by the House of the people by :
(*a*) Passing a substantive motion of no-confidence in the council of ministers
(*b*) Defeating the Government on a major issue of policy
(*c*) Passing an adjourment motion
(*d*) Any of the above

26. Who among the following enjoys the right to formulate the budget?
(*a*) Legislature
(*b*) Executive
(*c*) Judiciary
(*d*) None of the above

27. Administrative accountability means accountability of the administration to the
(*a*) Executive
(*b*) Judiciary
(*c*) Parliament
(*d*) None of the above

28. The constitution provides for an annual statement of the estimated receipts and expenditures to be placed before the :
(*a*) President
(*b*) Parliament
(*c*) Prime Minister
(*d*) None of the above

29. The Speaker shall vacate his office :
(*a*) If he ceases to be member of Lok Sabha
(*b*) If he sends his resignation to the Deputy Speaker
(*c*) If a resolution removing him has been passed in the Lok Sabha by majority of all the then members
(*d*) All of the above

30. The time immediately following the Question Hour in both Houses has come to be popularly knows as :
(*a*) Zero Hour
(*b*) Eleventh Hour
(*c*) Short Discussion Hour
(*d*) Emergency Hour

31. ------ was passed in 1985 by Parliament to put an end to the problem of political defection in our country.
(*a*) Private Law
(*b*) Common Law
(*c*) Anti-Defection Law
(*d*) None of the above

32. Which of the following is one of the types of resolutions?
(*a*) Private member's Resolutions
(*b*) Government Resolutions
(*c*) Statutory Resolutions
(*d*) All of the above

33. The Provision for the calling attention notices was first made in the year :
(*a*) 1954   (*b*) 1956
(*c*) 1955   (*d*) 1957

34. Which of the following is one of the categories of questions asked in both Houses of Parliament?
(*a*) Starred Questions
(*b*) Unstarred Questions
(*c*) Short Notice Questions
(*d*) All of the above

35. Which of the following questions are to be answered orally on the floor of the House?
(*a*) Starred Questions
(*b*) Unstarred Questions
(*c*) Short Notice Questions
(*d*) All of the above

36. An unstarred Question is so named because it does not carry a/an.
(*a*) Cross mark
(*b*) Tick mark
(*c*) Asterisk mark
(*d*) None of the above

37. Which of the following is a technique of Parliamentary surveillance over the administration practised in all the countries having representative parliamentary democracy?
(*a*) Zero Hour
(*b*) Parliamentary question
(*c*) Eleventh Hour
(*d*) Parliamentary immunity

38. Who among the following determines what matters are financial matters that fall within the exclusive jurisdiction of Lok Sabha?
   (*a*) Speaker
   (*b*) Vice-President
   (*c*) Chairman
   (*d*) Deputy Speaker

39. In Keshvananda's case, justice Sikri had tried to tabulate the basic features of the constitution including :
   (*a*) Supremacy of the Constitution
   (*b*) Republican and democratic form of Government
   (*c*) Secular Character of the Constitution
   (*d*) All of the above

40. The quorum to constitute a meeting of either House of parliament shall be ------ of the total number of members of the House.
   (*a*) One-fourth
   (*b*) One-third
   (*c*) One-tenth
   (*d*) One-fifth

41. Article 267 of the constitution empowers Parliament and the Legislature of a state to create :
   (*a*) A 'contingency fund' for India or for a state
   (*b*) Upper Chamber of a state legislature
   (*c*) All-India services
   (*d*) All of the above

42. Which of the following articles lays down norms regarding creation of All-India services?
   (*a*) Article 273
   (*b*) Article 119
   (*c*) Article 77
   (*d*) Article 312

43. The public account of India refers to :
   (*a*) Accounts to be audited by Comptroller and Auditor-General
   (*b*) Money received by an officer or court in connection with affairs of the Union
   (*c*) The record of incoming and outgoing money made by Accountant-General in a state
   (*d*) None of the above

44. Which of the following is a privilege of the House collectively?
   (*a*) Right to publish debates and proceedings
   (*b*) Freedom of attendance as witness
   (*c*) Right to disallow any motion what so ever
   (*d*) All of these

45. Article 107 prescribes :
   (*a*) Conditions to be elected as member of Rajya Sabha
   (*b*) Procedure regarding an ordinary bill
   (*c*) Impeachment of the President
   (*d*) None of the above

46. Which of the following is an expenditure charged on the consolidated fund of India?
   (*a*) Salary of a member of Parliament
   (*b*) Salary of Judges of the Supreme court
   (*c*) Emoluments of the President
   (*d*) Both (*b*) and (*c*)

47. Which Article says that two members may be nominated from the Anglo-Indian community by the President to the House of the people if he is of opinion that the Anglo-Indian community has not been adequately represented in the House of the people?
   (*a*) Article 300
   (*b*) Article 231
   (*c*) Article 331
   (*d*) Article 341

48. Section 135A of the criminal procedure code, as amended by Act 104 of 1976, exempts a member from arrest during the continuance of a meeting of the Chamber or committees and during a period of a certain number of days before and after such meeting or sitting. This number is :
   (*a*) 40
   (*b*) 50
   (*c*) 60
   (*d*) 90

49. A Parliamentary committee holds office for a period not exceeding one year or for a period specified by the speaker or until a new committee is nominated. Which of the following committees continue in office till reconstituted?
   (*a*) Business Advisory Committee
   (*b*) Committee on Petitions
   (*c*) Committee on privileges
   (*d*) All of the above

50. Which of the following is/are subject committee?
   (*a*) Committee on Agriculture

(b) Committee on Environment and forests
(c) Committee on Science and Technology
(d) All of these

51. Which of the following statements describes a 'Hung Parliament'?
(a) A Parliament in which no party has clear majority
(b) The Prime Minister has resigned but Parliament is not dissolved
(c) Parliament lacks quorum to conduct business
(d) A lame duck Parliament

52. The word 'Parliament' is derived from the french term :
(a) Parto　　　　　(b) Parler
(c) Parlem　　　　(d) None of the above

53. Who among the following is not an integral part of Parliament?
(a) Rajya Sabha　　(b) President
(c) Lok Sabha　　　(d) Vice-President

54. The maximum strength of the Lok Sabha as envisaged under the constitution is :
(a) 552　　　　　　(b) 562
(c) 545　　　　　　(d) 565

55. The total elected strength of the Lok Sabha is distributed among the states in such a way that :
(a) There is no discrimination between states regarding their representation
(b) All the states are equally represented
(c) The ratio between the number of seats and the population of any state is same for all states
(d) Both (a) and (b)

56. In the context of Parliament, 'delimitation' means :
(a) Fixing the minimum age limited for voting
(b) The process of re-adjusting the representation of the electoral constituencies
(c) Put an end to limitation of the maximum times a person can fight the election to the Lok Sabha
(d) None of the above

57. Parliament can assume legislative power with respect to a state subject only if :
(a) President issues an ordinance to this effect
(b) Lok Sabha passes a resolution to this effect
(c) The council of states passes a resolution to this effect supported by two-thirds of its members present and voting
(d) All of the above

58. Which of the following acts, among other things, as an organ of information?
(a) Parliament
(b) Ministry of Information and Broad casting
(c) Comptroller and Auditor-General
(d) None of the above

59. Power to authorise expenditures for the public services to specify the purposes to which that money shall be appreciated, to provide ways and means to raise the revenue required belong to :
(a) Both Houses of the Parliament
(b) Rajya Sabha
(c) Lok Sabha
(d) None of the above

60. Presidential power to dissolve the House of people is laid down under Article term represents :
(a) 56　　　　　　(b) 61
(c) 85　　　　　　(d) 92

61. Which of the following term represents termination of a session of the House of people?
(a) Adjournment　　(b) Prorogation
(c) Dissolution　　　(d) None of the above

62. A person who sits or votes in either House of Parliament knowing that he is not qualified may have to pay a penalty of :
(a) Rs. 500 per day
(b) Single day imprisonment
(c) Rs. 5000 per day
(d) None of the above

63. Disqualifications for being a member of the either House of Parliament are laid down under Article :
(*a*) 100
(*b*) 101
(*c*) 102
(*d*) 103

64. The Speaker or Deputy Speaker of the Lok Sabha normally hold their office :
(*a*) For two years
(*b*) Till they are removed
(*c*) During the life of the House
(*d*) All of the above

65. Provisions for removal of the Speaker and Deputy Speaker of Lok Sabha are laid down under Article :
(*a*) 69
(*b*) 74
(*c*) 89
(*d*) 94

66. Deputy Speaker presides over a sitting of the Lower House of Parliament only when
(*a*) Office of the Speaker is vacant
(*b*) Speaker is absent from the sitting
(*c*) Both (*a*) and (*b*)
(*d*) When president asks him to do so

67. The constitution says that the Lok Sabha shall meet at least :
(*a*) Once a year
(*b*) Twice a year
(*c*) Thrice a year
(*d*) As many times as desirable

68. The Speaker of the Lok Sabha is elected by :
(*a*) Elected members of Rajya Sabha
(*b*) Members of Lok Sabha
(*c*) Elected members of the state legislature
(*d*) None of the above

69. The House Committee of each House is concerned with :
(*a*) Maintenance of decorum in each House
(*b*) Residential accommodation of the members of Parliament.
(*c*) Communication between the Lok Sabha and Rajya Sabha
(*d*) None of the above

70. The Lok Sabha took the historic decision of introducing the standing committee system in the Indian parliamentary practice in the year :
(*a*) 1991
(*b*) 1992
(*c*) 1993
(*d*) 1977

71. Which of the following constitutes the final step in financial legislation?
(*a*) Appropriation Bill
(*b*) Money Bill
(*c*) Finance Bill
(*d*) None of the above

72. The Joint Committee on salaries and allowances of members of Parliament consist of :
(*a*) Ten members from Lok Sabha
(*b*) Five members from Rajya Sabha
(*c*) Both (*a*) and (*b*)
(*d*) Three members either from Lok Sabha or from Rajya Sabha

73. Which of the following is the best example of Adhoc Committees?
(*a*) Public accounts committee
(*b*) Select committee on bills
(*c*) Joint committee on bills
(*d*) Both (*b*) and (*c*)

74. A device which members can employ to draw attention to specific grievances or criticise particular policies of the Government is :
(*a*) Cut motion
(*b*) Interpellation
(*c*) No-Confidence motion
(*d*) All of the above

75. The functioning of parliament every day normally begins with :
(*a*) Zero hour
(*b*) Question hour
(*c*) Short Notice Question
(*d*) None of the above

76. Though the development of legislative bodies in India has been spread over a fairly long period, the evolution of parliamentary procedure and practice cannot be said to have begun earlier than :
(*a*) 1919
(*b*) 1921
(*c*) 1935
(*d*) 1909

77. The committee which is responsible for ensuring timely laying of various papers in

parliament in compliance of statutory obligations, fulfilment of assurances etc is called :
(*a*) Committee on papers
(*b*) Committee on subordinate Legislation
(*c*) Business Advisory committee
(*d*) None of the above

78. Which of the following Articles lay down norms regarding making of laws by the legislature?
(*a*) Article 107 (*b*) Article 108
(*c*) Article 245 (*d*) All of these

79. When a proclamation of Emergency is in force, the term of Lok Sabha can be extended by Parliament for a period of :
(*a*) Two months
(*b*) One year
(*c*) Six months
(*d*) None of the above

80. "Committee on Government Assurances" is a :
(*a*) House Committee
(*b*) Enquiry Committee
(*c*) Scrutiny Committee
(*d*) Service Committee

ANSWERS

1	2	3	4	5	6	7	8	9	10
(*b*)	(*a*)	(*b*)	(*c*)	(*a*)	(*b*)	(*d*)	(*d*)	(*d*)	(*c*)
11	**12**	**13**	**14**	**15**	**16**	**17**	**18**	**19**	**20**
(*a*)	(*d*)	(*a*)	(*c*)	(*b*)	(*b*)	(*c*)	(*b*)	(*a*)	(*d*)
21	**22**	**23**	**24**	**25**	**26**	**27**	**28**	**29**	**30**
(*d*)	(*b*)	(*d*)	(*d*)	(*d*)	(*b*)	(*c*)	(*b*)	(*d*)	(*a*)
31	**32**	**33**	**34**	**35**	**36**	**37**	**38**	**39**	**40**
(*c*)	(*d*)	(*a*)	(*d*)	(*a*)	(*c*)	(*b*)	(*a*)	(*d*)	(*c*)
41	**42**	**43**	**44**	**45**	**46**	**47**	**48**	**49**	**50**
(*a*)	(*d*)	(*b*)	(*a*)	(*b*)	(*d*)	(*c*)	(*a*)	(*d*)	(*d*)
51	**52**	**53**	**54**	**55**	**56**	**57**	**58**	**59**	**60**
(*a*)	(*b*)	(*d*)	(*a*)	(*c*)	(*b*)	(*c*)	(*a*)	(*a*)	(*c*)
61	**62**	**63**	**64**	**65**	**66**	**67**	**68**	**69**	**70**
(*b*)	(*a*)	(*c*)	(*c*)	(*d*)	(*c*)	(*b*)	(*b*)	(*b*)	(*c*)
71	**72**	**73**	**74**	**75**	**76**	**77**	**78**	**79**	**80**
(*a*)	(*c*)	(*d*)	(*a*)	(*b*)	(*b*)	(*a*)	(*d*)	(*b*)	(*c*)

9

THE JUDICIARY

1. Which of the following is a consequence of the judicial activism?
   (*a*) Corruption exposed in high places
   (*b*) Peral action initiated against top politicians and public servants
   (*c*) Strict enforcement of Environmental Laws leading to closure of relocation of a large number of industries
   (*d*) All of the above

2. What "is now, in a sense democracy's non-democratic alternative to representative government when the later bogs down in failure of inaction", according to Fehrendbacher?
   (*a*) Government by Judiciary
   (*b*) Government by Bureaucrats
   (*c*) Government by Legislature
   (*d*) None of the above

3. The concept of judicial activism can be seen to be reflecting from which of the following trends?
   (*a*) Expansion of rights of hearing in the administrative process
   (*b*) Expansion of judicial control over discretionary powers
   (*c*) Promotion of open government
   (*d*) All of the above

4. Consider the following judgements delivered by the Supreme Court in about a single month of 1993 and choose the correct answer by using the codes :
   1. It defined the constitutional powers of the Chief Election Commissioner
   2. It threatened multi-crore rupees industries with closure if they continued to pollute the Ganga and endanger the Taj Mahal
   3. It brought all government and semi-government bodies under the purview of the consumer protection Act :
   (*a*) 1 and 2 are correct
   (*b*) 1, 2 and 3 are correct
   (*c*) 1 and 3 are correct
   (*d*) 2 and 3 are correct

5. Which of the following Articles specifically declares that any law which contravenes any of the provisions of the part of Fundamental Rights shall be void?
   (*a*) Article 12   (*b*) Article 13
   (*c*) Article 14   (*d*) Article 15

6. The judicial control over administrative acts stem from the doctrine of :
   (*a*) Separation of powers
   (*b*) Judicial review
   (*c*) Rule of law
   (*d*) Delegated legislation

7. Which of the following are the two prime functions of Judicial Review?
   (*a*) Legitimising government and protect the government from undue litigation
   (*b*) Legitimising government action and to protect the constitution against undue encroachment by the government
   (*c*) Legitimising the encroachment upon fundamental rights and to justify the social policies of the government
   (*d*) None of the above

8. The power of courts to hold any law or executive order unconstitutional or ultra-vires on the ground that it is in conflict with the constitution is known as :
   (*a*) Rule of law

(*b*) Delegated legislation
(*c*) Judicial law
(*d*) Judicial Review

9. Which of the following is a Quasi Judicial authority?
(*a*) High Court of a state
(*b*) Lok Ayukta in a state
(*c*) Central vigilance commission
(*d*) Administrative tribunal

10. The judicial activism has led to the prosecution of a number of politicians and other public servants on various charges under the :
(*a*) Indian Penal Code
(*b*) Prevention of Corruption Act
(*c*) TADA
(*d*) All of the above

11. The first major case of judicial activism through social action litigation was the :
(*a*) Rural Litigation Vs State of U.P. Case
(*b*) Bihar Undertrials Case
(*c*) Minerva Mills Case
(*d*) None of the above

12. In public interest litigation—
(*a*) Only an aggrieved person can approach the court for redress.
(*b*) Public officials can approach the court of wrong allegation imposed against them.
(*c*) Only certain social welfare organisations can aproach the court for seeking justice on behalf of aggrieved citizen.
(*d*) Citizens as well as any public spirited organisation can lodge complaints in court against administrative injustice being done to other people or a group or a community

13. Who among the following Chief Justices of India is reported to have said that judicial activism has been more or less thrust upon the Indian Judiciary?
(*a*) Kuldip Singh   (*b*) A.M. Ahmadi
(*c*) N.P. Singh   (*d*) J.S. Verma

14. The important question today is not whether the Supreme Court could activise its judicial role, but to what extend could the concepts of judicial activism and creativity be exercised — this is the view of.
(*a*) Justice Verma
(*b*) Justice Pandian
(*c*) Justice Ahmadi
(*d*) None of the above

15. The institution of ------ originated in the U.S. in mid-1960s and legal aid to these litigations were provided by private foundations.
(*a*) Public Interest Litigation
(*b*) Judicial Review
(*c*) Judicial Activism
(*d*) None of the above

16. What makes it clear that any person who suffers an injury but is unable to reach the court is helped by public-minded citizens to reach the court to seek justice?
(*a*) Judicial Activism
(*b*) Public Interest Litigation
(*c*) Judicial Review
(*d*) None of the above

17. The petition of public interest litigation can be filed by :
(*a*) Any voluntary agency
(*b*) Government officials only
(*c*) A member of the public
(*d*) Both (*a*) and (*c*)

18. What has been regarded as the root of P I L (Public Interest Litigation)?
(*a*) Judicial Review
(*b*) Judicial Activism
(*c*) Rule of Law
(*d*) None of the above

19. Under which of the following Articles of the Constitution of India the High Court and the Supreme Court within their original jurisdiction can issue writs against the state to set right the grievance of an aggrieved party by issuing writs/orders/injunctions etc.?
(*a*) Articles 32 and 36
(*b*) Articles 24 and 222
(*c*) Articles 226 and 32
(*d*) Articles 22 and 24

20. PIL has enabled the Supreme Court to exercise affirmative action to vindicate those socio-economic rights traditionally considered unenforceable by the court and has thus enlarged the scope of ------ of the constitution.
(*a*) Articles 32   (*b*) Articles 31
(*c*) Articles 30   (*d*) Articles 33

21. What does SAL stand for?
(*a*) Social Action Litigation
(*b*) Steel Authority Limited
(*c*) Social Authority of Legislation
(*d*) School Authority Limited

22. In which of the following, petitions are made for the enforcement of the specific rights of a determinate class or group of people who are primarily injured by the impugned action?
(*a*) PIL   (*b*) SAL
(*c*) Judicial Review   (*d*) None of the above

23. In which of the following, there may be no direct specific injury to any member of the public?
(*a*) PIL
(*b*) SAL
(*c*) Affirmative action
(*d*) None of the above

24. Which of the following is an example of Social Interest Litigation?
(*a*) Prisoners under trial
(*b*) Workers in stone quarries
(*c*) Inmates of care centres or homes
(*d*) All of the above

25. Who among the following said that PIL is "the strategic arm of the legal aid movement and aims at bringing justice within the reach of the poor vulnerable masses and helpless victims of injustice"?
(*a*) D.D. Basu
(*b*) G. Austin
(*c*) M. Kumaramangalam
(*d*) P.N. Bhagwati

26. Which of the following statements is correct regarding PIL?
(*a*) PIL is meant to bring justice to the doorstep of the weak, the unorganised and exploited sections of society who have no access to the courts

(*b*) PIL is a part of participatory justice
(*c*) PIL was an opportunity for like-minded citizens to participate and reaffirm their faith in the legal process
(*d*) All of the above

27. In which of the following, the collective rights of the public are affected and redress is sought for such injury?
(*a*) SAL   (*b*) PIL
(*c*) Judicial activism   (*d*) None of the above

28. In which of the following, the injury suffered by members of a determinate class or group of people is direct?
(*a*) PIL
(*b*) Affirmative Action
(*c*) SAL
(*d*) None of the above

29. The most distinctive feature of the work of United States Supreme Court is its power of :
(*a*) Judicial activism   (*b*) Judicial review
(*c*) Judicial law   (*d*) Rule of law

30. The constitutional validity of the ------, ------ and ------ Amendments was challenged in the Fundamental Rights case (Keshvananda Bharti Vs. State of Kerala, 1973).
(*a*) 30th, 31st, 32nd   (*b*) 24th, 25th, 29th
(*c*) 20th, 21st, 22nd   (*d*) 24th, 25th, 26th

31. The Court's judgement in the cases of Golak Nath, Bank Nationalisation and privy purses were in favour of :
(*a*) Public Property
(*b*) Intellectual Property
(*c*) Private Property
(*d*) None of the above

32. Who among the following has observed that "Every judge is an activist either on the forward gear or on the reverse"?
(*a*) Justice A.M. Ahmadi
(*b*) Justice Venkatchalaiya
(*c*) Justice Krishna Iyer
(*d*) Justice Bharucha

33. Judicial activism can be said to be policy making in competition with :
(*a*) Policy making by executive
(*b*) Policy making by legislature

(*c*) Both (*a*) and (*b*)

(*d*) Policy making by local bodies

34. Which of the following events played a role in putting an end to the passivity of Indian Judiciary?

(*a*) Emergency

(*b*) Movement led by Jayaprakash Narayan

(*c*) Bangladesh War of 1971

(*d*) All of the above

35. Which among the following was the first major case of judicial activism through social action litigation?

(*a*) Bihar undertrials case

(*b*) Maneka Vs Union of India case

(*c*) Bommai Vs Union of India case

(*d*) None of the above

36. In the fifties and through half of the seventies the Supreme Court on the whole adopted a :

(*a*) Historical view of the constitution

(*b*) Judicial and structural view of the constitution

(*c*) Sociological view of the constitution

(*d*) Both (*a*) and (*c*)

37. In which of the following cases the Supreme Court of India took the view that the Executive had no right to tamper with the constitution and alter its basic features?

(*a*) Golak Nath case

(*b*) Keshvananda Bharti case

(*c*) Minerva Mills case

(*d*) None of the above

38. Which government referred to the Supreme Court the emotive and controversial issue of 27% reservation of jobs in central government and public sector undertakings?

(*a*) Narsimha Rao government

(*b*) V.P. Singh government

(*c*) Chandrashekhar government

(*d*) Deve Gowda government

39. According to the Supreme Court's decision altogether what per cent of jobs could be reserved for deprived and poor castes and classes?

(*a*) 50%   (*b*) 49%

(*c*) 51%   (*d*) None of the above

40. Who among the following played an important and judicially activist role in the Jain Hawala case?

(*a*) Justice M.N. Venkatchalliah

(*b*) Justice A.M. Ahmadi

(*c*) Justice S.P. Bharucha

(*d*) Justice J.S. Verma

41. Who among the following opined that judicial activism has been more or less thrust upon the Indian Judiciary?

(*a*) Justice A.M. Ahmadi

(*b*) Justice N.P. Singh

(*c*) Justice B.N. Kripal

(*d*) None of the above

42. Who must be consulted in the case of appointment of a judge other than the Chief Justice?

(*a*) Vice-President

(*b*) Speaker of Lok Sabha

(*c*) Chief Justice

(*d*) Deputy Chairperson of the Rajya Sabha

43. For long after the commencement of the constitution the appointment of the Chief Justice remained automatic in the sense that the senior most Judge of the Supreme Court was elevated to the highest judicial office on the retirement of the incumbent. In which year this convention was broken?

(*a*) 1965   (*b*) 1973

(*c*) 1981   (*d*) 1993

44. Who among the following was the first Supreme Court Judge to be appointed Chief Justice superseding his three senior colleagues?

(*a*) Justice Gajendra Gadkar

(*b*) Justice A.N. Ray

(*c*) Justice Sujata Manohar

(*d*) Justice A.M. Ahmadi

45. Which of the following Articles of the constitution provides for the appointment of ad hoc Judges?

(*a*) Article 91   (*b*) Article 127

(*c*) Article 231   (*d*) None of the above

46. Adhoc judges are required in the Supreme Court if :
  (*a*) A sudden vacancy arises in the Court
  (*b*) The session of the Supreme Court cannot be held or continued for want of a quorum
  (*c*) Both (*a*) and (*b*)
  (*d*) At any time there is great work-load in the Court

47. What is the minimum age prescribed for appointment as a Judge of the Supreme Court?
  (*a*) 38 years
  (*b*) 45 years
  (*c*) 55 years
  (*d*) There is no minimum age

48. What is the maximum age prescribed under the constitution attaining which a judge of the Supreme Court may cease to be a judge?
  (*a*) 60 years   (*b*) 62 years
  (*c*) 65 years   (*d*) 68 years

49. A Judge of Supreme Court may resign his office by writing addressed to :
  (*a*) The Chief Justice
  (*b*) The President
  (*c*) The Prime Minister
  (*d*) The Law Minister

50. A Judge of the Supreme Court can be removed from his position only on the ground of :
  (*a*) Proved misbehaviour
  (*b*) Incapacity
  (*c*) Either (*a*) or (*b*)
  (*d*) Insolvency

51. Under a federal constitution a Supreme Court is an essential part of the constitutional scheme. It is at once the highest interpreter of the constitution and a Tribunal for the final determination of disputes between the Union and its constituent units. Who among the following is authorised, under the constitution of India to change the number of judges?
  (*a*) Supreme Court itself
  (*b*) Parliament
  (*c*) President
  (*d*) Prime Minister

52. Mandamus is a Writ issued by the court—
  (*a*) Enquiring into the legality of claim of any person to public office.
  (*b*) Asking a person who has detained any other person unlawfully or illegally to produce before the court.
  (*c*) Asking a public official or any authority to perform legal duties.
  (*d*) Against any lower court not to do any acts in excess of their jurisdiction.

53. What is mean by Judicial Review?
  (*a*) Parliament's right to ask the Judiciary to review Judgements.
  (*b*) The president's right to seek the opinion of the supreme court on the constitutionality of law passed by parliament.
  (*c*) Judiciary's power to pronounce upon the constitutionality of laws passed by the Legislature and orders issued by the Executive.
  (*d*) Judiciary's right to review judgements passed by lower courts.

54. An All India Court was for the first time set up under :
  (*a*) Indian Independence Act, 1947
  (*b*) Second Constitution (Amendment) Act, 1951
  (*c*) Government of India Act, 1935
  (*d*) Government of India Act, 1919

55. Which of the following is the important consequence of judicial activism?
  (*a*) Exposure of corruption in high places
  (*b*) Initiation of penal action against top politicians and public servants
  (*c*) Enforcement of environmental laws leading to closure of relocation of many industries
  (*d*) All of the above

56. Who commented that—"Government by Judiciary is now, in a sense democracy's non-democratic alternative to representative government when the later bogs down in failure of in action"?
  (*a*) Chief Justice Huges
  (*b*) Fehrendbacher
  (*c*) Chief Justice Marshall
  (*d*) None of the above

57. A Judge of the High Court can be removed from office during his tenure by—
(*a*) The Governor, if the State Legislature passes a resolution to this effect by two-third majority.
(*b*) The president on the basis of a resolution passed by parliament by special majority.
(*c*) The Chief Justice of the Supreme Court on the recommendation of parliament.
(*d*) The president on the recommendation of the Chief Justice of the concerned High Court.

58. Judicial Review in India is based on—
(*a*) Procedure established by law.
(*b*) Due process of law.
(*c*) Rule of law.
(*d*) Precedents and conventions.

59. The grounds as mentioned under Article 124(4) on which a Judge of the Supreme Court can be removed by the president include :
(*a*) Immoral conduct
(*b*) Proved misbehaviour and incapacity
(*c*) Occupation of and office of profit
(*d*) All of the above

60. Which Article of the constitution grants an unlimited right to the Supreme Court to entertain appeal, by special leave, in any cause or matter determined by any court or tribunal in India, save military tribunals?
(*a*) Article 121　　(*b*) Article 131
(*c*) Article 136　　(*d*) Article 146

61. Which among the following institutions has the power to make laws regulating the constitution, organisation, jurisdiction and powers of the Supreme Court?
(*a*) President
(*b*) Parliament
(*c*) Lok Sabha
(*d*) Supreme Court itself

62. The original jurisdiction of the Supreme Court is dealt with in the Article :
(*a*) 121　　(*b*) 131
(*c*) 141　　(*d*) 151

63. With the coming into force of the Indian constitution, the Federal court of India was substituted by the Supreme Court. How many judges were there in the Supreme Court in 1950 when the Court was inaugurated with the new constitution?
(*a*) 8　　(*b*) 25
(*c*) 15　　(*d*) 32

ANSWERS

1	2	3	4	5	6	7	8	9	10
(*d*)	(*a*)	(*d*)	(*b*)	(*b*)	(*c*)	(*b*)	(*d*)	(*d*)	(*d*)
11	**12**	**13**	**14**	**15**	**16**	**17**	**18**	**19**	**20**
(*b*)	(*d*)	(*b*)	(*b*)	(*a*)	(*b*)	(*d*)	(*b*)	(*c*)	(*a*)
21	**22**	**23**	**24**	**25**	**26**	**27**	**28**	**29**	**30**
(*a*)	(*b*)	(*a*)	(*d*)	(*d*)	(*d*)	(*b*)	(*c*)	(*b*)	(*b*)
31	**32**	**33**	**34**	**35**	**36**	**37**	**38**	**39**	**40**
(*c*)	(*c*)	(*c*)	(*a*)	(*a*)	(*b*)	(*b*)	(*a*)	(*a*)	(*d*)
41	**42**	**43**	**44**	**45**	**46**	**47**	**48**	**49**	**50**
(*a*)	(*c*)	(*b*)	(*b*)	(*b*)	(*b*)	(*d*)	(*c*)	(*b*)	(*c*)
51	**52**	**53**	**54**	**55**	**56**	**57**	**58**	**59**	**60**
(*b*)	(*c*)	(*c*)	(*c*)	(*d*)	(*b*)	(*b*)	(*a*)	(*b*)	(*c*)
61	**62**	**63**							
(*b*)	(*b*)	(*a*)							

10

THE STATE EXECUTIVE

1. Who among the following said that the Governor "must be acceptable to the Government of the province"?
   (a) J.L. Nehru   (b) Gandhi
   (c) N.V. Gadgil   (d) V.V. Giri

2. Which of the following powers are enjoyed by the Governor?
   1. Executive powers
   2. Military powers
   3. Legislative powers
   4. Diplomatic powers
   5. Judicial powers
   Choose the correct answer from the codes given below :
   Codes :
   (a) 1, 2 and 3   (b) 1, 3 and 5
   (c) 2, 3 and 5   (d) 1, 2 and 4

3. Who among the following shall have the right to speak and to take part in the proceedings of, but no right to vote in, the Houses of the Legislature of the state?
   (a) Attorney-General
   (b) Auditor-General
   (c) Advocate-General
   (d) None of the above

4. In which of the following cases the supreme court held that the office of the Governor is not an office of profit under the Government?
   (a) Surya Narain Vs. Union of India
   (b) Hargovind Vs. Raghukul
   (c) Sanjeevi Vs. State of Madras
   (d) Sunit Kumar Vs. Government of West Bengal

5. The notorious misuse of ordinance-making power of the Governor was highlighted in the case of :
   (a) Hussain Vs. Najalingappa (1969)
   (b) K.M. Nanavati Vs. state of Bombay (1961)
   (c) D.C. Wadhava Vs. State of Bihar (1987)
   (d) None of the above

6. Normally, there shall be a Governor for each state, but an amendment of 1956 makes it possible to appoint the same person as the Governor for two or more states under :
   (a) Article 152   (b) Article 153
   (c) Article 253   (d) Article 254

7. Match List I with List II and select the correct answer by using the codes given below the lists :

	List I		List II
A.	Article 168	1.	Governor summons and prorogues the two Houses of the state legislature
B.	Article 174	2.	Governor addresses the members of the Legislature and may send messages
C.	Article 175-176	3.	The Governor is a part of the Legislature
D.	Article 200	4.	Without the Governor's assent, no Bill can become law

   Codes :

	A	B	C	D
(a)	1	2	3	4
(b)	4	3	2	1
(c)	3	1	2	4
(d)	3	1	4	2

8. What is the maximum possible strength of the Legislative Assembly of a State?

(*a*) 400 members   (*b*) 425 members
(*c*) 500 members   (*d*) 545 members

9. Which of the following union territories has its territorial areas spread in three states?
(*a*) Chandigarh   (*b*) Delhi
(*c*) Puducherry   (*d*) Lakshadweep

10. Under ------- the Governor may promulgate ordinances during the period when the House or both the Houses, where there are two Houses of state legislature, are not in session.
(*a*) Article 213   (*b*) Article 210
(*c*) Article 212   (*d*) Article 209

11. Which of the following Articles of the Indian Constitution says that there shall be a Governor for each State?
(*a*) Article 142   (*b*) Article 143
(*c*) Article 144   (*d*) Article 145

12. By the seventh constitutional amendment Act of 1956, it has been provided that :
(*a*) The same person can be appointed as Governor for more than one state
(*b*) The election of president or vice-president could not be challenged on the ground of any vacancy in the appropriate electoral college
(*c*) A High court should consider the question of granting a certificate for appeal to supreme court
(*d*) None of the above

13. Consider the following methods :
1. Election by adult suffrage
2. Election by the members of the lower House or both Houses of the state legislature either by the system of proportional representation or otherwise
3. Selection by the president out of a panel submitted by the lower house of the state legislature
4. Appointment by president
Which of the above are the alternative methods of selecting the Governor which the constituent assembly discussed before finally adopting "appointment by the president"?
(*a*) 1, 2 and 3   (*b*) 2 and 3
(*c*) 1 and 2   (*d*) 1, 2, 3, and 4

14. Which of the following Articles prescribes the term of office for a Governor as five years but he holds office at the pleasure of the president?
(*a*) Article 154   (*b*) Article 155
(*c*) Article 156   (*d*) Article 157

15. Who among the following was the only Governor appointed from a non-congress party upto 1964?
(*a*) Pattom Thanu Pillai
(*b*) Nurul Hassan
(*c*) Chintamani Panigrahi
(*d*) Khurshid Alam Khan

16. Which of the following commissions had recommended that a person who can be trusted to rise above party prejudicies and predilections should be considered for the post of Governor?
(*a*) Second Pay Commission
(*b*) The Administrative Reforms Commission
(*c*) Sarkaria Commission
(*d*) None of the above

17. Which of the following statements is not true regarding appointment of the Governor?
(*a*) Nath Pai suggested that the appointment of Governor should be subject to the approval of parliament
(*b*) The Setalwad study team is of the view that the Chief Minister should be consulted
(*c*) A.B. Vajpayee suggested that a panel of names should be placed before the Chief Minister to select one of them
(*d*) V.V. Giri expressed the view that the appointment should be made by the president

18. The study team of the Administrative reforms commission on union-state relations suggested that the following points ought to be observed :
1. The appointment of the Governor should be subject to parliament's approval
2. There should be practice of consulting the opposition leaders in the Lok Sabha on every selection of a Governor, before his appointment

3. The president should be given the right to select governor in his discretion. Choose the correct answer by using the codes given below :

Codes :
(*a*) 1 and 2
(*b*) 2 and 3
(*c*) 1 and 3
(*d*) 1, 2 and 3

19. Which of the following committees appointed by the DMK government in September 1969 suggested that a body of eminent jurists, lawyers and experienced administrators should be set up to select a Governor?
(*a*) Kripalani Committee
(*b*) Santhanam Committee
(*c*) Vohra Committee
(*d*) Rajmannar Committee

20. The Sarkaria commission recommended that a person to be appointed as a Governor should satisfy the following criteria :
1. He should be eminent in some walk of life
2. He should be a person from outside the state
3. He should be a person who has not taken too great a part in politics generally and particularly in the recent past
4. He should be a detached figure and not too intimately connected with the local politics of the state
Which of the above are correct? Choose the correct answer using the codes given below :
(*a*) 1, 2, 3 and 4
(*b*) 1, 2 and 3
(*c*) 1 and 2
(*d*) None of the above

21. Which Article of the Constitution makes a mention of the qualifications for membership of the state legislature?
(*a*) Article 173
(*b*) Article 283
(*c*) Article 169
(*d*) Article 174

22. Which Article of the constitution makes it clear that as a constitutional head of the state executive, governor has to act on the advice of the council of ministers?

(*a*) Article 256
(*b*) Article 163
(*c*) Both (*a*) and (*b*)
(*d*) Article 221

23. As regards matters on which the Governor is empowered to act in his discretion or on his 'special responsibility', the Governor will be under the complete control of the :
(*a*) President
(*b*) Prime Minister
(*c*) Chief Minister
(*d*) None of the above

24. Under Article 333 how many members of the Anglo-Indian community can be nominated by the Governor in the Legislative Assembly of the State if he is of the opinion that they are not adequately represented?
(*a*) One
(*b*) Two
(*c*) Three
(*d*) Indefinite

25. Who among the following is eligible for the office of the Governor?
(*a*) A member of the State Legislative Assembly
(*b*) A citizen of India who is over thirty-five years of age
(*c*) Any non-political persons
(*d*) None of the above

26. The term of office of the Governor is normally for five years. However, it can be terminated earlier by :
(*a*) Dismissal by the President
(*b*) Resignation
(*c*) Either (*a*) or (*b*)
(*d*) Impeachment

27. Which of the following is prohibited to a Governor?
(*a*) Holding any office of profit
(*b*) Holding governorship of any other state
(*c*) Membership of the union parliament or any state legislature
(*d*) Both (*a*) and (*c*)

28. Who makes laws relating to emoluments, allowances and privileges of the Governor?
(*a*) Parliament
(*b*) State Council of Ministers
(*c*) President
(*d*) None of the above

29. Which of the following articles of the constitution provides for a Governor for each state?
(*a*) Article 92 (*b*) Article 143
(*c*) Article 84 (*d*) Article 261

30. Article 155 of the constitution provides that the Governor of a state shall be appointed by the President by warrant under his hand and seal. But in actual practice he is appointed by :
(*a*) Lok Sabha
(*b*) State Council of Ministers
(*c*) Central Government
(*d*) None of the above

31. Which of the following offices has no Constitutional validity and legal sanction?
(*a*) Governor
(*b*) Chief Minister
(*c*) Deputy Chief Minister
(*d*) Speaker of the Assembly

32. Arunachal Pradesh became a state from the Union Territory in the year:
(*a*) 1983
(*b*) 1987
(*c*) 1994
(*d*) 1971

33. In a state, the minister is the political head of the department whose administrative head is :
(*a*) Deputy Minister
(*b*) Minister of state
(*c*) Secretary
(*d*) None of the above

34. Which among the following works is authored by Subhash C. Kashyap?
(*a*) The politics of power
(*b*) In pursuit of Lakshmi
(*c*) The Modernity of Tradition
(*d*) The Indian political system

35. Chief Minister of a state is the sole channel of communication between :
(*a*) Ministers and the Legislature
(*b*) Ministers and the Governor
(*c*) Both (a) and (b)
(*d*) Governor and the Legislature

36. Whips are maintained by the parties to :
(*a*) Discuss matters of national interest
(*b*) Discipline the members of legislature belonging to respective parties
(*c*) Act as a precautionary measure in case of an imminent threat of defection from the party
(*d*) Both (*b*) and (*c*)

37. The Chief Minister is ultimately responsible to :
(*a*) Electorate (*b*) Governor
(*c*) Legislature (*d*) Prime Minister

38. Which of the following has not been specified in the constitution?
(*a*) Size of the Council of Minister
(*b*) Salaries of the Council of Minister
(*c*) Both (a) and (b)
(*d*) Powers of the Chief Minister

39. Which Article of the Constitution discusses removal of the Governor?
(*a*) Article 155 (*b*) Article 156
(*c*) Article 157 (*d*) Article 158

40. Which Article of the constitution makes a mention of the Advocate-General for the state?
(*a*) Article 157 (*b*) Article 167
(*c*) Article 177 (*d*) Article 187

41. Which Article of the Constitution provides the procedure for the abolition of the second chamber of the Legislature (Legislative Council) in a state where it exists as well as for the creation of such a chamber in a state where there is none at present?
(*a*) Article 139 (*b*) Article 231
(*c*) Article 169 (*d*) None of these

42. Which of the following are necessarily the part of every State Legislature in India?
(*a*) Governor
(*b*) Governor and Legislative Assembly
(*c*) Legislative Assembly and Legislative Council
(*d*) Governor and Legislative Council

43. Of the total number of members of the Legislative Council in State what is the proportion of members nominated by the Governor of the State?

   (*a*) One-Fourth   (*b*) One-fifth

   (*c*) One-Sixth   (*d*) One-seventh

44. All decisions of the council of ministers in a state relating to the administration of the state of affairs and proposals of legislation are communicated to the Governor by :

   (*a*) Secretary of the Legislative Assembly

   (*b*) Chief Minister

   (*c*) Advisor to the Chief Minister

   (*d*) None of the above

45. Article 108 of the Constitution, inter alia prescribes that the assent of the president is mandatory for a Union Bill to become an Act. Which Article speaks of a similar provision for a State Bill?

   (*a*) Article 123   (*b*) Article 226

   (*c*) Article 157   (*d*) None of the above

46. Which Article confers upon the Governor the power to reserve a Bill pertaining to the state for consideration of the President?

   (*a*) Article 100   (*b*) Article 200

   (*c*) Article 111   (*d*) Article 179

47. The States having Bicameral Legislatures are :

   (*a*) Bihar, Rajasthan, Uttar Pradesh, Orissa and Jammu and Kashmir

   (*b*) Bihar, Maharashtra, Karnataka, Uttar Pradesh, Andhra Pradesh and Jammu and Kashmir

   (*c*) Rajasthan, Assam, Madhya Pradesh, Uttar Pradesh, Bihar, West Bengal

   (*d*) Tamil Nadu, Punjab, Kerala, Bihar, Jammu and Kashmir

48. Which Article of the Constitution confers upon the Governor of a state the power to make ordinances?

   (*a*) Article 123   (*b*) Article 213

   (*c*) Article 93   (*d*) None of the above

ANSWERS

1	2	3	4	5	6	7	8	9	10
(*a*)	(*b*)	(*c*)	(*b*)	(*c*)	(*b*)	(*c*)	(*c*)	(*c*)	(*a*)
11	**12**	**13**	**14**	**15**	**16**	**17**	**18**	**19**	**20**
(*b*)	(*a*)	(*d*)	(*c*)	(*a*)	(*b*)	(*d*)	(*d*)	(*d*)	(*a*)
21	**22**	**23**	**24**	**25**	**26**	**27**	**28**	**29**	**30**
(*a*)	(*b*)	(*a*)	(*a*)	(*b*)	(*c*)	(*d*)	(*a*)	(*b*)	(*c*)
31	**32**	**33**	**34**	**35**	**36**	**37**	**38**	**39**	**40**
(*c*)	(*b*)	(*c*)	(*a*)	(*b*)	(*b*)	(*a*)	(*b*)	(*b*)	(*c*)
41	**42**	**43**	**44**	**45**	**46**	**47**	**48**		
(*c*)	(*b*)	(*c*)	(*b*)	(*c*)	(*b*)	(*b*)	(*b*)		

11

INDIAN PARTY SYSTEM

1. Which of the following is the distinctive feature of the Indian party system?
(*a*) Weakness of non-congress parties
(*b*) Lack of the ideological commitment
(*c*) Factions within the parties
(*d*) All of the above

2. Consider the following problems of the political parties in India and choose the correct answer using the codes given below :
1. Organisational problems
2. Defections
3. Finances
4. More splits in parties

Codes :
(*a*) 1 and 2 are correct
(*b*) 1, 2, 3 and 4 are correct
(*c*) 2 and 3 are correct
(*d*) 1, 2 and 3 are correct

3. Rajni Kothari prefers to call the Indian party system as :
(*a*) Congress system
(*b*) One party Dominance system
(*c*) Multi-party system
(*d*) Both (a) and (b)

4. Which of the following is an example of adhoc parties?
(*a*) The Bangla Congress
(*b*) The Kerala Congress
(*c*) The BKD of Charan Singh
(*d*) All of the above

5. Consider the following statements regarding communal parties and choose the correct answer :
(*a*) They seek to protect and promote the interest of that particular community alone
(*b*) They are basically non-aggregative in their nature
(*c*) They generally mobilize their supporters by appealing to their particularist sentiments
(*d*) All of the above

6. Consider the following political parties of India—
1. DMK   2. CPI (M)
3. AGP   4. TDP
Which one of the following is the correct chronology of their formation?
(*a*) 1, 2, 4 and 3   (*b*) 1, 2, 3 and 4
(*c*) 2, 1, 4 and 3   (*d*) 4, 3, 2 and 1

7. Which of the following are called right parties?
(*a*) Traditional parties formed around religious community and caste
(*b*) Communist and socialist parties
(*c*) Regional and local parties
(*d*) Trans-regional and regional parties

8. What does DMK stand for?
(*a*) Delhi Munnetra Kazhagam
(*b*) Dravida Munnetra Kazhagam
(*c*) Dravida Manipur Kazhagam
(*d*) Dravida Megha Kerala

9. Which of the following is not a variant of the one party system?
(*a*) Where only one party is recognised
(*b*) Where one party represents the majority community
(*c*) Where one party prevails by restricting opposition parties or absorbing them
(*d*) Dominance of one party

10. Which of the following political parties does not belong to pondicherry?

(*a*) AIADMK
(*b*) DMK
(*c*) Pattali Makkal Katchi
(*d*) Shiv Sena

11. The Dravida Munnetra Kazhagam was founded in the year :
(*a*) 1945   (*b*) 1946
(*c*) 1947   (*d*) 1950

12. Who among the following said that 'party government is the vital principle of representative government'?
(*a*) Bryce   (*b*) Munro
(*c*) Bagehot   (*d*) Ogg

13. Which of the following countries have the two party system?
(*a*) Great Britain and USA
(*b*) India and Pakistan
(*c*) China and Japan
(*d*) None of the above

14. In which of the following countries one party prevails by restricting opposition parties or absorbing them?
(*a*) Myanmar   (*b*) Kenya
(*c*) Ghana   (*d*) All of these

15. Which of the following parties are considered as left parties?
(*a*) Liberal and Religious parties
(*b*) Local and Regional parties
(*c*) Socialist and Traditional parties
(*d*) Communist and Socialist parties

16. Consider the following statements—
1. Article 86(1) of the constitution provides that the president may address either house of parliament or both the Houses assembled together.
2. The provision for address by the Head of State to Parliament was made for the first time under the Government of India Act, 1935

Which of the statements given above is/are correct?
(*a*) 1 only   (*b*) 2 only
(*c*) Both 1 and 2   (*d*) Neither 1 nor 2

17. Which of the following is not a regional party of India?
(*a*) AIADMK
(*b*) Telugu Desam
(*c*) National Conference
(*d*) BJP

18. Nehru's classification of political parties includes :
(*a*) Communist party
(*b*) Communal parties
(*c*) Local parties
(*d*) All of the above

19. Which of the following parties may not survive very long, which may appear only for a short period and then disappear completely or merge into other parties?
(*a*) Communal parties (*b*) Regional parties
(*c*) Adhoc parties   (*d*) None of the above

20. Consider the following statements regarding regional parties and choose the correct one :
(*a*) Their power base and voting strength are confined to a particular geographic area
(*b*) These parties try to aggregate regional interests regardless of the caste and religious affiliations of their members
(*c*) These parties present national platform and emphasize national issues in the parliamentary elections
(*d*) Both (a) and (b)

21. During which of the following years, the Congress party has faced serious electoral reverses?
(*a*) 1967   (*b*) 1977
(*c*) 1989   (*d*) All of these

22. Which of the following can be designated as regional party?
(*a*) Akali Dal   (*b*) Congress
(*c*) BJP   (*d*) All of these

23. The work 'Democracy in India' is authored by
(*a*) Rajni Kothari
(*b*) Rasheeduddin Khan
(*c*) C.P. Bhambhri
(*d*) None of the above

24. Among the following, rule of the one party has been associated with :
- (*a*) Latin American countries
- (*b*) East European countries
- (*c*) West African countries
- (*d*) South East Asian Countries

25. An effective opposition appeared on the political-electoral scene in India during :
- (*a*) Second general election
- (*b*) Third general election
- (*c*) Fourth general election
- (*d*) Emergency

26. The thesis which see us to establish the relationship between electroral process and the party system is known as—
- (*a*) Duverger's thesis
- (*b*) Weber's doctrine
- (*c*) Mosca's thesis
- (*d*) None of the above

27. Which among the following is modern interest-cum-pressure group?
- (*a*) Municipality
- (*b*) Trade Union
- (*c*) Environmental groups
- (*d*) NGOs

28. Which of the following is the largest and most influential organisation of private capital in India?
- (*a*) Industrial Credit and Investment Bank of India
- (*b*) Federation of Indian Chambers of Commerce and Industry
- (*c*) National Alliance of Young Entrepreneurs (NAYE)
- (*d*) Sri Narayana Dharma Paripalanam (SNDP)

29. Identify the characteristics of the 'Congress System' as described by Rajni Kothari—
- (*a*) Faction-ridden party with charismatic leadership.
- (*b*) One-party dominance with weak opposition.
- (*c*) One-party dominance and factions in the party networking with the opposition.
- (*d*) One-party dominance and a strong regional leadership.

30. In the long drawn struggle against imperial domination, political parties represented an assertion of national solidarity of the Indian people. India's party system originated in :
- (*a*) Early twentieth century
- (*b*) Late nineteenth century
- (*c*) Mid-twentieth century
- (*d*) Early nineteenth century

31. Who of the following presidents of India was associated with the Trade Union Movement in India?
- (*a*) V.V. Giri
- (*b*) N. Sanjiva Reddy
- (*c*) K.R. Narayanan
- (*d*) Zakir Hussain

32. The Indian National Congress was a platform of loyalist reformers like cosmopolitan rich, the leisurely and influential community leaders etc from :
- (*a*) 1885 to 1904
- (*b*) 1904 to 1918
- (*c*) 1900 to 1925
- (*d*) None of the above

33. Which of the following best perform the function of interest articulation in a political system?
1. Trade Union and ethnic associations.
2. Organisations of businessmen and civic groups.
3. Judiciary and Law-making institutions

Select the correct answer using the codes given below :

Codes :
- (*a*) 1, 2 and 3
- (*b*) 2 and 3 only
- (*c*) 1 and 2 only
- (*d*) 1 only

34. At the time of independence who opined that "the Congress should flower into a Lok Sewak Sangh"?
- (*a*) Mahatma Gandhi
- (*b*) Jawahar Lal Nehru
- (*c*) V.B. Patel
- (*d*) Abdul Gaffar Khan

35. In Asian politics, the oldest political party is :
(*a*) Golkar party of Malaysia
(*b*) Indian National Congress of India
(*c*) Jiyuminken of Japan
(*d*) Awami league of Bangladesh, formely East Pakistan

36. Of the total votes polled in general elections in India since independence the electorally dominant political party has never governed with :
(*a*) More than 70% of the total votes polled
(*b*) Less than 50% of the total votes polled
(*c*) More than 60% of the total votes polled
(*d*) Less than 60% of the total votes polled

37. The Communist Party of India was established in the year :
(*a*) 1935   (*b*) 1950
(*c*) 1893   (*d*) 1920

38. The Bhartiya Jana Sangh revived under a new name-Bhartiya Janata Party (BJP) in the year :
(*a*) 1977   (*b*) 1980
(*c*) 1981   (*d*) 1990

39. In which year Communist Parties were got devided into CPI & CPI (M)?
(*a*) 1960   (*b*) 1964
(*c*) 1968   (*d*) 1972

40. In which year BSP led by Late Kanshi Ram was formed?
(*a*) 1978   (*b*) 1982
(*c*) 1984   (*d*) 1988

ANSWERS

1	2	3	4	5	6	7	8	9	10
(*d*)	(*b*)	(*d*)	(*d*)	(*d*)	(*a*)	(*a*)	(*b*)	(*b*)	(*d*)
11	**12**	**13**	**14**	**15**	**16**	**17**	**18**	**19**	**20**
(*a*)	(*c*)	(*a*)	(*d*)	(*d*)	(*c*)	(*d*)	(*d*)	(*c*)	(*d*)
21	**22**	**23**	**24**	**25**	**26**	**27**	**28**	**29**	**30**
(*d*)	(*a*)	(*b*)	(*b*)	(*c*)	(*a*)	(*b*)	(*b*)	(*b*)	(*b*)
31	**32**	**33**	**34**	**35**	**36**	**37**	**38**	**39**	**40**
(*a*)	(*a*)	(*c*)	(*a*)	(*c*)	(*a*)	(*d*)	(*b*)	(*b*)	(*c*)

12

GOVERNMENT AND TECHNOLOGY BUSINESS

1. The department of science and technology has been operating a scheme entitled 'Assistance for Development of State Councils on Science and Technology'
   (*a*) Since 1980   (*b*) Since 1970
   (*c*) Since 1982   (*d*) Since 1979

2. In the context of Indian defence **'Dhruv'** is—
   (*a*) Advance light Helicopter
   (*b*) Anti-craft Missile
   (*c*) Anti-Landmins Tank
   (*d*) None of these

3. International Science and Technology cooperation is realised at which of the following levels?
   (*a*) Bilateral cooperation with developed and developing countries
   (*b*) Regional cooperation such as with SAARC, ASEAN and BIMST countries
   (*c*) Multilateral cooperation through NAMS and T centre, COSTED, UNESCO etc.
   (*d*) All of the above

4. The India Meteorological Department (IMD) was establishment in the year :
   (*a*) 1877   (*b*) 1875
   (*c*) 1876   (*d*) 1880

5. What does NCMRWF stand for?
   (*a*) National Centre for Medium Range Weather Forecasting
   (*b*) National Centre for Marginal Range Weather Forecasting
   (*c*) Natural Centre for Medium Range Weather Forecasting
   (*d*) None of the above

6. **MCA-21** is a major initiative taken up by the Government of India in the field of—
   (*a*) Health
   (*b*) Education
   (*c*) Poverty Eradication
   (*d*) E-Governance

7. Which of the following is the principal organisation established for transferring technologies from Research and Development laboratories to industry?
   (*a*) Natural Research Development Corporation
   (*b*) National Research Development Commission
   (*c*) National Research Development Corporation
   (*d*) None of the above

8. The Council of Scientific and Industrial Research (CSIR) was constituted as an autonomous society in the year :
   (*a*) 1942   (*b*) 1945
   (*c*) 1946   (*d*) 1941

9. The Nuclear power programme of Department of Atomic Energy envisages building of pressurised ----- on commercial scale.
   (*a*) Heavy water reactors
   (*b*) Fast breeder reactors

(*c*) Thorium based reactors

(*d*) All of the above

10. The Department of Atomic Energy units engaged in the laser research and development programme are :

(*a*) CAT and NFC

(*b*) AMD and IGCAR

(*c*) CAT and BARC

(*d*) None of the above

11. Which of the following is one of the notable institutional structures which contributed to research and development being carried out in the country?

(*a*) The Council of Scientific and Industrial Research

(*b*) Council of Agricultural Research

(*c*) Indian Council of Medical Research

(*d*) All of the above

12. Council of Scientific and Industrial Research (CSIR) functions under the presidentship of:

(*a*) Prime Minister of India

(*b*) Home Minister of India

(*c*) Rural Development Ministry of India

(*d*) None of these

13. What does IRHPA stand for?

(*a*) Intensification of Research in High Priority Areas

(*b*) Industrial Research in High Priority Areas

(*c*) Industrial Research in Highly Productive Areas

(*d*) None of the above

14. The main objectives of TIFAC (Technology Information Forecasting and Assessment Council) include :

(*a*) Generation of Technology Forecasting and Technology Assessment

(*b*) Techno-market survey documents

(*c*) Enabling a Technology Information System

(*d*) All of the above

15. Centre for DNA Finger-printing and Diagnostics is located in:

(*a*) Kolkata   (*b*) Hyderabad

(*c*) Delhi   (*d*) Chennai

16. 'Hydrocarbon Vision-2025' is associated with:

(*a*) Storage of petroleum products

(*b*) Euro-II & Euro-III Vehicles

(*c*) Green house effect

(*d*) None of the above

17. The Natural Resources Data Management Programme is being implemented to upgrade the existing data management methodologies at the :

(*a*) Village level

(*b*) District level

(*c*) Block level

(*d*) None of the above

18. The headquarters of the Department of Space (DOS) and Indian Space Research Organisation (ISRO) are located at

(*a*) Hyderabad   (*b*) Goa

(*c*) Lucknow   (*d*) Bengaluru

19. Which of the following countries is emerging as a global power in Information Technology (IT) as one of the largest generators and exporters of Software in the World?

(*a*) Japan   (*b*) India

(*c*) Germany   (*d*) Italy

20. Which one of the following is not a space Satellite?

(*a*) SLV-3   (*b*) RS-D1

(*c*) IRS-1D   (*d*) INSAT-2D

21. Which one of the following regions of India in now regarded as an 'ecological hot spot'?

(*a*) Western Himalayas

(*b*) Eastern Himalayas

(*c*) Eastern Ghats

(*d*) Western Ghats

22. T E Marshall links one person one vote for citizenship with:

(*a*) Social class in the context of capitalism and its by-product, the market

(*b*) Suffragist movement of the nineteenth century

(*c*) Emergence of Marxism
(*d*) Rise of political parties

23. Kymlicka's theory of citizenship is based on:
(*a*) Culturally differentiated rights
(*b*) One person one vote
(*c*) Weightage in voting for the minorities
(*d*) The philosophy of uniform citizenship

24. The first operational long range forecast of seasonal monsoon rainfall (June-September) of India was issued by India Meteorological Department in the year :
(*a*) 1988
(*b*) 1986
(*c*) 1985
(*d*) 1987

25. Which of the following programmes has been initiated to promote innovation among enterpreneurs?
(*a*) Entrepreneur promotion programme
(*b*) Programme for Entrepreneur promotion
(*c*) Technopreneur promotion programme
(*d*) None of the above

26. ELISA Test is carry out for detection of:
(*a*) Aids
(*b*) Typhoid
(*c*) Cancer
(*d*) Pregnancy

27. The Information Technology (IT) Act, which provides legal framework for recognition of electronic contracts, prevention of computer crimes, electronic filling of documents and digital signature, came into effect on :
(*a*) 19th June 2000
(*b*) 14th August 2000
(*c*) 18th October 2000
(*d*) 15th May 2000

28. ------ is the only Government organisation in India, at present, offering network services over C-band and K4-band (TDMA, FTDMA and SCPC) VSATs, wireless Metropolitan Area Networks (MANs) and Local Area Networks (LANs).
(*a*) Multi-media Information Centre
(*b*) National Informatics Centre
(*c*) Computer Informatics Centre
(*d*) None of the above

29. India tested its first Nuclear device on—
(*a*) 15 May, 1972
(*b*) 18 May, 1974
(*c*) 20 May, 1975
(*d*) 26 May, 1976

30. In which of the following years, a separate Department of Biotechnology was established under the Ministry of Science and Technology?
(*a*) 1986
(*b*) 1987
(*c*) 1988
(*d*) 1985

31. What does SEETOT stand for?
(*a*) Scheme to Enhance the Efficiency of Technology Transfer
(*b*) Scientific Economic Establishment to Transfer Technology
(*c*) Scheme to Enhance the Efficacy of Transfer of Technology
(*d*) None of the above

32. National informatics centre was set up in the year :
(*a*) 1976
(*b*) 1977
(*c*) 1975
(*d*) 1974

33. ------- of the Ministry of Information Technology is a premier science and Technology organisation of the Government of India in the field of informatics services and Information Technology (IT) applications in India.
(*a*) National Informatics Centre
(*b*) National Information Centre
(*c*) National Computer Centre
(*d*) None of the above

34. 'The National Science Day' is observed on:
(*a*) February 28
(*b*) March 8
(*c*) March 15
(*d*) March 31

35. An advisory committee for the Ministry of Information Technology Comprising professionals from Indian IT industry was set up on :
(*a*) 18th December 1999
(*b*) 17th January 2000
(*c*) 20th June 2000
(*d*) 21st July 1999

36. Match List I with List II and select the correct answer using the codes given below :

	List I		List II
A.	Indian Academy of Sciences	1.	New Delhi
B.	Indian National Science Academy	2.	Allahabad
C.	Indian National Academy of Engineering	3.	Kolkata
D.	National Academy of Science	4.	Bangluru
E.	Indian Science Congress Association	5.	New Delhi

Codes :

	A	B	C	D	E
(a)	1	2	3	4	5
(b)	4	1	5	2	3
(c)	5	4	3	1	2
(d)	4	1	2	3	5

37. The acronym IRHPA stand for :
(a) Integrated Rural Housing personnel Association
(b) International Research on Heavy plutonium and Argon
(c) Intensification of Research in High Priority Areas
(d) None of the above

38. Scientific and technological activities in India are carried out under a wide set-up. A part from the Central Government and the State Governments it mainly consists of :
(a) Higher educational sector
(b) Public and Private Sector Industry
(c) Non-profit institutions and associations
(d) All of the above

39. The Apex Institution in the Sphere of agriculture Credits is—
(a) State Bank of India
(b) Reserve Bank of India
(c) NABARD
(d) Regional Rural Bank

40. The acronym TIFAC stands for :
(a) Tata Institute of Fundamental Agro-Climatic Research
(b) Technology Information Forecasting and Assessment Council
(c) Tropical Information Facility and Agricultural Centre
(d) None of the above

41. What are EKASWA-A and EKASWA-B?
(a) Hybrid varieties of Barley
(b) Heavy-water atomic reactors
(c) Cloning technologies being worked out in India
(d) CD ROM databases brought out by patent Facilitating cell

42. The Central Drug Research Institute, CDRI, is located at :
(a) New Delhi   (b) Kolkata
(c) Lucknow   (d) Nagpur

43. The Technology Day falls every year on :
(a) 23rd October
(b) 11th May
(c) 2nd January
(d) None of the above

44. The 'National Award for successful commercialisation of indigenous technology' has been instituted by :
(a) Confederation of Indian Industry
(b) Department of Science and Technology
(c) By (a) and (b) jointly
(d) Technology Development Board

45. 'Siddha' is :
(a) A short range surface to surface missile being developed by DRDO
(b) A system of medicine
(c) A hybrid variety of sorghum
(d) None of the above

46. Vigyan Prasar was established in :
(a) 1952   (b) 1966
(c) 1989   (d) 1993

47. Which of the following Scientific organisations was set up in 1767?
(*a*) Survey of India
(*b*) Indian Council for Agricultural Research
(*c*) Defence Research and Development organisation
(*d*) Vigyan Prasar

48. India is not a member of—
(*a*) Commonwealth of Nations
(*b*) SAARC
(*c*) NAM Organisation
(*d*) OPEC Organisation

49. Which of the following is situated at Kalpakkam?
(*a*) Indira Gandhi Centre for Atomic Research
(*b*) Council for Scientific and Industrial Research
(*c*) National Research Development Corporation
(*d*) All of the above

50. Who was the First Speaker of Independent India's Lok Sabha?
(*a*) Hukam Singh
(*b*) Bali Ram Bhagat
(*c*) Rabi Ray
(*d*) G.V. Mavalankar

51. To meet the heavy water requirements of the Indian nuclear power and research reactors, heavy water plants have been installed at several places. One of the place is :
(*a*) Jodhpur
(*b*) Shimla
(*c*) Manuguru
(*d*) Kalpakkam

52. Atomic power reactors have been commissioned, among other places, at kakrapar and kaiga which are respectively situated in the states of :
(*a*) Maharashtra and Karnataka
(*b*) Karnataka and Madhya Pradesh
(*c*) Gujarat and Karnataka
(*d*) Tamil Nadu and Uttar Pradesh

53. DREAM 2047 is :
(*a*) A monthly newsletter launched by Vigyan Prasar focussing on its activities
(*b*) A book authored by K. Kasturirangan in which he has laid down a development blue print for India
(*c*) A fifty year programme to increase sericulture in India
(*d*) None of the above

54. The term STEP stands for :
(*a*) Science and Technology Entrepreneurship Park
(*b*) State Transport Employment Programme
(*c*) Solar Technology and Energy Project
(*d*) None of the above

55. The National seismological database centre has been established at :
(*a*) Indore
(*b*) New Delhi
(*c*) Srinagar
(*d*) Chamoli

56. The Indian space programme was formally organised in 1972 with the setting up of :
(*a*) Department of space
(*b*) Space Commission
(*c*) Both (*a*) and (*b*)
(*d*) ISRO

57. Which one of the following is not correctly matched?
(*a*) Kalpakkam – Tamil Nadu
(*b*) Rana Pratap Sagar – M.P.
(*c*) Narora – U.P.
(*d*) Tarapore – Maharashtra

58. Which one is not correctly matched?
(*a*) Sriharikota – Andhra Pradesh
(*b*) Thumba – Kerala
(*c*) BARC – Karnataka
(*d*) Pokhran – Rajasthan

59. The term **SETS** stand for—
(*a*) Science and Ecology Testing Scheme
(*b*) Society of Electronic Transactions & Security
(*c*) Social and Economical Transformation Scheme
(*d*) None of these

60. In which part of the country, the community Information centres have been set up by the Ministry of Information Technology, for the Socio-Economic development of the region?
(*a*) Rajasthan
(*b*) North-East
(*c*) Sikkim
(*d*) Both (*b*) and (*c*)

61. The INSAT is a multi-purpose satellite system for telecommunications, meteorological observations and data relay etc. It is a joint venture of :
(*a*) Department of Space and Department of Telecommunications
(*b*) Indian Meteorological Department
(*c*) All India Radio and Doordarshan
(*d*) All of the above

62. Indian National Satellite System (INSAT) was established in :
(*a*) 1979   (*b*) 1981
(*c*) 1983   (*d*) 1985

63. The Acronym NNRMS stands for :
(*a*) National Natural Resources Management System
(*b*) Natural Non-Regional Management System
(*c*) New Narcotics Research Manpower System
(*d*) None of the above

64. To function as a nodal department for organising, coordinating and promoting ocean development activities in the country, the Department of Ocean Development was created in :
(*a*) 1971   (*b*) 1981
(*c*) 1991   (*d*) 1891

65. India's pace launching base **'Sriharikota'** is located in—
(*a*) Andhra Pradesh
(*b*) Karnataka
(*c*) Tamil Nadu
(*d*) Orissa

66. The name of the Indian station situated in Antarctica is :
(*a*) Dhanush   (*b*) Maitri
(*c*) Shila   (*d*) None of the above

67. The Acronym FORV stands for :
(*a*) Fertile Organic Reorientation Value
(*b*) Fishery and Oceanographic Research Vessel
(*c*) Fuel and Ozone Research Vehicle
(*d*) All of the above

68. 'Sagar Sampada' is
(*a*) Ocean research vessel
(*b*) Ocean exploration project
(*c*) Newest rig installed by India
(*d*) Latest expeditions sent to Antarctica

69. The computer system which links and stores information among different countries in the world through a satellite is known as—
(*a*) Apollo
(*b*) INSAT 2D
(*c*) Internet
(*d*) Nicnet

70. A technology to enhance solar energy output in the country :
(*a*) A technology to enhance solar energy output in the country
(*b*) An institution of higher scientific research dedicated to nuclear technology
(*c*) A fellowship to enable talented persons to pursue research in front-line areas of science and technology
(*d*) None of the above

71. Securities and Exchange Board of India (SEBI) was established in the year
(*a*) 1992   (*b*) 1989
(*c*) 1988   (*d*) 1980

72. Which one of the following is NOT a capital market instrument?
(*a*) Debentures
(*b*) Shares
(*c*) Public Sector Bonds
(*d*) Treasury Bill

ANSWERS

1	2	3	4	5	6	7	8	9	10
(*a*)	(*d*)	(*d*)	(*b*)	(*a*)	(*d*)	(*c*)	(*a*)	(*d*)	(*c*)
11	**12**	**13**	**14**	**15**	**16**	**17**	**18**	**19**	**20**
(*d*)	(*a*)	(*a*)	(*d*)	(*b*)	(*a*)	(*b*)	(*d*)	(*b*)	(*a*)
21	**22**	**23**	**24**	**25**	**26**	**27**	**28**	**29**	**30**
(*d*)	(*a*)	(*a*)	(*b*)	(*c*)	(*a*)	(*c*)	(*b*)	(*b*)	(*a*)
31	**32**	**33**	**34**	**35**	**36**	**37**	**38**	**39**	**40**
(*c*)	(*b*)	(*a*)	(*a*)	(*b*)	(*b*)	(*c*)	(*d*)	(*c*)	(*b*)
41	**42**	**43**	**44**	**45**	**46**	**47**	**48**	**49**	**50**
(*d*)	(*c*)	(*b*)	(*d*)	(*b*)	(*c*)	(*a*)	(*d*)	(*a*)	(*d*)
51	**52**	**53**	**54**	**55**	**56**	**57**	**58**	**59**	**60**
(*c*)	(*c*)	(*a*)	(*a*)	(*b*)	(*c*)	(*b*)	(*c*)	(*b*)	(*d*)
61	**62**	**63**	**64**	**65**	**66**	**67**	**68**	**69**	**70**
(*d*)	(*c*)	(*a*)	(*b*)	(*a*)	(*b*)	(*b*)	(*a*)	(*c*)	(*c*)
71	**72**								
(*c*)	(*d*)								

13

LOCAL SELF GOVERNMENT

1. The entire concept of community development was conceived by the :
(a) State Government
(b) Local Government
(c) Union Government
(d) None of the above

2. The administration of the community Development programme was entrusted to a newly created agency called ------- located in the planning commission :
(a) Community Development Commission
(b) Community Project Administration
(c) Community Development Administration
(d) None of the above

3. The essential elements of the community Development Programme include :
(a) All-round development of the people in rural areas
(b) People's participation
(c) Political empowerment of women
(d) Both (a) and (b)

4. Which of the following committees was appointed by the government to review the working of the community Development programme?
(a) Balwant Rai Mehta committee
(b) Ashok Mehta committee
(c) Santhanam committee
(d) None of the above

5. Consider the following recommendations of Balwant Rai Mehta committee on democratic decentralisation :
1. There should be genuine transfer of power and responsibility to these institutions of local government
2. Adequate resources should be transferred to these bodies to enable them to discharge those responsibilities
3. The whole system of Panchayati Raj should facilate further devolution and dispersal of power, responsibilities and resources in the future
4. There should be a three-tier structure of local self-government
Which of the above are correct? Choose the correct answer using the codes given below :
(a) 1, 2 and 3   (b) 1, 2 and 4
(c) 2 and 4   (d) 1 and 2

6. Which of the following is not true regarding Gram Sabha?
(a) Gram Sabha is a meeting of all the adult residents in the panchayat circle
(b) The Gram Sabha is the base of the Panchayati Raj system
(c) This body is found at the block level
(d) It is obligatory for every panchayat to convene, at least twice in a year, meetings of the Gram Sabha

7. Which of the following is the main source of income of the panchayats?
(a) Grants from Government
(b) Taxes on buildings
(c) Tax on commercial crops
(d) All of the above

8. The Chief Executive of the Panchayat Samiti is the :
(a) Block Development Officer
(b) Chairman
(c) Sarpanch
(d) None of the above

9. Which of the following governments at the centre appointed a committee, under the chairmanship of Ashok Mehta, to review the working of the Panchayati Raj set up?
(*a*) Congress Government
(*b*) Janata Government
(*c*) BJP Government
(*d*) Communist Government

10. Consider the following recommendations of the Ashok Mehta committee appointed in 1977 :
1. It recommended the creation of the two-tier system of Panchayati Raj in the place of the existing three-tier system
2. The committee recommended that the Nyaya Panchayats should be kept as separate bodies
3. It made specific recommendations about the composition of various tiers of panchayats
4. Panchayati Raj elections should be conducted by the Chief Election Officer
Which of the above are correct? Choose the correct answer using the codes given below.
(*a*) 1 and 2　　　　(*b*) 2 and 3
(*c*) 1, 2, 3 and 4　(*d*) 2 and 4

11. Committee appointed under the Chairmanship of G.V.R Rao in 1985 suggested :
(*a*) Appropriate improvement in the representative character
(*b*) Strengthening of the capability of the people's representatives
(*c*) Administrative personnel in the Panchayati Raj institutions
(*d*) All of the above

12. Consider the following features of the 73rd Constitutional Amendment Act.
1. Panchayati Raj bodies will receive finance from state government in the form of grants
2. One-third seats of the total seats in Panchayati Raj bodies will be reserved for women
3. All states will have three-tier Panchayati Raj system

4. Panchayati Raj bodies will prepare plans for economic development, social justice and social welfare
Which of the above are correct? Choose the correct answer using the given codes :
(*a*) 1, 2, 3 and 4　　(*b*) 2 and 4
(*c*) 1 and 2　　　　　(*d*) 1, 2 and 3

13. L.M. Singhvi suggested that Panchayati Raj should primarily be viewed as the :
(*a*) Rural self-government system
(*b*) Local self-government system
(*c*) Urban self-government system
(*d*) Political self-government system

14. Which statement is not correct regarding the 73rd amendment (Panchayati Raj)?
(*a*) M.L.As. M.L.Cs. and M.Ps. have been included from the membership of Panchayat bodies at all levels
(*b*) Provision has been made for a Finance Commission in every State
(*c*) One-third seats have been reserved for women at all levels
(*d*) The Panchayat bodies have been given a fixed term of five years

15. Which of the following statements is not true?
(*a*) B.D.O is assisted by a group of extension officers immediately below him
(*b*) B.D.O is the captain of the team of officers in the block administrative organisation
(*c*) B.D.O is not the chief executive officer of the block administration
(*d*) B.D.O is described as the "miniature collector" so far as the development administration in the block is concerned

16. Which of the following committees recommended that the collector should be closely associated with the new institutions of Panchyati Raj and he should be the chairman of the Zila Parishad?
(*a*) Santhanam Committee
(*b*) Balwant Rai Mehta Committee
(*c*) Ashok Mehta Committee
(*d*) None of the above

17. In which of the following states, reorganisation of the Panchayati Raj system took place after 73rd Constitutional Amendment Act. 1992?
 (*a*) Karnataka (*b*) Andhra Pradesh
 (*c*) Madhya Pradesh (*d*) All of these

18. The corporations are headed by elected :
 (*a*) Representatives (*b*) Chairman
 (*c*) Mayors (*d*) Councillors

19. Which of the following is one of the different names of municipal councils in different parts of the country?
 (*a*) Municipal committee
 (*b*) Municipal board
 (*c*) Municipality
 (*d*) All of the above

20. Municipalities have which of the following authorities?
 (*a*) The council and its committees
 (*b*) Chairman/president
 (*c*) Chief Executive Officer/Chief Municipal Officer
 (*d*) All of the above

21. Which of the following play an active and positive role in providing information skill and resources for evolving and establishing grass root women's organisations?
 (*a*) Women studies centres
 (*b*) Agricultural universities
 (*c*) Non-Government organisations
 (*d*) All of the above

22. Mahila Milap, Sampark Samiti, Forum for women in politics, Semakaya in Gujarat, women and Development in Rajasthan are successful examples of :
 (*a*) Networking
 (*b*) Government agencies
 (*c*) International women organisation
 (*d*) None of the above

23. Which of the following committees not only recommended representation of women in Panchayati Raj institutions but also mooted the idea of statutory all women panchayats at village level as a transitional measure for responding to rural women's critical needs of literacy/education, especially about their legal rights, new avenues of employment etc?
 (*a*) Committee on Empowerment of women
 (*b*) Committee on women upliftment
 (*c*) Committee on 'status of women in India
 (*d*) None of the above

24. Match List I with List II and select the correct answer by using the codes given below the lists :

List I	List II
(Women organisation)	(Base)
A. Stree Adhar Kendra	1. Maharashtra
B. Sampark Samiti	2. Bangluru
C. Vimochana	3. Andhra Pradesh
D. Aware	4. Mumbai

Codes :

	A	B	C	D
(*a*)	4	1	2	3
(*b*)	1	2	3	4
(*c*)	2	1	4	3
(*d*)	4	1	3	2

25. Many groups have prepared women's menifestos and have conducted voters education campaign and exposure programmes on 'know The candidate' and made an appeal to women to vote fearlessly and consciously in :
 (*a*) Delhi, Bangluru and Chennai
 (*b*) Ahmedabad, Kolkata and Bhubaneswar
 (*c*) Bangluru, Ahmedabad and Pune
 (*d*) Mumbai, Pune and Kolkata

26. Which of the following statement is correct regarding Town Area Committees?
 (*a*) It is a semi-municipal authority which is constituted for small towns
 (*b*) They are governed by a separate Act of the State Legislature
 (*c*) The members of the committee are partly elected and partly nominated
 (*d*) All of the above

27. Urban areas where troops are stationed are known as :

(*a*) Cantonments   (*b*) Tents
(*c*) Camps   (*d*) Dormitories

28. Municipal administration, like all public administration, may be based on :
(*a*) Area or extension
(*b*) Area of function
(*c*) Extension of function
(*d*) Any of the above

29. Which of the following councils was established under Article 263 of the constitution by an order of the President in September 1954?
(*a*) The Central Council of Rural Self-Government
(*b*) The Local Council of Urban Self-Government
(*c*) The Central Council of Local Self-Government
(*d*) None of the above

30. Consider the following duties of the central Council of local self-government and find out which of them is correct?
(*a*) To consider and recommended broad lines of activity relating to local self-government in all its aspects
(*b*) To make proposals for legislation in fields of activity relating to local self-government matters
(*c*) To make recommendations to the Central government regarding the allocation of available Financial assistance to local bodies
(*d*) All of the above

31. Which of the following committees recommended induction of two women members in panchayats to carry on the specific programmes for women and children?
(*a*) Administrative Reforms Commission
(*b*) Santhanam Committee
(*c*) Balwant Rai Mehta Committee
(*d*) Narashimham Committee

32. First concrete, measure to give constitutional sanction to empowerment of women in Panchayati Raj Institutions was taken by Rajiv Gandhi's government by introducing 64th constitutional Amendment Bill on local government on :
(*a*) 15th July, 1990
(*b*) 15th May, 1989
(*c*) 13th November, 1988
(*d*) 15th June, 1987

33. Seventy-Third Amendment Act is extremely important for political empowerment of :
(*a*) Women   (*b*) Scheduled Castes
(*c*) Scheduled Tribes (*d*) All of these

34. Operation Barga in ------- can be called a unique example of bringing about an attitudinal change in village and block level bureaucracy.
(*a*) Rajasthan   (*b*) Orissa
(*c*) West Bengal   (*d*) Andhra Pradesh

35. National Law School in ------- has taken a lead in organising legal training programmes with contexturalisation of women specific dimensions to ensure gender justice.
(*a*) Delhi   (*b*) Bangalore
(*c*) Chandigarh   (*d*) Chennai

36. Which of the following parts of the constitution envisages a three-tier system of panchayats?
(*a*) Part IX   (*b*) Part VII
(*c*) Part XI   (*d*) Part VI

37. Article 243 D provides that seats are to be reserved for :
(*a*) Scheduled Castes (*b*) Scheduled Tribes
(*c*) Ex-service men   (*d*) Both (a) and (b)

38. Which of the following acts was passed by the British Government for giving powers of self-government to panchayats in rural areas and municipalities in urban areas?
(*a*) The Bengal village Self-Government Act, 1919
(*b*) The Bengal Municipal Act, 1884
(*c*) The Bengal local Self-Government Act, 1885
(*d*) All of the above

39. Which of the following amendments inserted parts IX and IX A in the Constitution?
(*a*) 72 and 73rd   (*b*) 70th and 71st
(*c*) 73rd and 74th   (*d*) 18th and 19th

40. Which of the following commission of 1949 recommended the launching of a national extension service movement covering the entire country?
(*a*) Fulton commission
(*b*) Fiscal commission
(*c*) Finance commission
(*d*) None of the above

41. Which of the following was described as the method of rural extension and the agency through which the transformation of the social and economic life of villages was to be initiated?
(*a*) Community Development
(*b*) Self-Government
(*c*) Rural Development
(*d*) Political Empowerment

42. Not less than ------- of the total number of seats to be filled by direct elections in every panchayat shall be reserved for women.
(*a*) One-fourth   (*b*) One-third
(*c*) One-sixth   (*d*) One-fifth

43. Match List I with List II and select the correct answer by using the codes given below the lists :

List I	**List II**
A. Article 243k	1. This Article provides that seats are to be reserved for (a) scheduled castes, and (b) scheduled tribes
B. Article 243F	2. State legislatures have the legislative power, to confer on the panchayats
C. Article 243D	3. This Article is designed to ensure free and fair elections to the panchayats
D. Article 243G-243H	4. This Article provides that all persons who are qualified to be chosen to the state legislature shall be qualified to be chosen as a member of a panchayats

Codes :

	A	B	C	D
(*a*)	2	3	4	1
(*b*)	1	2	3	4
(*c*)	3	4	1	2
(*d*)	3	4	2	1

44. Which of the following has the power to legislate on all matters relating to elections to panchayats?
(*a*) Union Parliament   (*b*) State Legislature
(*c*) Village Panchayat   (*d*) District Board

45. Under ----- courts shall have no jurisdiction to examine the validity of a law, relating to delimitation of constituencies or the allotments of seats, made under Article 243k.
(*a*) Article 329   (*b*) Article 320
(*c*) Article 328   (*d*) Article 321

46. Part IX A which has come into force in 1993 gives a Constitutional foundation to the local self government units in :
(*a*) Villages
(*b*) Rural areas
(*c*) Urban areas
(*d*) None of the above

47. Institutions of self-government, called by a general name "municipalities", are :
(*a*) Nagar panchayats, for transitional areas, i.e. an area which is being transformed from a rural area to an urban area
(*b*) Municipal councils for smaller urban areas
(*c*) Municipal corporations for larger urban areas
(*d*) All of the above

48. Part IX of the Indian constitution relates to the -----, containing Articles 243-A to 243-ZG.

(*a*) Panchayats
(*b*) Municipalities
(*c*) Municipal corporation
(*d*) None of the above

49. Community Development Programme was launched on :
(*a*) October 9, 1953
(*b*) December 3, 1957
(*c*) November 27, 1952
(*d*) October 2, 1952

50. Among the institutions of governance the presence and participation of women in formal democratic process is inadequate at :
(*a*) Union Level
(*b*) State level
(*c*) Local or grassroot level
(*d*) All of the above

51. The issue of adequate participation of women in Panchayati Raj Institutions was first raised by :
(*a*) Santhanam Committee Report
(*b*) Ashok Mehta Committee Report
(*c*) Balwant Rai Mehta Committee Report
(*d*) All of the above

52. To start with, women joined the Panchayati Raj Institutions in many states as :
(*a*) Elected members
(*b*) Nominated members
(*c*) Co-opted members
(*d*) Ex-officio members

53. How many women members were recommended to be inducted in panchayats to carry on the specific programmes for women and children?
(*a*) Two   (*b*) Three
(*c*) Four   (*d*) Five

54. Which of the following states first resorted to reservation of women in Panchayati Raj Institutions?
(*a*) Andhra Pradesh   (*b*) Karnataka
(*c*) Maharashtra   (*d*) All of the above

55. It mooted the idea of statutory all women panchayats at village level. It was
(*a*) Balwant Rai Mehta committee

(*b*) The committee on 'status of women in India.'
(*c*) National commission for women
(*d*) None of the above

56. Which among the following was the first concrete measure sought to be taken by the Government to give constitutional sanction to the Panchayati Raj Institutions?
(*a*) 64th Constitutional Amendment Act
(*b*) 73rd Constitutional Amendment Act
(*c*) 74th Constitutional Amendment Act
(*d*) Both (b) and (c)

57. Operation Barga is associated with which of the following states?
(*a*) Andhra Pradesh   (*b*) West Bengal
(*c*) Asom   (*d*) Karnataka

58. Which part of the constitution contains the following statement?
"The state shall take steps to organise village panchayats and endow them with; such powers and authority as may be necessary to enable them to function as units of self-government".
(*a*) Part II   (*b*) Part III
(*c*) Part IV   (*d*) Part VI

59. During which prime minister's tenure it was first decided by the Union Government to provide local self-governing institutions a Constitutional basis?
(*a*) Jawaharlal Nehru
(*b*) Indira Gandhi
(*c*) Rajiv Gandhi
(*d*) P.V. Narsimha Rao

60. What is the minimum age that a person must attain to be eligible to be a member of a panchayat?
(*a*) 18 years   (*b*) 21 years
(*c*) 25 years   (*d*) 30 years

61. If a question arises as to whether a member of a panchayat has become subject to any disqualification, the question shall be referred to :
(*a*) Governor
(*b*) Speaker of the state legislative Assembly

(*c*) Such authority as the State Legislature may provide by law

(*d*) None of the above

62. The Constitution provides that the qualifications that a person should have to be chosen as a member of a panchayat are same as are required of a person to be chosen to :

(*a*) Rajya Sabha

(*b*) State Legislature

(*c*) Lok Sabha

(*d*) State Legislative Council

63. Who is authorised by the constitution to make law to reserve seats or offices of chair-persons in the panchayat at any level in favour of backward classes of citizens?

(*a*) State Legislature (*b*) Governor

(*c*) Parliament (*d*) Zila Parishad

64. Which of the following articles contains provisions regarding reservations favouring the scheduled castes and Tribes in the institutions of local government?

(*a*) Article 201 (*b*) Article 334

(*c*) Article 139 (*d*) None of the above

65. Provisions of the 73rd and 74th Constitutional Amendment Acts do not apply to :

(*a*) Jammu and Kashmir

(*b*) Meghalaya and Mizoram

(*c*) Nagaland

(*d*) All of the above

66. Provisions inserted in the constitution by the 73rd and 74th Constitutional Amendments are in the nature of basic provisions which are to supplemented by :

(*a*) Laws made by respective State Legislatures

(*b*) Ordinances issued by State Governor from time to time

(*c*) Relevant provisions of the constitution

(*d*) All of the above

67. Which of the following are the matters as listed in the Eleventh schedule on which a panchayat can take decisions?

(*a*) Minor irrigation

(*b*) Animal Husbandry

(*c*) Both (a) and (b)

(*d*) Land revenue

68. Which of the following schedules distributes powers to legislature between the State Legislature and the panchayat?

(*a*) VIIth Schedule (*b*) IXth Schedule

(*c*) XIth Schedule (*d*) XIIth Schedule

69. A panchayat can levy collect and appropriate taxes, duties, tolls etc in accordance with the procedure and limits laid down by :

(*a*) Law of State Legislature

(*b*) Law of parliament

(*c*) Constitution

(*d*) Ordinance issued by the Governor of the State

70. Panchayati Raj Institutions have been assigned multifarious duties and several sources of income to fulfil those duties one of which is grants-in-aid. These may be given to panchayats from :

(*a*) Consolidated Fund of India

(*b*) Contingency Fund of India

(*c*) Consolidated Fund of the State

(*d*) Any of the above

71. The 73rd and 74th Constitution Amendments provide for a finance commission to ensure financial viability of the Panchayati Raj Institutions. These provisions are modelled on which Article of the Constitution?

(*a*) Article 123 (*b*) Article 280

(*c*) Article 350 (*d*) Article 300

72. Part IX-A of the Constitution which gives a Constitutional Foundation to the local self-government units in urban areas came into force in :

(*a*) June 1992 (*b*) June 1993

(*c*) April 1993 (*d*) January 1994

73. Which of the following articles of the Constitution is relevant to the institutions of urban local self-government?

(*a*) Article 243Q (*b*) Article 243ZX

(*c*) Article 243ZE (*d*) All of these

74. In ancient India the decline of the republic and representative institutions began with :
(*a*) Coming of Alexander, the Great
(*b*) Rise of the Mauryan Empire
(*c*) Decline of Gupta Dynasty
(*d*) All of the above

75. Which of the following phenomenon of the electoral politics at the grassroot level tend to vitiate the practice of the provisions of the seventy-third Constitution Amendment Act?
(*a*) Money and muscle power
(*b*) Expensive, violent and corrupt nature of elections in India
(*c*) Conservative attitude of the electoral machinery at the state
(*d*) Both (a) and (b)

76. The Panchayati Raj is based on the principle of—
(*a*) Decentralisation
(*b*) Deconcentration
(*c*) Democratic Centralism
(*d*) Democratic Decentralisation

77. Which of the following are deemed as important for enabling women to become an effective pressure group and leveller of power?
(*a*) Networking amongst themselves as members of a gender group
(*b*) Pooling of resources
(*c*) Both (a) and (b)
(*d*) Statutory recognition of their equal position compared to men's

78. What is the maximum period provided in the 73rd Constitution Amendment Act within which election to a panchayat must be held in the event of its dissolution?
(*a*) Six months   (*b*) Four months
(*c*) Two months   (*d*) One year

79. Which of the following office bearers in the Panchayati Raj Institution are elected through an indirect election?
(*a*) Chairperson of Panchayat Samiti
(*b*) Chairperson of Zila Parishad
(*c*) Ex-officio member at each level of the PRIs
(*d*) Both (a) and (b)

80. Which of the following Constitution Amendment Bills was the first concrete measure envisaged by the Government to revitalise Panchayati Raj Institutions?
(*a*) 24th Amendment Bill, 1971
(*b*) 73rd Amendment Bill, 1992
(*c*) 64th Amendment Bill, 1989
(*d*) None of the above

81. The seventy-third constitution Amendment Act which includes various provisions for strengthening panchayats at all levels, provides for compulsory three-tier system in all the states except where the population does not exceed :
(*a*) 50 Lakhs   (*b*) One Crore
(*c*) 20 Lakhs   (*d*) 75 Lakhs

82. Which one of the following is not an attribute of Local Self Government?
(*a*) Statutory Status
(*b*) General purpose
(*c*) Power to raise Finance
(*d*) Sovereignty

83. In the history of India, the village panchayats survived throughout the centuries till the :
(*a*) Advent of English East India company
(*b*) Moghul Rule
(*c*) Rise of freedom struggle
(*d*) None of the above

84. Which of the following scriptures of ancient India give an account of one hundred twenty Janapadas of Bharatvarsha?
(*a*) Ramayana
(*b*) Mahabharat
(*c*) Vayu Purana
(*d*) Chhandogya Upanishad

85. Which committtee was set up at the union level by the Rajiv Gandhi Government to write a concept paper on Panchayati Raj in 1985?
(*a*) Balwant Rai Mehta Committee
(*b*) Gargi Committee
(*c*) L.M. Singhvi Committee
(*d*) Pylee Committee

86. A study team on Community Development and National Extension service was appointed

to review the working of the community development programme. It was headed by :
(*a*) Ashok Mehta
(*b*) L.M. Singhvi
(*c*) Balwant Rai Mehta
(*d*) S.N. Mishra

87. India's experiment with democratic decentralisation started in Rajasthan with the formal inauguration of Panchayati Raj by the then Prime Minister Pt. Jawaharlal Nehru at Nagaur on :
(*a*) January 2, 1960
(*b*) October 2, 1959
(*c*) December 30, 1957
(*d*) June 1, 1961

88. Which among the following states have the traditional council of village elders instead of the routine Panchayati Raj Institutions?

(*a*) Meghalaya
(*b*) Mizoram
(*c*) Nagaland
(*d*) All of these

89. Which of the following is the main source of income for the Municipal Committee?
(*a*) Income tax
(*b*) Octroi duty
(*c*) Assistance from the centre
(*d*) Excise duty

90. Which Article is designed under the 73rd Constitution (Amendment) Act to ensure free and fair elections to the panchayats?
(*a*) Article 121C
(*b*) Article 234B
(*c*) Article 243K
(*d*) None of the above

ANSWERS

1	2	3	4	5	6	7	8	9	10
(*c*)	(*b*)	(*d*)	(*a*)	(*b*)	(*c*)	(*d*)	(*a*)	(*b*)	(*c*)
11	**12**	**13**	**14**	**15**	**16**	**17**	**18**	**19**	**20**
(*d*)	(*a*)	(*b*)	(*a*)	(*c*)	(*b*)	(*d*)	(*c*)	(*d*)	(*d*)
21	**22**	**23**	**24**	**25**	**26**	**27**	**28**	**29**	**30**
(*d*)	(*a*)	(*c*)	(*a*)	(*c*)	(*d*)	(*a*)	(*b*)	(*c*)	(*d*)
31	**32**	**33**	**34**	**35**	**36**	**37**	**38**	**39**	**40**
(*c*)	(*b*)	(*d*)	(*c*)	(*b*)	(*a*)	(*d*)	(*d*)	(*c*)	(*b*)
41	**42**	**43**	**44**	**45**	**46**	**47**	**48**	**49**	**50**
(*a*)	(*b*)	(*c*)	(*b*)	(*a*)	(*c*)	(*d*)	(*a*)	(*d*)	(*d*)
51	**52**	**53**	**54**	**55**	**56**	**57**	**58**	**59**	**60**
(*c*)	(*c*)	(*a*)	(*d*)	(*b*)	(*a*)	(*b*)	(*c*)	(*c*)	(*b*)
61	**62**	**63**	**64**	**65**	**66**	**67**	**68**	**69**	**70**
(*c*)	(*b*)	(*a*)	(*b*)	(*d*)	(*a*)	(*c*)	(*c*)	(*a*)	(*c*)
71	**72**	**73**	**74**	**75**	**76**	**77**	**78**	**79**	**80**
(*b*)	(*b*)	(*d*)	(*b*)	(*d*)	(*d*)	(*c*)	(*a*)	(*d*)	(*c*)
81	**82**	**83**	**84**	**85**	**86**	**87**	**88**	**89**	**90**
(*c*)	(*d*)	(*b*)	(*c*)	(*c*)	(*c*)	(*b*)	(*d*)	(*b*)	(*c*)

14

BUREAUCRACY AND DEVELOPMENT

1. Which of the following is one of the features of the administrative sub-systems in more developed countries?
   (a) There is a high degree of task specialisation
   (b) Government activity expends over a wide range of public and personal affairs
   (c) Popular interest and involvement in public affairs is widespread
   (d) All of the above

2. Who among the following describes the growth of bureaucracies from structural functional angle in colonial and non-colonial developing countries?
   (a) Riggs (b) Eisenstadt
   (c) Weidner (d) Fainsod

3. Which of the following countries has a system of administrative courts that is distinct from the civil court system in other countries?
   (a) France (b) Germany
   (c) U.S.A (d) Both (a) and (b)

4. _____ ordinarily involves the establishment of machinery for planning economic growth and mobilizing and allocating resources to expand national income.
   (a) Public administration
   (b) Financial administration
   (c) Development administration
   (d) Planning commission

5. The Chief Election Commissioner of India can be removed from his office during his tenure by—
   (a) The Chief Justice of India if Some Charges are proved against him
   (b) The President on the basis of a resolution of the Union Cabinet
   (c) A Committee Consisting of the Chief Justice of India, Law Minister of India and the Vice-President of India
   (d) The president on the basis of resolution passed by parliament by special majority

6. Which of the following is one of the aims and objectives of community development programme started in 1952?
   (a) To develop local leadership and self-governing institutions
   (b) To develop, in total, the human and capital resources of rural areas
   (c) to increase agricultural production in order to raise the living-standards of the rural people
   (d) All of the above

7. Which of the following is one of the major functions of the Panchayati Raj Institutions?
   (a) Administrative (b) Political
   (c) Development (d) All of these

8. The rationale of decentralised planning lies in :
   (a) Failure of centralised planning
   (b) Diversities, details and information costs
   (c) Socio-political aims like people's participation
   (d) All of the above

9. Who among the following described community development programme as "one of the most beneficient revolutions in the peasantry's life that have been known so far to history"?
   (a) Oscar Lewis (b) Toynbee
   (c) Wilson (d) Douglas

10. Which of the following programmes was started in order to create employment opportunities for unemployed and under-employed?
    (*a*) National Rural Employment programme
    (*b*) Food for work programme
    (*c*) Rural landless employment guarantee programme
    (*d*) All of the above

11. Which of the following committees suggested a two-tier structure ______ the zila parishad should serve as the first point of decentralisation and the unit of planning and mandal panchayat below the district as the implementing agency?
    (*a*) Santhanam Committee
    (*b*) Balwant Rai Mehta Committee
    (*c*) Ashok Mehta Committee
    (*d*) None of the above

12. The concept of 'development administration' was first introduced by :
    (*a*) Riggs
    (*b*) Weidner
    (*c*) Palombara
    (*d*) Waterson

13. Today development administration is concerned with the formulation and implementation of the four p's which are :
    (*a*) Plans, policies, programmes and projects
    (*b*) Plans, priorities, policies and projects
    (*c*) Public, priorities, plans and projects
    (*d*) Parties, parliament, plans and policies

14. Which of the following is not correct regarding the characteristics of bureaucracies in more developed countries as given by Ira Sharkansky?
    (*a*) Bureaucracy is considered to be professional a sign of specialisation among bureaucrats
    (*b*) Bureaucracy accepts directions from other legitimate branches of government
    (*c*) Bureaucracies are large
    (*d*) Widespread discrepancy between form and reality

15. The term "development administration" was first coined by Goswami in the year :

16. Who among the following has defined development administration as an "action-oriented goal-oriented administrative system"?
    (*a*) F.W. Riggs
    (*b*) La Palombara
    (*c*) Edward Weidner
    (*d*) Albert Waterson

    (*a*) 1956
    (*b*) 1955
    (*c*) 1957
    (*d*) 1958

17. Who among the following has said that bureaucracy for development tends to be characterised by flexibility in place of excessive emphasis on rationality?
    (*a*) Blau
    (*b*) Merton
    (*c*) Ghidyal
    (*d*) Marx

18. Which of the following were regarded as essentials of development administration?
    (*a*) Modernisation
    (*b*) Institution-building
    (*c*) Socio-economic development
    (*d*) All of the above

19. According to Fred W. Riggs, _____ refers both to administrative problems and governmental reform.
    (*a*) Development administration
    (*b*) Public administration
    (*c*) Personnel administration
    (*d*) None of the above

20. Who among the following observes, "Administration cannot normally be improved very much without changes in the environmental constraints that hampers its effectiveness, and the environment itself cannot be changed unless the administration of development programmes is strengthened"?
    (*a*) C. Stoner
    (*b*) Glenn Stahl
    (*c*) F.W. Riggs
    (*d*) Weidner

21. Which of the following is one of the major characteristics of national bureaucracies in the developing countries as given by Ferrel Heady?
    (*a*) The basic pattern of administration is imitative rather than indigenous
    (*b*) The bureaucracies are deficient in skilled manpower necessary for developmental programmes

(*c*) Operational autonomy
(*d*) All of the above

22. The members of which one of the following standing Committees are chosen exclusively from the members of the Lok Sabha?
(*a*) Public Accounts Committee
(*b*) Committee on Public Undertakings
(*c*) Committee on Estimates
(*d*) Committee on Delegated Legislation

23. Which of the following is the goal of the process of economic development?
(*a*) A higher rate of growth
(*b*) Reduction of population living below the poverty line
(*c*) An enlargement of employment potential leading to full employment
(*d*) All of the above

24. The civil service in India is expected to play which one of the following roles?
(*a*) It is the focal point of stability and order in the shifting hands for politics
(*b*) It is an instruments of modernisation and social change
(*c*) It is an instrument of planning and economic development
(*d*) All of the above

25. Who among the following said that the best way to enforce accountability is to develop institutions that vigorously monitor the actions of public bureaucracy and punish those guilty of maladministration?
(*a*) Levine (*b*) Hart
(*c*) Thompson (*d*) Finer

26. The word 'accountable' seems to have come into usage in the English language for the first time in the year :
(*a*) 1583 (*b*) 1589
(*c*) 1586 (*d*) 1580

27. The example of external formal controls is :
(*a*) Audit
(*b*) Legislative surveillance
(*c*) Judicial review
(*d*) All of the above

28. Which of the following is a limitation accountability?

(*a*) Professional ethics of a person may come into conflict with his administrative ethics
(*b*) Accountability, being culture oriented operates within the cultural atmosphere of a political system
(*c*) Administrative accountability is conditioned by the political structure of a country
(*d*) All of the above

29. _____ is the outcome of delegation of responsibility and authority.
(*a*) Propriety (*b*) Accountability
(*c*) Efficacy (*d*) None of the above

30. Which of the following means to give an account of one's action and to report on the achievement of the declared objectives?
(*a*) Accountability
(*b*) Control
(*c*) Ordinance
(*d*) None of the above

31. Which of the following is vital to accountability?
(*a*) Decentralisation (*b*) Devolution
(*c*) Delegation (*d*) All of these

32. ____ is interchangeably used with accountability.
(*a*) Control (*b*) Responsibility
(*c*) Delegation (*d*) None of these

33. Which of the following is a form of accountability?
(*a*) Legislative accountability
(*b*) Judicial accountability
(*c*) Political accountability
(*d*) All of the above

34. Who among the following has defined 'civil service' as a "professional body of officials, permanent, paid and skilled"?
(*a*) White (*b*) Finer
(*c*) Willoughby (*d*) Presthus

35. Which of the following, according to the Fulton Committee Report, is the task of the civil service accompanied by a change in the nature of its role?

(*a*) It engages in research and development both for civil and military purposes

(*b*) It provides comprehensive social services and is now expected to promote the fullest possible development to individual human potential

(*c*) Through nationalisation it more directly controls a number of basic industries

(*d*) All of the above

36. Which of the following Articles of the Constitution provides for the Constitution of two services, the IAS and the IPS :
(*a*) Article 310   (*b*) Article 315
(*c*) Article 312   (*d*) Article 325

37. Who among the following defines 'Administrative Adjudication' as the process by which administrative agencies settle issues arising in the course of their work when legal rights are in question?
(*a*) White   (*b*) Dimock
(*c*) Gorwala   (*d*) Robson

38. The Central Administrative Tribunal was set up in :
(*a*) May 1982   (*b*) July 1983
(*c*) June 1981   (*d*) November 1985

39. Which of the following commissions recommend the establishment of subordinate services commission that came into existence in 1975?
(*a*) Planning commission
(*b*) Second pay commission
(*c*) Administrative Reforms Commission
(*d*) None of the above

40. Which of the following is the duty of the collector?
(*a*) Direction and fulfilment of development of plans
(*b*) To carry on development activity or programmes of the government
(*c*) Maintenance of law and order in the district
(*d*) All of the above

41. ______ is the Returning Officer for elections to parliament and vidhan sabha constituencies, and has the responsibility for coordination of election work at the district level
(*a*) Election Commissioner
(*b*) Collector
(*c*) Divisional Commissioner
(*d*) None of the above

42. What is the function of the collector, as an Administrative officer?
(*a*) He is incharge of the treasury and the district stamp office
(*b*) He is responsible for implementation of government orders
(*c*) He is the principal agency of government in matters of general administration in the district
(*d*) All of the above

43. Which of the following reports recommended the establishment of the Indian Institute of Public Administration?
(*a*) Gorewala Report
(*b*) Appleby Report
(*c*) Pay Commission Report
(*d*) None of the above

44. Under the British rule, the ______ was the basis of administration?
(*a*) District
(*b*) Village
(*c*) State
(*d*) None of the above

45. Consider the following tasks of district administration :
1. Regulatory tasks
2. Development tasks
3. Residuary tasks
4. Conducting elections
5. Emergency tasks
6. Tasks concerning local bodies

Which of the above are correct? Choose the correct answer using the codes given below :

Codes :
(*a*) 1 and 2   (*b*) 1, 2, 3, 4, 5 and 6
(*c*) 2, 3 and 4   (*d*) 4, 5 and 6

46. Who is the first Law Officer of the Government of India?
(*a*) The Chief Justice of India
(*b*) Union Law Minister
(*c*) Attorney General of India
(*d*) Law Secretary

47. The administrator of which Union Territory is called Chief Commissioner?
(*a*) Puducherry   (*b*) Chandigarh
(*c*) Delhi   (*d*) Lakshadweep

48. In which year the Indian Economic Service was created?
(*a*) 1960   (*b*) 1961
(*c*) 1970   (*d*) 1971

49. Though the nature and scope of governmental functions around the world has accompanied the development of human civilization, an accelerated growth of such functions is noted since :
(*a*) The Russian Revolution of 1917
(*b*) The First World War, 1914-1918
(*c*) The French Revolution of 1789
(*d*) The Second World War, 1939-1945

50. Who has made the observation that "The heart of administration is the management of programmes designed to serve the general welfare"?
(*a*) L.D. White   (*b*) Henery Hart
(*c*) Paul Brass   (*d*) Paul H. Appleby

51. Important cause of strain between the Minister and the secretary in the Indian government has been :
(*a*) Difference in the class background of politicians and civil servants
(*b*) Difference in approach and manner of work of politicians and civil servants
(*c*) Difference in the educational attainments of the politicians and civil servants
(*d*) Both (a) and (c)

52. Which of the following central services was created in the year 1961?
(*a*) Indian statistical service
(*b*) Indian Audit and Account service
(*c*) Indian Defence Account service
(*d*) All of the above

53. In India as in other democratic countries the role of public officials is becoming increasingly :
(*a*) Political   (*b*) Technical
(*c*) Managerial   (*d*) All of these

54. Which of the following was recommended by the Fulton committee of 1968?
(*a*) Technocratic control over the generalists
(*b*) Generalist control of the scientists and technocrats
(*c*) Professionalisation of civil service
(*d*) All of the above

55. The Traditional concept of the civil servant, in a parliamentary Democracy has been that of :
(*a*) An anonymous servant of his Minister
(*b*) An appointed personnel run the policy-making apparatus
(*c*) A Manager in a community situation
(*d*) Both (*b*) and (*c*)

56. The Bureaucratic model set-up in India by the British Government was based on the theory given by :
(*a*) Weber   (*b*) Macaulay
(*c*) Michels   (*d*) None of these

57. Who among the following has characterised public administration as the "heart of the problem of modern government"?
(*a*) Herman Finer   (*b*) L.D. White
(*c*) Paul Appleby   (*d*) Parkinson

58. The work 'Crisis in Command Management in the Army' is authored by :
(*a*) R.A. Gabriel   (*b*) Girth and Mills
(*c*) P.L. Savage   (*d*) Both (a) and (c)

59. In the Pre-Independence India, a new cadre of class I posts was introduced in addition to the existing Imperial services by :
(*a*) Government of India Act of 1909
(*b*) Montford Reforms
(*c*) Government of India Act, 1935
(*d*) None of the above

60. In the British India, the doors of civil service at the high levels were not open to all. A few persons of Indian extraction were allowed to fill these posts only in :
(*a*) Second quarter of the twentieth century

(*b*) Second quarter of the nineteenth century

(*c*) Last quarter of nineteenth century

(*d*) First quarter of the twentieth century

61. In a parliamentary Democracy, Ministers are confident of obtaining loyal service from the civil servants irrespective of what political party is in power. This phenomenon proves the fact that in a democracy civil servants are :

(*a*) Homogenous   (*b*) Neutral

(*c*) Partial   (*d*) Authoritarian

62. Which of the following is an essential feature of the concept of civil service neutrality.

(*a*) Public confidence in the freedom of the civil service from all political bias

(*b*) Personal control of the politicians over the civil servants

(*c*) Perks and privileges to a civil servant commensurate with his or her duties

(*d*) None of the above

63. An unhealthy development in the Indian Bureaucracy is the emergence of personal affiliations leading to an element of 'politicisation' among civil servants. This evil came in a big way during :

(*a*) The Prime Ministership of L.B. Shastri

(*b*) Emergency

(*c*) Operation Blue Star

(*d*) None of the above

64. The Minister of Government must protect the civil servant in certain cases, especially, where :

(*a*) There is an explicit order of the Minister which the civil servant has carried out

(*b*) There is no breach of privilege of the members of the legislatures

(*c*) The civil servant acts properly in accordance with the policy laid down by the Minister

(*d*) Both (*a*) and (*c*)

65. With the increasing complexity of the functions of government in independent India, which of the following has been questioned and challenged seriously during recent years?

(*a*) The neutrality of the civil servants

(*b*) The Trevelyan-macaulay philosophy

(*c*) The subordinate-superior relationship between the administrative and political executive

(*d*) Both (*a*) *and* (b)

ANSWERS

1	2	3	4	5	6	7	8	9	10
(*d*)	(*b*)	(*d*)	(*c*)	(*d*)	(*d*)	(*d*)	(*d*)	(*b*)	(*d*)
11	**12**	**13**	**14**	**15**	**16**	**17**	**18**	**19**	**20**
(*c*)	(*b*)	(*a*)	(*d*)	(*b*)	(*c*)	(*c*)	(*d*)	(*a*)	(*c*)
21	**22**	**23**	**24**	**25**	**26**	**27**	**28**	**29**	**30**
(*d*)	(*c*)	(*d*)	(*d*)	(*d*)	(*a*)	(*d*)	(*d*)	(*b*)	(*a*)
31	**32**	**33**	**34**	**35**	**36**	**37**	**38**	**39**	**40**
(*d*)	(*b*)	(*d*)	(*b*)	(*d*)	(*c*)	(*b*)	(*d*)	(*c*)	(*d*)
41	**42**	**43**	**44**	**45**	**46**	**47**	**48**	**49**	**50**
(*b*)	(*d*)	(*b*)	(*a*)	(*b*)	(*c*)	(*b*)	(*b*)	(*b*)	(*d*)
51	**52**	**53**	**54**	**55**	**56**	**57**	**58**	**59**	**60**
(*b*)	(*a*)	(*c*)	(*c*)	(*a*)	(*a*)	(*b*)	(*d*)	(*b*)	(*d*)
61	**62**	**63**	**64**	**65**					
(*b*)	(*a*)	(*b*)	(*d*)	(*b*)					

CHALLENGES TO INDIAN DEMOCRACY

1. Which of the following is the cause of corruption, according to Klitgaard?
   (a) Cultural   (b) Structural
   (c) Bureaucratic   (d) All of these

2. Which of the following committees pointed out "corruption can exist only if there is someone willing to corrupt and capable of corrupting"?
   (a) Kripalani committee
   (b) Santhanam committee
   (c) Narshimhan committee
   (d) None of the above

3. Who among the following said that "men steal when there is lot of money lying around loose and no one is watching"?
   (a) Wilson   (b) White
   (c) Laski   (d) Swaminathan

4. Which of the following reports pionted out that there exists in India a nexus between the politicians, bureaucrats and criminals?
   (a) Appleby Report
   (b) Gorwala Report
   (c) Vohra committee Report
   (d) None of the above

5. At present the corruption cases are dealt with under the :
   (a) Civil services conduct Rules
   (b) Prevention of corruption Act, 1947
   (c) Indian penal code
   (d) All of the above

6. The Central vigilance commission was set up in the year :
   (a) 1964   (b) 1963
   (c) 1962   (d) 1961

7. Which of the following commission had recommended that Bombay should remain a bilingual state, but also suggested the creation of a separate state of Vidharbha, by adding some areas of Madhya Pradesh?
   (a) Administrative Reforms commission
   (b) Planning commission
   (c) States reorganisation commission
   (d) None of the above

8. Which one of the following goes against the idea of Socialism?
   (a) Nationalism
   (b) Land Consolidation
   (c) Abolition of Zamindari
   (d) Grant of Privy Purse

9. The main cause for the outbreak of the Andhra agitation in 1973 was the supreme court's decisions of 3rd October, 1972 on :
   (a) The mulki Rules
   (b) Conduct Rules
   (c) State Rules
   (d) None of the above

10. _____ are the largest single tribal community in the north-east.
    (a) Nagas   (b) Bhutias
    (c) Bodos   (d) Lepchas

11. The States Reorganisation Commission recommended that ____ should be a separate state, but that a provision should be made for its union with Andhra Pradesh after the third general election.
    (a) Vidharbha
    (b) Telangana
    (c) Mysore
    (d) None of the above

12. In December 1969, the Assam reorganisation Bill was passed by the parliament and the Hill state of _____ was created as an autonomous unit with Asom.
   (*a*) Meghalaya   (*b*) Manipur
   (*c*) Tripura   (*d*) Mizoram

13. _____ can be defined as a social phenomenon in which a section of the society is unable to fulfil even its basic necessities of life.
   (*a*) Unemployment
   (*b*) Poverty
   (*c*) Unequal distribution
   (*d*) None of the above

14. Which of the following is "a defined territorial unit including particular language or languages, jatis, ethnic groups or tribes, particular social setting and cultural pattern, folk dance, music, folk arts, etc"?
   (*a*) Region
   (*b*) Nation
   (*c*) YIX Area
   (*d*) None of the above

15. Which of the following is one of the factors for the growth of regionalism in India?
   (*a*) India lacked a balanced economic growth of all parts and regions
   (*b*) Difference in the per capita income
   (*c*) Creation of linguistic states which reinforced regionalism and stirred demands for increased state autonomy
   (*d*) All of the above

16. Who among the following said that communalism came to India with the British?
   (*a*) Mahatma Gandhi   (*b*) Gokhale
   (*c*) Sardar Patel   (*d*) Tilak

17. _____ is the antagonistic assertiveness in political, social and economic spheres by one aggregation of individuals against another after being organised along religious caste or other ascriptive lines.
   (*a*) Regionalism
   (*b*) Communalism
   (*c*) Nationalism
   (*d*) None of the above

18. Jawaharlal Nehru once described communalism as the Indian version of :
   (*a*) Fascism   (*b*) Apartheid
   (*c*) Nazism   (*d*) None of the above

19. Which of the following is one of the main factors of the growth of communalism in contemporary India?
   (*a*) Communal parties and organisations
   (*b*) Political opportunism
   (*c*) Separatism and isolationism among muslims
   (*d*) All of the above

20. What is the most appropriate meaning of the term **'Secularism'** in the Indian context?
   (*a*) Separation of religion from politics
   (*b*) Freedom of religion
   (*c*) There shall not be any religion of the state
   (*d*) Equality of all religions

21. _____ means love of a particular region or state in preference to the country as a whole.
   (*a*) Nationalism   (*b*) Regionalism
   (*c*) Ethnicism   (*d*) None of the above

22. Which of the following acts is punishable under the prevention of corruption Act, 1947?
   (*a*) Habitual taking of illegal gratification to influence a public servant
   (*b*) Possession of wealth disproportionate to the known source of income
   (*c*) Criminal misconduct by public servant in the discharge of official duty
   (*d*) All of the above

23. The Punjab Administrative Reforms Commission (1966) mentioned which of the following causes of corruption?
   (*a*) Complicated and dilatory procedures
   (*b*) Lack of proper education and training of civil servants
   (*c*) Political patronage of officials
   (*d*) All of the above

24. Which of the following committees was appointed by the Government of India in 1962 on corruption?

(*a*) Gorwala committee
(*b*) Kripalani committee
(*c*) Santhanam committee
(*d*) None of the above

25. As per the provisions of Article 25, which one of the following is not mentioned as a ground to impose restriction on the right to freedom of religion?
(*a*) Health
(*b*) Public Order
(*c*) Morality
(*d*) Contempt of the Court

26. Which of the following five year plans used the concept of 'poverty gap' developed by World Bank to measure the severity of poverty?
(*a*) Second
(*b*) Third
(*c*) Ninth
(*d*) Fourth

27. Which one of the following is the characteristics of a pressure group?
(*a*) It tries to capture power
(*b*) It contests elections
(*c*) It pressurises the government to fulfil public interest
(*d*) It pressurises the government to fulfil its own specific interests

28. The _____ made an attempt to have a more inclusive concept of poverty line.
(*a*) Fourth Finance Commission
(*b*) Sixth Finance Commission
(*c*) Seventh Finance Commission
(*d*) Third Finance Commission

29. Who among the following was the Chairman of the Expert Group constituted by the planning commission in 1989 to consider methodological and computational aspects of estimation of proportion and number of poor in India?
(*a*) P.K. Bardhan
(*b*) D.T. Lakdawala
(*c*) Montek Ahluwalia
(*d*) V.M. Dandekar

30. India is republic because—
(*a*) The Head of the State is elected directly or indirectly by the people
(*b*) The Head of the Government is nominated by the parliament
(*c*) The Government is responsible to parliament
(*d*) The Constitution of India is Supreme and mady by a Constituent Assembly

31. Which of the following secessionist groups operates in the state of Manipur?
(*a*) Meite National Front
(*b*) Meithei Marup
(*c*) Pan Manipuri Youth League
(*d*) All of the above

32. Which of the following five-year plans did not refer to the problem of regional disparities?
(*a*) First five-year plan
(*b*) Third five-year plan
(*c*) Second five-year plan
(*d*) None of the above

33. Which of the following are the important socio-economic factors of regional imbalance in India?
(*a*) Per Capita Income
(*b*) Regional Location of industries
(*c*) Population below poverty line
(*d*) All of the above

34. Which of the following is the most important factor for the backwardness of the Himalayan States?
(*a*) Inaccessibility
(*b*) Political negligence
(*c*) Lack of resources
(*d*) Negative public attitude

35. Which of the Five Year Plans has laid emphasis on 'Faster, Sustainable and Inclusive Growth'?
(*a*) Seventh Five Year Plan
(*b*) Ninth Five Year Plan
(*c*) Eleventh Five Year Plan
(*d*) Twelfth Five Year Plan

36. The _____ enjoys more powers than the Finance Commission in recommending resources transfer from the centre to the states :
(*a*) Pay Commission
(*b*) Regulatory Commission
(*c*) Planning Commission
(*d*) None of the above

37. Special plans schemes have been formulated with central assistance to develop :
  (*a*) Hilly areas
  (*b*) Tribal areas
  (*c*) Drought-prone areas
  (*d*) All of the above

38. Which of the following incentives has been provided by the Government of India to promote private investment in backward areas?
  (*a*) Income tax concession
  (*b*) Central Investment subsidy scheme
  (*c*) Transport subsidy scheme
  (*d*) All of the above

39. Which of the following is one of the three major public sector Financial institutions?
  (*a*) IDBI   (*b*) IFCI
  (*c*) ICICI   (*d*) All of these

40. What does ICICI stand for?
  (*a*) Industrial Credit and Investment Corporation of India
  (*b*) Industiral Co-operation and Investment Corporation of India
  (*c*) Indian Cultural and Investment Corporation of India
  (*d*) None of the above

41. Which authority decides about the state's share in central taxes?
  (*a*) Finance Commission
  (*b*) Planning Commission
  (*c*) Election Commission
  (*d*) None of these

42. According to 2011 census the least densely population area is :
  (*a*) Sikkim
  (*b*) Nagaland
  (*c*) Arunachal Pradesh
  (*d*) Jammu and Kashmir

43. The population of India has grown rapidly after 1971 because :
  (*a*) Birth rate has increased rapidly
  (*b*) There is influx of people from foreign countries

  (*c*) Death rate has declined rapidly
  (*d*) All of the above

44. Which of the following countries has introduced 'direct democracy'?
  (*a*) Russia   (*b*) India
  (*c*) France   (*d*) Switzerland

45. Census in India is being held regularly after every :
  (*a*) 10 years   (*b*) 13 years
  (*c*) 5 years   (*d*) 15 years

46. The Fundamental Rights in our constitution are inspired by the consititution of—
  (*a*) USA   (*b*) UK
  (*c*) Switzerland   (*d*) Canada

47. Which of the following states is placed at the bottom on literacy ground?
  (*a*) Uttar Pradesh   (*b*) Madhya Pradesh
  (*c*) Bihar   (*d*) Nagaland

48. What is/are the ground or grounds mentioned in the Constitution to initiate impeachment proceedings against the president of India?
  (*a*) Proved misbehaviour incapacity
  (*b*) Corruption
  (*c*) Violation of the Constitution
  (*d*) All of the above

49. Which one of these is not a keyword of Gandhian Economy?
  (*a*) Self-Sufficiency
  (*b*) Decentralised production
  (*c*) Equitable distribution
  (*d*) Centralized production

50. Which of the following Acts form the legal basis for conduct of censuses in independent India?
  (*a*) The population Act, 1949
  (*b*) The Census Act, 1948
  (*c*) The population Growth Act, 1947
  (*d*) None of the above

51. Arrange the following countries in the decreasing order of their population :
  1. China   2. India
  3. USA   4. Indonesia

Select the correct answer from the following :
(*a*) 1, 2 3, 4 (*b*) 2, 3, 1, 4
(*c*) 4, 3, 2, 1 (*d*) 1, 2, 4, 3

52. The population census is a _____ subject in India.
(*a*) State (*b*) Union
(*c*) Concurrent (*d*) None of these

53. In which of the following ministries the census organisation has been functioning on a permanent footing ever since 1961?
(*a*) Welfare Ministry
(*b*) Health Ministry
(*c*) Human Resource Development Ministry
(*d*) Union Home Ministry

54. Which State of India occupies the third position in terms of the area?
(*a*) Rajasthan (*b*) Bihar
(*c*) West Bengal (*d*) Maharashtra

55. The central notion of citizenship as having the cappacity to bear arms, to own property and for self-government is considered fundamentally flawed by which of the following groups of political theorists?
(*a*) Anarchists (*b*) Communitarians
(*c*) Neo-liberals (*d*) Feminists

56. Which one of the following Articles about Fundamental Rights is directly related to the exploitation of children?
(*a*) Art. 17 (*b*) Art. 19
(*c*) Art. 23 (*d*) Art. 24

57. The Public Account Committee submits its report to :
(*a*) The Minister for Parliamentary Affairs
(*b*) The Comptroller and Auditor General
(*c*) The President of India
(*d*) The Speaker of Lok Sabha

58. The first Expert Committee on population, projections was set up by the planning commission in the year :
(*a*) 1958 (*b*) 1960
(*c*) 1959 (*d*) 1962

59. Civic republican view of citizenship supports:
(*a*) Active, responsible and virtuous citizenship
(*b*) Self-reliance and criticizes the Welfare State
(*c*) The view that in a class-divided society, the idea of equal citizenship is a sham
(*d*) Equal rights and equal access for all

60. The marxists and the radical feminists do not share which one of the following views on State power?
(*a*) Both deny that the State is an autonomous entity
(*b*) Both maintain that the ideology of the State can be understood by reference to the power structure in a society
(*c*) Both are based on institutionalized structures of stratification
(*d*) Both agree on the location of structures of inequality and exploitation in society

61. What does MFAL stand for?
(*a*) Marginal Farmers and Agricultural Labour
(*b*) Manpower, Farming and Agricultural Land
(*c*) Marginal Families of Large Areas
(*d*) None of the above

62. Which of the following programmes was introduced by the Government in order to ameliorate the conditions of the under-privileged people?
(*a*) SRDA (*b*) MFAL
(*c*) DPADP (*d*) All of these

63. Training of Rural Youths for Self-Employment (TRYSEM) was initiated in the year :
(*a*) 1976 (*b*) 1981
(*c*) 1979 (*d*) 1978

64. The Supreme Court of India enunciated the Doctrine of Basic Structure in the—
(*a*) Shankari Prasad Case
(*b*) Sajjan Singh Case
(*c*) Golakh Nath Case
(*d*) Keshwanand Bharti Case

65. Which one of the following is a subject of the Concurrent List?
(*a*) Police
(*b*) Criminal Matters
(*c*) Radio and Television
(*d*) Foreign Affairs

66. Cabinet Mission Came to India in the year—
(*a*) 1946 (*b*) 1945
(*c*) 1942 (*d*) 1940

67. In 2011 the density of India was :
(a) 110   (b) 70
(c) 382   (d) 95

68. Which of the following is one of the causes of economic inequality?
(a) Private property   (b) Unemployment
(c) Inflation   (d) All of these

69. Which of the following Articles of the Directive Principles in the constitution urges the state to provide free and compulsory education for all the children until they complete 14 years of age?
(a) Article 45   (b) Article 38
(c) Article 46   (d) Article 39

70. The population aged ____ years and above only is to be classified as literate or illiterate.
(a) Six   (b) Four
(c) Seven   (d) Eight

71. The Constitutional Amendment of ____ included education in the concurrent list, the official list of subjects for which the centre and the states assume joint responsibility.
(a) 1972   (b) 1975
(c) 1973   (d) 1976

72. Economic equality may become a possibility by :
(a) Collection of taxes faithfully
(b) Checking offences like smuggling
(c) Bringing out the black money
(d) All of the above

73. Which of the following is one of the causes of regional imbalances?
(a) Economic backwardness
(b) Lack of proper management of industry
(c) Too much of dependence on agriculture
(d) All of the above

74. Article 370 of the Constitution became operative on Nov. 17, 1952. How can it be made inoperative?
(a) By the Amendment Act passed by Parliament
(b) By the president on the recommendations of the Legislative Assembly of J & K.

(c) By the order of the president on the recommendations of the Constituent Assembly of J & K.
(d) None of the above

75. Which of the following programmes is included under "beneficiary-oriented" programmes?
(a) SFDA   (b) MFAL
(c) IRDP   (d) All of these

76. "Since wars begin in the minds of men, therefore, defences of peace should be built in the mind of men" was stated in the :
(a) UNESCO Charter
(b) League of Nations Charter
(c) UNICEF Charter
(d) Human Rights Charter

77. If the name of a tribe has to be excluded from the list of Scheduled Tribes. Who has the power for such exclusion?
(a) President
(b) Parliament
(c) Union Council of Ministers
(d) National Commission for Scheduled Castes and Scheduled Tribes

78. Which of the following arenas of violence is not found in India?
(a) Inter-caste   (b) Inter-racial
(c) Inter-communal   (d) Inter-linguistic

79. Which of the following is a cause of deforestation?
(a) Shifting or Jhuming cultivation
(b) Overgrazing
(c) Lumbering
(d) All of the above

80. The Integrated conservation Research, a U.S. ecological research group has suggested elaborate programmes for the betterment of forests, including :
(a) Agroforestry
(b) Ethnobotany
(c) Natural history-oriented tourism
(d) All of the above

81. Which of the following are an example of sociological pollution?
(*a*) Crimes   (*b*) Communal riots
(*c*) Perpetual quarrels (*d*) All of these

82. Who among the following defined political crime as a politically motivated law-breaking behaviour by altruistic individuals?
(*a*) Austin Turk   (*b*) Rand Mc Nally
(*c*) William Minor   (*d*) Myron Weiner

83. Since _____ we have a prevention of corruption Act which defines categories that constitute culpable corruption.
(*a*) 1947   (*b*) 1952
(*c*) 1950   (*d*) 1948

84. The Election Commission reported booth-capturing in Bihar for the first time during the :
(*a*) Fifth General Elections
(*b*) Fourth General Elections
(*c*) Second General Elections
(*d*) Third General Elections

85. Which of the following Acts permitted company donations to parties?
(*a*) Industrial Act, 1986
(*b*) Labour Act, 1982
(*c*) Companies (Amendment) Act, 1985
(*d*) Company Act, 1948

86. Who among the following made use of the Brown-shirts and even of the Gestapo to swell his rank of supporters?
(*a*) Hitler   (*b*) Lenin
(*c*) Mao   (*d*) Marx

87. Who among the following launched the satya shodhak movement which tried to organise the non-Brahmanical castes, particularly the Marathas, as a political force?
(*a*) Jyotiba Phule
(*b*) Baba Amte
(*c*) B.R. Ambedkar
(*d*) None of the above

88. Which of the following section of the Representation of People Act puts a limit on election expenses incurred by a candidate?
(*a*) Section 74   (*b*) Section 77
(*c*) Section 71   (*d*) Section 72

89. The right to vote available to Indian Citizens under the Constitution is a—
(*a*) Fundamental Right
(*b*) Civil Right
(*c*) Political Right
(*d*) Political Duty

90. What is/are the ground/grounds given in the Constitution to disqualify a citizen from exercising his voting rights?
(*a*) Non-residence
(*b*) Unsoundness of mind
(*c*) Crime or corrupt or illegal practice
(*d*) All of the above

91. Communalism is based on and promotes
(*a*) Differences between different castes
(*b*) Similarities between ethnic groups
(*c*) The idea of an inherent antagonism between religious communities and irreconcilability of interests between them
(*d*) Patronage of propertied classes

92. Who made the statement :
''Communalism is the Political assertiveness of a Community to maintain its identity in a Plural society undergoing modernization''
(*a*) Robert Melson   (*b*) Thomas Hevrdy
(*c*) Howard Wolpe   (*d*) Both (a) and (c)

93. The famous work 'Communalism in Modern India' is authored by :
(*a*) Rumki Basu
(*b*) Ashutosh Varshney
(*c*) Bipan Chandra
(*d*) None of the above

94. Communalism is opposed to :
(*a*) Secular change
(*b*) Racial conflict
(*c*) Amity between classes
(*d*) All of the above

95. Communalism in India was born, nurtured and promoted by :
(*a*) Muslim League
(*b*) British Imperialism
(*c*) Congress politics
(*d*) All of the above

96. British imperialism perceived India as essentially a conglomeration of :
(*a*) Feudal principalities
(*b*) Religious communities
(*c*) Racial groups
(*d*) Both (a) and (b)

97. What was the most damaging blow which the British colonial administration dealt to the emerging body politics of India?
(*a*) Separatism in politics
(*b*) Politicization of religious communities
(*c*) Both (*a*) and (*b*)
(*d*) Ethnic separatism

98. As a political strategy, communalism is opposed to :
(*a*) Nationalism   (*b*) Regionalism
(*c*) Localism   (*d*) Internationalism

99. Communalism is opposed to :
(*a*) Rational civic basis of party formations and political system
(*b*) Secularism as a pattern of socio-cultural co-existence
(*c*) Humanism and compassion
(*d*) All of the above

100. As a political orientation what does communalism recognise as the focal point of political allegiance?
(*a*) Religious community
(*b*) Caste group
(*c*) Nation-State
(*d*) None of the above

101. Who among the following has analysed the phenomenon of communalism in the socio-economic perspective?
(*a*) Humayun Kabir
(*b*) Asghar Ali Engineer
(*c*) Nissar Ali
(*d*) All of the above

102. During the British period the emergence of communalism was centred around :
(*a*) The question of share in the loaves of offices
(*b*) Provincial administration
(*c*) Differences between various caste-groups
(*d*) None of the above

103. Economically, muslims in India have failed to produce :
(*a*) Surplus capital
(*b*) A viable capitalist class
(*c*) Adequate per capita income
(*d*) Industrial growth

104. Regionalism means :
(*a*) Love of a particular region or state in preference to the country as a whole
(*b*) Giving precedence to local issue over national issues
(*c*) Love of the community in preference to the nation
(*d*) Both (*a*) and (*c*)

105. More than anything else, a region is characterised by :
(*a*) Religious commonality
(*b*) A widely shared sentiment of 'togetherness' in the people
(*c*) Ethnic similarity
(*d*) Language communion

106. Who among the following has held regionalism as an example of micro-nationalism?
(*a*) Yogesh Atal   (*b*) Yogendra Yadava
(*c*) Yogesh Alagh   (*d*) None of the above

107. A region is characterised by a feeling of togetherness in the people which is internalised from which of the following sources?
(*a*) Common prosperity
(*b*) Comraderie developed in a common struggle
(*c*) Idea of separateness from others
(*d*) All of the above

108. Which of the following problems most fostered regionalism in India?
(*a*) Social   (*b*) Economic
(*c*) Religious   (*d*) Both (*a*) and (*b*)

109. The backward parts of India are so because they have been a neglected most in the matter of :
(*a*) Education
(*b*) Setting up of plants and factories
(*c*) Allocation of central funds and grants
(*d*) Job opportunities

110. 'Sub-nationalism' in India is most readily associated with :
(*a*) Language   (*b*) Caste
(*c*) Region   (*d*) Class

111. The extreme form of regionalism in India is :
(*a*) Lingual chauvinism
(*b*) Sentiment of secession from the union
(*c*) Inter-state dispute
(*d*) All of the above

112. Who among the following maintained that the people of south India were of a different stock from that of the North?
(*a*) M.G. Ramchandran
(*b*) K. Karunanidhi
(*c*) C.N. Annadurai
(*d*) All of the above

113. An unequal society is most prone to :
(*a*) Racial riots   (*b*) Class conflict
(*c*) Structural violence   (*d*) Both (*a*) and (*b*)

114. Shiva Sena which raised the slogan of Maharashtra for Maharashtrian's was founded in :
(*a*) 1965   (*b*) 1966
(*c*) 1967   (*d*) 1968

115. After Independence, which was the first state in India created on the linguistic basis—
(*a*) Tamil Nadu   (*b*) Karnataka
(*c*) Andhra Pradesh   (*d*) Kerala

116. Important socio-economic indicators which reflect regional imbalance in India include :
(*a*) Per Capita Income
(*b*) Population below poverty line
(*c*) Regional location of industries
(*d*) All of the above

117. How many finance commissions have so far been appointed?
(*a*) 10   (*b*) 16
(*c*) 12   (*d*) 14

118. In India the basic criterion for estimating the number of people below poverty line is :
(*a*) A person's nutritional requirements in terms of calories
(*b*) Per Capita gross domestic product
(*c*) Human Development Index
(*d*) All of the above

119. Which of the following governmental programmes are aimed at eradication of poverty?
(*a*) Integrated Rural Development Programme
(*b*) Jawahar Rozgar Yojana
(*c*) Employment Assurance Scheme
(*d*) All of the above

120. Which one of the following North-East States was the last to get the status of a full-fledged state?
(*a*) Mizoram
(*b*) Manipur
(*c*) Nagaland
(*d*) Arunachal Pradesh

121. In the census operations prior to 1991, what was the minimum age considered in making literacy estimates?
(*a*) 4 years   (*b*) 5 years
(*c*) 6 years   (*d*) 7 years

122. The powers of Parliament in respect of passage of the Budget are enshrined in the constitution in—
(*a*) Art. 114   (*b*) Art. 113 & 203
(*c*) Art. 265 & 267   (*d*) Art. 112 & 117

123. Which one of the following recommended the abolition of the post of Governor of a state?
(*a*) the Rajamannar Committee
(*b*) The Sarkaria Commission
(*c*) The First Administrative Reforms Commission
(*d*) None of these

124. Which Article of the Constitution of India directs the State to make effective provision for securing the Right to work?
(*a*) Article 16   (*b*) Article 38
(*c*) Article 41   (*d*) Article 43

125. The 'Rolling Plan' concept in national planning was introduced by—
(*a*) Indira Gandhi   (*b*) Janta Government
(*c*) NDA Government   (*d*) None of these

126. Which among the Indian states occupy top spots respectively in male literacy and female literacy?

    (*a*) Manipur   (*b*) Goa
    (*c*) Kerala   (*d*) Mizoram

127. Which among the following is most adversely impacted by the widespread illiteracy?
    (*a*) Family planning programme
    (*b*) Poverty alleviation programmes
    (*c*) Per capita gross domestic product
    (*d*) All of the above

128. Which of the following is not a regional party of India?
    (*a*) BJP
    (*b*) DMK
    (*c*) Telugu Desam
    (*d*) National Conference

129. Which one of the following is not in conformity with liberalism?
    (*a*) Welfare State
    (*b*) Bourgeois state
    (*c*) Representative Government
    (*d*) Limited Government

130. The remark—"power corrupts and absolute power tends to corrupt absolutely" is attributed to :
    (*a*) Plato   (*b*) Lord Acton
    (*c*) Laski   (*d*) Winston Churchill

131. Which among the following Indian states have the largest number of poor in absolute terms?
    (*a*) Bihar
    (*b*) Orissa
    (*c*) Uttar Pradesh
    (*d*) None of the above

132. Which one of the following is not the ground mentioned in the Constitution to impose reasonable restrictions on the right to form association or unions?
    (*a*) Friendly relations with foreign states
    (*b*) Public order
    (*c*) Morality
    (*d*) Sovereignty and integrity of India

133. Which one of the following preventive detention Acts is still in force?
    (*a*) NSA
    (*b*) TADA
    (*c*) MISA
    (*d*) Preventive Detention Act

134. Who among the following observed that corruption may help in assimilating new groups into the system and thus serve as a substitute for reform?
    (*a*) K. Subramaniam
    (*b*) Samuel Huntington
    (*c*) Margaret Thatcher
    (*d*) None of the above

135. Who among the following sees corruption as reducing the rigidities of bureaucracy and making it relatively flexible?
    (*a*) Myron Weiner
    (*b*) Francise Frankel
    (*c*) W.H. Morris Jones
    (*d*) Morris Janohatz

136. How many different types of embezzlement like bribery, graft, favouritism etc. are identified by Kautilya?
    (*a*) Ten   (*b*) Thirteen
    (*c*) Thirty   (*d*) Forty

137. Which of the following Governor-General of India was impeached in Britain for his economic misdemeanours in India?
    (*a*) Lord Clive   (*b*) Warren Hastings
    (*c*) Lord Cornwallis (*d*) Wellesly

138. The institution of Lok Ayukta at state level was first created in :
    (*a*) Bihar   (*b*) Punjab
    (*c*) Maharashtra   (*d*) Uttar Pradesh

139. The first country to appoint an ombudsman was :
    (*a*) Finland   (*b*) Denmark
    (*c*) Norway   (*d*) Sweden

140. Which of the following can be described as characteristic sociological unit of primordial cohesion peculiar to India?
    (*a*) Community   (*b*) Caste
    (*c*) Ethnic group   (*d*) Tribe

141. Caste system is :
    (*a*) Hierarchical
    (*b*) Segmentary
    (*c*) Marked by a dichotomy between purity and pollution
    (*d*) All of the above

142. The Central Administrative Tribunal and State Administrative Tribunals were set up through a law passed in :
 (*a*) 1986   (*b*) 1985
 (*c*) 1984   (*d*) 1983

143. Who made the comment that the caste system is not merely a division of labour, it is a division of labourers?
 (*a*) M.N. Shrinivas
 (*b*) B.R. Ambedkar
 (*c*) C.N. Annadurai
 (*d*) None of the above

144. The importance attached to the jatis which is the dominant caste in a village, region or state is due to :
 (*a*) Their rank in chaturvarnashrama
 (*b*) Their material wealth and control of land
 (*c*) The political patronage they receive
 (*d*) All of the above

145. Which of the following caste groups are regarded as the so-called "twice born"?
 (*a*) Brahmins   (*b*) Kshatriyas
 (*c*) Vaishyas   (*d*) All of these

146. Which of the following jatis are dominant in most of the Uttar Pradesh?
 (*a*) Thakurs and Jats
 (*b*) Yadavs and Ahirs
 (*c*) Gujjars and Kurmis
 (*d*) All of the above

147. Socially dominant castes of Bihar are :
 (*a*) Bhumihars and Kayasthas
 (*b*) Yadavas and Kurmis
 (*c*) Rajputs and Koeris
 (*d*) All of the above

148. As socially dominant caste-groups the Rajputs, Kayasthas and Marwaris are Dominant in :
 (*a*) Rajasthan   (*b*) Gujarat
 (*c*) Madhya Pradesh   (*d*) All of the above

149. Which among the following recommended appointment of a Lokpal at the centre and a Lok Ayukta in every state?
 (*a*) Administrative Reforms Commission
 (*b*) Santhanam Committee
 (*c*) Sarkaria Commission
 (*d*) M.C. Setalvad Committee

150. Of the Hindus, Muslims, Christians, Jains, Sikhs, and Buddhists which is the numerically smallest community?
 (*a*) Sikhs   (*b*) Budhists
 (*c*) Jains   (*d*) Christians

151. It can be said that a casteist conceives of India basically as a Federation of :
 (*a*) States
 (*b*) Jatis
 (*c*) Free and equal citizens
 (*d*) Tribes

152. The 'Izhavas' and 'velamos' are socially dominant caste groups in :
 (*a*) Kerala
 (*b*) Kerala and Andhra Pradesh respectively
 (*c*) Andhra Pradesh
 (*d*) Andhra Pradesh and Kerala respectively

153. The Anti-Brahmin movement by the DK and DMK in Tamil Nadu was basically a movement against :
 (*a*) Jati   (*b*) Class
 (*c*) Gotra   (*d*) Varna

154. The word ombudsman is derived from the root 'ombud' which is swedish and which mean :
 (*a*) Conscience-keeper
 (*b*) A person who acts as a representative of another person
 (*c*) Upholder of law and morality
 (*d*) All of the above

155. In short, political crime can be described as :
 (*a*) Crime by politicians
 (*b*) Politically motivated law-breaking behaviour by altruistic individuals
 (*c*) Crime committed in pursuit of politics
 (*d*) Any of the above

156. Caste system, which over the centuries became a more or less rigid endogamous group, presumably originated in :
 (*a*) Division of labour
 (*b*) Occupational classes
 (*c*) Both (*a*) and (*b*)
 (*d*) None of the above

157. Mainly, corruption involves :
- (*a*) Misuse of official position or authority
- (*b*) Deviation from rules, laws and norms
- (*c*) Non-action when action is required and personal gain for selfish motives
- (*d*) All of the above

158. The apex advisory body in the field of wildlife conservation in India headed by the Prime Minister is :
- (*a*) Environment Impact Assessment Board
- (*b*) National Wildlife Conservation Board
- (*c*) Indian Board for Wildlife
- (*d*) None of the above

159. Among the states in India, Kerala retained its position by being on top with a 93.91% literacy rate. Which state closely follows Kerala?
- (*a*) Meghalaya
- (*b*) Goa
- (*c*) Karnataka
- (*d*) Mizoram

160. Important hurdles to Government efforts for poverty alleviation include :
- (*a*) Lack of education and infrastructure
- (*b*) Anachronistic administrative and financial procedures
- (*c*) Rapid population growth
- (*d*) All of the above

161. Which political formations among the following was in the forefront of the campaign to make the Madras state an independent sovereign state?
- (*a*) DMK
- (*b*) Non Tamil
- (*c*) Tamil Arasu Kazhagam
- (*d*) AIADMK

162. Economic backwardness is an important cause of the growth of regionalism. What is the most common test of relative backwardness of a region?
- (*a*) Disjunction in political aspirations
- (*b*) Difference in the per capita income
- (*c*) Dichotomy between social collectivities
- (*d*) All of the above

163. Which one of the following triggered of the reorganisation of the provinces on linguistic lines in India after independence?
- (*a*) Dhar Committee Report
- (*b*) Justice Wanchoo Committee Report
- (*c*) Death of P. Sriramulu
- (*d*) None of these

164. Regional disparities in income and wealth have been responsible for rise of disturbances in :
1. Kashmir
2. Asom
3. Telangana
4. Jharkhand

Select the correct answer from the following:
- (*a*) 1 and 2
- (*b*) 1 and 3
- (*c*) 1, 2 and 3
- (*d*) 2, 3 and 4

165. Most of all, the progress of the national economy is reflected in :
- (*a*) Incremental sectoral development
- (*b*) The rate of growth released by different regions
- (*c*) Gradual elimination of class difference
- (*d*) Both (*b*) and (*c*)

166. Which among the following is modern interest-cum-pressure group?
- (*a*) Municipalities
- (*b*) Trade Union
- (*c*) Environmental groups
- (*d*) NGOs

167. Which one of the following devices draw the attention of minister towards a matter of public importance?
- (*a*) Special discussion
- (*b*) Budget discussion
- (*c*) Calling attention motion
- (*d*) Meeting of committee of petitions

168. The system of influencing the government through pressure groups is most prevalent in—
- (*a*) France
- (*b*) Britain
- (*c*) U.S.A.
- (*d*) India

169. A group of positions sufficiently similar with respect to difficulty of duties and responsibilities is known as :
- (*a*) Series
- (*b*) Class
- (*c*) Service
- (*d*) Grade

170. Which of the following is the distinctive feature of the Indian Party system?
   (*a*) Weakness of non-congress parties
   (*b*) Lack of the ideological commitment
   (*c*) Fractions within the parties
   (*d*) All of the above

171. Which of the following is the main source of income of the Panchayats?
   (*a*) Grants from government
   (*b*) Taxes on buildings
   (*c*) Tax on commercial crops
   (*d*) All of the above

172. According to which theory, participation represents the process by which goals are set and means are chosen in relation to all sorts of social issues?
   (*a*) Socialist theory
   (*b*) Marxist theory
   (*c*) Democratic theory
   (*d*) None of the above

173. In short, political crime can be described as—
   (*a*) Crime by Politicians
   (*b*) Politically motivated law-breaking behaviour by altruistic individuals
   (*c*) Crime committed in pursuit of politics
   (*d*) All of the above

174. Match the following—

List-I	List-II
A. Central Vigilance Commission	1. Consitutional
B. Lokayukta	2. Resolution of government of India
C. Central Bureau of Investigation	3. Statutory Appeals
D. High Court	4. Resolution of Home Ministry

Codes :

	A	B	C	D
(*a*)	3	2	1	4
(*b*)	3	1	2	4
(*c*)	2	3	4	1
(*d*)	1	4	2	3

175. The institution of Lokayukt was created for the first time in 1971 in the state of—
   (*a*) Orissa   (*b*) Bihar
   (*c*) Karnataka   (*d*) Maharashtra

ANSWERS

1	2	3	4	5	6	7	8	9	10
(*d*)	(*b*)	(*a*)	(*c*)	(*d*)	(*a*)	(*c*)	(*d*)	(*a*)	(*c*)
11	**12**	**13**	**14**	**15**	**16**	**17**	**18**	**19**	**20**
(*b*)	(*a*)	(*b*)	(*a*)	(*d*)	(*a*)	(*b*)	(*a*)	(*d*)	(*d*)
21	**22**	**23**	**24**	**25**	**26**	**27**	**28**	**29**	**30**
(*b*)	(*d*)	(*d*)	(*c*)	(*d*)	(*c*)	(*d*)	(*c*)	(*b*)	(*a*)
31	**32**	**33**	**34**	**35**	**36**	**37**	**38**	**39**	**40**
(*d*)	(*a*)	(*d*)	(*a*)	(*c*)	(*c*)	(*d*)	(*d*)	(*d*)	(*a*)
41	**42**	**43**	**44**	**45**	**46**	**47**	**48**	**49**	**50**
(*a*)	(*c*)	(*c*)	(*d*)	(*a*)	(*a*)	(*c*)	(*c*)	(*d*)	(*b*)
51	**52**	**53**	**54**	**55**	**56**	**57**	**58**	**59**	**60**
(*a*)	(*b*)	(*d*)	(*a*)	(*a*)	(*d*)	(*d*)	(*a*)	(*a*)	(*c*)
61	**62**	**63**	**64**	**65**	**66**	**67**	**68**	**69**	**70**
(*a*)	(*d*)	(*c*)	(*d*)	(*b*)	(*a*)	(*c*)	(*d*)	(*a*)	(*c*)

71	72	73	74	75	76	77	78	79	80
(d)	(d)	(d)	(d)	(d)	(a)	(b)	(b)	(d)	(d)
81	82	83	84	85	86	87	88	89	90
(d)	(c)	(a)	(a)	(c)	(a)	(a)	(b)	(c)	(d)
91	92	93	94	95	96	97	98	99	100
(c)	(d)	(c)	(a)	(b)	(d)	(c)	(a)	(b)	(a)
101	102	103	104	105	106	107	108	109	110
(b)	(a)	(b)	(a)	(b)	(a)	(d)	(d)	(c)	(a)
111	112	113	114	115	116	117	118	119	120
(b)	(c)	(c)	(b)	(c)	(d)	(d)	(a)	(d)	(d)
121	122	123	124	125	126	127	128	129	130
(b)	(d)	(a)	(c)	(b)	(c)	(a)	(a)	(b)	(b)
131	132	133	134	135	136	137	138	139	140
(c)	(a)	(a)	(a)	(a)	(d)	(b)	(c)	(d)	(b)
141	142	143	144	145	146	147	148	149	150
(d)	(b)	(b)	(b)	(d)	(d)	(b)	(a)	(a)	(c)
151	152	153	154	155	156	157	158	159	160
(b)	(b)	(d)	(b)	(b)	(c)	(d)	(c)	(d)	(d)
161	162	163	164	165	166	167	168	169	170
(a)	(b)	(a)	(d)	(b)	(b)	(c)	(c)	(b)	(d)
171	172	173	174	175					
(d)	(c)	(b)	(c)	(d)